PERSONAL SOCIAL
AND EMOTIONAL
DEVELOPMENT
OF CHILDREN

The Open
University

Personal, Social and Emotional Development of Children forms part of the Open University course ED209 *Child Development*. The icons that appear in the margin of this text refer to other elements in the course such as television programmes, study guides and a methodology handbook. For further information about this course, please write to Open University Educational Enterprises Limited, 12 Cofferidge Close, Stony Stratford, Milton Keynes MK11 1BY, United Kingdom. Other titles in the series are:

1   *The Foundations of Child Development* edited by John Oates

3   *Children's Cognitive and Language Development* edited by Victor Lee and Prajna Das Gupta

4   *Influencing Children's Development* edited by Dennis Bancroft and Ronnie Carr

PERSONAL, SOCIAL AND EMOTIONAL DEVELOPMENT OF CHILDREN

EDITOR
PETER BARNES

The Open University

BLACKWELL
Oxford UK & Cambridge USA

Copyright © The Open University, 1995

First published 1995 by Blackwell Publishers Ltd in association with
The Open University

Reprinted 1997, 1998

The Open University
Walton Hall
Milton Keynes MK7 6AA, UK

Blackwell Publishers Ltd
108 Cowley Road
Oxford OX4 1JF, UK

Blackwell Publishers Inc.
350 Main Street
Malden, Massachusetts 02148, USA

Cover illustration
Mary Cassatt, *The Family*, ca 1892, oil on canvas, 32x26 1/8 inches;
The Chrysler Museum, Norfolk, Virginia. Gift of Walter P. Chrysler, Jr. 71.498.

British Library Cataloguing in Publication Data
A CIP catalogue record for this book is available from the British Library

Library of Congress Cataloging in Publication Data
Personal, social and emotional development of children/
editor Peter Barnes
p.   cm. — (Child development: 2)
Includes bibliographical references and index.
ISBN 0–631–19423–1 (alk. paper) — ISBN 0–631–19424–X (pbk: alk. paper)
1. Identity (Psychology) in children. 2. Identity (Psychology) in adolescence.
3. Self-perception in children. 4. Self-perception in adolescence.
5. Child development. I. Barnes, Peter, 1946– .
BF723.156P47   1995   94-33967
155.4'18—dc20   CIP

Edited, designed and typeset by The Open University
Printed in the United Kingdom by Alden Press Ltd, Oxford and Northampton

This book is printed on acid-free paper

CONTENTS

INTRODUCTION vi

1 **CHILD CARE AND ATTACHMENT** 1
Helen Cowie

2 **DISTURBING BEHAVIOUR IN YOUNG CHILDREN** 41
Martin Woodhead

3 **GROWING UP IN FAMILIES** 83
Prajna Das Gupta

4 **DEVELOPMENTAL PERSPECTIVES ON EMOTION** 135
Martin Woodhead, Peter Barnes, Dorothy Miell and John Oates

5 **DEVELOPING A SENSE OF SELF** 187
Dorothy Miell

6 **PLAY, SELF AND THE SOCIAL WORLD** 231
Dorothy Faulkner

7 **GROWTH AND CHANGE IN ADOLESCENCE** 287
Peter Barnes

READING: STUDYING RELATIONSHIPS AND SOCIAL UNDERSTANDING 335
Judy Dunn

ACKNOWLEDGEMENTS 348

NAME INDEX 352

SUBJECT INDEX 353

INTRODUCTION

Peter Barnes

This book addresses an area of psychological enquiry that has grown rapidly in recent years: children's personal, social and emotional development. This increase in interest is due, in part, to a greater recognition of how patterns of family care can affect psychological adjustment and social integration. Notable factors include arrangements for child care; the roles of mothers, fathers and other caregivers, both within and outside the family; and patterns of marital separation, divorce and remarriage. All these have repercussions for children's experiences of relationships, their understanding of their social world and their sense of self.

However, this new interest is undoubtedly also due to a major theoretical shift within psychology itself. This has seen moves away from a consideration of the cognitive, social and emotional realms in isolation – with an emphasis on the cognitive – towards a more integrated perspective. This transformation can be seen in the growth of interest in the social constructivist perspective on cognitive development, the study of social cognition, symbolic interactionist theories of the self, and 'theory of mind'. New perspectives are being brought to bear on familiar topics: for example, the idea of an 'internal working model' addresses cognitive dimensions of attachment; studies of early social relations are clarifying the capacity for perspective-taking; and the experience of play is now considered to be important for the construction of self. At the centre of these perspectives is a belief that social and emotional development does not just happen in parallel with cognitive development, but that all three may be closely interlinked and mutually dependent.

These changes in emphasis are well illustrated by the first topic addressed in the book: attachment. The early relationships established between young children and significant adults – most notably the children's mothers – have long been the focus of psychologists' attention because of the power they have been seen to exert in shaping children's social and emotional development. Chapter 1 traces some of the history of this subject, from the work of John Bowlby through to more recent studies of early attachment experiences and their possible links to behaviour and relationships in adulthood. Important examples include the current interest in building on Bowlby's idea of the 'internal working model' and in extending the concept of attachment to other relationships and to later stages of the life-cycle.

One reason for this interest is the belief that early relationships which are distorted in some way may predispose children to develop psychological difficulties. Chapter 2, however, demonstrates how the issues surrounding the origins of such disturbed behaviour in childhood are often much more complex. It is argued that psychological development – including disturbed development – is best understood in terms of a complex, continuous *transaction* between individual and social processes.

In practice, the vast bulk of research and theorizing has concentrated on dyadic relationships (usually mother–child). Psychologists have recently begun to take account in their research and theorizing of the self-evident fact that children develop within the context of multiple relationships, notably relationships within the family. This context is the topic of Chapter 3 which, while acknowledging the dangers that accompany attempts to generalize about the significance of the family, introduces some of the approaches that have been taken to describing its influence. Early research took the theme of 'socialization' as the starting point for studies of how styles of parenting, especially control and discipline, might affect children's behaviour. The goal of identifying the most effective strategies proved elusive because insufficient account was taken of the impact of cultural context in defining the adaptiveness of parental strategies and children's behaviour, and because children's own roles in the process were undervalued.

In their various ways, the first three chapters of the book are concerned with how children's emotional worlds are shaped by their experiences. Chapter 4 provides a more detailed appraisal of developmental psychologists' accounts of the origins and growth of emotional understanding. In particular, it draws on Judy Dunn's observations of the significance of young children's everyday experiences and encounters at home, and Paul Harris's investigations into the nature of children's understanding of other people's emotional states. In both instances, recent explorations of children's 'theory of mind' have become important.

The study of the development of a sense of self and of self-identity during childhood has engaged psychologists since the early days of the discipline and continues to be of significance. Chapter 5 reflects this historical continuity in its introduction both to classic accounts of the self as subject and the self as object, and to more recent experimental investigations of these same themes, notably in relation to the development of gender identity. Once again, the important role played by social relationships in these processes is emphasized.

One kind of social relationship common to children around the world is that found when they play together. Chapter 6 considers the influences of socio-dramatic and fantasy play in home and playground on the development of the self and the growth of social competence. Research on the significance of children's play experiences is set against a background of the theoretical perspectives of Piaget, Vygotsky and Mead. The chapter raises questions about the centrality of play for social development and the routes by which its impact may be expressed.

Finally, in Chapter 7, the focus shifts to a consideration of personal and emotional development during the period of adolescence. The nature of adolescence is explored first as a number of independent processes of physical and psychological development. The concept of adolescent identity receives particular attention, especially through the work of Erik Erikson and his followers. The chapter also considers whether it is necessarily appropriate to regard adolescence as a stage of development characterized by personal upheaval. An account of how adolescence can be a relatively harmonious experience for the majority of young people recognizes the role of other family members in anticipating and accommodating the adolescent's changing needs.

A recurring theme throughout this book is the significance of children's day-to-day experiences for their continuing development. Though at first sight run-of-the-mill, these experiences may also be highly influential. In recent years an extensive and important contribution to the documentation and interpretation of these experiences has been made by Judy Dunn. Her research is regularly referred to throughout the book, and an autobiographical account of a series of her studies – how they came to be, and how they relate to each other and to wider issues in developmental psychology – concludes this volume.

Helen Cowie

CONTENTS

1 INTRODUCTION 2

2 ATTACHMENT THEORY – THE EARLY YEARS 4
2.1 The maternal deprivation hypothesis 6
2.2 Critique of the maternal deprivation hypothesis 9
Summary of Section 2 12

3 PATTERNS OF ATTACHMENT 13
3.1 Sensitive mothering: a controversial idea? 17
Summary of Section 3 18

4 WIDER RELATIONSHIPS 19
4.1 Children and day care 19
4.2 Variations in day care 21
4.3 Relationships with other family members 23
4.4 The wider context of secure and insecure attachments 27
Summary of Section 4 28

5 ATTACHMENT BEYOND INFANCY 28
5.1 The internal working model 28
5.2 Into childhood 30
5.3 Attachment in adult life 32
Summary of Section 5 34

6 CONCLUSION 34

FURTHER READING 36

REFERENCES 36

> **OBJECTIVES**
>
> When you have studied this chapter, you should be able to:
>
> 1 understand and critically evaluate the early formulations of attachment theory;
> 2 examine patterns of secure and insecure attachment behaviour in infancy and beyond;
> 3 link these patterns to qualities of sensitivity on the part of primary caregivers;
> 4 describe the effects on young children of day care outside the home;
> 5 describe the role of different family members in the development of young children;
> 6 review the concept of the child's internal working model of relationships.

1   INTRODUCTION

Everyone, it seems, has views on what is best when it comes to caring for young children. Theories of child care have evolved over centuries and across cultures to form a backdrop against which parents and other caregivers engage in the process of child rearing. In western cultures in the 20th century, views on child development have been strongly influenced by the work of child psychologists whose ideas have had a particular impact on the practice of parenting. Yet there is disagreement amongst these theorists and practitioners and many, not least the caregivers themselves, are confused – intimidated, even – by the array of competing theories and the huge output of research in this expanding field. Underlying all these theories and research is a series of questions about:

(a) the characteristics of the caring relationship between children, their parents and other caregivers;
(b) the function of these relationships in promoting 'normal', 'healthy' psychological development; and the immediate and long-term effects on children of various kinds of breakdown in these relationships.

In this chapter I do not attempt to give 'right' answers to these questions, but rather aim to provide an opportunity to look critically at some key ideas which have influenced thinking and practice around these relationships between caregiver and child. I hope that you will find through your reading, through discussion, through reflections on your own experience and, if possible, through observations of children and adults interacting with one another, a deeper understanding of relationships and their long-term implications for development throughout the lifespan.

Psychologists have employed a wide range of concepts in the study of early relationships (*inter-subjectivity, meshing, proto-conversation, scaffolding*, to name but a few). When it comes to thinking about the significance of these relationships for children's psychological welfare, one concept in particular has a special place – *attachment*. Attachment theory originated in the work of the British psychiatrist John Bowlby (1907–90) who argued that the propensity to form strong emotional bonds with particular individuals was a fundamental characteristic of human young; it had survival value by bringing nurturance, protection and security to the infant. In Section 2 I describe the early formulations of attachment theory and the controversial *maternal deprivation* hypothesis which was associated with them.

In more recent years, developmental psychologists have gone on to explore and refine an understanding of early attachments and in particular the relationships between secure or insecure attachments in infancy and later emotional and cognitive development. Some of this work, particularly that of Mary Ainsworth and her colleagues, is considered in Section 3. This research has, in its turn, generated much debate and Section 4 provides an account of this. From it has emerged a much greater emphasis on the cognitive aspects of attachment in addition to the behavioural and emotional aspects, especially through the concept of the *internal working model*. Accordingly, Section 5 is concerned with evidence about children's capacity to represent and construct their world – an internal working model of relationships and the effects of early attachments on other relationships within and without the family. The wheel comes full circle since some of the longer-term implications of certain patterns of early attachment, for example the risks of psychopathology, are just as central to the contemporary debate as they were for Bowlby. This important subject is explored in more detail in Chapter 2.

Despite the changing fortunes of attachment theory there is a sustained interest in the idea that early experiences of relationships with significant others have long-term implications for a child's future social and emotional development. In its recent formulation, attachment theory has a *life span* dimension to it which has challenging implications for the constructivist view of development. It gives insights into continuities and discontinuities between one generation and another and provides explanations for recurring themes in the development and maintenance of interpersonal relationships. From this perspective, the formation of an attachment bond is not simply a developmental task to be resolved in infancy and then left behind; rather children, and later, adults, are 'continually renegotiating the balance between being connected to others and being independent and autonomous as they encounter each new developmental phase' (Cicchetti *et al.*, 1990, p. 3).

ACTIVITY 1

Allow about 20 minutes

RECALLING EARLY ATTACHMENTS

Before going further, consider this emotional aspect of your own early childhood – your very first close relationships with significant caregivers. A word of caution: if you anticipate that this may stir up painful memories then you might want to move on to the next section. It may in any case be helpful to share your recollections with someone who is understanding and supportive and who has time to listen.

Try to recall your early childhood:

Who cared for you?

To whom were you especially attached?

To whom did you turn when you were distressed? Who comforted you?

What words would you use to describe one particular person to whom you felt close?

Can you remember a time when you were separated from that person? What feelings are evoked by that memory?

Responses to these questions, are of course, individual to each reader. But keep them in mind as you progress through this chapter and relate them to the unfolding story of attachment and child care. You should also reflect on some of the terminology you have used. I have used 'attached' several times already in this chapter; you may have used the term 'bond'. Both can be interpreted in a rather mechanical, 'adhesive' way; what does that imply?

2 ATTACHMENT THEORY – THE EARLY YEARS

EXAMPLE 1
REACTIONS TO A STRANGER

Judith is at home with Tanya, her 1-year-old child, when a visitor arrives. At first, Tanya stays close by her mother. Later she sits apart and plays as her mother and the visitor talk. Tanya looks at her mother quite frequently; sometimes she smiles. Every so often she stops in her play and calls to her mother or points to something in the room. From time to time Tanya toddles over to Judith and stays close before returning to her toys. On one occasion when Judith leaves the room for a few moments, Tanya follows her, ignoring the visitor's friendly invitation to play. On another occasion when Judith leaves Tanya cries, again resists the friendly advances of the visitor and, on her mother's return, greets her with a hug.

John Bowlby

The brief account in Example 1 is typical of the regular experience of many young children in our society and others like it. Look first at the *behaviour* that is reported. Tanya smiles and vocalizes preferentially to her mother; she cries and attempts to follow when her mother leaves the room; she greets and hugs her when she returns. She is wary of the stranger. Taken together this is an example of a secure *attachment relationship*. Judith, the caregiver, is perceived as a secure base from which to explore the environment and as a place of refuge to return to for comfort when feeling threatened. The relationship is two-way and is mutually satisfying to both parties. The child plays an active part in this process and both adult and child become reciprocally attached.

John Bowlby developed and refined the concept of attachment over a number of years (e.g. Bowlby, 1958, 1969, 1973, 1980). He drew on ideas from the *psychodynamic* theory of Sigmund Freud and from *ethology* – the study of animal behaviour – to create a theory about the *bonding* relationship that develops between parents and their children, and the disruption to that relationship which can occur through separation, bereavement or emotional deprivation. He argued that affectional ties between children and their parents or caregivers have a biological and evolutionary basis. There is a predisposition in babies to maintain proximity to their caregivers and to behave in ways that attract their attention and engage their involvement.

Bowlby thought of attachment in the early years of life as a behavioural system which has as a set goal the maintenance of appropriate proximity to the primary caregiver. Separation from the caregiver activates the attachment system in order to restore proximity. But in the first year of life the child's *proximity-promoting behaviours* – crying, vocalizing, clinging – become organized into a *goal-oriented* system focused on a specific caregiver, usually, but not necessarily, the mother. When the attachment system has achieved its goal – being in sufficiently close contact with the caregiver – then attachment behaviours subside. The child no longer needs to cry or reach out to the caregiver.

Bowlby also hypothesized that infants have a predisposition to explore the world around them. This need to explore and play takes the child away from the primary caregiver and counteracts the need for proximity. A balance is struck between the two opposing tendencies. Infants play an active part in this process and normally the attachment is reciprocal. The balance shifts when the child is distressed by some experience. In a situation of threat, such as separation from the caregiver or being in an unfamiliar setting or when the child is ill, the attachment behaviours are activated. The child will cry, cling, call out and behave in ways that are likely to bring about close proximity to the caregiver.

This brief summary encapsulates some of the major principles of attachment. For much of this chapter we will be exploring more recent theory and research that builds on Bowlby's original theory. But before doing so we need to acknowledge an earlier phase of his work, when he proposed a highly influential and controversial set of ideas that have come to be known as the *maternal deprivation hypothesis*.

2.1 The maternal deprivation hypothesis

One of Bowlby's early publications (1944) was a retrospective study of the childhood experiences of delinquent adolescent boys. Deprivation of maternal care appeared to be a recurring theme; these young people shared a history of being taken into care, growing up in institutions or moving from one temporary mother-figure to another. Bowlby was given the opportunity to elaborate on this theme when asked by the World Health Organization to prepare a report on the needs of homeless children. This was originally published in 1951 and popularized as *Child Care and the Growth of Love* in 1953. The book contained the much quoted assertion:

> What is believed to be essential for mental health is that an infant and young child should experience a warm, intimate, and continuous relationship with his mother (or permanent mother-substitute – one person who steadily 'mothers' him) in which both find satisfaction and enjoyment.

(Bowlby, 1953, p. 13)

The power of this set of ideas was greatly strengthened when Bowlby began to incorporate principles derived from the field of *ethology*. For example, Konrad Lorenz had shown how young birds and mammals learn the characteristics of a moving object during the period soon after birth or hatching; they then follow the object around.

This process of learning which object to follow became known as *imprinting*. Lorenz (1966) also introduced the concept of the *critical period* to describe the restricted time interval during which, it was believed, imprinting took place – in ducklings, for instance, this is from nine hours to seventeen hours after birth. Usually the mother is the first moving figure which the young encounter during this critical period and being imprinted on the mother in this way has an obvious survival value. Lorenz concluded that imprinting was irreversible after the critical period.

By applying these ideas to the young child, Bowlby was able to offer an apparent explanation for the deleterious effects of the loss of maternal care. He proposed a critical period between around 6 months and 3 years of age. During that time, he argued, the child needs continuous love and care from one person, the mother or a permanent mother-substitute. Significant separations between the child and this primary caregiver would have a serious deleterious effect on the emotional and social development of the child. In his view, an absent mother cannot be sensitive since, through her absence, she is not available to meet the child's needs.

Young goslings imprinted on Konrad Lorenz.

Much research has been carried out since Bowlby first formulated the maternal deprivation hypothesis and although he extensively developed his own thinking about attachment theory in the course of his life, he is often quoted as if his ideas had become fossilized in the 1950s. Bowlby's strongest critics have tended to fasten on to the maternal deprivation hypothesis even though most present-day practitioners and researchers have long since abandoned it. Nevertheless, policy issues have continued to be influenced by this early work and versions of the maternal deprivation hypothesis are regularly presented in the media and by politicians to justify certain approaches to child care.

ACTIVITY 2 Allow about 20 minutes	**WHAT DOES 'MATERNAL DEPRIVATION' ENTAIL?** Look again at the oft-quoted sentence from *Child Care and the Growth of Love* reproduced above and think about the questions listed below: (a) What conditions did Bowlby consider were essential for satisfactory parenting? (b) What did he mean by 'mothering', 'warm, intimate and continuous', 'mental health' and 'satisfaction and enjoyment'? (c) To what extent are these ideas congruent with views on parenting today? (d) Is the hypothesis still identifiable in current thinking and policy-making forty years and more on from when it was written? (e) How does contemporary society view the care of young children? (f) How is the concept of 'unsatisfactory parenting' used to explain disturbed or disturbing behaviour in older children? If possible, collect extracts from newspapers and magazines on the theme of parenting: what sources of evidence do the writers draw upon to reach their conclusions?

What led Bowlby to propose the maternal deprivation hypothesis? He drew on a number of sources of evidence:

(a) In his work with children he had noticed that by around 9 months the infant not only seemed to use the mother as a secure base but was also beginning to display separation protest and fear of strangers. Both of these phenomena are rare before 5 or 6 months, are at their peak at around 12 to 16 months, and then decline. This timing suggested that the infant had formed a clear attachment to the primary caregiver (usually the mother).

(b) The separation protest and fear of strangers served a function in that they were likely to prevent subsequent attachment bonds from being formed. Bowlby was drawn to the view that the infant becomes attached primarily to just one caregiver, usually the mother; this is known as *monotropism*. Furthermore, separation from this attachment figure will have serious outcomes for the child.

(c) Observations of young children who had been separated from their parents – for example when in hospital – suggested that there could be adverse effects. They exhibited a characteristic sequence of responses:

protest, though with the possibility of being comforted;

despair and being inconsolable;

denial and *detachment* with the appearance of being unconcerned at the separation by denying any sign of affection or responsiveness when reunited with the parent.

These three stages were vividly illustrated in a series of films made by James and Joyce Robertson (1967–73), colleagues of Bowlby at the Tavistock Clinic in London.

Research also indicated that children in long-term institutional care experienced delays to their social, emotional and cognitive development. One particularly influential study is described in Research Summary 1.

RESEARCH SUMMARY 1
GOLDFARB'S STUDY OF THE EFFECTS OF EARLY EXPERIENCES

During the 1940s an American psychiatrist, William Goldfarb, took the opportunity to follow up the development of thirty children who had been separated from their natural mother before the age of 9 months. Half of them had been cared for by foster parents. The other half had been cared for in an institution until about the age of 3½, when they were placed with foster parents who looked after them for the remainder of their childhood.

The quality of the later foster care was judged to be comparable for the two groups, so the implication was that any differences between them were attributable to their contrasting experiences in infancy. Goldfarb's assessments carried out when the children were aged between 10 and 14 years showed that those who had lived in an institution during their early years were retarded in terms of intelligence, speech, reading and arithmetic. They were also more frequently found to be restless, unable to concentrate, fearful, unpopular with other children and craving for adult affection.

(Goldfarb, 1947)

Bowlby's interpretation of this research was that:

> The comparative success of many babies adopted between six and nine months who have spent their first half-year in conditions of deprivation makes it virtually certain that, for many babies at least, provided they receive good mothering in time, the effects of early damage can be greatly reduced. What Goldfarb's work demonstrates without any doubt is that such mothering is almost useless if delayed until after the age of two years six months. In actual fact this upper age limit for most babies is probably before twelve months.

(Bowlby, 1951, p. 49)

(d) Further support came from research with animals. Harry Harlow (1958; and Harlow and Harlow, 1969) showed that when infant rhesus monkeys were separated from their mothers and reared in isolation they became extremely disturbed, were usually terrified of other monkeys, and displayed aggressive or withdrawn behaviour. If the separation from the mother continued beyond the age of three months the effects seemed to be irreversible. By adolescence these monkeys were usually unable to mate, and in those instances where females did produce offspring they were unable to care for them adequately.

(e) Studies of human adolescents with acute behaviour disorders indicated that in their earlier childhood they had often experienced separation from their primary caregivers (for example, through divorce, death of a parent, hospitalization). Bowlby argued that the early experience of separation from the mother caused the later difficulties.

In reflecting on these various influences on thinking about the nature and significance of early mothering it is important to recognize that Bowlby was, in effect, bringing together a number of trends that were already under way, rather than initiating them himself. It is also significant to view these trends within the wider social context of their time. The Second World War had a disruptive impact on family life and on children in particular and there was a public wish in many quarters not just to restore the positive experience of family life but to complement it with what was perceived to be a growing knowledge of what was needed for the *psychological* welfare of children. In some quarters this was expressed in terms of 'mothering' being as necessary for children's healthy development as a proper diet and medical care. Note, too, a politically and economically inspired source of encouragement for these moves; whereas there had been a national need for women to work in factories and on the land while the men were engaged in fighting the war, the troops' return in search of work meant that a peacetime role had to be recreated for women.

2.2 Critique of the maternal deprivation hypothesis

There have been many criticisms of the maternal deprivation hypothesis in the years since Bowlby first proposed it and as a result it has become largely discredited (though this does not discredit attachment theory in general). These criticisms have arisen from a number of sources:

(a) Ethologists have replaced the notion of the critical period by the more flexible concept of a *sensitive period* when certain learning occurs more readily than at other times in an animal's life. The all-or-nothing feature of the critical period has thus been modified.

(b) Further research with rhesus monkeys indicated that, under certain conditions, the effects of the social and sensory deprivation could be overcome (Suomi and Harlow, 1972). At 6 months monkeys that had been reared in isolation were withdrawn and depressed and, when placed with adult monkeys or peers, they were attacked and did not respond to others appropriately. However, when these deprived 6-month-olds were placed with normally-reared 3-month-old monkeys there was a striking difference. The 3-month-olds typically clung to the isolates, so preventing the stereotypic responses of rocking, huddling or clasping themselves. Instead, the isolates began to move about, to explore their environment and to engage in social play. After a few weeks the rate of stereotypic behaviour had decreased, and after 6 months the isolated monkeys were scarcely presenting any social deficits. These findings raised challenging questions about the positive contribution to social and emotional competence of same-age and younger peers.

(c) Research on human infants has shown that Bowlby over-simplified the typical response to a stranger. Although it does occur in the way he described and can be observed in a range of different cultures, the *intensity* of the response varies greatly depending on the experiences which the child has already had. More crucially, evidence indicates that 1- to-2-year-olds are perfectly able to form new social relationships with adults and, for example, older children, and that these relationships can be strong and enduring.

(d) The concept of *monotropism* has also been found wanting. Children do form attachments with more than one adult, even if one of them appears stronger than the others. Separation from the primary caregiver can be compensated for if another attachment figure is present. The expressions of protest, despair and denial which appeared in the Robertsons' films can be substantially alleviated if the child is placed in the care of other adults with whom there is already a bond. Furthermore, stays in hospital can be made much less distressing to the child by regular visits from significant attachment figures.

(e) Studies of child-rearing in institutions have also been re-evaluated. The reason the children studied by Goldfarb suffered (Research Summary 1) was not necessarily separation from their primary caregivers. These children were typically reared in conditions where the environment was generally unstimulating, there was a high turnover of caregivers and the caregivers were often discouraged from forming close relationships with the children in their charge. Research by Barbara Tizard and colleagues (Research Summary 2) suggests that experiencing a large number of caregivers may disrupt children's capacity to form close relationships, which has consequences for their later social adjustment. While there is evidence (e.g. Clarke and Clarke, 1976) that children can make remarkable recoveries from severe deprivation, it is still clearly a matter of concern that should be addressed when considering the needs of children in care. So, Bowlby's predictions were not completely upheld by the evidence from institutions which provided a stimulating, supportive environment for the children. Improved arrangements for institutional care have resulted in significantly

> ### RESEARCH SUMMARY 2
> ### FOLLOWING THE DEVELOPMENT OF CHILDREN IN CARE
>
> Barbara Tizard and colleagues followed the development of 65 healthy babies who were admitted into institutional care before the age of 4 months and remained there until at least 2 years of age. By the age of 4½ years 24 had been adopted, 15 had been restored to their natural mothers and 26 remained in institutional care. It was therefore possible to compare their development and assess the effects of institutional care.
>
> The institutions were judged to provide a reasonably stimulating environment with books, toys and opportunities for varied experiences beyond their walls. In this they differed significantly from the orphanages studied earlier by Goldfarb. When the children's cognitive and linguistic development was measured at 4½ they performed at about the same level as a comparable group of London working-class children (the control group), thus indicating that there was no obvious adverse effect on cognition associated with their institutional experience.
>
> In terms of their social and emotional development the behaviour of the children who had experienced early maternal deprivation was judged to be on a par with that of the control group in a number of respects. However, there were some important differences. One notable feature of the institutions was the extent of shared care; by the age of 2 years the 26 children who were to remain in institutions for the duration of the study had had, on average, 24 nurse carers and by 4½ this had risen to 50. At that point 18 of the 26 (69 per cent) were described by staff as 'not to care deeply about anyone'. Eleven (42 per cent) were judged to be 'markedly attention seeking' compared with 20 per cent of the control group. When followed up at 8 years the institutional group children were seen by their teachers as 'severe problems' and as attention-seeking, restless, unpopular and anti-social.
>
> (Tizard and Rees, 1975; Tizard and Hodges, 1978)

fewer adverse effects than those investigated in earlier studies. It is now widely recognized that the care of young children can be shared by more than one adult but that there are limits to the number of adults with whom young children can form a meaningful relationship. As Tizard *et al*'s studies show, children in institutional care are not given the opportunity to form stable attachments to just one or two adults, and this appears to have consequences for their ability to form relationships in later life.

(f) Research has not confirmed a straightforward link between early experiences of separation from mother and disordered behaviour in adolescence. In a major review of maternal deprivation research the psychiatrist Michael Rutter (1981) has argued that it is important to distinguish between different constellations of early experience because they are associated with different outcomes. The first distinction is between what he terms *privation* of affectional bonds, where children growing up in institutions may be denied the opportunity of establishing such bonds, and *disruption* of affectional bonds, where, having been established, maternal care is lost. A second distinction is between the *disruption* of relationships (e.g. resulting from the mother's death) and the *distortion* of relationships which may surround the break-up of a family through separation and divorce, even though the mother is physically present.

Evidence suggests that children who have experienced long-term institutional care since soon after birth (privation) are more likely to have difficulty in making relationships in later childhood than children who, though growing up in institutions, spend at least the first year of life with their mothers and are able to maintain some sort of relationship with them subsequently. Distinguishing between disruption and distortion, research shows, for instance, that the delinquency rates for boys who had lost a parent by death was not different from those in normal intact families, whereas the rate for boys whose parents had separated or divorced was twice that figure.

Rutter has offered the following explanation:

> Early events may operate by altering sensitivities to stress or in modifying styles of coping which then protect from, or predispose towards, disorder in later life only in the presence of later stress events. The suggestion, then, is not that there is any direct persistence of good or ill effects but rather that patterns of response are established that influence the way the individual reacts to some later stress or adversity.
>
> (Rutter, 1985, p. 363)

Bowlby's early statements about the importance of the mother or single caregiver for children's emotional and social needs prompted a great deal of debate and research. One outcome of this is that the factors in children's experiences and relationships which appear to have short-term and long-term consequences have become more clearly identified. This is important not only for answering questions about the practicalities of the care of children but also for gaining a clearer understanding of the psychological mechanisms through which the effects are realised. The study of patterns of attachment which forms the focus of the next section is a part of that developing story.

SUMMARY OF SECTION 2

- Bowlby maintained that there is a predisposition in babies to maintain proximity to their caregivers. In order to achieve this, babies engage in behaviour which attracts the attention of the caregiver.

- Children have a need to explore the environment and play an active part in maintaining a balance between proximity to the caregiver and exploring the outside world.

- Young children perceive separation from the caregiver as a threat and this is likely to activate attachment behaviours.

- The maternal deprivation hypothesis says that between the age of 6 months and 3 years children need continuous love from a primary caregiver, usually the mother. Significant separation from the primary caregiver has a serious effect on the children's emotional development. Research has not, on the whole, confirmed the maternal deprivation hypothesis.

- Attachment theory has generated a great deal of research. Current research investigates the impact of early relationships with significant caregivers on later emotional and cognitive development.

- 1- and 2-year-old children are capable of forming healthy, lasting relationships with adults and older siblings. Separation from the primary caregiver can be compensated for if children are left in the care of other adults with whom they have formed a stable relationship.

- Studies of monkeys have shown that early isolation and separation from the mother can be compensated for, in part, by placement with younger infants.

- Rutter's work indicates that there is not a direct causal link between early experiences of separation from parents and later emotional distress. The critical factor is whether young children are sensitively supported through an experience of separation from parents, not the separation in itself.

- Studies of children in care indicate that shared care of young children by large numbers of adults can have an adverse effect on their capacity to form close relationships

3 PATTERNS OF ATTACHMENT

One very important extension of Bowlby's early work on the maternal deprivation hypothesis has been a focus on the nature of the attachment relationship. Foremost in this research has been Mary Ainsworth, originally a student of Bowlby's, who has studied the patterns of attachment shown by young children in different contexts and over time, emphasizing the *quality* of the carer-child relationship (Ainsworth, 1985; Ainsworth and Bell, 1974; Ainsworth *et al.*, 1978). Her research indicates that the behaviour of the primary caregiver – usually but not always the mother – in the early years of the child's life can predict the type of relationship that this mother–child dyad will have later on. From observational studies, begun in Uganda, Ainsworth developed the central concept of the *secure base*; subsequent research in the US confirmed and extended this idea.

In the early months of life it is usually – though not inevitably – the mother who carries most of the responsibility for a child being able to maintain the balance between closeness to the caregiver and exploration of the environment. From studying the way in which a mother responds to her child's needs it is possible to rate her in terms of *sensitivity*.

Ainsworth argued that mothers who are more sensitive, responsive, accessible and co-operative during their child's first year are likely to have a child who develops a secure attachment. This, in turn, forms the basis within the child for feelings of self-worth and self-confidence.

How can security of attachment be measured? In her observations of 1-year-old children in their home settings Ainsworth noted variations in the extent to which they used their mother as a base from which to explore the world; their response when mother left the room and again when she returned; and their response to the entry of a stranger (Ainsworth and Wittig, 1969). This should remind you of the Example which began Section 2. These observations led to the development of a laboratory-based *Strange Situation* technique which has played a key role in much subsequent research into attachment throughout the world. The technique is described in Example 2, which you should look at now.

On the strength of her observations Ainsworth became particularly interested in children's behaviour on the two occasions of reunion with the mother. She identified three contrasting patterns of attachment:

The most frequently found reaction was for children to cry during separation from their mothers but then to be easily soothed upon reunion. The children actively sought and maintained proximity, contact or interaction with their mothers, especially during the reunion episode. Any distress shown during the separation period was clearly related to the mother's absence. The child preferred the mother to the stranger. Ainsworth classified this as a *secure* attachment pattern (and it has come to be know as Type B).

By contrast, some infants shunned contact with their mothers upon reunion. They either ignored her when she returned to the room or mingled welcome with responses such as turning away, moving past her or averting their gaze. The stranger and the mother were treated in very similar ways throughout the experimental situation. This was described as an insecure attachment pattern of the *anxious/avoidant* type (Type A).

A third pattern of response was typified by infants who were very upset when their mother left the room but, in contrast to Type B, were not easily comforted on her return. They resisted contact but combined this with some seeking of proximity. Some showed anger towards their mother at reunion and gave the impression of being ambivalent about reunions after separations. They also resisted comfort from the stranger. This was described as another form of insecure attachment, with an *anxious/ambivalent* pattern (Type C).

Subsequent studies using the Strange Situation technique (e.g. Main and Solomon, 1990) have added a further insecure pattern which is seen most frequently in families where there is parent pathology, child abuse or very high social risk. Here, the child appears dazed, confused or apprehensive, and shows no coherent system for dealing with separation and reunion. This behaviour suggests fear or confusion about the relationship and prompts the label *disorganized* attachment pattern (Type D).

EXAMPLE 2
AINSWORTH'S STRANGE SITUATION TECHNIQUE

The procedure consists of a series of episodes involving collaboration between experimenter and mother. Throughout, the infant's behaviour is recorded either on video tape or by an unseen observer sitting behind a two-way mirror.

1 The infant and her mother are brought into a comfortably furnished laboratory playroom and the child has an opportunity to explore this new environment.

2 Another female adult, whom the child does not know, enters the room and sits talking in a friendly way, first to the mother and then to the child.

3 While the stranger is talking to the child the mother leaves the room, unobtrusively, at a prearranged signal.

4 The stranger tries to interact with the child

5 Mother returns and the stranger leaves her together with the child.

6 Mother then goes out of the room leaving the child there alone.

7 Stranger returns and remains in the room with the child.

8 Mother returns once more.

Each of these separate episodes lasts for three minutes at the most, but less if the child becomes very distressed.

The video record is scored in terms of the child's behaviour directed towards the caregiver:

- seeking contact
- maintaining contact
- avoidance of contact
- resistance to contact

Like Bowlby, Ainsworth claimed that attachment between infant and one or more specific caregivers was universal and had biological roots; the attachment behaviours of the helpless, vulnerable infant and the corresponding responses of the caregivers evolved as a means of protecting young from danger. When she replicated her Uganda study with a contrasting sample of families in the US city of Baltimore she found many similarities. As with the Ugandan families, American 1-year-olds tried to stay close to their mothers, especially when they were in a situation of threat; in both cultures they used the primary caregiver as a secure base from which to explore their environment. She also found a very similar distribution of the three patterns: 70 per cent securely attached (Type B), 20 per cent avoidant (Type A) and 10 per cent ambivalent (Type C).

However, evidence from a wider range of countries and cultures indicates rather greater variation. Some data gathered together by Marinus van IJzendoorn and Pieter Kroonenberg (1988) are summarized in Table 1.

TABLE 1   Cross-cultural comparisons of secure and insecure attachments based on thirty-two studies

Country	No. of studies	Percentage of attachment types		
		Secure (Type B)	Avoidant (Type A)	Ambivalent (Type C)
West Germany	3	57	35	8
UK	1	75	22	3
Holland	4	67	26	6
Sweden	1	75	22	4
Israel	2	64	7	29
Japan	2	68	5	27
China	1	50	25	25
USA	18	65	21	14
Overall average		65	21	14

Source: adapted from Van IJzendoorn and Kroonenberg, 1988, pp.150–51.

ACTIVITY 3

Allow about 10 minutes

INTERPRETING CROSS-CULTURAL DATA ON ATTACHMENT

What do the data in Table 1 show about differences among cultures in the quality of attachment between mothers and infants?

What cautions need to be applied when making comparisons of this sort?

Comment

There are some broad similarities but also some sizeable variations. Secure attachments (B) are the commonest in each of the countries, though the incidence varies from 50 per cent in China to 75 per cent in the UK and Sweden. There are variations in patterns of insecure attachments: avoidant patterns (Type A) tend to be commoner in Western Europe and the US, and ambivalent patterns (Type C) commoner in Israel and Japan.

But are we comparing like with like? Is the Strange Situation equally valid in different cultures? For example, one explanation of the pattern of results from Japanese studies is that the infants were very distressed in the Strange Situation because, in their culture, they are never normally left alone at 12 months (Takahashi, 1990). There was no opportunity for them to show avoidance patterns (Type A) since at reunion the mothers typically went straight to them and picked them up immediately. This meant that an unusually high number of Japanese infants were scored as Type C at 12 months, yet in other settings they did not appear to be insecurely attached.

It is also important to note – though it cannot be deduced from Table 1 – that variation *within* these cultures (e.g. comparing different socio-economic groups, or distressed and non-distressed families) is greater than the variation *between* cultures (see Clarke-Stewart, 1988, p. 297).

From these comparisons it would appear that there are some common factors in the mother–child relationship which contribute to secure and insecure attachments. However, there are also wide cultural differences in the ways in which these patterns are expressed.

3.1 Sensitive mothering: a controversial idea?

Ainsworth followed Bowlby in arguing that the development of secure attachments is founded on consistently accessible 'sensitive' mothering during the first year of life. The primary caregiver, usually the mother, mediates between the child's competing needs for proximity on the one hand and exploration on the other. The contradiction for the child is overcome with the help of the supportive, sensitive caregiver who, in the child's early years at least, is almost always 'available'. But what are the implications of this apparent need for constant 'availability'? There are certainly important ones for mothers.

> If he [the child] leaves her [the mother], he knows she will remain available. In this way, very early on, the gulf is firmly asserted between the *outside world* – school and work – on the one hand, where we are supposed to be independent and self-reliant, and the *inside world* – family and mother – on the other hand, where we expect emotional availability. This emotional regulation is characteristic of our culture.
>
> (Singer, 1992, p. 135–6)

There is evidence that the parent – invariably the mother – who gives up work outside the home to care for young children can experience depression and loss of identity when faced with this task (Boulton, 1983). On top of that, the obligation to aspire to the ideal of the sensitive, available, responsive caregiver can be overwhelming. For some women 'sensitive parenting' does not come naturally and their experience of parenting may well include boredom, depression and hostility rather than the ideal of mutual fulfilment. While over half the mothers in Boulton's sample found that the experience of parenting gave them fulfilment, a large minority did not.

Woollett and Phoenix (1991) are also highly critical of this emphasis on maternal sensitivity and the lack of concern displayed for the feelings and experiences of mothers themselves. Sensitivity of this type, they say, is offered to children at a price – the mothers' self-esteem, career aspirations and adult relationships. And although the term 'parenting' is often used in the attachment theory literature, in practice, Woollett and Phoenix argue, given the power of relationships between men and women, sensitivity is normally related to the characteristics of mothers rather than fathers.

One alternative is the greater sharing of the role of parenthood and the reframing of issues of responsibility for children. If children receive (and come to expect) only part-time availability from both fathers and mothers, then, it is argued, the adults too can keep the balance between home and the outside world. Of course, any change in the cultural arrangements for the care of young children will have implications for patterns of attachment. This issue is being more strongly debated in relation to the provision of day care, which is the subject of the next section.

SUMMARY OF SECTION 3

- Ainsworth has emphasized the importance of the parent as a secure base for the child. She has described parental qualities which facilitate the child's security of attachment.

- According to Ainsworth, secure attachments in infancy form the basis for children's feelings of self worth.

- Ainsworth's Strange Situation Technique is a standard procedure for assessing the extent and quality of an infant's attachment to the parent.

- Researchers using this technique have identified four distinct patterns of attachment: Type A – anxious/avoidant; Type B – secure; Type C – anxious/ambivalent; Type D – disorganized.

- Cross-cultural comparisons suggest that there are certain common factors in parent–infant relationships across all cultures. However, there are differences in the patterns of interaction which appear to contribute to secure and insecure attachment.

- The concept of sensitive parenting has come under some criticism. A significant proportion of women do not find the role of sensitive, available caregiver a satisfying one.

4 WIDER RELATIONSHIPS

4.1 Children and day care

One of Bowlby's original concerns related to the welfare of young children in long-term *residential* care in homes and nurseries which, by today's standards, would be considered understaffed and failing to meet children's psychological needs. Others, however, translated the general direction of his thinking into messages about the risks to children's development if their mothers went out to work and placed them in *day care* or a nursery before the age of 3 years. For example, his 1951 WHO report claimed that the use of day nurseries would result in 'permanent damage to the emotional health of a future generation' (WHO, 1951; quoted in Tizard, 1991, p. 64). Whether or not these concerns had any foundation in the l950s, the more important question concerns whether they have any foundation today.

Researchers have compared children who are cared for at home with those who spend time in day care while their mothers go out to work. Most studies conducted in the 1970s and 80s found that day care need not have a bad effect on young children. For example, one conclusion of Jay Belsky and Laurence Steinberg's (1978) extensive review of studies done in the US was that 'the total body of evidence [...] offers little support for the claim that day care disrupts the child's tie to his mother' (cited in Belsky, 1988, p. 236). Young children whose mothers work do still form attachments to them and, indeed, prefer their mothers to their other caregivers (Clarke-Stewart and Fein, 1983).

However, the debate does not stand still. In 1988 Belsky published a paper in which he reconsidered the accumulating evidence on the effects of day care and revised the conclusion he had reached ten years earlier (Belsky, 1988). Belsky was struck, in particular, by the reported incidence of insecure attachments amongst very young children who experienced more than twenty hours of non-maternal care per week. Table 2 combines and summarizes the data from a number of studies.

Table 2 shows that the rate of insecure attachments is 1.6 times greater when infants have more than twenty hours of non-maternal care per

TABLE 2 Security of infant–mother attachment and extent of non-maternal care

	Extent of non-maternal care	
	More than 20 hours/week	Less than 20 hours/week
Secure attachment	59%	74%
Insecure attachment	41%	26%
N = 464		

Source: Belsky, 1988, p. 247.

week than when they have less than twenty hours or virtually none at all. Belsky offered the following preliminary conclusion:

> particularly in studies reported since 1980, there is an *emerging* pattern, in which 20 hours or more per week of non-maternal care – especially when initiated in the first year either at home or in centers – is associated with the infant's tendency to avoid or maintain a distance from the mother after a series of brief separations.
> (Belsky, 1988, p. 248)

ACTIVITY 4
Allow about 10 minutes

INTERPRETING DATA ON THE CONSEQUENCES OF CHILD CARE

What explanations can you offer for the differences summarized in Table 2? What questions do comparisons of this kind raise? Look back to the description of the Strange Situation; is it possible that children's reactions to this situation might reflect their familiarity with 'safe' separations and reunions in day care, rather than the security of their attachments?

Taken at face value, the higher levels of insecure attachment might imply that the separations between working mothers and their young children lead the latter to doubt their mothers' availability and responsiveness and to develop a coping style that masks their anger. This is the sort of explanation that Belsky leans towards. Other commentators, such as Clarke-Stewart, take the view that, though plausible, this sort of explanation is highly speculative and would be difficult to substantiate (Clarke-Stewart, 1988).

A second question concerns whether the difference can properly be attributed to the day-care experience alone. There may be other relevant differences between mothers who choose or need to work and those who do not, and it may be these that relate to security of attachment. The earlier account of different reactions to the 'ideals' of sensitive mothering may be one case in point.

We also need to consider whether there is a danger of placing too much emphasis on the importance of attachment to mother and neglecting other attachment relationships. Even if the levels of insecure attachment to mother are higher for children in day care this does not necessarily mean that they are emotionally insecure in general. And, allied to that, another of Clarke-Stewart's concerns is that there is a danger of getting the scale of the differences in Table 2 out of proportion. Though the difference in this particular sample is 'both substantial and significant' (1988, p. 300) overall percentages of insecure attachments amongst infants of working mothers are virtually identical to the normal range reported for the US in Table 1. She concludes that the difference 'is not large enough to conclude that infants are in danger if their mothers work' (Clarke-Stewart, 1988, p. 300).

Belsky's interpretation is rather different and is of particular interest because it represents something of a change of heart. His first analysis led him to conclude that few risks seemed to be associated with day care; however, the later refocus concluded that 'risks seem to be associated with extensive non-maternal care in the first year' (Belsky, 1988, p. 266). At the same time he recognizes the complexity and variability of experience that resides behind labels like 'day-care':

> Infants in day care are likely to be found in a variety of arrangements (usually resulting from their mothers working outside of the home), for a variety of reasons, and with a variety of feelings and family practices associated with the care arrangement. Thus infant day care refers to a complex ecological niche, and probably to several niches. This means, then, that any developmental outcomes associated with care are also related to a host of other factors. It would be misguided to attribute any 'effects' of non-maternal care to the care *per se* or even to the mother's employment.
>
> (Belsky, 1988, p. 257)

Furthermore, there is plenty of room for interpretation of the seemingly objective data and this in turns gets associated with particular political and ideological positions. Sometimes this is quite overt, at other times it is not; but it is always necessary to be alert to this dimension when interpreting and evaluating contributions to the debate. In that respect little has changed since Bowlby's ideas first appeared on the scene.

4.2 Variations in day care

I've already noted that the label 'day-care' is used to cover a range of provision for young children and it is possible to identify a number of variables that might have a bearing on children's reaction to that experience and its impact on their development.

ACTIVITY 5

Allow about 10 minutes

VARIATIONS IN CARE

Make a note of the different care arrangements for young children that you can think of and identify what you consider to be the significant ways in which they vary. Which of these would you anticipate having an effect – positive or negative – on the children? How do you think that effect might come about?

Comment

Some differences that come to mind are whether the care is provided in the familiar surroundings of the child's own home or in some other setting, the size of the group of children being cared for, the ratio of adults to children, the level of training and experience of the staff, the care 'regime' that is provided and the quality of the physical environment. These variables, and others besides, are just the ones that have been considered when researchers have attempted to evaluate the effects of day care. One such study is described in Research Summary 3.

RESEARCH SUMMARY 3
THE THOMAS CORAM RESEARCH UNIT STUDY

Researchers at the Thomas Coram Research Unit in London followed 255 two-parent families and their first-born children from birth until they were 3 years old. All of the women were in work before their child was born and three-quarters of them returned to full-time work before the child was 9 months old. About a third of these children were cared for by a relative, half by a childminder and the remaining 20 per cent attended a nursery.

The children's development was assessed in different ways at two points. When they were 18 months old, and after they had been in one of the four day-care environments for some months, they were observed during 'free-play' periods and their caregiver was interviewed. These observations showed that some behaviour was the same across all settings, for example, the extent of physical contact, individual play and crying. But others varied: attention and vocalization (to and from the child in both instances) was greatest in the home, followed by the relative, then the childminder and least in nurseries. For activities involving the simultaneous participation of two or more people the trend was in the opposite direction, with the highest incidence in the nurseries. Affection, both to and from the child, was lowest in nurseries and aggression was highest (related to the fact that there were many more children available to be the subject of it).

Also, at 18 months an assessment was made of the children's socio-emotional development, including an experience akin to the Strange Situation. The behaviour of the children on reunion was comparable for all groups, though it was noted that those in nursery care seemed less excited and showed less positive signs of emotion when approached by the stranger. Other observations indicated that the nursery sub-group showed less orientation to people and more negative mood.

Further measures were taken when the children were 3 years old. Affectionate interactions were more frequent where mothers and relatives were providing the care than in nurseries. But the nursery children were more likely to demonstrate positive social characteristics such as sharing and empathy with others.

The researchers noted variations in the quality of care. In particular, the nursery care was considered to be of poor quality; the low level of responsiveness and adult–child interaction contrasted with the other care environments and was judged likely to affect developmental progress. The adult–child ratio was best for care by a relative (average of 1.3:1) the lowest for nursery care (average of 4.6:1). One consequence of poorer ratios was that staff became more involved in controlling children than interacting with them. Other potentially significant factors noted were that over half of the nurseries complained about inadequacies in their accommodation, the staff were younger than the other caregivers in the study and only a third had children of their own in contrast to almost all the relatives and childminders, who were mothers. A further potentially disadvantageous feature of the nurseries was the proportionately higher turnover of staff, with the effect that had on the stability and consistency of the care environment as experienced by the children.

(Melhuish *et al.*, 1990a, 1990b)

4.3 Relationships with other family members

Much of the discussion thus far has been about young children's attachments to their mothers and the consequences of disturbances to those attachments. But, the vast majority of children grow up in environments which provide them with the opportunity of a much wider range of potential close relationships than this. One study of 186 contemporary non-industrial societies found only five in which the child was looked after almost exclusively by the mother (Weisner and Gallimore, 1977). And closer to home, fathers, grandparents, older siblings and other adult family members may play significant roles in young children's social and emotional lives. Are these roles different from those of the mother? Do they have different implications for development? What follows serves to introduce some of the issues, many of which are taken up in subsequent chapters.

Fathers

Research suggests that typically fathers do not play such a large part in child-rearing and domestic tasks as do mothers (Lamb, 1987). Even in societies which pride themselves on their egalitarianism, such as Sweden, mothers still perform a larger share of child care responsibilities. Nevertheless, when fathers do interact with their newly-born children they use a similar repertoire of behaviours to those employed by mothers – bouncing, talking, cuddling – and the same sort of mutual pleasure in the interaction is commonly seen (Parke and Tinsley, 1981). However, as the children grow older, a differentiation in roles appears between the parents (Parke and Tinsley, 1987). The father's role includes more boisterous play activity and more games, in contrast to quieter interactions and routine care giving on the part of the mother. One explanation of these differences is that they are part of the more widespread sex-role differentiation in our culture. Alternatively, and perhaps more prosaically, it could simply be that the mother, who does most of the routine care giving, has less time for playful activities.

When we look at children's attachment to their fathers, it seems that the intensity of that attachment depends on such factors as his sensitivity to the infant's signals, his playfulness and the amount of time spent in face-to-face interaction (Chibucos and Kail, 1981). In general, infants prefer either the father or the mother to a stranger; however, when frightened they are more likely to turn to the mother than the father (Lamb, 1981). Lewis (1986) has suggested that the more time fathers spend in care giving and becoming sensitively attuned to the baby's needs, then the stronger will be the child's attachment.

Siblings

In many societies older siblings may be expected to take on the role of caregiver. Typically, they demonstrate tolerance for younger children and can be important role models for them. In nuclear families, too, siblings play a role, though it is only relatively recently that developmental psychologists have begun to recognize its potential significance and to investigate it in detail.

READING: STUDYING SIBLINGS

The most sustained study of siblings and their significance in psychological development has been conducted by Judy Dunn and her colleagues. This research will be referred to at intervals throughout the book and the reading at the end of the book provides an account of the background to each stage. You should read all of this reading now and then you will be asked to read specific sections of it again at set points in subsequent chapters.

As you read it for the first time, look out for those aspects of sibling relationships that appear to relate to issues of attachment.

Note that in Section 2 Dunn was interested to see whether 'children's early relationships experiences with their siblings show any systematic links with their later development or relationships'.

The Cambridge study indicated that the arrival of a sibling is an event of considerable emotional significance to a first-born child. Example 3 gives some examples of children's reactions to their new brothers and sisters. Note how the children display a range of reactions, including ambivalent and hostile feelings as well as empathy and concern.

In most cases, however, children soon become reconciled to their younger sibling and through the experience of interacting with them come to understand others and learn how to influence or even manipulate them. From an early age siblings seem to be acquiring knowledge of how to tease, placate, comfort or get their own way with a brother or sister. Dunn and Kendrick's study shows, however, that it may take some time for children to become genuinely attached to a new sibling.

EXAMPLE 3
OLDER SIBLINGS' VIEWS OF THE NEW BABY

MOTHER OF BOY: He's started feeding himself – first time for months he *insists* on feeding himself. Also he will go and play in the garden if she's in the pram .

MOTHER OF GIRL: There's a new independence. She's started talking to people in the shops, which she never used to.

MOTHER OF BOY: He's generally more depressed, more quiet, more touchy. I'm expecting him to play more on his own than he used to – I'm not giving him so much attention. What he finds as occupations tend to be the 'come and stop me' ones. I try not to let it escalate, but quite often it does.

GIRL TO BABY: All right, baby (caressing him). (To mother) Smack him.

BOY (standing on edge of pram, rocking it) …

MOTHER: Don't stand on there, there's a good boy, or you'll tip her out.

BOY: I want her out.

BOY (baby playing with a balloon): He's going to pop it in a minute. And he'll cry. And he'll be frightened of me too. I *like* the pop.

(Dunn and Kendrick, 1982)

One way of investigating the attachment relationship between siblings is to use a variant of the Strange Situation test. In one such study (Stewart, 1983) the older siblings were left alone with the infants after the mothers left the room. Within seconds of the mother's departure just over half of the older siblings showed care giving behaviour by hugging or reassuring the infant or drawing attention to toys; the rest ignored the infant or moved away and did not respond to the child's distress in a caring way. Stewart's study, like Dunn and Kendrick's, found that young children do not automatically form good relationships with their siblings shortly after birth.

Grandparents

For many of the new-borns in Dunn and Kendrick's Cambridge sample, their grandparents formed a recurring presence in their lives. Half of the children saw their maternal grandmother at least once or twice a week and their father's mother was also a regular if somewhat less frequent visitor. More widely, the extent and nature of the grandparent's role varies considerably depending on geography, mobility and age; it is worth remembering that many grandparents are in their fifties when their grandchildren are young and may well have the time and opportunity to have frequent and active contact with them. A study in Germany (Sticker, 1991) found, perhaps unsurprisingly, that the frequency of contact varied according to the age of the grandchild; in this sample 64 per cent of the grandparents of children under the age of 2 years had contact with them more than once a week.

As with the study of siblings, psychologists' interest in the significance of grandparents in children's development is relatively recent (see Smith, 1991). Even then it is interesting to note that the majority of studies have focused on grandmothers, and particularly maternal grandmothers; few studies examine the role of grandfathers. Grandparents can act as surrogate parents to young grandchildren, for example, as baby-sitters or child-minders when parents are at work. In the Thomas Coram Study (Research Summary 3), for example, 22 per cent of mothers who returned to work chose relations to look after their children. The grandparents' role is especially important in lone parent families; here the greater likelihood of poverty is a significant factor. Many single mothers live with or near their family of origin. Sharing child care arrangements with relations is one way of reducing the impact of poverty, and it has important implications for the pattern of attachment relationships developed by children. Research Summary 4 gives a brief survey of research in other cultural settings which highlights the significance of acknowledging attachment relationships beyond the parent–child dyad.

RESEARCH SUMMARY 4
CROSS-CULTURAL STUDIES INTO THE ROLE OF GRANDPARENTS

(a) Research into black extended families in the US (reviewed by Werner, 1991) places emphasis on the role of the maternal grandmother. The black grandmother is perceived by herself and the daughter as being actively involved in child rearing and, where the mother is in employment, is often the grandchild's primary caregiver.

(b) Among native Americans, where a biological grandparent is absent, children and parents may adopt an unrelated elder into the family to provide guidance and discipline for the grandchildren. Werner (1991) notes that social welfare professionals (usually middle-class Caucasians) can ignore this valuable resource and place native American children in foster-care rather than into the care of their grandparents when the parents are unable to care for their own children.

(c) Research in Poland emphasizes that grandparents are not simply alternative attachment figures to parents. Their family status, age and experience permits a unique relationship to develop. For example, they can pass on family and social history to their grandchildren. Tyszkowa (1991) indicates that almost 20 per cent of her sample of Polish students 'reported that grandparents told them about the country's past: in childhood – legends and historical episodes; later – most often the history of the Second World War [...] Lively knowledge, shown through the filter of personal experience' (Tyszkowa, 1991, p. 62).

So far we have discussed the role of fathers, siblings and grandparents as an extended network of attachment relationships that can be important to young children in varying degrees in different families, societies and cultures. But the picture is more complex than this, requiring a more *systemic* view of the family relationships (Hinde and Stevenson-Hinde, 1988). For example, besides being attachment figures to their grandchildren, grandparents can serve a supportive function in fostering and maintaining children's attachments to their primary caregivers. Similar patterns of mutual support can extend throughout the family network. Of course we need to acknowledge that in some situations these influences can be less benign, for example, where there is conflict between parents, or other stresses within the family. In these circumstances a child's attachment relationship with grandparents can serve to buffer their emotional distress. Situations of family breakdown and divorce provide a clear example. Wallerstein and Kelley (1980) found that the paternal grandmother can sometimes maintain the relationship with grandchildren when their father finds it difficult to do so. Regardless of age, children who coped well in school and kept good relationships with peers and teachers during a family break-up were more likely to have positive relationships with grandparents who lived near them and who were concerned about their needs.

4.4 The wider context of secure and insecure attachments

The emphasis of this chapter has been on the significance of parents, other family members and professional caregivers for the development of attachment security. I would like, briefly, to draw your attention to the important ways in which the wider social context can, in varying degrees, support or weaken these relationships, which can have important implications for the welfare of children. For example, the proportion of secure attachments is smaller in families living in conditions of poverty and chronic stress (Spieker and Booth, 1988).

Belsky (1984) has suggested a model which distinguishes three main influences on the quality of parent–child relationships. These are:

(a) Personal psychological resources of the parent, including mental health, the quality of internal representations of relationships (see below) and their developmental history.

(b) Contextual sources of support, including the social network of support from partner, relatives and friends, and job conditions and financial conditions.

(c) Characteristics of the child, in particular easy or difficult temperament.

 Belsky's model is represented in Figure 1. Note that the classic attachment literature tends to concentrate on the first influence, with the emphasis on maternal sensitivity (as discussed above). In subsequent chapters more attention is given to the role of wider family functioning in children's social and emotional development as well as examining the contribution of children themselves to these processes.

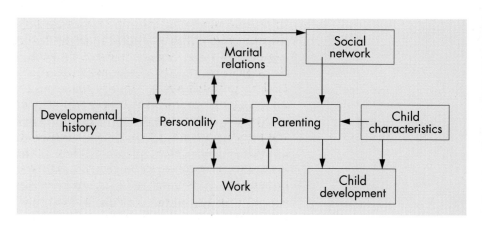

FIGURE 1 A process model of the determinants of parenting. Source: Belsky, 1984.

SUMMARY OF SECTION 4

- There is an on-going debate about the impact on children's social and emotional development of being cared for outside the home in the early years.

- Belsky has warned that twenty hours or more of non-maternal care outside the home may be associated with patterns of insecure attachment in children in the first year.

- Clarke-Stewart is sceptical of Belsky's conclusion and suggests that factors other than separation from the mother may have an effect.

- Research by Melhuish *et al.* has investigated the significance of such variables as the quality of day care provision, staff ratios and the training and experience of caregivers.

- The significance of children's relationships with other family members is important for children's development.

- The broader social context within which children form close relationships cannot be ignored. Factors such as economic and social conditions, as well as children's temperament, have an impact on the nature of parental functioning.

5 ATTACHMENT BEYOND INFANCY

5.1 The internal working model

One question which pervades much of the research on attachment concerns the means by which the child's early attachment experiences come to predict later relationships. Bowlby (1969) proposed that from a very early age children develop *internal working models* of their relationships with their primary caregivers and that these persist, relatively unchanged, throughout life. These are cognitive structures, mental models or representations which embody the day-by-day interactions with the attachment figure. They are schemes which guide the child's actions with the attachment figure based on previous interactions and which incorporate the expectations and emotional experiences associated with them. I will use some of Ainsworth's research to illustrate how this idea might be developed.

We saw earlier how Ainsworth found that the caregivers' sensitivity to the infant's signals (e.g. quickness of response) and their respect for the infant's autonomy (e.g. co-operative as opposed to intrusive care) predicted the infant's confidence in the reliability of the parent's responsiveness to distress. When caregivers are sensitively attuned to their babies' needs, the children are 'freed from the disorganizing effects of intense emotional arousal and are able to explore their world' (Crittenden, 1992, p. 580). This is the normal pattern of interaction between caregiver and infant. Ainsworth suggested that securely attached infants (Type B) build up an internal working model of their caregivers as available and responsive to their needs. But what happens when the caregiver fails to give the child this basic sense of security? Ainsworth suggested that the intense emotional arousal which ensues disorganizes the child and leaves them not only distressed emotionally but unable to process information in the normal way. Thus, the problem facing the insecurely attached infant is how to maintain attachment with a caregiver who is unpredictable or rejecting. For such children the internal working model is constructed to help them cope with and accommodate to a caregiver who is often 'unavailable' to meet their needs or who is cold and rejecting.

What about the anxious/avoidant infant's (Type A) typical response to unavailability? If the caretaker rarely provides the comforting response which the infant needs in order to be calmed, then, Ainsworth argued, eventually the infant learns to block off the information which leads to such distress. Eventually the baby stops screaming and, by ceasing to express distress through crying, may actually inhibit the emotional experience (Ekman, 1992). Avoidant babies learn to defend themselves against rejection by showing little emotion and by avoiding the caregiver on reunion. The capacity for cognitive development may actually be enhanced since, by cutting themselves off from distressing emotions, they are free to interact with their environment. The outcome sets the pattern for a 'dispassionate quality of cognitive activity' (Crittenden, 1992) combined with difficulty in engaging in close, intimate relationships with others.

Anxious/ambivalent children (Type C), by contrast, learn to adapt to the unavailability of the mother by intensifying their cries of distress. This will eventually result in the caregiver appearing in order to calm the baby, but though in the short term this response reduces discomfort, in the longer term, if the pattern persists, the attention of such insecurely attached babies is likely to be focused on their feelings at the expense of mutual sharing. Ainsworth argued that they construct an internal working model of their caregivers as inconsistently available and responsive. These babies are difficult in everyday situations because they are never sure whether their caregiver will return after a separation. During reunions they are likely to be angry because they are afraid of disappointment. This explains the ambivalent nature of their response to the mothers on reunion. Because they are so preoccupied by their distress at the quality of the relationship, they have less time and opportunity to explore their environment in a calm, relaxed way.

The idea of the internal working model has aroused interest in part because it offers a way of bringing together cognitive and affective (emotional) aspects of development. It attempts to relate the mental models, beloved by cognitive psychologists, with both psychodynamic concerns for the importance of mother–child relationships and the increasing attention being paid to the development of children's social understanding. However, the idea is not without its critics who argue that it is so vaguely conceived that it can be used to explain almost everything (Dunn, 1993). Although the above account of Ainsworth's three types in terms of the children's internal working model may have a certain plausibility, the model itself doesn't lead to any directly testable hypotheses about the pattern of findings in studies of relationships, nor does it shed light on which aspects of relationships with parents might be linked to which dimensions of children's other relationships.

5.2 Into childhood

As the child develops, Ainsworth argues that the workings of the attachment system are modified to allow for greater separation from the caregivers. The child is developing his or her internal working model reflecting experiences in primary attachment relationships. The quality of the early relationships influences the child's concept of self as well as attitudes towards others and expectations of existing and future relationships.

EXAMPLE 4
FROM HOME TO SCHOOL

At 5, Tanya is ready to make the transition from home to school. She is not too distressed when she first goes to school as her family have prepared her for this new experience. She is used to being cared for by a number of members of her close family and has often stayed overnight with her grandmother. She has been attending nursery since she was three and has made good friends with peers. At school Tanya remains an open and friendly child who soon settles down to her new environment. She is good at her work and enjoys sports. Everyday conflicts are taken in her stride. She soon becomes a popular member of her class. Tanya and her family are African–Caribbean and they all have a strong sense of their cultural identity. Tanya sees herself very positively so when she encounters discrimination she perceives it as injustice and not as a personal failing. For example, when all the girls, including Tanya, are deliberately left out of a football game by the boys Tanya explains it in terms of the boys' jealousy of the girls' skill and organizes her own game. The next day boys and girls play football together. When she encounters some racist name-calling in the playground, she is understandably angry and upset. She is proactive in challenging the bullies and in telling adults who can intervene. Later she takes active steps to befriend other children who are victims of bullying by accompanying them in the playground and by making sure that responsible adults know what is happening. Tanya remains a popular member of the class, friendly with boys and girls. She retains her strong sense of positive self-identity founded in the secure base which she experienced within the family from her earliest years.

ACTIVITY 6

Allow about 10 minutes

APPLYING THE INTERNAL WORKING MODEL

Example 4 charts the progress of the fictional Tanya, first encountered as a 1-year-old in Example 1. How can this account be related to the idea of an internal working model?

Comment

Tanya is likely to maintain the pattern of secure attachment in later life because she feels secure with her primary caregivers. She can separate from them and develop her own style of living. Secure pre-schoolers and 5 to 7-year-olds respond positively to a parent on reunion and seem to be able to combine attention to the parent with the capacity to explore the environment and relate to other adults and children. In terms of the internal working model, separation is less stressful to these children than it was when they were younger since they seem to have developed a model which assumes that the parent will be there when needed but which allows for reasonable separation, for example when attending nursery or first school, or playing at a friend's house. Reunions are happy and conversation is natural and free-flowing.

This sort of illustration is supported by systematic research which indicates longer-term implications of early attachments for children's social relationships in later life. For example, Erickson *et al.* (1985) have shown that the quality of attachments at 12 months predicts teacher ratings of the child, the extent of behaviour problems and the quality of peer relationships during the first school years.

Several studies have attempted to measure attachment quality in older children. Variants of the Strange Situation have been used with 3- to 6-year-olds (Main and Cassidy, 1988). They found that children who have had a warm, satisfying experience of relationships are likely to see themselves as lovable, will expect others to like them and will place a value on close, intimate relationships with others. Those who have had a harsh experience of relationships, who have been rejected, and who have not been comforted when in distress are likely to see themselves as unlovable, will have low expectations of relationships and will act in ways which are likely to elicit rejection. Avoidant pre-schoolers and 5- to 7-year-olds seem to be more interested in activities than in the reunion with their parents after a separation. They may respond conventionally with a greeting but there is a lack of eye contact and a coldness of response to parental approaches. The characteristic strategy appears to be to remain as neutral as possible and to do little to attract attention to the relationships. Among older children the anxious/ambivalent pattern is characterized by a preoccupation with the relationship rather than with activities. The parent and child will engage in drawn-out arguments; the child will be whiny and clingy. Even by school age the anxious/ambivalent child is likely to be upset by separations from the parent.

In older children the disorganized (Type D) pattern of relationship with parents emerges in one of two ways. One is related to care-giving. The child may be exceptionally but unnaturally enthusiastic on reunion as if to make sure of pleasing the parent, for fear of what might happen. The other is punitive. The child is directly hostile to the parent or ignores the parent. For further work on this disturbing aspect of parent–child relationships see Chapter 2.

5.3 Attachment in adult life

Do the patterns of attachment endure right into adulthood? Some attachment theorists maintain that the nature of the attachment established in childhood can strongly influence significant adult relationships, and can even be transmitted to the next generation. For example, Mary Main and her colleagues devised the Adult Attachment Interview (AAI) as a way of tapping the internal working models of parents with respect to attachment. Main and Goldwyn (1984) claim that a mother's recollection of the quality of her childhood relationship with her mother is related to the quality of the relationship that she has with her own child (as classified in the Strange Situation); the patterns and relationships are summarized in Example 5.

EXAMPLE 5
FOUR MAJOR PATTERNS OF ADULT ATTACHMENT BASED ON RESPONSES TO THE ADULT ATTACHMENT INTERVIEW (AAI)

(a) Autonomous-secure
Persons who can recall their own earlier attachment-related experiences objectively and openly, even if these were not favourable; these tended to be parents of securely attached children. These adults openly expressed their valuing of relationships.

(b) Dismissing-detached
Persons who dismissed attachment relationships as of little concern, value or influence; these tended to be parents of anxious/avoidant children. They gave brief accounts, had few childhood memories and often idealized their childhood without being able to provide any supporting evidence.

(c) Preoccupied-entangled
Persons who seemed preoccupied with dependency on their own parents and still actively struggled to please them; these tended to be parents of anxious/ambivalent children. They gave inconsistent, often incoherent accounts of childhood. The conflicts they described were often unresolved and still an on-going issue with them.

(d) Unresolved-disorganized
Persons who had experienced traumatic separation from the attachment figure and not worked through the mourning process; or who had experienced severe neglect and abuse. These tended to be parents of children who show an insecure disorganized pattern of behaviour in the Strange Situation.

(Main and Goldwyn, 1984)

According to Main and Goldwyn, if adults have easily accessible memories of their relationship with their own parents and are able to talk openly about the positive and negative aspects of that relationship, then they are more likely to have a secure relationship with their own children. By contrast, if they find it difficult to get in touch with their feelings about their parents or if they are still preoccupied with issues which were unresolved in their own childhood, then they are more likely to have an insecure attachment with their own children. Secure adults value relationships and can talk easily about them. If their childhood was secure, they can acknowledge the failings of their parents in an accepting way. If their childhood was difficult, they have worked through their unhappiness and come to an understanding of how it came to happen; they have been able to form new adult relationships of significance. Main and Goldwyn found that 75 per cent of securely attached infants had mothers who were rated 'secure-autonomous'.

As adults, *dismissing-detached* people will not appear to place high value on intimate relationships. They will avoid closeness and appear untouched by rejections. They will show little concern for unhappy experiences in their own childhood, and may even be unable to speak about them. At the same time they will often idealize the past with statements like 'My childhood was a very happy one' yet be unable to think of any examples to illustrate this assertion.

The *preoccupied-entangled* adult remains trapped by unresolved struggles with parents and may well experience a loss of identity when separated from family. The unfinished business with parents makes it difficult to break free and can overshadow adult relationships. It is difficult for them to reach an objective evaluation of their own childhood and they remain preoccupied with the past in a way which makes it difficult to focus on present relationships.

In adulthood, the *unresolved-disorganized* pattern is expressed through mourning over the loss of the attachment figure or the loss of childhood. This loss may be through abrupt separation from the parent or through separation due to illness or break-down of the parents' relationship. It may be that the parent, though present, was experienced by the child as being absent, by not meeting the child's needs, through abuse or violence or neglect. The adults may still be so preoccupied with unresolved issues from the past that it is difficult to meet the needs of their own children. They may expect their young child to meet their needs in highly inappropriate ways.

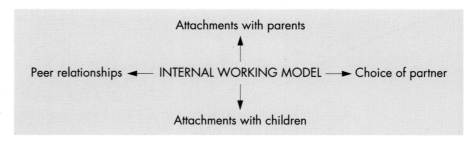

FIGURE 2 Attachment through the life span

Research studies of this kind reflect a growing interest in the impact which early attachment has on the pattern for later adult–parent relationships and also for adult relationships, for example, with friends, partners and with other children. These studies offer some evidence that the pattern established in infancy seems to endure (see Figure 2 for a diagrammatic summary.

SUMMARY OF SECTION 5

- Recent work focuses on the nature of the child's internal working model of relationships. This is a hypothetical cognitive structure based on the child's experiences of interacting with significant others.
- The child's internal working model is rooted in the experience of accommodating to the primary caregivers. If the relationship is secure, the infant will have an internal working model of caregivers and others as being responsive to his or her needs.
- Insecurely attached infants will develop an internal working model of caregivers who are unavailable or unresponsive to their needs, which has a strong influence on the child's later emotional and social development.
- The internal working model changes as the child develops, accommodating larger numbers of relationships and longer periods of separation.
- Main's research using the Adult Attachment Interview indicates links between the quality of a mother's relationships with her parents and the quality of her relationships with her own child.
- Four major patterns of adult attachment are identified by this research – secure-autonomous, dismissing-detached, preoccupied-entangled and unresolved-disorganized.

---

6 CONCLUSION

In this chapter we have begun to explore a crucial aspect of the process of caring for young children – the development of patterns of secure and insecure attachment. We have reviewed a model which suggests that effective caregivers are sensitive and responsive to their children and give them a secure base from which to venture out into the world. We have examined the nature of these secure and insecure attachments and critically reviewed the idea that they are indeed linked to qualities of sensitivity on the part of primary caregivers. We have also looked at the caregivers themselves and explored the influence that their own experiences of parenting can have on their capacity to care for young children. We have discussed the role of other family members in facilitating the social and emotional development of children, in particular the impact of fathers, siblings and grandparents. Looking beyond the family, we have overviewed the debate on day-care and the conditions under which it may be considered wise to delegate the care of young children beyond primary caregivers.

We have also considered the possibility that there may be continuities between early experience and later adult relationships. Here the concept of the internal working model offers some insights. In Bowlby's original formulation the internal working model was based on the quality of the early relationship between parent and child. Attachment theorists continue to believe that through the experiences of relationships with important caregivers the child builds up an expectation of the quality of his or her relationships with other people, including the self. This concept has been widely adopted by therapists working in the attachment theory tradition. The emphasis here is on unconscious processes and on the impact which stressful childhood experiences and unresolved conflicts can have on relationships. In particular, from this perspective, it is held that the repressed conflicts from childhood are likely to be repeated in the next generation unless the individual takes steps to work through them.

Erickson *et al.* (1992) indicate some difficulties with the concept of the internal working model, although they stress that it is a flexible idea with great potential for giving us insights into the processes of emotional and social development in childhood. Many new questions emerge that are beyond the scope of this chapter. Are the cognitive processes generalized models of the world, models of relationships or models of individuals, including the self? Does the model change as the child develops? To what extent do the child's experiences of the wider social world – for example, of adult carers other than the parents – influence the internal working model and modify the impact of the parent–child relationship? Is there an interaction between unconscious levels of processing and the explicit surface levels of thought? If so, how does it develop? Do the unconscious levels provide a scaffolding for conscious levels? The answers to these questions can only come from continued longitudinal and intervention work.

Attachment theory is only one of a number of influential developmental theories in psychology. The studies which we have looked at in this chapter suggest some of the factors which may lie at the heart of emotional strength and the capacity to face up to life's vicissitudes – a sense of security, the experience of loving and being loved, the sense of being valued and being of worth, the sense of being rooted in a secure base. Not all psychologists agree with this particular way of looking at the person. Perhaps in the following chapters you will come to integrate and synthesize these differing perspectives.

FURTHER READING

HOLMES, J. (1993) *John Bowlby and Attachment Theory*, London, Routledge.

SCHAFFER, H. R. (1990) *Making Decisions about Children*, Oxford, Blackwell.

SINGER, E. (1992) *Childcare and the Psychology of Development*, London, Routledge.

REFERENCES

AINSWORTH, M. (1985) 'Patterns of infant–mother attachments: antecedents and effects on development', *Bulletin of New York Academy of Medicine*, **66**(9), pp. 771–90.

AINSWORTH, M. and BELL, S. M. (1974) 'Mother–infant interactions and the development of competence' in CONNOLLY, K. and BRUNER, J. (eds) *The Growth of Competence*, London, Academic Press.

AINSWORTH, M., BLEHAR, M. C., WATERS, E. and WALL, S. (1978) *Patterns of Attachment: a Psychological Study of the Strange Situation*, Hillsdale, NJ, Lawrence Erlbaum.

AINSWORTH, M. and WITTIG, B. A. (1969) 'Attachment and exploratory behaviour of one-year-olds in a strange situation' in FOSS, B. M. (ed.) *Determinants of Infant Behaviour*, Vol. 4, London, Methuen.

BELSKY, J. (1984) 'The determinants of parenting: a process model', *Child Development*, **55**, pp. 83–96.

BELSKY, J. (1988) 'The "effects" of infant day care reconsidered', *Early Child Research Quarterly*, **3**, pp. 235–72.

BELSKY, J. and STEINBERG, L. D. (1978) 'The effects of day care: a critical review', *Child Development*, **49**, pp. 929–49.

BOULTON, M. G. (1983) *On Being a Mother: a study of women with preschool children*, London, Tavistock.

BOWLBY, J. (1944) 'Forty-four juvenile thieves: their characters and home life', *International Journal of Psychoanalysis,* **25**, pp. 1–57 and 207–28.

BOWLBY, J. (1951) *Maternal Care and Mental Health*, Report to the World Health Organization, New York, Shocken Books.

BOWLBY, J. (1953; second edn 1965), *Child Care and the Growth of Love*, Harmondsworth, Penguin.

BOWLBY, J. (1958) 'The nature of the child's tie to his mother', *International Journal of Psychoanalysis*, **39**, pp. 350–73.

BOWLBY, J. (1969) *Attachment and Loss: attachment,* New York, Basic Books.

BOWLBY, J. (1973) *Attachment and Loss: separation,* New York, Basic Books.

BOWLBY, J. (1980) *Attachment and Loss: loss, sadness and depression,* New York, Basic Books.

CHIBUCOS, T. and KAIL, P. (1981) 'Longitudinal examination of father–infant interaction and infant–father interaction', *Merrill-Palmer Quarterly,* **27**, pp. 81–96.

CICCHETTI, D., CUMMINGS, E. M., GREENBERG, M. T. and MARVIN, R. (1990) 'An organizational perspective on attachment beyond infancy: implications for theory, measurement and research' in GREENBERG, M. T., CICCHETTI, D. and CUMMINGS, E. M. (eds) *Attachment in the Preschool Years,* Chicago, University of Chicago Press.

CLARKE, A. M. and CLARKE, A. D. B. (1976) *Early Experience: myth and evidence,* London, Open Books.

CLARKE-STEWART, A. (1988) 'The "effects" of infant day care reconsidered: risks for parents, children and researchers', *Early Childhood Research Quarterly,* **3**, pp. 292–318.

CLARKE-STEWART, A. and FEIN, G. G. (1983) 'Early childhood programs' in HAITH, M. M. and CAMPOS, J. J. (eds) *Handbook of Child Psychology,* Vol. 2, New York, Wiley.

CRITTENDEN, P. M. (1992) 'Treatment of anxious attachment in infancy and early childhood', *Development and Psychopathology,* **4**, pp. 575–602.

DUNN, J. and KENDRICK, C. (1982) *Siblings: love, envy and understanding,* London, Grant McIntyre.

DUNN, J. (1993) *Young Children's Close Relationships Beyond Attachment,* London, Sage.

EKMAN, P. F. (1992) 'Facial expression of emotions: new findings, new questions', *Psychological Science,* **3**, pp. 34–8.

ERICKSON, M. F., EGELAND, B. and SROUFE, L. A. (1985) 'The relationship between quality of attachment and behaviour problems in preschool in a high-risk sample' in BRETHERTON, I. and WATERS, E. (eds) 'Growing points in attachment theory and research' , *Monographs of the Society for Research in Child Development,* **50**, pp. 147–86.

ERICKSON, M. F., KORFMACHER, J. and EGELAND, B. R. (1992) 'Therapeutic intervention with mother–infant dyads', *Development and Psychopathology,* **4**, pp. 495–507.

GOLDFARB, W. (1947) 'Variations of adolescent adjustment of institutionally reared children', *American Journal of Orthopsychiatry,* **17**, pp. 449–57.

HARLOW, H. (1958) 'The nature of love', *American Psychologist*, **13**, pp. 673–85.

HARLOW, H. and HARLOW, M. (1969) 'Effects on various mother–infant relationships on rhesus monkey behaviours', in FOSS, B. M. (ed.) *Determinants of Infant Behaviour*, Vol. 4, London, Methuen.

HINDE, R. A. and STEVENSON-HINDE, J. (1988) (eds) *Relationships within Families: mutual influences*, Oxford, Clarendon.

LAMB, M. (1981) 'The development of father–infant relationships' in LAMB, M. E. (ed.) *The Role of the Father in Child Development* (2nd edn), New York, Wiley.

LAMB, M. (1987) 'Introduction: the emergent American father' in LAMB, M. E. (ed.) *The Father's Role: cross-cultural perspectives*, Hillsdale N.J., Lawrence Erlbaum.

LEWIS, C. (1986) *Becoming a Father*, Milton Keynes, Open University Press.

LORENZ, K. (1966) *On Aggression*, London, Methuen.

MAIN, M. and CASSIDY, J. (1988) 'Categories of response to reunion with the parent at age 6: predictable from infant classifications and stable over a 1-month period', *Developmental Psychology*, **24**, pp. 415–26.

MAIN, M. and GOLDWYN, R. (1984) 'Predicting rejection of her infant from mother's representation of her own experience: implications for the abused-abusing inter-generational cycle', *Child Abuse and Neglect*, **8**, pp. 203–17.

MAIN, M. and SOLOMON, J. (1986) 'Discovery of an insecure/disorganised attachment pattern' in BRAZELTON, T. B. and YOGMAN, M. W. (eds) *Affective Development in Infancy*, Norwood, N.J., Ablex.

MAIN, M. and SOLOMON, J. (1990) 'Procedures for identifying infants as disorganised/disoriented during the Ainsworth Strange Situation' in GREENBERG, M. T. CICCHETTI, D. and CUMMINGS, E. M. (eds) *Attachment in the Preschool Years*, Chicago Ill., University of Chicago Press.

MELHUISH, E. C., MOONEY, A., MARTIN, S. and LLOYD, E. (1990a) 'Type of childcare at 18 months – I. Differences in interactional experience', *Journal of Child Psychology and Psychiatry*, **31**, pp. 849–59.

MELHUISH, E. C., LLOYD, E., MARTIN, S. and MOONEY, A. (1990b) 'Type of childcare at 18 months – II. Relations with cognitive and language development', *Journal of Child Psychology and Psychiatry*, **31**, pp. 861–70.

PARKE, R. D. and TINSLEY, B. J. (1981) 'The father's role in infancy: determinants of involvement in caregiving and play' in LAMB, M. E. (ed.) *The Role of the Father in Child Development* (2nd edn), New York, Wiley.

PARKE, R. D. and TINSLEY, B. J. (1987) 'Family interaction in infancy' in OSOFSKY, J. D. (ed.) *Handbook of Infant Development* (2nd edn), New York, Wiley.

RUTTER, M. (1981, 2nd edn) *Maternal Deprivation Reassessed*, Harmondsworth, Penguin.

RUTTER, M. (1985) 'Family and school influences on behavioural development', *Journal of Child Psychology and Psychiatry*, **26**, pp. 349–68.

SINGER, E. (1992) *Childcare and the Psychology of Development*, London, Routledge.

SMITH, P. K. (ed.) (1991) *The Psychology of Grandparenthood: an international perspective*, London, Routledge.

SPIEKER, S. J. and BOOTH, C. L. (1988) 'Maternal antecedents of attachment quality' in BELSKY, J. and NEZWORSKI, T. (eds) *Clinical Implications of Attachment*, Hillsdale, NJ, Lawrence Erlbaum.

STEWART, R. B. (1983) 'Sibling attachment relationships: child–infant interactions in the strange situation', *Developmental Psychology*, **19**, pp. 192–9.

STICKER, E. J. (1991) 'The importance of grandparenthood during the life cycle in Germany' in SMITH, P. K. (ed.) *The Psychology of Grandparenthood,* London, Routledge.

SUOMI, S. J. and HARLOW, H. F. (1972) 'Social rehabilitation of isolate-reared monkeys', *Developmental Psychology*, **6**, pp. 487–96.

TAKAHASHI, K. (1990) 'Are the key assumptions of the 'strange situation' procedure universal? A view from Japanese research', *Human Development*, **33**, pp. 23–30.

TIZARD, B. (1991) 'Working mothers and the care of young children' in WOODHEAD, M., LIGHT, P. and CARR, R. (eds) *Growing up in a Changing Society*, London, Routledge.

TIZARD, B. and HODGES, J. (1978) 'The effect of early institutional rearing on the development of eight-year-old children', *Journal of Child Psychology and Psychiatry*, **19**, pp. 99–118.

TIZARD, B. and REES, J. (1975) 'The effect of early institutional rearing on the behaviour problems and affectional relationships of four-year-old children', *Journal of Child Psychology and Psychiatry*, **16**, pp. 61–74.

TYSZKOWA, M. (1991) 'The role of grandparents in the development of grandchildren as perceived by adolescents and young adults in Poland' in SMITH, P. K. (ed.) *The Psychology of Grandparenthood: an International Perspective*, London, Routledge.

VAN IJZENDOORN, M. H. and KROONENBERG, P. M. (1988) 'Cross-cultural patterns of attachment: a meta-analysis of the Strange Situation', *Child Development*, **59**, pp. 147–56.

WALLERSTEIN, J. S. and KELLEY, J. B. (1980) *Surviving the Break-up: how children and parents cope with divorce*, New York, Basic Books.

WEISNER, T. S. and GALLIMORE, R. (1977) 'My brother's keeper: child and sibling caretaking', *Current Anthropology*, **18**, pp. 169–90.

WERNER, E. (1991) 'Grandparent–grandchild relationships amongst US ethnic groups' in SMITH, P. K. (ed.) *The Psychology of Grandparenthood: an international perspective*, London, Routledge.

WOOLLETT, A. and PHOENIX, A. (1991) 'Psychological views of mothering' in PHOENIX, A., WOOLLETT, A. and LLOYD, E. (eds) *Motherhood: meanings, practices and ideologies*, London, Sage.

Martin Woodhead

CONTENTS

1	**INTRODUCTION**	**42**
2	**NORMAL AND PROBLEM BEHAVIOUR**	**46**
2.1	Issues of measurement	48
2.2	An epidemiological study	52
	Summary of Section 2	59
3	**THE ROLE OF THE FAMILY**	**60**
3.1	Maternal responsiveness	61
3.2	Maternal attitudes	65
	Summary of Section 3	67
4	**THE ROLE OF THE CHILD**	**68**
4.1	Directions of effect in human processes	68
4.2	A transactional model	72
4.3	The influence of temperament	73
	Summary of Section 4	78
5	**CONCLUSION**	**78**
	FURTHER READING	**79**
	REFERENCES	**79**

OBJECTIVES

When you have studied this chapter, you should be able to:

1 analyse the concept of 'normal' and 'disturbing' behaviour, and highlight the issues surrounding the identification of psychological difficulties;

2 describe research on the incidence of psychological difficulties, including some issues surrounding attempts to evaluate their stability, and to introduce the concept of risk factors;

3 understand the potential contribution of maternal behaviour, attitudes and mental state to the development of difficulties within the context of wider family and social factors;

4 recognize the role of the child in the process – in particular, the way child temperament can interact with parental responsiveness;

5 discuss the relevance of a transactional model for describing these parent–child processes;

6 explain the relevance of vulnerability, resilience, protective mechanisms, gateways and amplifiers in the context of studies of behavioural difficulties.

1   INTRODUCTION

Chapter 1 examined the role of attachment in social development and included some consideration of whether insecure attachments contribute to the development of psychological difficulties. In this chapter I shall focus directly on children whose development becomes a cause for concern. Their behaviour may become challenging and difficult, they may appear isolated, anxious and fearful, or they may seem unhappy or disturbed. I shall be looking at the characteristics of these problems, at some of the explanations that have been offered for their development, and at the assumptions that underlie the judgements that we as adults make of children as 'a problem', 'abnormal', 'pathological' or 'disturbed'.

ACTIVITY 1

Allow about 25 minutes

THINKING ABOUT DISTURBED DEVELOPMENT

This first activity introduces four 3-year-old children and raises questions about how – if at all – their behaviour is a problem. The following descriptions are taken from a major research project carried out by Naomi Richman *et al.* (1982) which you will study in detail in Section 2. Richman *et al.* made a clinical assessment of each of these children and this assessment is given after the description.

As you study these cases consider the following questions.

(a) What constitutes 'a problem'? When do problems of growing up justify labels like 'disturbed'?

(b) Whose problem is it: a problem for the child, a problem for the adult who cares for the child, or a problem in the relationship between adult and child?

(c) What do you think might be the causes of these kinds of problems?

(d) What kinds of professional intervention, treatment or therapy might be helpful?

(e) What do you think is the likelihood of these children continuing to present problems later in childhood?

1 Michael

Michael is the youngest child and has three older grown-up brothers and sisters. His mother works and he is looked after by his sister. He goes to bed at 10 p.m., though his mother would prefer him to go much earlier. He gets into his parents' bed every other night. He is very active and is said to be hardly ever still. His concentration is short, but he can amuse himself. He can be disobedient, and have tempers but this happens rather rarely. He is not usually difficult and mixes pretty well. He seems to have no worries and there are no difficulties over separation.

Clinical rating – No problem.

2 Sandra

Sandra is the youngest of five, her brothers and sisters being considerably older than she is. She soils and wets herself, and is not a happy child. She cannot amuse herself and follows her mother around all the time. She is a very poor eater and faddy. She has some difficulties in settling at night and is generally restless with poor concentration. She can be left with others though only with some difficulty. When frustrated she goes on and on screaming until her mother gives in for the sake of peace. She will scream and shout in the street. She has tempers if thwarted two or three times a day and has quite a number of fears. She screams and shouts if her older brothers and sisters will not play with her and consequently she irritates them. She cannot play with other children because she has no idea of give and take. Her mother had to give up work because Sandra fretted for her and lost weight.

Clinical rating – Mild problem.

3 Moira

She is the younger of two girls. Moira was said by her mother never to do what she was told, but to run around the room, never still, climbing on the table at mealtime etc. She has a smallish appetite and eats inappropriate materials such as tissues. She takes about half an hour to get to bed and then sleeps through the night. She is a very active girl with poor concentration and is always playing with things that she shouldn't. She seems to annoy her mother deliberately. She is uncontrollable at times, for example when her mother takes her out shopping. She has infrequent tempers but is often grizzly, whiney and moody, and her moods may last up to an hour. She fights with her sister a good deal and is generally boisterous and tends to get into fights with other children from whom she has to be separated. She wears both her parents out. She has no fears. She tends to dominate the other members of the family.

Clinical rating – Moderate problem.

4   Peter

Peter is the older of two boys. He is very over-active and is said to 'run around like a madman'. He is reported to be very wild, and totally out of control, having a tantrum whenever he is frustrated. He torments his nine-month-old brother so that he cannot be left with him. He will not play with other children, but only fights with them. It is impossible to take him out. He follows his mother around all day. He has a poor appetite, is faddy, and he occasionally eats paint. It takes a very long time to settle him at night, and he often gets into his parents' bed. He shows facial grimacing at times. He can amuse himself but he is disinclined to do this. He cannot be left for long with others, and is irritable if he doesn't get his own way. He worries that his mother might die, and is also frightened of monsters and of noises at night. He has many other fears as well as nightmares. He frequently shouts and screams, and the neighbours and other children will not have anything to do with him.

Clinical rating – Marked problem.

(Richman *et al.*, 1982, pp. 19–20)

Activity 1 provides an overview of many of the issues to be examined in this chapter. I shall address each set of questions, with the exception of those about intervention, treatment and therapy. To help clarify your initial thinking I offer the following brief contrast between two perspectives. Think about how each perspective represents a different set of answers to the questions posed in Activity 1.

Perspective 1: Adherents to the first perspective might describe the problems in terms of 'disorders', thereby locating them firmly *within* the child, as part of the child's psychological make-up. The emphasis of this approach is on describing symptoms, making a diagnosis and prescribing treatment, which might include drugs or psychotherapy offered to an individual child in the setting of a Child Guidance Clinic. This *medical* model dominated the field during the middle decades of this century, but was subsequently the subject of much criticism. It is not difficult to think why. Emotional and behavioural difficulties are not like medical conditions. In some cases, of course, there may be an underlying neurological problem, chromosomal abnormality or psychiatric disorder; but in many more cases there are no clear-cut organic causes. And even when a child is born with or develops an identifiable disorder, the expression of that disorder in emotional and behavioural difficulties is the product of developmental processes that take place in the context of social relationships, in the family, at school and so on.

Perspective 2: The second perspective is wary of projecting labels like 'disturbed' onto the child, whose problems are thought more likely to reflect 'disturbed' patterns of parental care. Whereas in the medical model the child is the focus of explanation, in this *social environment* model the attention is on such issues as impoverished home circumstances, inadequate or abusive parental care, or a lack of discipline at school. The theory of maternal deprivation (as discussed in Chapter 1) is a fine illustration of this perspective, which was highly influential in the construction of post-war social policy about the functions of the family, and especially the role of women as mothers, in promoting the mental health of children. The emphasis of intervention within this perspective would be on support and training for parents, the placement of children in a therapeutic community in which a more stable social environment can be constructed to support their development or, as a last resort, taking children into care.

In the sections that follow I shall argue that neither a 'medical' nor a 'social environment' model can provide a satisfactory account of the development of disturbed behaviour on its own. While a narrow emphasis on psychological disorders within the child is in most cases inappropriate, explanations that single out particular features of the child's social environment can be equally misleading. Psychological development comprises a complex, continuous *transaction* between individual and social processes. This is as true of disturbed as it is of normal development. Simplistic attempts to attribute causes to either 'child' or 'environment' make little sense. The challenge is to understand the interrelationships between these sources of influence.

ACTIVITY 2

Allow about 5 minutes

DISTURBING BEHAVIOUR

Think carefully about the title of this chapter. The phrase 'disturbing behaviour' is provocative, and you may find it puzzling at first. Does it suggest more than one meaning to you? Is it about young children whose behaviour is being disturbed? Or is it about young children whose behaviour is disturbing to others? Could it be about both?

FIGURE 1 Which perspective dominates our thinking?

The phrase 'disturbing behaviour' is deeply ambiguous, intentionally so. Like the paradoxical picture in Figure 1 (Wittgenstein's duck/rabbit) it has multiple meanings which are difficult to hold simultaneously in consciousness. On one reading, 'disturbing behaviour' suggests a compassionate view, that of the child as a victim whose behaviour is the product of external forces, perhaps inadequate or abusive parenting.

But another reading reverses the perspective, producing an image of the child as the cause of the problem, someone whose difficult behaviour needs to be contained and modified. Each view reflects a different aspect of the relationship between children and their social world. A major goal of this chapter is to highlight both aspects through a consideration of relevant theory and research. I hope that by the end you will be able to offer a partial resolution to the paradox!

In summary, this chapter is about the concept, causes and progress of disturbances in young children's emotional, social and behavioural development. My perspective is that these children are both disturbing to, as well as disturbed by, family, school and society. They are troublesome as well as troubled, disorderly as well as disordered. The rationale for adopting this perspective will become clearer if I now turn to look at attempts to define and measure the incidence of problem behaviour.

2 NORMAL AND PROBLEM BEHAVIOUR

In this section I shall look at some examples of attempts to measure the characteristics and prevalence of disturbed behaviour in young children. My attention will be focused on the more common social, emotional and behavioural difficulties that have no obvious organic root. So I shall not be considering those generally quite severe conditions that are associated with recognized clinical disorders – such as chromosomal abnormalities, metabolic disorders or the autistic spectrum of disorders (see Barker, 1988). I shall start with issues of diagnosis. What constitutes 'a problem'?

FIGURE 2 Where is the borderline between everyday difficulties and problem behaviour?

In a leading textbook of clinical child psychology, Martin Herbert (1991, p. 13) argues that: 'Childhood signs of psychological abnormality are, by and large, manifestations of behavioural, cognitive and emotional responses common to all children. Their quality of being dysfunctional lies in their inappropriate intensity, frequency and persistence.' In other words, whether a child's behaviour is identified as a problem becomes a judgement about where to draw the line between normality and abnormality, health and pathology, integration and disturbance. But the problems of assessment are more complicated than this. Expressions of difficulty are also inherently unstable, and are associated with developmental issues related to particular age groups, as the following activity should make clear.

ACTIVITY 3

Allow about 10 minutes

DEVELOPMENTAL STAGE OR PSYCHOLOGICAL DISTURBANCE?

Think about the following 'problems' of early childhood: first, as they might be described by the parents of a 1-year-old child; then as they might be described by the parents of a 5 year old. How might parental concerns and professional advice about the possibility of psychological disturbance be affected by consideration of the child's age?

- bed wetting
- temper tantrums
- night waking
- clinging to parents

Take the example of 'clinging to parents'. The clinging 1-year-old child might be seen as a sign of secure attachment; the 5 year old showing the same behaviour might be viewed as over-dependent. In other words, the criteria for disturbance need to take account of not only the severity of the difficulties presented by a child, but also their relationship to the developmental expectations for that age group. These complexities of assessment apply to all clinical work, and especially to the larger-scale research to which I now turn.

Most assessments of childhood difficulties carried out within the context of research have been based on rating scales of children's behaviour completed by parents, teachers and/or clinicians. One of the most widely used rating scales was originally designed for completion by teachers of 10 and 11 year olds, and was used in conjunction with an equivalent instrument for parents as part of a pioneering epidemiological study of children living on the Isle of Wight by Rutter, Tizard and Whitmore (1970). By way of illustration, eight items from a revised 26-item version of the scale are reproduced here.

Extracts from Child scale B(2)

TO BE COMPLETED BY TEACHERS

STATEMENT	0 Doesn't apply	1 Applies somewhat	2 Certainly applies
1 Very restless, has difficulty staying seated for long	☐	☐	☐
4 Often destroys or damages own or others' property	☐	☐	☐
6 Not much liked by other children	☐	☐	☐
7 Often worried, worries about many things	☐	☐	☐
15 Is often disobedient	☐	☐	☐
20 Has stolen things on one or more occasions in the past 12 months	☐	☐	☐
21 Unresponsive, inert or apathetic	☐	☐	☐
23 Has had tears on arrival at school *or* has refused to come into the building in the past 12 months	☐	☐	☐

Source: copyright © Michael Rutter

Some of the items in the scale have been found to reflect two reasonably stable and widely replicated broad groupings of children's behavioural difficulties: *neurotic*, that is, fearful, emotional and anxious; and *antisocial*, that is, non-compliant, deceitful and aggressive. (There are also, of course, many children with problems who do not fall neatly into either category.) In subsequent research this distinction has been reframed as one between 'internalizing' and 'externalizing' disorders (Cicchetti and Toth, 1991). For the rest of this section I shall be concerned with both these categories of problem. What can research tell us about their incidence?

2.1 Issues of measurement

ACTIVITY 4

Allow about 10 minutes

THREE BRITISH STUDIES

I have briefly summarized below the findings of three major UK studies that have attempted to assess the incidence of disturbed development. What do you conclude about the incidence of problems? What difficulties are there in drawing conclusions from these studies?

Study 1   The Isle of Wight study

You have already been introduced to the pioneering study carried out on the Isle of Wight by Rutter, Tizard and Whitmore (1970). From judgements made by parents and teachers (based on Child scale B), they concluded that approximately 6 per cent of 10 to 11 year olds showed significant emotional and behavioural problems.

A further study carried out in an inner London borough using the same scale suggested rates of disorder nearly twice as high as those found in the Isle of Wight (Rutter *et al.*, 1975).

Study 2   The National Child Development Study

The National Child Development Study followed the progress of a cohort of British children born in 1958. Teacher assessments when the children were 7 indicated that 22 per cent were showing some symptoms of maladjustment and 14 per cent were considered to present serious problems. This study also found, in common with other research, that levels of maladjustment were higher in boys than girls and more common in children from social classes IV and V (Davie *et al.*, 1972).

Study 3   The Thomas Coram Research Unit Study

A more recent study of children in inner London infant schools by the Thomas Coram Research Unit, University of London, reported 16 per cent of 4 to 7 year olds to have definite behaviour problems in the eyes of their teachers, and a further 17 per cent to have mild behaviour problems (Tizard *et al.*, 1988). There was a marked increase in the number of children considered to have a problem between the reception class and the middle infant year. The teachers' perceptions were confirmed by direct observations in the classroom.

These studies provide valuable information about the incidence of disturbed behaviour in British children, especially drawing attention to the variations in levels of difficulty associated with the age of child, gender and social background. But statistics like these must be treated with extreme caution. There can be no direct comparison between the percentages reported in Study 1 and those in Study 2 or Study 3. Their methods of assessing problems were different, in terms of both the kinds of problems assessed and the source of the assessment (parents at home, teachers at school, psychologists at clinics and so on). Increasingly, clinicians and researchers are standardizing the assessment of emotional and behavioural problems. But while criteria may become dictated by convention, in the final analysis there is no universal standard for behaviour and social integration, no narrow set of rules that define children with behavioural problems. To take the case of Rutter's Child scale B(2), the rating of items reflects the expectations that particular schools place on particular pupils at a particular age, not the behaviour of children in any absolute sense. In other words, their disturbance is *normatively* defined, where normality comprises a wide variety of ways of functioning which fit within broad boundaries of social or moral acceptability for particular age groups. Children are deemed to present problems when their behaviour falls outside the range of tolerance and age-appropriateness. That range may be more or less wide depending both on the context and on the attitudes of those making such judgements. To put it bluntly, many children are only seen as having problems when they become a problem to others. So, whose problem is it? Where does the problem reside?

Problems are context-embedded and normatively defined

One straightforward way of addressing these questions is to compare the judgements of teachers, parents and others about what constitutes 'a problem'. You may know of cases in which children who have been reported as 'playing-up' at school present few problems at home, or vice versa. Achenbach *et al.* (1987) collected together the findings of over 100 systematic studies of the way various parental and professional groups judge children's behavioural problems. From this procedure (technically known as *meta-analysis*) they concluded that there was only a very modest agreement between these groups. Average correlations were as follows:

> r = +.24 between parents and mental health workers
>
> r = +.27 between parents and teachers
>
> r = +.34 between teachers and mental health workers
>
> (where r = 0 would mean no association and r = +1.0 would be a perfect positive association).

Furthermore, when the judgements of children's problems made by these adult groups were compared with children's own perceptions of their problems the correlations were even lower.

How would you interpret such low levels of agreement? One interpretation would be that this is a problem of reliability, that the assessment procedures used were insufficiently sensitive to identify problems clearly, or that the various adults making the judgements lacked sufficient information about the children concerned. This interpretation would point to the unsatisfactory nature of clinical assessment procedures that depend too heavily on one informant's view of a child's problems. A comprehensive assessment clearly needs to take account of more than one perspective on behavioural problems, but the issue isn't simply about improving inter-judge reliability amongst perspectives. Achenbach *et al.* argue that low correlations highlight a very different interpretation of the issue, one which centres on the relationship between behaviour and social context. There are several respects in which problems can be seen as context-embedded and normatively defined.

(a) Different contexts offer different opportunities and place different demands on children, in terms of physical setting, social groupings, activities and routines. Children may behave differently in the context of home as opposed to school.

(b) Standards of behaviour expected of children vary. There are different rules, rituals and regulations, partly related to the age of the child. A child may cope in one situation but not in another.

(c) Those making the judgements may vary in their expectations of children's behaviour, their tolerance of difficulties and the effectiveness of their approach to maintaining discipline.

(d) Relationship patterns will differ in various contexts. The characteristics of the caregiver and the characteristics of the child may interact to produce harmony in one setting, but discord in another.

Each of the above factors will modify the expression and identification of disturbed behaviour. Difficulties arise when the behaviour and goals of the child lack 'goodness of fit' with the social environment to which the child is expected to adapt (Chess and Thomas, 1984; Richardson, 1994). Goodness of fit doesn't just apply at one particular point in time. Each child brings to a given situation an internalized history of experiences, feelings and behaviours evoked by comparable situations in the past (for example, confronting an authority figure, coping with separation, integrating with a peer group). On each occasion there will have been greater or lesser degrees of goodness of fit. In short, any particular 'problems' that a child might present need to be understood in terms of the demands of the context, the biography of similar experiences faced by the child, and the biography of the adult who finds the child's behaviour disturbing. (The concept of 'goodness of fit' will be discussed in more detail in Section 4.)

These principles can also be illustrated from a broader cross-cultural perspective. Weisz *et al.* (1993) used a standardized behaviour checklist to compare parents' perception of 'problems' in their 11 to 15 year olds in Kenya, Thailand and the USA. They found that white American parents often reported their offspring as disobedient and argumentative, whereas Kenyan (Embu) parents' concerns often centred on their children's fears and anxieties. Such variations can be interpreted in terms of some combination of variation in child behaviours and parental expectations between the two societies. Weisz *et al.* note that while American children are growing up in a relatively more permissive and child-centred atmosphere, Kenyan child-rearing patterns are much more strict and controlling.

Adopting a cross-cultural perspective has important implications for the clinical assessment of 'disturbed' behaviour. Behaviour that is adapted to one social or cultural context may be maladjusted in another. It may be fruitful to work flexibly within a concept of the 'ecological adaptiveness' of behaviour (after Bronfenbrenner, 1979) – a concept which recognizes that social adjustment solutions to the tasks of growing up may vary at cultural, sub-cultural and individual levels.

FIGURE 3 Behaviour that is normal in one setting might be cause for concern in another.

I can summarize the arguments so far in terms of the first two questions in Activity 1. For most emotional and behavioural difficulties there is no clear-cut boundary between health and pathology. The diagnosis of a problem is a judgement made by adults and will depend on who is making that judgement and in what context. It will also depend crucially on issues to do with the age and maturity of the child, since some difficulties are linked to specific developmental issues. In short, 'problems' are defined through the relationship between children, their social context and the beliefs of the adults who make the judgement. These principles apply to the clinical diagnosis of individual children as well as to large-scale studies of emotional and behavioural disturbances. For the rest of this section I shall concentrate on one context-specific British study of problem behaviour in young children.

2.2 An epidemiological study

Epidemiology employs techniques of population screening originally developed for the study of major diseases. But it has also been applied in influential studies of psycho-social disorders in children. You have already seen how rating scales were used in the Isle of Wight epidemiological study (Rutter *et al.*, 1970). A more recent British study was carried out by Naomi Richman, Jim Stevenson and Philip Graham. They identified a representative sample of over 700 families with 3 year olds growing up in an outer London borough (Waltham Forest) during the 1970s (Richman *et al.*, 1982). They then carried out a longitudinal study of these children, providing valuable data on the *incidence* of behaviour problems, the *stability* of those problems and the *risk factors* that appear to contribute to the problems. The four descriptions used in Activity 1 are taken from their research report.

Incidence

The first aim of the research was to obtain an accurate assessment of the incidence of difficulties. Parents were asked about potential problem areas using a specially developed behaviour checklist, followed up by semi-structured interviews. The checklist was similar in design to Rutter's Child scale B(2) (reproduced in part on page 48), but the content was quite different, reflecting the problem areas experienced by parents of 3 year olds. The main problems covered were:

feeding – for example, poor appetite and faddiness

wetting – day and/or night

soiling – bowel control

sleeping – for example, ease of settling/night waking

activity level – for example, restlessness, concentration

independence – for example, clinging, attention seeking

sibling relations – for example, squabbling

discipline – for example, difficult to control, temper tantrums

temperament – for example, irritability, anxiety, fears.

From the information gained, Richman *et al.* made a clinical assessment of each child based on 'the frequency and duration of the problem behaviour as well as on the amount of suffering apparent within the child and affecting his relationships with adults and children, ability to play, and independence' (Richman *et al.*, 1982, p. 17).   As a guide to Richman *et al.*'s ratings of severity, turn back to the four descriptions in Activity 1.

ACTIVITY 5

Allow about 15 minutes

INCIDENCE OF PROBLEMS

Richman *et al.*'s basic findings are given in Table 1.

1   Compare the findings in Table 1 with the findings of the research projects described in Activity 4.

2   Note the evidence of differences between girls and boys in the diagnosis of moderate and severe problems. Gender differences are a feature of this topic (and of later chapters of this book).

TABLE 1   Behaviour problems in urban pre-school children.

Clinical rating of severity	Boys (%)	Girls (%)	Total (%)
No problem/dubious problem	76.0	79.0	77.6
Mild problem	14.6	15.4	15.0
Moderate problem	7.6	4.9	6.2
Severe problem	1.7	0.5	1.1

Source: Richman *et al.*, 1982, p. 18.

Transient or enduring problems?

A second aim of Richman *et al.*'s research was to assess the degree of stability in the problems presented by children. (This was question 4 of Activity 1, and was also addressed in Activity 3.) Would the behavioural difficulties identified for 3 year olds be specific to that stage of their development? After all, parents expressing concern are often greeted with the reassuring advice: 'Don't worry, it's only a phase – they'll grow out of it.' Richman *et al.* wanted to find out whether they do, in fact, grow out of it. There are several aspects to this question: the continuity of behaviour, the stability of the difficulties, and clusters of problems.

(i) Continuity of behaviour

There are respects in which a problem at 3 could continue to be a problem at 5, or even at 25. A fearful child could grow up to become a timid adult. A deceitful child could grow up to become a dishonest adult. One of the ways in which Richman *et al.* looked into the question of continuity was to follow the progress of sub-samples of the 100 most problematic cases, along with a control group randomly drawn from the remainder of the main sample. The data are based on interviews with parents at two stages: just before the children were 4, and just before they were 8.

ACTIVITY 6

Allow about 15 minutes

CONTINUITY OF BEHAVIOUR

Table 2 contains data on continuity for both problem and control groups. Please note the data in this table only represent a selection of the areas of problem behaviour covered in Richman *et al.*'s study. Consider the following questions for both groups of children.

(a) Which kinds of problem mainly affect 3-year-old children?

(b) Which kinds of problem mainly affect 8-year-old children?

(c) Which kinds of problem do not appear to be age-specific, being equally problematic at both 3 and 8?

(d) For which kinds of problem is there evidence of continuity from 3 to 8 – that is, children who experience the problem at 3 are also likely to experience it at 8?

(e) To what extent are the same patterns of continuity found for control and problem groups?

Table 2 indicates quite clearly that many problems are transient and age-specific. Night waking and night wetting are major issues for the parents of 3 year olds, but they are rarely a problem for 8 year olds. By 8, different problems are emerging – notably relationships with siblings in the case of the control group. Other difficulties do not appear to be so age-related. This is especially true of 'fears' which are a problem for some children at 3, and different children at 8, with no evidence of continuity for either control or problem behaviour group.

Turning to those items on which there *is* evidence of continuity, the picture is somewhat different for the two groups. In the control group, for whom by definition there was low incidence of problems at 3, there is relatively little evidence that problems persist; exceptions include faddy eating, attention seeking and relations with siblings. For these children there is some truth in the conventional wisdom that they will 'grow out' of any early childhood problems. In other words, for *control group* children, problems at 3 reflect developmental issues for this age group. They are about emotional and physical dependence versus growing mobility and autonomy, about the assertion of an emerging sense of self, and about the gradual inner regulation of basic life rhythms. There is some truth in conventional wisdom about the 'terrible 2's' and the 'troublesome 3's'. Testing the boundaries of emerging independence isn't just normal; it is an important part of development (see Chapter 4, Section 3).

The idea that the pre-school years are a period in which parents experience increased 'difficulties' in caring for their children is well illustrated in research by Jenkins *et al.* (1984). They interviewed parents and doctors of children at seven intervals between 6 weeks and 4 years 6 months. During the early years, the incidence of problems was relatively low, at most affecting 13 per cent of the children as judged by parents, or 10 per cent as judged by doctors. But at 3 years of age these rates rose dramatically (to 23 per cent and 27 per cent respectively). However, by 4 years 6 months they had already started to decline again.

TABLE 2 Persistence of selected items of problem behaviour from 3 to 8 years of age in the control group and the 'problem' group of the Waltham Forest Study.

| | Percentage of children with item of problem behaviour | | | | | |
| | Control group | | | 'Problem' group | | |
	3 years only	3 and 8 years	8 years only	3 years only	3 and 8 years	8 years only
Faddy eating	10	4	8	22	9	18
Difficulty settling at night	9	2	7	15	14	17
Waking at night	11	0	2	26	3	2
Sleeping in parents' bed	4	3	2	19	1	2
Over-active, restless	5	3	8	41	13	4
Attention seeking	2	5	5	31	10	16
Difficult to control	1	1	8	38	15	1
Tempers	1	1	4	13	10	12
Fears	7	0	2	21	0	32
Relations with siblings	4	4	15	19	16	16
Night wetting	32	1	4	38	11	1

Source: adapted from Richman *et al.*, 1982, pp. 89–90.

Table 2 also indicates that conventional wisdom about children growing out of their problems does not apply so well to the most disturbing cases. For a significant number of children in this *'problem' group* there is a consistent pattern of continuity in the persistence of specific items of difficulty between 3 and 8 years of age, notably in the areas of feeding, settling at night, controllability, temper tantrums, relations with siblings and night wetting. What is also notable from Table 2 is that even where there is no continuity in the specific difficulties presented by the behaviour problem group, there is still a continuation of problems. This suggests a second way of approaching the question of whether behaviour difficulties are transient or enduring: the question now becomes whether there is continuity in a deeper sense, perhaps as problems expressed at one stage of development in one way become transmuted into later development and are expressed in a different way.

To convey this idea of enduring psychological difficulties that transcend specific difficulties, I shall introduce a different term, 'stability', in the sense used by Stevenson and Oates (1994). This term will be used to refer to persistence in the severity of problem behaviour in general, by contrast with 'continuity' which refers to the persistence of particular kinds of problem.

(ii) Stability of difficulties

I can address the issue of stability as a question: Were children placed in the problem category at 3 still causing difficulties at 8, irrespective of the particular nature of those difficulties? The answer, for the majority of the children, is 'yes'. 62 per cent of 'problem' children at 3 were still judged to show mild, moderate or severe disorders at 8, while the remaining 38 per cent no longer showed significant problems. Conversely, some children who had been placed in the control group at 3 were now judged to present difficulties that constituted a 'problem'. The persistence of problems was much more evident for the boys than the girls. Some 73 per cent of boys in the 'problem' group continued to present difficulties at 8, compared with only 48 per cent of girls. In other words, assessments made at 3 years of age have considerable predictive value for boys, while there is much higher probability of a change in the fortunes of girls during the next five years. It appears that boys are more vulnerable than girls in two respects: they are more likely to be diagnosed as presenting problems; and these problems are more likely to persist.

Richman *et al.* conclude:

> It seems from our findings that, once a child's behaviour is established in a maladaptive pattern, it does not readily change. Further, young children who show even slight signs of difficult behaviour are at increased risk for developing behaviour and emotional problems in school life. We do not wish to suggest that parents of children who show minor problems should be unnecessarily alarmed, for the chances of their children developing serious difficulties later on are in fact rather small, but it is of interest that even minor disturbance in young children predisposes to later difficulties in some degree.
>
> (Richman *et al.*, 1982, pp. 195–6)

(iii) Clusters of problems

This leads us to a final set of questions about continuity. In Richman *et al.*'s research, children with severe problems typically presented *several* symptoms of difficulty. Is there any pattern to these symptoms? In other words, do particular sets of symptoms tend to occur together, perhaps reflecting particular types of underlying difficulty? How many distinctive patterns is it possible to detect in such young children?

Richman *et al.* were already able to detect some patterns at 3 years of age. Some clusters appear to be short-lived and are associated with developmental problems (for example, those centred on bed wetting). But one cluster, representing 10 per cent of the sample, appeared to have an enduring significance. These 18 children presented a picture of restlessness, over-activity, tantrums, discipline problems, poor concentration, negative moods, and difficulties with siblings. By the age of 8, 16 out of the 18 children were still considered to have clinically significant problems.

When Richman *et al.* carried out a cluster analysis on the data for 8 year olds (a statistical technique that identifies patterns of association in large numbers of variables), two patterns became clear (coinciding with the distinction between antisocial and neurotic disorders introduced at the beginning of this section). They found that 8-year-old antisocial children (mainly boys) had more often been restless and over-active at 3, whereas children with neurotic disorders had more often shown symptoms of fearfulness and temper tantrums at 3. Other research has identified stronger patterns along similar lines. Antisocial symptoms are often associated with risk factors such as a broken home, parental inconsistencies and rejection. Neurotic symptoms are often associated with over-protective parenting and maternal depression (Rutter, 1965).

I would now like to look more closely at Richman *et al.*'s evidence on the risk factors associated with behaviour problems. In doing so, note that we are now turning to the issues raised by question (c) of Activity 1, and that these issues will be the major theme of the rest of this chapter.

Risk factors

ACTIVITY 7

Allow about 10 minutes

RISK FACTORS IN PROBLEM BEHAVIOUR

As you read the following summary of the risk factors associated with problem behaviour at 3 years of age, consider carefully the processes through which social, marital and parenting variables might influence the development of behavioural disturbance.

(a) **Social background**. Richman *et al.* report data on two broad indicators: parental occupation and housing. The parental occupation data are summarized in Table 3.

TABLE 3   Percentage of 3-year-old children with behaviour problems by parental occupation.

	Manual (%)	Non-manual (%)
Girls	14.8	6.9
Boys	19.2	14.4
Total	17.0	10.4

Source: adapted from Richman *et al.*, 1982, p. 21.

Housing data showed that rates of disturbance were higher in those living in council accommodation (20 per cent) than those in owner-occupied housing (13 per cent). The risk of behaviour problems was especially high in those living on the fourth floor and above in tower-block flats: 26 per cent of these children gave cause for concern. Boys were especially at risk in this environment.

(b) **Marital relationship.** Ratings made by the interviewers based on comments from the mother as well as direct observation revealed that 40 per cent of the children in the 'problem' group were living with parents with a poor or very poor marital relationship, compared with 19 per cent of the control group.

(c) **Mother's mental state.** This was measured by questions to mothers about mood, anxiety, fears, worries, energy levels and so on, when the children were 3. Some 39 per cent of the mothers of problem-group children reported moderate or marked levels of depression, compared with 20 per cent of the mothers of the control-group children.

(d) **Parental attitudes to the child.** Criticism and irritation were much more commonly expressed by both mothers and fathers towards 'problem' children than towards children in the control group. These attitudes were also reflected in the incidence of negative feelings and actions towards the child (for example, scolding, smacking and so on). In the case of the mothers these attitudes were often reflected in their fear of losing control, or actually losing control, when irritated by their child.

Table 4 brings together a selection of these findings concerning parental attitudes and family relationships.

Richman *et al.*'s research offers considerable insight into the way social factors are associated with problem behaviour. But great caution is needed before drawing conclusions about the *causal* processes through which these factors might influence the development of disturbance. First, we do not have data for a comprehensive set of measures of social background and family process; other, unmeasured, variables might be more strongly associated with disturbance. Second, we are dealing with very different kinds of measure, from socio-economic indicators that are relatively far removed from the symptoms of behaviour problems to ratings of parental attitude that seem closely linked to parental judgements about problem behaviour. Third, these various measures are not statistically independent. For a complete picture we need to know about the *interactions* involved – for example, the interactions between marital disharmony and parental hostility. Fourth and most important, these are only associations; the patterns of causation are unclear. It is for this reason that it is best to avoid talking about 'causes'; associations are best described in terms of 'risk factors'.

For the rest of this chapter we shall be looking in more detail at some of the 'risk factors' identified by Richman *et al.* My treatment of this major topic is necessarily selective, and is designed to stimulate your thinking about the complex range of pathways to disturbed behaviour. I shall be concentrating on research into 'maternal mental state' and 'parental attitudes', although you should note that a third risk factor, 'marital relationship', will be treated further in both Chapters 3 and 4. As a starting point, turn back to the simple contrast made between the 'medical' and 'social environment' models in Section 1. Consider which model fits most closely to Richman *et al.*'s elaboration of social background, marital relationship, mother's mental state and parental attitude as risk factors? 'Social environment', I think. In the next section I shall expand on this theme, reviewing evidence about the contribution that the young child's family and social environment can make to the development of difficulties, especially in the case of antisocial/externalizing disorders. Then, in Section 4, I shall turn to the question of what influence characteristics of the child might have on the development of these disorders.

TABLE 4 Family relationships and problem behaviour at 3 years of age.

| | Percentage of children experiencing adverse family relationships | | |
	Behaviour problem group (n = 94)	Control group (n = 91)	Significance level p*
Mothers' attitudes:			
Mother moderately/markedly critical of child	34.0	8.9	< 0.001
Mother shows little or no warmth to child	37.2	10.0	< 0.001
Mother smacks child more than once a day	34.0	11.1	< 0.001
Fathers' attitudes:			
Father moderately/markedly critical of child	27.2	8.9	< 0.01
Father shows little or no warmth to child	21.7	8.9	< 0.05
Father smacks child at least once a day	15.2	3.3	< 0.05
Marital disharmony:			
Poor or very poor family relations	40.3	18.9	< 0.01
Frequently disagree over punishing child	28.3	11.2	< 0.01
Parents punish the child equally often	22.8	38.2	< 0.05

*Significance level of chi-square test, d.f. = 1.
Source: adapted from Richman *et al.*, 1982, p. 40.

SUMMARY OF SECTION 2

- The emphasis of this chapter is on psychological problems that do not appear to originate in a recognized organic disorder.
- Rating scales are widely used to assess these kinds of disturbed behaviour, completed by parents, teachers and others.
- Precise classification of problems and measurements of their incidence are not straightforward. Problems are context-embedded and normatively defined.
- Richman *et al.* (1982) carried out a major epidemiological study following up children from 3 to 8 years. Boys appear particularly vulnerable to presenting difficulties.
- A major issue for this study was how far problems are transient or enduring. This can be looked at in terms of (i) continuity of specific problems; (ii) stability of problem behaviour; and (iii) clustering of problems.
- Risk factors associated with problem behaviour include (i) social background; (ii) marital relationships; (iii) mother's mental state; and (iv) parental attitudes to the child.

3 THE ROLE OF THE FAMILY

BBC Radio 4's reports of *Yesterday in Parliament* frequently include noisy exchanges between MPs in the House of Commons. On one occasion the BBC presenter followed a particularly disorderly incident with the cryptic comment 'I blame it on their parents'. In so doing, he was parodying the enduring cultural belief that the proper focus for an explanation of aberrant human behaviour lies within early childhood and the home environment, especially in the quality of parenting provided. This belief draws attention away from the role that children themselves might play in their problems (thereby reinforcing the concept of childhood innocence and perfection), and it also draws attention away from a collective social responsibility for the welfare of children (and their parents). Responsibility is placed squarely on the shoulders of parents, especially mothers. Most importantly, this belief is not just a feature of a particular ideology; it has become the foundation stone of influential psychological theories about the processes of normal and disturbed development. It is most clearly illustrated by the theory of maternal deprivation (as discussed in Chapter 1).

In an influential article written in 1979, William Kessen examined the way modern western faith in the objectivity of scientific psychology has been grafted onto cultural beliefs about child development that reflect a particular society and culture. The danger is that cultural ideology can become merged with scientific endeavour and vice versa. Writing in the American context, he argued that two cultural beliefs – namely, the importance of good mothering, and the critical influence of early experiences on development – have been combined with a third belief, that mothers are responsible for their children's welfare, to produce a powerful weapon of social control.

> The assumption of essential maternity and the assumption of the determining role of early experience join to support yet another underdebated postulate of child psychology. If something goes wrong in the course of a child's development, it is the primary responsibility of the mother (or whoever behaves as mother), and […] if a social problem is not repaired by modification of the child's first years, the problem is beyond repair. The working of the postulate has produced ways of blaming mothers that appear in all theoretical shapes […]
>
> (Kessen, 1979, p. 819)

In other words, beware of ideologies that masquerade as psychological knowledge. This doesn't apply only to the theory of maternal deprivation. I would encourage you to bear Kessen's caution strongly in mind when you draw conclusions from research that has examined the contribution of difficulties in mother–child relationships to the development of disturbed behaviour.

One final word of caution. I realize that for those of you with personal experience of these issues, the discussion that follows may be worrying and distressing. As you will see later, I am not arguing that maternal behaviour in itself causes emotional and behavioural problems in children. The causal process is altogether more complex than that. Indeed one of the reasons for paying attention to maternal behaviour, attitude and mental state is that it can provide a bridge to a discussion of other risk factors, including those associated with the child (as discussed in Section 4).

3.1 Maternal responsiveness

Lynne Murray has carried out a series of investigations into the way disturbed behaviour in small children can be related to difficulties in the relationship with their mother, and may reflect the mother's mental state (Murray and Stein, 1991).

The first study involved introducing a temporary experimental disruption to normal patterns of maternal behaviour and observing the impact on infants 1 to 2 months old. There is now extensive evidence about the significance of normal patterns of complex, reciprocal relationships for infant development (see Oates, 1994). Mothers were invited to bring their infants to the laboratory and engage in normal face-to-face communication. Murray then studied the impact of three kinds of disruption.

Condition 1. During a period when the mother was actively involved with her infant, the experimenter distracted the mother by initiating a conversation so that the mother ceased to engage with her infant's communications.

Condition 2. The mother was asked to continue to face her infant, but remain still and adopt a blank, unresponsive facial expression.

Condition 3: By means of a live video-link, normal forms of maternal responsiveness were set out of phase with the infant's behaviour, so that the mother's expressions were no longer synchronized with the infant's.

ACTIVITY 8

Allow 10 minutes

THE EFFECTS OF DISRUPTION

Which forms of disruption would you expect to disturb the infant most? Consider how far each would match with infant expectations about the patterns in a relationship.

Murray draws an important distinction between disruptions which are a normal part of everyday communication ('natural perturbations', as in Condition 1) and those which violate the infant's expectations about relationships ('unnatural perturbations', as in Conditions 2 and 3). In Condition 1 infants typically quietened and watched the communication between mother and experimenter. Even though the mother changed her behaviour markedly, turned her face away from her infant and altered her speech patterns, the infants showed no distress. By contrast, in Condition 2 a blank expression typically provoked a strong reaction from the infants, who initially attempted to engage their mother's attention, frowning and thrashing their arms about, and later became passively self-absorbed. The mismatches of timing between infant initiatives and maternal responses in Condition 3 caused confusion in the infants, who typically made short darting glances at the mother's face before turning away, becoming avoidant, self-absorbed and often distressed.

The conclusions of this experimental research, that even very young infants are highly sensitive to the form and timing of their mothers' responses, led Murray to enquire about the impact on infants of a disruption in the normal patterns of maternal responsiveness outside the laboratory. She carried out a longitudinal study on the impact of postnatal depression, screening a large population of women with 6-week-old infants to identify a sample of 58 mothers suffering postnatal depression, along with a control group of 42 mothers with no previous psychiatric history or current depression (Murray, 1992). Both groups of mothers and infants were followed up when the infants reached 18 months old, using a comprehensive battery of assessment procedures linking postnatal depression to aspects of infant development.

Murray found that 18-month-old infants whose mothers had suffered bouts of postnatal depression were much more likely to be assessed as 'insecurely attached' in the 'Strange Situation' (see Chapter 1). This effect was particularly evident for the boys in the sample. Insecure attachment has been consistently linked with psychological difficulties (Sroufe, 1988; see also Greenberg et al., 1993).

Murray also found that the 18-month-old children with depressed mothers were already more likely than controls to present behaviour difficulties as assessed using a Behavioural Screening Questionnaire (adapted from the instrument used by Richman et al., 1982). The overall levels of difficulty were not high, and it must be borne in mind that they were based on mothers' reports of behaviour problems. Nonetheless, as an indicator of the early impact of relationship difficulties, there is some significance in the finding that these infants were more often reported to have temper tantrums, eating difficulties, to suffer sleep disturbance and to be overly clinging.

A feature of Murray's research is that it points to the *processes* through which maternal mental state may be influencing aspects of infant development. Murray videotaped interactions between a sub-sample of mothers and infants throughout the 18-month period. Analyses of maternal speech during play with children at 2 months of age show that depressed mothers were less responsive to their infants: their speech more often reflected the personal experiences with which they were preoccupied than their infant's needs. These mothers were less likely to respond to their infant's own behaviour and signals, expecting compliance with the mother's agenda, and were more likely to show hostility to their infant's behaviour (Murray and Stein, 1991).

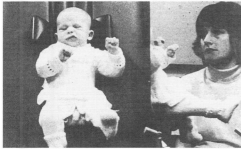

FIGURE 4

(reproduced courtesy of Lynne Murray,
Winnicott Research Unit, University of
Cambridge).

Murray's evidence that infants are highly sensitive to the
mental state and interactive style of their mothers is
broadly confirmed in research carried out by Tiffany Field
in the USA. Field *et al.* (1988) have also shown that the
defensive or avoidant strategies adopted by 3 to 6-month-
old infants with depressed mothers are not specific to that
particular adult. When infants were videotaped
interacting with a non-depressed adult their tendency to be
more withdrawn and show less positive affect appeared to
generalize.

The research discussed so far has focused on mothers and
very young infants. For a longer-term perspective on the
way maternal mental state can affect maternal
responsiveness we now turn to a study by Tony Cox and his
collaborators (Cox *et al.*, 1987). Their research involved an
urban working-class population in Britain. Depressed
mothers were identified when their children were already 2
years old. One particular feature of this research is the
concept of 'links', an attempt to measure the degree of
reciprocity or contingency in the mother–child relationship:
in other words, the extent to which mothers pick up the
cues in their children's behaviour or utterances. A *link*
occurs when the response of one partner to the interaction
is judged to be relevant to the other's utterance and
behaviour and expands or extends the meaning of that
behaviour.

This measure clearly differentiated the 'depressed' mothers
from a control group. Links offered by depressed mothers
were much less likely to be followed by an appropriate
response from their child, compared with links offered by
an equivalent group of non-depressed mothers. Cox *et al.*
argue that low levels of links can be interpreted as a failure
on the mother's part to recruit, sustain and expand the
young child's attention and concentration. This failure can, in due
course, leave parent and child with a disturbed relationship. If mothers
are preoccupied, inactive, unresponsive and indecisive, their small
infants are also likely to turn away, becoming more self-directed but
also more 'whiney'. Maternal behaviour may become negative, the
mother may ignore the child, or at other times, attempt to control the
child, in response to toddler behaviour which may be disturbed,
demanding or, in some cases, coercive towards the mother. At worst,
the child's resistent behaviour and the mother's attempts to assert
control could result in an incident that borders on child abuse.

Before moving on, I would like to re-emphasize that the case of maternal
depression has served as a vehicle for discussing the significance of
maternal responsiveness. I am not implying that there is a simple
causal relationship between depression, responsiveness and child
disturbance. First, not all depressed mothers develop difficulties in

their relationships with their offspring. In Cox *et al*.'s study, a wide range of maternal styles was observed, especially in depressed mothers (Cox *et al*., 1987). And in American research, Zahn-Waxler *et al*. (1990) have identified a sub-group of depressed mothers who appear to be able to maintain a responsive style of care towards their child despite their personal preoccupations.

Second, the extent of the longer-term consequences of maternal depression for childhood disturbances is far from clear. One recent review of this topic concluded that during the period of maternal depression there is evidence of an association with child behaviour disorder. However, once the depression is past, there is much less evidence of a long-term effect, except in the context of other family and social adversities which continue to feed the disturbed relationship (Cummings and Davies, 1994).

Third, the research by Murray and Cox has highlighted a single variable. For a fuller picture, maternal depression needs to be understood as part of a network of risk factors impinging on the developmental process. Its significance may lie in the immediacy of its association with relationship patterns, but you need to be aware of the impact of other variables. For example, like Richman *et al*., Cox *et al*. reaffirm the central significance of a mother's wider relationship difficulties for her mental state and her relationship with her children. Depression is strongly associated with marital disharmony and a long history of attachment problems. A much higher percentage of the depressed women in Cox's sample reported that they themselves had experienced poor relationships with their own parents, with less warmth and harsher discipline, as well as a high incidence of separations and disruptions, and more emotional and schooling difficulties as children. They also reported having married younger, having had their first child younger than mothers in the control group, and they perceived marital disharmony as a major cause of their depression. Once these wider sets of variables are taken into account, the inappropriateness of thinking in terms of maternal mental state (or any other single variable) as the *cause* of disturbed behaviour becomes apparent. Indeed, an alternative view would be that the mother's depression, the child's disturbance and the difficulties in their relationship are all the *effects* of deeper, longer-standing problems of social stress and family discord.

Fourthly, the network of variables associated with maternal depression only represents one pathway to disturbed behaviour, albeit a pathway which can be associated with the development of insecure attachments in infancy and may result in longer-term relationship and behaviour difficulties. A second pathway, which has been most extensively elaborated by Patterson (1986), traces the origins of antisocial behaviour to harsh and inconsistent discipline, and ineffective parental control strategies which unwittingly reinforce the child's negative (coercive) behaviour. It is this pathway that I want to elaborate on next.

3.2 Maternal attitudes

In our discussion of maternal responsiveness we mainly c[
on behavioural indicators of disturbed relationships. But the parties
to a relationship aren't just *behaving* towards each other. They are
thinking about each other. In the terminology of attachment theory
(Chapter 1), they have an Internal Working Model of the relationship.
In other words, we need to take account of the cognitive as well as the
social and emotional dimensions of the relationship. This is especially
true of the mother, who may be trying to make sense of her child's
behaviour, as well as reflecting on her sense of adequacy as a mother;
but it is also true of the child as he or she begins to construct
expectations of his or her caregiver's behaviour and attitude (Stern-
Bruschweiler and Stern, 1989). The contribution of parents' beliefs
and attitudes as a risk factor was one of the major findings of Richman
et al.'s study (Section 2). For the rest of this section I would like you to
consider two pieces of research that provide a deeper insight into the
character of these beliefs and attitudes and their contribution to
disturbed relationships.

The starting point of the first piece of research was not disturbed
behaviour in children, but the related topic of abusive behaviour in
parents. Stratton and Swaffer (1988) investigated beliefs about
relationship difficulties in a sample of British mothers whose 3 to 5-
year-old children had been identified as having been physically
abused. Mothers of non-abused children from a similar catchment
area served as a control; and mothers of children with special needs
provided a comparison group of parents who were coping, despite
being under higher than normal levels of stress. The research focused
on the mothers' beliefs about the causes of their children's difficult
behaviour.

The main findings were based on 15-minute structured interviews
with the mother about what the child was like at home. Stratton and
Swaffer found that the special-needs group presented a pattern of
beliefs which was distinctively different from that of either the abused
or the control group. These mothers tended to see the causes of
problems as internal to the child, but not within the child's control.
Nor did their statements suggest that they held themselves personally
responsible to the same extent as the mothers in the other groups.
They were also more likely to see stability in the causes of problems.
Like the special-needs mothers, the mothers of abused children were
also more likely than the control-group mothers to see causes as
internal to the child and not under their (that is, the mother's) own
control. But they were much more likely than either control or
special-needs mothers to believe that what happened, and the
difficulties they experienced, were in their child's control. In other
words, these mothers presented a picture of impotence and
helplessness, which the authors argue was associated with their
desperate, abusive attempts to re-establish control.

> The mothers in the abuse group could be seen as protecting their own self image by perceiving causes as outside themselves and their control. Blame is directed at their children [...] This can be seen as a workable adaptation for much of the time but having a high likelihood that when things go wrong, efforts to bring about change will largely be in the form of attempts to influence the child, with the risk that when this fails to solve the problem, the child will be scapegoated and eventually attacked.
>
> (Stratton and Swaffer, 1988, p. 212)

This illustrates in a high-risk group the way negative maternal beliefs about a child may feed into a vicious circle of perceptions, behaviours and responses. However, there is a limitation to this research, namely that it only focuses on one party to the relationship. For a complete account, we also need to consider the contribution of the child's beliefs about and perceptions of the mother.

American research by MacKinnon-Lewis *et al.* (1992) illustrates the point very clearly and builds on the model of *pathways* to antisocial behaviour elaborated by Patterson (1982). In this model, weak parenting skills are believed to encourage the child to become non-compliant to parental requests and to make unreasonable (coercive) demands on parents and other members of the family. The growing negative attention given to the child's inappropriate behaviours combines with a failure to reward positive behaviours to produce an escalating cycle of parent–child conflict.

MacKinnon-Lewis *et al.* have attempted to extend Patterson's analysis beyond the behavioural to the cognitive and emotional aspects of relationships. They studied 104 mother–son pairs. First, the boys (aged 7 to 9 years) were interviewed individually on a standardized procedure designed to elicit their beliefs about their mother's intentions and reactions in potential conflict/discipline situations. They were told a series of stories about a boy (with whom they were invited to identify) and his mother. In each case, the boy behaved in a way that might be construed by a parent as 'naughty'. The mother's disciplinary response was left ambiguous, and the child was invited to give his interpretation of the mother's actions, his understanding of her intentions and his likely response to them. The child's response to each story was then scored on a five-point scale of perceived maternal attitude (ranging from hostile to positive). Second, mothers were interviewed about their response to a series of equivalent hypothetical stories in which the child's behaviour was ambiguous, but could be construed as provocative. Mothers were asked about the boy's intentions, and again these were scored on a scale of perceived child attitude (from hostile to positive).

Mother–son interactions were then video-recorded during 20-minute sessions in which they were invited to play two games: one was highly competitive; the second demanded close co-operation. These interactions were later analysed in terms of the frequency of positive, negative and neutral behaviours by mother and son (including verbal and non-verbal behaviour as well as facial expressions and so on). Results showed that there was a strong association between mothers' and sons' perceptions of each other's hostile intent. These perceptions are also closely linked to the negativity of their behaviours towards each other. In other words, the aggressive interactions between mothers and sons were being sustained, at least in part, by mutual, negative, affective cognition. Most significantly, children's *beliefs* about their mother's hostility appeared to be influential, over and above their *actual* hostility, in fuelling children's negative behaviour. Having said that, this research still leaves many fascinating questions unanswered about the interrelationships between cognition, feelings and behaviour in the genesis of disturbed relationships between parents and their children.

In this section I have taken two of the risk factors identified in Richman *et al.*'s research and looked in more detail at research into the processes through which they might contribute to the development of disturbed behaviour. As we leave this section it is important to reaffirm that there are multiple pathways to disturbed behaviour and that maternal mental state and attitudes represent just two amongst a constellation of social context, family and parental risk factors that have been found to be associated with childhood difficulties. MacKinnon-Lewis *et al.*'s research is also a timely reminder of the need to take account of the role of the child in the process. In the discussion so far, this has been a major missing element, a source of influence that is at the centre of the process and yet is often overlooked. In the next section I want to look at how family and parenting variables can interact with the characteristics of the child, and at how, through the way they shape their environment, children can be the 'producers of their own development' (Lerner and Busch-Rossnagel, 1981).

SUMMARY OF SECTION 3

- Much psychological research and theory has been linked to wider cultural beliefs in family responsibility for child development (especially maternal responsibility).

- Experimental studies of disrupted maternal responsiveness illustrate the potential impact of maternal depression on child development.

- Maternal depression can be associated with insecure attachment and early indicators of behaviour difficulties; it can also feed the development of a vicious cycle of disturbed relationships.

- Research into long-term effects is inconclusive. Maternal depression is one of many risk factors that can contribute to disturbed development. Simple cause and effect models are misleading.

- Parents and their children develop an Internal Working Model, a set of beliefs about each other's actions and intentions and about their relationship, which can itself feed the growth of disturbed behaviour.

4 THE ROLE OF THE CHILD

I began Section 3 by drawing attention to the enduring cultural belief that the proper focus for enquiry into the causes of disturbed and disturbing behaviour lay in some aspect of children's early environment, especially the adequacy of the parenting and the role of the mother. In reviewing the relevant research I encouraged you to beware of thinking in terms of simple cause and effect influences, favouring instead the expression 'risk factors' which is less deterministic and acknowledges multiple patterns of influence. As we start Section 4 I want to return to these issues of causality.

4.1 Directions of effect in human processes

Beliefs about the family and parenting as *the cause* of aberrant child behaviour reflect a 'social environment' perspective, in which the child is seen as the passive victim of circumstances. This perspective also shapes the design of research which has traditionally set out to address questions about the effects of environmental variables on children's development and adjustment. For example, in Chapter 1, Section 3, studies by Goldfarb and Tizard set out to measure the effects of institutional care on children's social, emotional and intellectual development. And in Section 2 of this chapter, the study by Richman *et al.* highlighted the influence of social background, marital relationship, maternal mental state and parental attitudes on the development of problem behaviour.

For some years now scepticism has been growing about the validity of this way of asking questions about causality in human development. One of the first challengers to convention was Bell (1968); for a more recent discussion see Shaw and Bell (1993). Bell took the example of a classic study by Sears, Maccoby and Levin (1957) into the effects of parental style on aggressive behaviour in children. Sears *et al.* had reported a close association between these variables. Parents of aggressive children were found to use punitive discipline strategies, but at the same time they also tended to be permissive. By contrast, the parents of non-aggressive children were much less punitive in their discipline, but they had higher expectations of their children's behaviour. How would you interpret these results?

In their report, Sears *et al.* offered a 'social environment' interpretation, arguing that it was the combination of permissiveness and punitiveness in parents that caused their children to become aggressive. This seems plausible enough. After all, a highly permissive style means that children lack clear guidance on appropriate behaviour, and a highly punitive style means that, at the same time, they may have been frustrated by bouts of severe punishment. Bell (1968) offered a very different interpretation. He argued persuasively for reversing the direction of effect, claiming that it was the child's temperamental characteristics that determined how aggressive it was, and that parental discipline strategies were an attempt to modify the child's nature. So those parents with difficult youngsters got tough with them, while those with compliant offspring had no need to resort to severe methods. Bell's paper set in motion a healthy scepticism about simplistic interpretations of the direction of cause and effect relationships.

ACTIVITY 9
Allow about 10 minutes

REVERSING THE DIRECTION OF EFFECT

Look back over the research we discussed in Section 3. Might the concept of 'direction of effect' suggest a different interpretation of the evidence on the relationship between the mental state and attitudes of mothers and the disturbed behaviour of children?

A striking example of unexpected directions of effect is provided in a long-term research programme directed in the USA by Russell Barkley. Barkley *et al.* (1985) identified a group of six-year-old children who were presenting problems of restlessness, impulsivity and a short attention span. They were observed interacting with their mothers in a laboratory playroom with a standardized set of play possibilities. Mothers were asked to spend the first 20 minutes in free play with their child. Then the experimenter asked the mothers to work with their child in a series of tasks and situations, such as tidying up the toys, copying a series of geometric designs and asking the child to play quietly on their own while the mother read a magazine.

Initial research had shown that while there was little to distinguish the 'problem' child–mother dyads from a control group in the free-play situation, significant differences emerged once the mothers were asked to accomplish specific tasks. In the 'problem' group, interactions were much less smooth and co-operative. Mothers were more directive towards their children, with many more commands and more negative behaviour, including frequent reprimands. At the same time, they were much less responsive to their child's general social interactions. These children, in turn, were more often negative and disobedient; they were less likely to comply with their mother's requests and commands, and when they did comply, their attention to the task was shorter than for a control group. How would you explain the association between maternal style and child behaviour? To what extent do the negative interactions originate in the mothers' behaviour and attitude?

In summarising Barkley *et al.*'s study I omitted one piece of information. The 'problem' children had been selected for study because their behaviour over the preceding 12 months met criteria for a clinical diagnosis as 'hyperactive'. How does this label alter your view of cause and effect in Barkley's data? By labelling the problem 'hyperactivity' our attention is redirected to the children's behaviour as 'the cause' of the problem. The second stage of Barkley *et al.*'s research can help us disentangle cause and effect (for this group of children at least).

In this second stage Barkley *et al.* (1985) evaluated the short-term therapeutic potential of the drug Ritalin (Methylphenidate). Ritalin is a stimulant drug which has been widely used in North America (although not without controversy). In children it has the effect of reducing motor activity and improving attention and concentration. Sixty boys aged between 5 and 9 (and diagnosed hyperactive) were assigned either to a control (no drug) condition or to one of three experimental conditions (placebo, low dose and high dose). After seven days of drug treatment the boys and their mothers were asked to return to the laboratory playroom, and their interactions observed following the procedure already described.

ACTIVITY 10

Allow about 10 minutes

EFFECTS OF MEDICATION ON INTERACTION

Table 5 summarises the results of Barkley *et al.*'s observations of mother–child interaction for just two of the groups (placebo and high dose). Study the table carefully and think about the implications of these results for the way we think about the causes of disturbed behaviour.

TABLE 5 Mother–child interaction for placebo and high-dose medication groups.

Observations	Placebo	High dose
Mother initiates interactions – average frequency	47	5
Mother–child contingencies	(%)	(%)
Mother directs – child complies	89	94
Child complies – mother controls	45	30
Child off-task – mother attends	18	35
Child off-task – mother controls	45	30

Source: adapted from Barkley *et al.*, 1985, p. 711.

The first measure ('mother initiates interactions') is a summary measure of the average number of interactions initiated by the mother during the observation period. The rest of the table contains a more sophisticated measure of interaction called 'contingency'; this measures the degree of reciprocity or cohesion in the mother–child relationship. For example, instead of just recording how often mothers attempted to direct their child's behaviour (say, by issuing a command), the researchers were able to record the percentage of these commands that were complied with by the child. Or, to look at contingencies of mother on child behaviour, the observation system recorded, for instances where the child's behaviour drifted off-task, how often this was followed up by the mother attempting to bring the child's behaviour back on course (mother control) or the mother showing some positive interest in the child's activity (mother attends). These measures of 'contingency' are similar to the measure of 'links' discussed in Section 3.

We might expect that mothers with 'difficult to manage' children would be locked into a 'high-control' style of interaction, whereas Barkley *et al.*'s results suggest that even after only seven days' treatment, the impact of the drug on children's behaviour had already produced a marked effect on their mother's interaction style. The mothers of children in the placebo group were preoccupied with the problem of managing their child's behaviour, entailing a very high level of 'initiates interaction'. The high-dose group no longer required that level of basic control. Furthermore, within an interaction they were more likely to comply with their mother's directions. Conversely, on those occasions when they did not comply, this was less likely to be met with a 'control' response from their mothers. The final two contingencies illustrate that when children's attention went 'off-task', they were likely to meet a different response according to whether their behaviour was being modified by the influence of high-dose Ritalin. Mothers of the children receiving Ritalin were more willing to show an interest in their child's behaviour when the child strayed off-task, rather than scolding them in an effort to maintain the desired behaviour, which was more common in the placebo group.

The therapeutic and ethical issues associated with the use of drugs to control problem behaviour are beyond the scope of this chapter (see Barker, 1988), The value of Barkley *et al.*'s research for this chapter is in illustrating the dangers of adopting a deterministic attitude to the risk factors associated with disturbed behaviour, and presuming particular directions of causality. In our earlier discussion of the environmental risk factors identified in Richman *et al.*'s research, there was an implicit assumption that these variables were in some sense causing the child's problems. Yet as we have seen, there may be situations where it is characteristics of the child that are contributing to family stress, modifying parental attitudes and shaping maternal behaviour.

We must be careful not to take the argument too far. Bear in mind that Barkley's research was with a group of children clinically defined as hyperactive, whereas this chapter has concentrated mainly on children with behavioural difficulties that are not strongly associated with known clinical disorders. The issue is not about whether the direction of effect runs from child to mother or from mother to child; *it is about their mutual influence as partners in a relationship*. In short, children as well as parents play an active role in the process of development; *interactive* patterns of influence will apply in all cases. The relative influence of parenting behaviour versus child behaviour will vary, according to the characteristics of the child, the characteristics of the parent and the circumstances affecting both. Patterns of functional and dysfunctional interaction are not fixed. They are linked to the developmental process. Their influence may shift as child, parent and circumstances change. Problems may be amplified by new stresses or attenuated by effective intervention and support.

4.2 A transactional model

This picture of how difficult behaviour develops has much in common with the transactional model elaborated by Sameroff (1991).

FIGURE 5
A transactional model
(adapted from Sameroff,
1991).

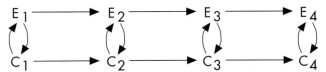

Figure 5 is an attempt to capture the essential features of the model in a simple, abstract way. The child is represented by the symbol 'C', their social environment by the symbol 'E'. Figure 5 depicts the interrelationship of child and environment over several time intervals. The young child is actively relating to the environment and being acted upon by the environment, which includes major caregivers. Interactions at time 1 not only modify the way the child behaves at time 2, they also modify the environment for subsequent development. So difficult behaviour at time 1 will modify the way a parent or teacher treats the child at time 2. Transactional processes don't just affect the child in terms of the quality of their interactions; they can also result in a more fundamental change in their environment – for example, in extreme cases, by being excluded from school, taken into care, or referred to special education. The emerging configuration at time 2 will in turn shape child/environment relationships at time 3, and so on.

ACTIVITY 11

Allow about 10 minutes

APPLYING THE TRANSACTIONAL MODEL

Think about this model in relation to the theme of this chapter, 'what causes disturbed behaviour?' Or try applying it to another aspect of development that interests you – for example, achievement in school, or the development of a skill of some kind. In each case, think about the way influences on a child at one point in time can be understood in a longer-term transactional perspective.

Sameroff (1991) provides the following example.

A complicated childbirth may have made an otherwise calm mother somewhat anxious. The mother's anxiety during the first months of the child's life may have caused her to be uncertain and inappropriate in her interactions with the child. In response to such inconsistency the infant may have developed some irregularities in feeding and sleeping patterns that give the appearance of a difficult temperament. This difficult temperament decreases the pleasure that the mother obtains from the child and so she tends to spend less time with the child. If there are no adults interacting with the child, and especially speaking to the child, the child may not meet the norms for language development and score poorly on pre-school language tests. In this case the outcome was not determined by the complicated birth nor by the mother's consequent emotional response. If one needed to pick a cause it would be the mother's avoidance of the child, yet one can see that such a view would be a gross oversimplification of a complex developmental sequence.

(Sameroff, 1991, p. 174)

With this framework in mind let us turn to other research that has examined the child's role in the transactional process. The hyperactive children in Barkley's research served as an extreme example of the way a specific behavioural disorder can shape the character of the child's interactions with the environment. Other clinically identified disorders – for example, autism, epilepsy or other syndromes and inherited disorders – place caregivers under different adaptive pressures. But many children who develop disturbing behaviour do not suffer from a readily identifiable pathology. In so far as they influence the course of their development it must be through the impact on caregivers of more subtle individual characteristics, notably their temperament.

4.3 The influence of temperament

The significance of temperament in accounting for individual differences is controversial (Stevenson and Oates, 1994). Quite strong associations have been found between a 'difficult' temperament at 4 or 5 years of age and behavioural difficulties in later childhood; indeed, it is unclear where we should draw the line between a 'difficult temperament' and 'behaviour disorder' (Chess and Thomas 1984; Maziade *et al.,* 1989). But there is much less stability during the years before 5. The evidence suggests that a 'difficult' or 'irritable' temperament is best thought of as another risk factor, a vulnerability to relationship difficulties which affects boys especially, who (as we have seen) are much more likely than girls in Western society to become identified as presenting difficulties during the pre-school years. Whether a 'difficult' infant becomes a disturbed child appears to depend on the appropriateness of environmental adaptations to that temperament. As noted in Section 2, Chess and Thomas introduced the concept of 'goodness of fit' to describe the transactional relationship between child and environment.

> When the organism's capacities, motivations and style of behaving and the demands and expectations of the environment are in accord, then goodness of fit results. Such consonance between organism and environment potentiates optimal positive development. Should there be dissonance between the capacities and characteristics of the organism on the one hand and the environmental opportunities and demands on the other, there is poorness of fit, which leads to the maladaptive functioning and distorted development. Goodness of fit and consonance, poorness of fit and dissonance are never abstractions. They have meaning only in terms of the values and demands of a given socio-economic group or culture.

(Chess and Thomas, 1984, p. 21)

Figure 6 is an illustration of the way characteristics of the child can interact with features of the environment in the production of disturbed behaviour.

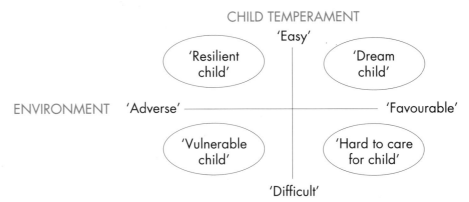

FIGURE 6 The interaction of child and environmental variables.

On this model difficult temperament is a risk factor, but its impact depends on the caring qualities of the family environment in which the child is growing. Conversely, the relative impact of adverse family experiences depends on the child's ability to adapt and cope with difficulties. This is, of course, a gross oversimplification. Child 'temperament' and 'environment' are not single, bipolar variables, nor are they static in time. Nonetheless, this model should give you a feel for the power of a transactional perspective.

Much current research is dedicated to elucidating the complex interactions amongst a host of child, parent, family and social environment variables, which predispose some children to become vulnerable to disorder, while other children who present a slightly different picture of temperament and adversities may appear resilient. To illustrate this theme, we can return to the issue of gender. You will recall that Richman *et al.* identified more 3-year-old boys than girls with behaviour difficulties, and that these problems were more likely to persist in the boys until the age of 8. Rutter (1987) has tried to tease out some of the reasons for this widespread finding, focusing on the impact of family discord. He presents evidence for several respects in which boys are more *vulnerable* than girls to the adverse impact of family discord: (i) they are more susceptible to a neurological disorder which renders them less able to cope with stress; (ii) temperamental characteristics make them more likely to become caught up in family discord (and be the object of parental criticism); (iii) in cases of family breakdown they are more likely to be placed in institutional care than girls; (iv) they are more likely to react to family stress by presenting difficulties that cannot be overlooked – that is, externalizing (antisocial) rather than internalizing (neurotic) disorders (boys are characterised as 'warriors' and girls as 'worriers' by Zahn-Waxler, 1993); and (v) their difficult behaviour is more likely to provoke a parental reaction. However, note that set against these adversities are *protective* factors (such as a good relationship with at least one parent or positive educational experiences at pre-school or school level) which can temper the impact on the child.

The interplay between risk and protective factors is not static. It needs to be understood within a developmental perspective in which children are susceptible to different patterns of influence at different stages and transition points in life. For example, going to nursery or school is often an important *gateway* through which the 'disturbed' status of a troublesome child becomes confirmed. This is not just because the child's behaviour is publicly assessed and labelled, possibly leading to a Statement of Special Educational Needs. The particular demands, pressures and expectations for 'good' classroom behaviour (Klein and Ballentine, 1988) often *amplify* a child's problems of social integration. The educational goals and professional orientation of teachers (combined with the physical and social constraints of managing large groups of children in the confined space of a classroom) place distinct adaptive pressures on their pupils.

To summarize the argument of this section so far, a transactional perspective on the development of behavioural difficulties overcomes the issue of direction of effect by acknowledging continuous patterns of mutual influence between characteristics of the child and characteristics of the environment. A clear example is provided by research into temperament, especially the concept of 'goodness of fit'. A new generation of research is now dedicated to teasing out the interaction of risk factors in longitudinal perspective, guided by concepts such as vulnerability, resilience, protective mechanisms, gateways and amplification (Robins and Rutter, 1990; Rutter and Casaer, 1991). Finally in this chapter, I would like to explore some of these themes via research that has traced the interrelationship of temperament with other variables, notably attachment and parental responsiveness, in the generation of disturbance.

Temperament, attachment, maternal support and difficult behaviour

As you know from Chapter 1, attachment to one or a small number of consistent caregivers is generally recognized as a prerequisite of social adjustment. Attachment is a 'secure base', a pattern of relationships through which the infant can learn, from which the infant can explore, and to which it can return for security and comfort. As you also know from Section 3, insecure attachment is associated with depressed maternal mental state and is predictive of problem behaviour.

Conventional interpretations of the causes of insecure attachment generally refer to the mother's unavailability, insensitivity or lack of reciprocity. However, there have been some attempts to disentangle the infant's contribution to the process. Notable amongst these was a study by Crockenburg (1981) which built on earlier work by Waters *et al.* (1980). Waters *et al.* assessed one hundred newborn infants using a neonatal paediatric screening procedure, and followed this up a year later with Ainsworth's Strange Situation procedure. Those 1 year olds classified as insecurely attached were found to have shown signs of 'irritability' as newborns (in terms of responsiveness, motor immaturity and physiological regulation).

Crockenburg (1981) took the same basic design, but extended it to show how characteristics of the infant interact with qualities of the environment in the production of relationship difficulties. Forty-eight middle-class mothers and their infants took part in this study, which involved four sets of measurements:

(a) a paediatric assessment made shortly after birth, on which basis the sample was broadly divided into two groups: high irritability and low irritability

(b) home observations of the way mothers responded to their infants' distress signals, which led to them being classified as high responsive or low responsive

(c) mother's perceptions of the extent of social support, in relation to stress, given to them by family, neighbours, friends and so on

(d) security of attachment on the Strange Situation at 1 year of age.

TABLE 6 Frequency of securely and insecurely attached infants in social support/irritability sub-groups.

	High irritability		Low irritability	
	Low support	High support	Low support	High support
Securely attached	2	12	7	13
Anxiously attached	9	1	2	2

Source: Crockenburg, 1981, p. 862.

Crockenburg's first finding was that the more irritable (that is, vulnerable) infants were less likely to attract responsive care from their mothers, and were in turn more likely to show insecure attachments. But, as Table 6 shows, the impact of irritability was strongly affected by the degree of social support perceived by the mother. This effect did not apply to the low irritability group who were generally securely attached irrespective of support to the mother (that is, they were resilient). In the high irritability group, vulnerability to insecure attachment appears to have been moderated by maternal support, which can be seen as a 'protective factor' for vulnerable infants.

> Unresponsive mothering does indeed appear to be one mechanism through which a child's trust is undermined and his attachment to his mother rendered anxious. But whether a mother behaves unresponsively appears to be influenced by the infant's irritability and her attitudes as well as the social support available to her as a mother.
>
> (Crockenburg, 1981, p. 864)

Multiple pathways

In this chapter we have looked at some of the pathways to disturbed behaviour that have received the greatest attention from recent research. I have concentrated on variables to do with social circumstances, marital relationships, maternal depression, parental attitudes and child temperament, as these affect the quality of mother–child relationships in the early years. I have argued against a deterministic view of these variables, favouring a more dynamic, transactional model, which acknowledges that problem behaviour is the product of a relationship history between children and their caregivers to which both actively contribute at the level of behaviour, beliefs and feelings; for a more extended discussion of the model see Shaw and Bell (1993). But this is still a far from complete picture, in two key respects.

First, it is arguable that current research is still overemphasizing the significance of the mother–child dyad at the expense of other relationship patterns: disturbed behaviour frequently applies to father–child, grandparent–child and sibling–child relationships (Patterson, 1986). Also, disturbed behaviour in children may result from wider relationship difficulties – for example, discord between parents can have serious repercussions for the child. Indeed, Hinde and Stevenson-Hinde (1988) have cogently argued that it is these complex systems of relationships within families, rather than merely the development of children, that should be the starting point for research – a perspective that is closely aligned to the 'systems theory' approaches that inform family therapy (for example, Bentovim *et al.*, 1987). The influence of wider family relationships is one of the themes of Chapter 3.

FIGURE 7

Second, you should not be misled into assuming that, because a child presents social and emotional problems, those problems necessarily originate in a disturbance in their social and emotional development. There are other, quite different, pathways that feed into the process of becoming disturbed. One of the best established pathways concerns children with language disorders. There is an extensive research literature on the learning difficulties faced by children with various kinds of language disorder, and language disorders are often closely linked to behavioural difficulties (Rutter and Casaer, 1991). This example serves as a reminder that while courses on child development may divide the subject up into discrete sections (cognitive, emotional, social and so on), the process of development itself is a great deal more integrated and dynamic. Of course, this applies to normal as much as to disturbed development.

> ### SUMMARY OF SECTION 4
>
> - Conventional beliefs about the impact of parenting on the child have been modified by re-analyses of directions of effect.
> - Studies of the effects of drug therapy on mother–child interaction in hyperactive children illustrate the potential impact of child variables on the development of disturbed behaviour.
> - A transactional model best encapsulates these processes, which are examined through a case study of the interaction between infant temperament and environmental support, in terms of 'goodness of fit'.
> - Other concepts have been introduced, notably vulnerability, resilience, protective mechanism, gateways and amplification; and these concepts have been applied to research into the mutual influence of temperament, maternal responsibility and social support on the security of attachment.

5 CONCLUSION

ACTIVITY 12

Allow about 10 minutes

DISTURBING BEHAVIOUR

At the beginning of this chapter (Activity 2) I asked you to think about the ambiguities implicit in the phrase 'disturbing behaviour'. Think again about this phrase in the light of a transactional model.

As we come to the end of this chapter I hope that some of the issues of causality in the study of disturbed behaviour have become clearer. Explanations which focus on linear causes, either in the child's social environment or in their own make-up, are a gross oversimplification. Interaction involving a number of risk factors is always the rule. The child is disturbing to others at the same time as they are being disturbed. Disturbed behaviour can best be understood as a spectrum of patterns of deviant development. At one end of the spectrum the problems may be strongly linked to developmental disorders or a difficult temperament which place extraordinary pressures on even the most well-resourced and well-prepared parents. In the middle of the spectrum is the majority of cases, where there may be a mild developmental issue or irritable temperament, but where behaviour problems and relationship difficulties are also being strongly shaped by family factors (discord, maternal depression, negative attitudes) which, in turn, may be amplified by stresses in the social environment (notably inadequate family support, housing, poverty and lack of access to public services). At the other extreme of the spectrum are those cases where gross deprivation, neglect, distorted patterns of care or abuse create an adverse environment in which even the most resilient child develops disturbed patterns of adaptation.

FURTHER READING

HERBERT, M. (1991) *Clinical Child Psychology*, Chichester, Wiley.

NICOL, R., STRETCH, D. and FUNDUDIS, T. (1993) *Pre-School Children in Troubled Families*, Chichester, Wiley.

RICHMAN, N., STEVENSON, J. and GRAHAM, P. J. (1986) *Pre-School to School: a behavioural study*, London, Academic Press.

RUTTER, M. and RUTTER, M. (1992) *Developing Minds: challenge and continuity across the life span*, Harmondsworth, Penguin (especially Chapters 1 to 5).

ROLF, J., MASTEN, A., CICCHETTI, D., NUECHTERLEIN, N. and WEINTRAUB, S. (eds) (1990) *Risk and Protective Factors in the Development of Psychopathology*, New York, Cambridge University Press.

WEBSTER-STRATTON, C. and HERBERT, M. (1994) *Troubled Families – Problem Children: working with parents: a collaborative process*, Chichester, Wiley.

REFERENCES

ACHENBACH, T. M., McCONAUGHY, S. H. and HOWELL, C. T. (1987) 'Child adolescent behavioral problems: implications of cross-informant correlations for situational specificity', *Psychological Bulletin*, **102**, pp. 213–32.

BARKER, P. (1988) *Basic Child Psychiatry*, Oxford, Blackwell.

BARKLEY, R. A., KARLSSON, J., POLLARD, S. and MURPHY, J. (1985) 'Developmental changes in the mother–child interactions of hyperactive boys: effects of two doses of Ritalin', *Journal of Child Psychology and Psychiatry*, **26**, pp. 705–15.

BELL, R. Q. (1968) 'A reinterpretation of the direction of effect in studies of socialization', *Psychological Review*, **75**, pp. 81–95.

BENTOVIM, A., GORELL-BARNES, G. and COOKLIN, A. (1987) *Family Therapy: complementary frameworks of theory and practice*, London, Academic Press.

BRONFENBRENNER, U. (1979) *The Ecology of Human Development*, Cambridge, Massachusetts, Harvard University Press.

BUGENTAL, D. B., BLUE, J. and LEWIS, J. (1990) 'Caregiver beliefs and dysphoric affect directed to difficult children', *Developmental Psychology*, **26**, pp. 631–8.

CHESS, S. and THOMAS, A. (1984) *Origins and Evolution of Behaviour Disorders*, New York, Brunner Mazel.

CICCHETTI, D. and TOTH, S. L. (1991) 'Internalizing and externalizing expressions of dysfunction', *Rochester Symposium on Developmental Psychopathology*, **2**, Hillsdale, New Jersey, Lawrence Erlbaum Associates.

COX, A. D., PUCKERING, C., BOND, A. and MILLS, M. (1987) 'The impact of maternal depression in young children', *Journal of Child Psychology and Psychiatry,* **28**, pp. 917–28.

CROCKENBERG, S. B. (1981) 'Infant irritability, mother responsiveness, and social support influences on the security of infant–mother attachment', *Child Development*, **52**, pp. 857–65.

CUMMINGS, E. M. and DAVIES, P. T. (1994) 'Maternal depression and child development', *Journal of Child Psychology and Psychiatry*, **35**, pp. 73–112.

DAVIE, R., BUTLER, N. and GOLDSTEIN, H. (1972) *From Birth to Seven*, London, Longman.

DUNN, J. (1988) *The Beginnings of Social Understanding*, Oxford, Blackwell.

FIELD, T., HEALY, B., GOLDSTEIN, S., PERRY, S., BENDELL, D., SCHANBERG, S., ZIMMERMAN, E. A. and KUHN, C. (1988) 'Infants of depressed mothers show "depressed" behaviour even with nondepressed adults', *Child Development,* **59**, pp. 1569–79.

GREENBERG, M. T., SPELTZ, M. L. and DEKLYNEN, M. (1993) 'The role of attachment in the early development of disruptive behavior problems', *Development and Psychopathology*, **5**, pp. 191–213.

HERBERT, M. (1991) *Clinical Child Psychology*, Chichester, Wiley.

HINDE, R. A. and STEVENSON-HINDE, J. (1988) *Relationships within Families: mutual influences*, Oxford, Clarendon.

JENKINS, S., OWEN, C., BAX, M. and HART, H. (1984) 'Continuities of common behaviour problems in pre-school children', *Journal of Child Psychology and Psychiatry,* **25***,* pp. 75–89.

KESSEN, W. (1979) 'The American child and other cultural inventions', *American Psychologist*, **34**, pp. 815–20.

KLEIN, H. A. and BALLANTINE, J. H. (1988) 'The relationship of temperament to adjustment in British infant schools', *Journal of Social Psychology*, **128***,* pp. 585–95.

LERNER, J. M. and BUSCH-ROSSNAGEL, N. A. (1981) *Individuals as Producers of Their Own Development: A Lifespan Perspective*, New York, Academic Press.

MACKINNON-LEWIS, C., LAMB, M. E., ARBUCKLE, B., BARADARAN, L. P. and VOLLING, B. L. (1992) 'The relationship between biased maternal and filial attributions and the aggressiveness of their interactions', *Development and Psychopathology*, **4**, pp. 403–15.

MAZIADE, M., COTE, R., BERNIER, H., BOUTIN, P. and THIVIERGE, J. (1989) 'Significance of extreme temperament in infancy for clinical status in preschool years', *British Journal of Psychiatry*, **154**, pp. 535–43.

MURRAY, L. (1992) 'The impact of post-natal depression on infant development', *Journal of Child Psychology and Psychiatry,* **33**, pp. 543–61.

MURRAY, L. and STEIN, A. (1991) 'The effects of postnatal depression on mother–infant relations and infant development' in WOODHEAD, M., CARR, R. and LIGHT, P. (eds) *Becoming a Person*, London, Routledge.

OATES, J. (ed.) (1994) *The Foundations of Child Development*, Oxford, Blackwell/The Open University (Book 1 of ED209).

PATTERSON, G. R. (1982) *A Social Learning Approach, Vol. 3, Coercive Family Process*, Eugene, Oregon, Castalia Publishing Company.

PATTERSON, G. R. (1986) 'The contribution of siblings to training for fighting' in OLWEUS, M. D. and RADKE-YARROW, M. (eds) *Development of Anti-Social and Prosocial Behaviour*, Orlando, Academic Press.

RICHARDSON, K. (1994) 'Interactions in development' in OATES, J. (ed.) *The Foundations of Child Development*, Oxford, Blackwell/The Open University (Book 1 of ED209).

RICHMAN, N., STEVENSON, J. and GRAHAM, P. J. (1982) *Pre-School to School: a behavioural study*, London, Academic Press.

ROBINS, L. N. and RUTTER, M. (eds) (1990) *Straight and Devious Pathways from Childhood to Adulthood*, Cambridge, Cambridge University Press.

RUTTER, M. (1965) 'Classification and categorization in child psychiatry', *Journal of Child Psychology and Psychiatry*, **6**, pp. 71–83.

RUTTER, M. (1967) 'A children's behaviour questionnaire for completion by teachers', *Journal of Child Psychology and Psychiatry*, **8**, pp. 1–11.

RUTTER, M. (1987) 'Psychosocial risk and protective mechanisms', *American Journal of Orthopsychiatry,* **57**, pp. 316–31.

RUTTER, M. (ed.) (1988) *Studies of Psycho-Social Risk: the power of longitudinal data*, Cambridge, Cambridge University Press.

RUTTER, M. and CASAER, T. (eds) (1991) *Biological Risk Factors for Psycho-social Disorders*, Cambridge, Cambridge University Press.

RUTTER, M., COX, A., TUPLING, C., BERGER, M. and YULE, W. (1975) 'Attainment and adjustment in two geographical areas. I The prevalence of psychiatric disorder', *British Journal of Psychiatry*, **126**, pp. 493–509.

RUTTER, M., TIZARD, J. and WHITMORE, K. (1970) *Education, Health and Behaviour*, London, Longman.

SAMEROFF, A. J. (1991) 'The social context of development' in WOODHEAD, M., CARR, R. and LIGHT, P. (eds) *Becoming a Person*, London, Routledge.

SEARS, R. R., MACCOBY, E. E. and LEVIN, H. (1957) *Patterns of Child Rearing*, Evanston, Illinois, Row Peterson.

SHAW, D. S. and BELL, R. Q. (1993) 'Developmental theories of parental contributors to anti-social behaviour', *Journal of Abnormal Child Psychology*, **21**, pp. 493–518.

SROUFE, L. A. (1988) 'The role of infant–caregiver attachment in development' in BELSKY, J. and NEZWORSKI, T. (eds) *Clinical Implications of Attachment*, Hillsdale, New Jersey, Lawrence Erlbaum Associates.

STERN-BRUSCHWEILER, N. and STERN, D. N. (1989) 'A model for conceptualizing the role of the mother's representational world in various mother–infant therapies', *Infant Mental Health*, **3**, pp. 142–56.

STEVENSON, J. E. AND OATES, J. (1994) 'Infant individuality' in OATES, J. (ed.) *The Foundations of Child Development*, Oxford, Blackwell/The Open University (Book 1 of ED209).

STRATTON, P. and SWAFFER, R. (1988) 'Maternal causal beliefs for abused and handicapped children', *Journal of Reproductive and Infant Psychology*, **6**, pp. 201–16.

TIZARD, B., BLATCHFORD, P., BORKE, J., FARQUHAR, C. and PLEWIS, I. (1988) *Young Children at School in the Inner City*, Hillsdale, New Jersey, Lawrence Erlbaum Associates.

WATERS, E., VAUGHN, B. E. and EGELAND, B. R. (1980) 'Individual differences in infant–mother attachment relationships at age one: antecedents in neonatal behaviour in an urban, economically disadvantaged sample', *Child Development*, **51**, pp. 208–16.

WEISZ, J. R., SIGMAN, M., WEISS, B. and MOSK, J. (1993) 'Parental reports of behavioural and emotional problems among children in Kenya, Thailand and the United States', *Child Development*, **64**, pp. 98–109.

ZAHN-WAXLER, C., IANNOTTI, R. J., CUMMINGS, E. M. and DENHAM, S. (1990) 'Antecedents of problem behaviours in children of depressed mothers', *Development and Psychopathology*, **2**, pp. 271–91.

ZAHN-WAXLER, C. (1993) 'Warriors and worriers: gender and psychopathology', *Development and Psychopathology*, **5,** pp. 79–89.

CHAPTER **3** GROWING UP IN FAMILIES

Prajna Das Gupta

CONTENTS

1 FAMILIES AND SOCIALIZATION — **84**
1.1 What is a family? — 84
1.2 What is socialization? — 86
Summary of Section 1 — 87

2 STYLES OF PARENTING — **88**
Summary of Section 2 — 96

3 PARENTAL CONTROL — **97**
Summary of Section 3 — 101

4 SOCIALIZATION ACROSS CULTURES — **102**
4.1 The six cultures study — 103
4.2 Parental expectations of children — 106
4.3 Transactional theory in cross-cultural perspective — 108
Summary of Section 4 — 111

5 MULTIPLE INFLUENCES IN INTERPERSONAL RELATIONSHIPS — **111**
5.1 Marital discord, separation, divorce and remarriage — 114
5.2 Siblings: investigating triadic relationships — 119
Summary of Section 5 — 124

6 CONCLUSION — **124**

FURTHER READING — **126**

REFERENCES — **126**

READING A: SOCIALIZATION AND THE FAMILY: CHANGE AND DIVERSITY — **130**

READING B: THE CHILD'S ENTRY INTO A SOCIAL WORLD — **132**

1 FAMILIES AND SOCIALIZATION

> We are moulded and remoulded by those who have loved us; and though the love may pass, we are nevertheless their work, for good or ill.
>
> (Francois Mauriac)

'Those who have loved us' may be parents, siblings, grandparents, other relatives, teachers or peers. Although other groups and social factors affect socialization, the family is typically seen as the most influential agency in the socialization of the child. It is the context within which the most direct and intimate relationships are forged. Our concept of family is greatly influenced by our personal experiences and our culture. Before I look at research on families and socialization, therefore, it might be helpful to explore what the terms 'family' and 'socialization' mean to us.

1.1 What is a family?

Casual observation suggests that families differ from one another. Activity 1 asks you to reflect on some of these differences. This will form a base from which to consider research on children and families.

ACTIVITY 1

Allow about 10 minutes

FAMILIES: SIMILARITIES AND DIFFERENCES

Describe your own family in terms of its members and their relationships to one another.

Now describe a family – perhaps one you know – which is different in certain significant respects from your own.

What, if anything, do these two families have in common?

Family structures

There has always been a variety of family patterns but, owing to economic, social and legal changes (for example, changes in family size and changes in the divorce laws), family structures are more variable today than they were even 50 years ago. Table 1 describes some of the different types of family structure that can be found in the UK today.

TABLE 1   Family structures.

Family type	Description
Conjugal nuclear	Married couple, or married couple with children (also called 'traditional'). Exists only as long as its two focal members (husband and wife) remain together; when either partner dies or leaves, it becomes a lone-parent family.
Non–conjugal nuclear	As above, but the couple are not legally married. Also referred to as 'co-habiting' (living together) or common-law marriage.
Lone parent	The majority are lone mothers with at least one child, and are formed as a result of the death of the partner, separation or divorce. A minority of lone-parent families are made up of a mother and child/children who have not entered into a relationship with a single partner.
Reconstituted	The combination of two previously lone-parent families (step-family), or a family created following the marriage/remarriage of a lone parent.
Extended	More than one generation of parents and children living together. It could also include aunts, uncles, cousins, not necessarily living in the same household, but living in close proximity. Following marriage/remarriage the extended family includes the relatives of both partners.

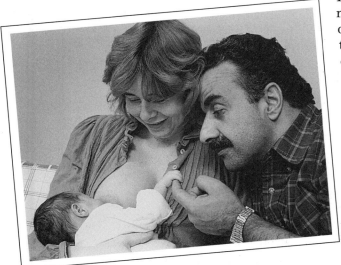

The range of family patterns shown in Table 1 is not exhaustive (you may be able to think of others). The definitions of the family types in the table, however, include three important elements: marriage, residence and parenthood. These elements identify some of the assumptions built into our definitions of 'family'. For example, some people assume that a family is made up of a married couple (marriage) and their child or children (parenthood) who live together (residence). Others may define a family as one adult who lives with their child (parenthood, residence). Any explanation of the significance of families for child development should acknowledge both the diversity of family patterns and the ways in which these patterns are subject to change. This is the theme of the first reading.

READING

You should now study Reading A, 'Socialization and the family: change and diversity' by David Morgan, at the end of this chapter. Note the different uses of the term 'family' and the meanings associated with them. Note also that Morgan talks of family processes in terms of a 'life-cycle': people moving through different life stages in the course of which they enter and leave different sets of family relationships. A simplified family life-cycle might involve the stages shown in Figure 1 but, increasingly, for some people it includes cohabitation, separation, divorce, lone-parenthood, remarriage and step-parenthood. The population at any given time is made up of families at different stages of the family life-cycle.

A consideration of the variety of family patterns and the different shades of meaning associated with the term 'family' also indicates that any generalizations about the family should be viewed critically. Much of the work carried out by psychologists in the area of family and socialization has tended to concentrate on the conjugal nuclear family and, within that, on the mother–child dyad (Schaffer, 1984). Family patterns may affect children in different ways (see Section 5 for examples). It is important to remember this, although much of the research discussed in this chapter is about relationships in nuclear families. Sections 2 and 3 describe studies on parent–child (mostly mother–child) relationships in the UK and USA, and Section 4 discusses studies of this relationship in other cultures. Section 5 describes recent trends in research that take into account multiple relationships within families and consider the effects of changing family structures on children.

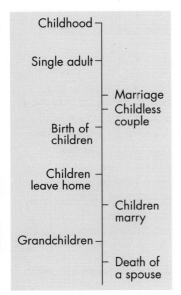

FIGURE 1 Stages in a family life-cycle (Family Policy Studies Centre, 1982).

1.2 What is socialization?

Mauriac's view of socialization, expressed in the quotation at the beginning of this chapter, as a process by which parents mould or influence children is echoed in Hetherington and Parke's (1993, p. 418) definition of socialization as 'the process whereby an individual's standards, skills, motives, attitudes and behaviour are influenced to conform to those regarded as desirable and appropriate for his or her present or future role in society'. This is a popular view of socialization. Some psychologists, however, have questioned whether parents have (or should have) such apparent omnipotence in the process of child rearing, preferring instead to emphasize the *mutual* influences between parents and children, and the situational and cultural influences on their behaviour, beliefs and relationships (Hinde and Stevenson-Hinde, 1988; LeVine, 1974).

This chapter will review different perspectives on the process of growing up in families. I shall take as a starting point three models summarized by Rudolf Schaffer (1984).

READING

Three contrasting models of socialization are summarized in Reading B at the end of this chapter. You should read it now.

Note the principal way in which the models differ in terms of the extent and nature of the caretaker's role.

Schaffer distinguishes between theories of socialization which are based on a model of parents using rewards and punishments to shape the behaviour of the malleable, growing child in socially acceptable and desirable directions, and theories which see the child as a more active participant, but one still needing control and guidance from adults in order to fit into society (what he calls the 'conflict model'). This model has influenced a lot of the research you will come across in the following sections, and this research, in turn, has strengthened the acceptance of this model.

More recent views (for example, the transactional model which you have already come across in Chapter 2) see the child as an active agent in the process of socialization from a very early age. According to this view, the path that an individual develops along in the process of becoming an adult is a product of what both the child and his or her adult caretakers bring to the interactions which continuously take place between them.

SUMMARY OF SECTION 1

- Cultural variation, as well as the variety of family patterns, makes it difficult to generalize about 'the family'.

- Assumptions that the conjugal nuclear family is the 'ideal' or typical family have influenced research on the family and socialization, leading to a focus on the mother–child relationship.

- Socialization is the process by which children acquire a range of values, skills and behaviours which are necessary for their development as members of a particular society.

- Within the family, parents are seen as the primary agents of socialization, influencing the child both directly and indirectly.

- Behaviourism and psychoanalytic theory both influenced early research on socialization. Despite fundamental differences, the two positions emphasized the importance of parental influences and portrayed children as passive recipients of the socialization process.

- A transactional model, by contrast, emphasizes the reciprocal nature of interactions in the family and the ways in which parents and children influence each other. Children are considered active participants in the socialization process.

2 STYLES OF PARENTING

Schaffer (1984) identified three models of socialization which have influenced our thinking about the effects of child rearing on development. In this section I shall look at how far research has succeeded in identifying a relationship between styles of child rearing or parenting and child behaviour. The implicit agenda for much of this research was to establish whether particular styles of parenting were in some senses 'better' or 'more effective' than others.

I shall start with a pioneering study carried out in the United States in the 1950s by Robert Sears, Eleanor Maccoby and Harry Levin (Sears *et al.*, 1957). (This study was briefly described in Chapter 2, Section 4.) Sears *et al.* interviewed the mothers of nearly 400 5-year-old children and asked them about their child-rearing practices at different points in their children's lives. As well as seeking information about feeding and potty training they also asked about their methods of discipline and about how they handled aggression and dependent behaviour. The children's personality characteristics were measured separately.

When the data were analysed very few associations were found between the child-rearing practices and the children's personalities. However, one positive outcome from this research was the identification of different *patterns* and *dimensions* in the ways in which parents behaved towards their children. Two dimensions, in particular, stood out:

Warmth–coldness: mothers varied in the extent to which they demonstrated affection to their children, whether they used reason when disciplining them, whether they accepted their children's dependency, and whether they were outwardly 'playful' in their relationship with their children.

Permissiveness–restrictiveness: mothers also varied in how tolerant they were of aggression and their expectations of being obeyed and of

the child showing 'good manners'. They varied, too, in their use of physical punishments in maintaining discipline.

These two dimensions of maternal behaviour, the quality of the emotional relationship (warmth–coldness) and the degree of control that the mother exercises (permissiveness–restrictiveness), have continued to be identified as significant in socialization research (Maccoby and Martin, 1983).

Activity 2 provides an opportunity to relate these dimensions to a real-life example.

ACTIVITY 2

Allow about 10 minutes

IDENTIFYING DIMENSIONS OF PARENTAL BEHAVIOUR

Read the following account of 3-year-old Daniel's experience of contrasting styles of adult supervision. Use the two dimensions described above to describe the ways in which his mother and grandmother behave towards him in terms of (a) their emotional relationship with Daniel and (b) their attitudes towards discipline and control.

> I once took my three-year-old Daniel to stay with my mother for two days, not without some misgivings for I knew that my mother had been a great one for discipline and attached great importance to good manners. On the other hand she was very fond of Daniel, and he of her because when she came to stay with us she liked to read him stories. However, when I picked him up after those two days he said to me in the car: 'I don't want to stay with Grandma anymore.' Astonished, I asked him why, and he replied: 'She hurt me.' …
>
> The story was perfectly simple: The dessert was Daniel's favourite, cottage-cheese soufflé. When he had finished the helping he had been given, he picked up the serving spoon and reached out to help himself to some more. He always does this at home, taking great pride in his independence. But now my mother held him back, gently placing her hand, as she told me, on his and saying: 'You must first ask whether you may have some and whether there is enough for others.' 'Where are the others?' asked Daniel, and began to cry. He threw down the spoon and refused to eat any more, although my mother urged him to: he said he wasn't hungry anymore and wanted to go home. My mother tried to calm him, but he threw a real tantrum. After a few minutes his rage was spent, and he said: 'You hurt me, I don't like you. I want to go to Mommy.' After a while he asked: 'Why did you do that? I know how to help myself.' 'Yes,' said my mother, 'but you must first ask whether you may.' 'Why?' asked Daniel. 'Because you must learn good manners.' 'What for?' asked Daniel. 'Because one needs them,' replied my mother. Daniel then said quite calmly: '*I* don't need them. With Mommy I can eat when I'm hungry.'
>
> (quoted in Miller, 1990, pp. 177–8)

Comment

There appears to be some difference between Daniel's mother and grandmother on the permissiveness–restrictiveness dimension. Daniel's mother allows him to help himself at the table and she obviously values independent behaviour. Daniel's grandmother, on the other hand, thinks it is important for the child to learn social rules because 'one needs them'; and she also values obedience.

You may have found relating this incident to the warmth–coldness dimension more difficult. There is nothing to suggest that the relationship between Daniel and his grandmother has not been a warm one. This illustrates an important point, namely that it may be misleading to attempt to classify parental behaviour in terms of single, discrete dimensions. Indeed, the American psychologist Diana Baumrind (1973), who has carried out numerous studies of parenting styles, argues that it is pointless studying parental attributes like 'warmth' and 'control' in isolation.

Baumrind's own studies of adult leadership styles led her to propose that the most effective style combined elements of democracy with elements of authority. She applied this proposal to her studies of childhood socialization. She was particularly interested in finding out how different types of emotional relationship between parents and children, and differences in the type of control exercised by parents, interact to influence children's behaviour. One of her studies (Baumrind, 1971) is described in Example 1.

EXAMPLE 1
DIMENSIONS OF PRE-SCHOOL CHILDREN'S BEHAVIOUR

Baumrind (1971) observed pre-school children in their nursery schools over a 14-week period and rated their behaviour on the following dimensions:

- *hostile–friendly* (selfish versus understands other child's position);
- *resistive–co-operative* (impetuous and impulsive versus can be trusted);
- *dominant–submissive* (peer leader versus suggestible);
- *achievement-oriented–not achievement-oriented* (gives best to play and work versus does not persevere when encounters frustration).

The children's parents were also interviewed, and they were observed interacting with their children, both in the natural setting of the home and in a research laboratory.

In addition to rating the children's behaviour, Baumrind also devised a scale for rating their parents' behaviour according to specified criteria, some of which are listed in Example 2. These criteria were seen as indicative of more general styles of parenting behaviour. So, for example, the existence of a fixed bedtime (item 2) was taken as a sign of parents structuring children's activities; and not being coerced by the child (item 5) was seen as evidence of being in control of the child's behaviour.

EXAMPLE 2
SAMPLE ITEMS FROM BAUMRIND'S (1971)
PARENTAL HOME OBSERVATION RATING SCALE

1. Set standards of excellence
2. Fixed bedtime hour
3. Clear ideals for child
4. Stable firm views
5. Cannot be coerced by child
6. Gives reasons with directives
7. Firm enforcement of rules
8. Use negative sanctions when defied
9. Force confrontation when child disobeys
10. Encourages independence
11. Solicit child's opinions
12. Become inaccessible when displeased

From these interviews and observations Baumrind (1973) identified three parenting styles, which she labelled *permissive, authoritarian* and *authoritative*. This is how she defined the three styles:

Permissive parents do not set strict standards for the child's behaviour and do not believe in restricting the child's autonomy. They exercise less control over their children than is apparent with other styles, allow children to determine their own schedules and activities, demand less achievement and tolerate more immature behaviour than other parents. Permissive parents rate low on items such as 'fixed bedtime hour' or 'firm enforcement' (items 2 and 7).

Authoritarian (or *autocratic*) parents value obedience and believe in limiting the child's autonomy and independence. They stress obedience to authority, have set standards of behaviour, and favour punitive measures to control children's 'wilful' behaviour. The type of control exerted by these parents is 'restrictive'. Such parents rate high on the 'firm enforcement of rules' (item 7), but low on the 'encourages independence' (item 10) measures of the scale.

Authoritative parents also set standards for the child's behaviour and value compliance, but they also respect the child's autonomy and independence. They tend to believe in reciprocal rights for parents and children, explain rules and decisions, exert control by reasoning with children, listen to the child's point of view and value self-assertion. The type of control exerted by these parents is 'demanding', in the sense that it makes demands on the child to behave in developmentally appropriate ways. Such parents would rate high on both 'firm enforcement' and 'encourages independence' (items 7 and 10).

The relationship between these parental styles and the behaviour displayed by the children is summarized in Table 2.

TABLE 2 Parenting styles and children's behaviour.

Parental type	Children's behaviour
Permissive-indulgent parent	*Impulsive-aggressive children*
Rules not enforced	Resistive, noncompliant to adults
Rules not clearly communicated	Low in self-reliance
Yields to coercion, whining, nagging, crying by the child	Low in achievement orientation
Inconsistent discipline	Lacking in self-control
Few demands or expectations for mature, independent behaviour	Aggressive
Ignores or accepts bad behaviour	Quick to anger but fast to recover cheerful mood
Hides impatience, anger, and annoyance	Impulsive
Moderate warmth	Aimless, low in goal-directed activities
Glorification of importance of free expression of impulses and desires	Domineering
Authoritarian parent	*Conflicted-irritable children*
Rigid enforcement of rules	Fearful, apprehensive
Confronts and punishes bad behaviour	Moody, unhappy
Shows anger and displeasure	Easily annoyed
Rules not clearly explained	Passively hostile and guileful
View of child as dominated by uncontrolled antisocial impulses	Vulnerable to stress
Child's desires and opinions not considered or solicited	Alternates between aggressive, unfriendly behaviour and sulky withdrawal
Persistent in enforcement of rules in the face of opposition and coercion	Aimless
Harsh, punitive discipline	
Low in warmth and positive involvement	
No cultural events or mutual activities planned	
No educational demands or standards	
Authoritative parent	*Energetic-friendly children*
Firm enforcement of rules	Self-reliant
Does not yield to child coercion	Self-controlled
Confronts disobedient child	High energy level
Shows displeasure and annoyance in response to child's bad behaviour	Cheerful
Shows pleasure and support of child's constructive behaviour	Friendly relations with peers
Rules clearly communicated	Copes well with stress
Considers child's wishes and solicits child's opinions	Interest and curiosity in novel situations
Alternatives offered	Co-operative with adults
Warm, involved, responsive	Tractable
Expects mature, independent behaviour appropriate for the child's age	Purposive
Cultural events and joint activities planned	Achievement-oriented
Educational standards set and enforced	

Source: Baumrind, 1967, reprinted in Hetherington and Parke, 1993, p. 431, Table 13.2.

ACTIVITY 3

Allow about 10 minutes

PARENTAL STYLE AND CHILDREN'S BEHAVIOUR

Look at the relationships between parental style and children's behaviour as set out in Table 2.

Extract what you consider to be the main features of the relationships between parental style and children's behaviour.

Note down any reservations you have about making generalizations from this study.

Hetherington and Parke's summary of Baumrind's results in Table 2 indicates that, compared with children with 'autocratic' and 'permissive' parents, children with 'authoritative' parents showed greater social responsibility (as measured by friendliness towards peers and co-operativeness towards adults, for example). They also tended to show more independence (for example, social dominance, non-conforming behaviour). Baumrind (1973) has suggested that authoritative parents balance high control with high responsiveness (warmth), and that this balance is a critical factor in determining the nature of children's behaviour.

Surprisingly, perhaps, the permissive pattern, where parents exercise less control, did not foster independence in children. Indeed, Baumrind found that both permissiveness and over-protection were associated with dependence in children. She stressed that firm control did not inhibit social maturity and independence; on the contrary, it helped to promote individuality and independence, provided it occurred in an environment in which the child felt secure and loved.

Other studies since have supported Baumrind's basic findings. Authoritative parenting has been associated with what are judged to be positive consequences for children, such as social responsibility, high self-esteem (see Chapter 5), a desire to achieve, and cognitive competence (Grusec and Lytton, 1988).

Interest in the relationship between parental styles and children's behaviour is not limited to short-term outcomes. On the contrary, the more general personal and public concern is for what happens in the longer term as children become increasingly independent and make their own way in the world.

When Baumrind followed up some of her sample from the pre-school period through to adolescence she found that parental styles were related to children's social competence in the long term. In particular, *autocratic* styles of parenting had more negative long-term outcomes, particularly for boys, while *authoritative* styles continued to be associated with positive outcomes in adolescence. Authoritative styles seemed especially important for the development of competence in boys (Baumrind, 1991).

I have discussed Baumrind's research in detail as representative of a particular approach to studying socialization which has been influential in shaping ideas about what constitutes effective parenting. However, there are some serious limitations to this approach. I shall summarize the main points here and expand on them in later sections.

Parental style and children's behaviour: linear or reciprocal influence?

The relationships that research such as Baumrind's establishes between parental styles and children's behaviour are largely *correlational* — particular styles are more closely associated with some outcomes than with others. All too often, however, the conclusions drawn from such research are that a particular parental style *causes* the subsequent child outcomes. For example, my summary of Baumrind's follow-up studies reads 'autocratic styles of parenting had more negative long-term outcomes', and 'authoritative styles seemed especially important for the development of competence in boys' (page 93). Yet here, as elsewhere in psychological research, finding a link between two variables is not a sufficient basis for attributing *causality* (see the discussion on 'direction of effects' in Chapter 2).

Also, more recent research suggests that simple, unidirectional, causal models are not sufficiently sophisticated to explain the complex effects children and adults have on each other. It is clear, for example, that certain types of child behaviour elicit particular types of parental behaviours. This has been demonstrated by research which has examined the effects of child temperament on parent–child relationships in infancy (Stevenson and Oates, 1994). Two-way models which explain the ways in which children and parents exert a mutual influence on each other's behaviour and reactions are known as *transactional* models and were introduced in Chapter 2. Transactional models make prediction and explanation a good deal more difficult than the more straightforward, linear model of causality, but as Schaffer explains:

> we need a 'transactional model' ... if we are to understand the course of child development – transactional in the sense that we recognize the constant and progressive mutual modifications of parent and child at all stages of growth. The fact that a child is weaned early (or undergoes a period of separation, or has minimal brain damage, or loses a parent through death) will not by itself tell one about the eventual outcome. *The child is too much part of his immediate social environment to justify disregard of the effect that he has on his caretakers and of the effect that their reaction in turn will have on him* [italics added]. Both parents and child operate within a system of mutuality where the behaviour of one produces effects on the other that in turn modify the behaviour of the first.

(Schaffer, 1977, p. 30)

Schaffer sees children as playing an active part in their own socialization. They are individuals who initiate as well as respond to the behaviours of others, and who shape the behaviour of their parents, as well as being shaped by it. Therefore, to understand the influence of parental styles on children's behaviour, psychologists must take into account the contribution of the child as well as that of the parents (see also Chapter 2, Section 4).

Social context and parental style

The sample that Baumrind studied contained largely white, reasonably affluent, suburban families with two parents. The conditions under which such families live are quite different from those of parents and children living in impoverished circumstances, or those of a sole parent, or those of families from different cultural and social groupings. It could well be the case that samples drawn from these groups would show alternative parenting styles which might not fit neatly into Baumrind's three-way classification.

One reason for this is that not all societies or families value the sort of independence that is held up as a positive end-product of Baumrind's authoritative style. These different values are most notable when comparisons are made between cultures, but they are also apparent within a culture when comparisons are made between families from different ethnic, religious and socio-economic backgrounds (Newson and Newson, 1976; White and Woollett, 1992). It is important to recognize that psychological research is not value-free. Where a researcher has drawn his or her sample from a particular subset of a population, the findings will necessarily reflect particular cultural, religious and economic assumptions and biases. We must be careful, therefore, about over-generalizing the findings as applying to all families everywhere.

Style as parental attribute or pattern of relationships

A final criticism is that the classification of parenting into three discrete styles implies that these are distinctive and consistent attributes of parents – features of their personality, attitudes and behaviour. This impression, however, may in part be an artefact of particular research methods. First, there may be a gap between what parents say they do in interviews and what they actually do in practice.

Second, the parental behaviour an observer records during the relatively brief observations at home may not sample the full range of parental interactions. Finally, both interviews and observational techniques encourage parents to show consistency and to present what they think is a socially desirable attitude or behaviour, that is, what they think they 'ought to do', or what the interviewer 'ought to hear' in the context of a research project.

A closer look at family interactions suggests that parents do not use just one style of control in a consistent way. Although a parent may tend to use one style more than others, most parents use some mixture of all these styles. So classifying a mother as *permissive,* for example, may be misleading. She may well be permissive about the child's bedtime, but be very demanding about toilet training. Parents also deal differently with toddlers, school-age children and adolescents; they may be more *permissive* with younger children, and be more prepared to tolerate 'immature' behaviour which would be unacceptable coming from an older child. Furthermore, parental styles may fluctuate over time, and be influenced by characteristics of the child, as parents discover what 'works best' with individual children at different times. They may also vary according to the situation. Libraries and supermarkets, for example, place different expectations on parents from playgrounds and parks, and being at home alone with a child is a very different situation from being at home with a child and a relative stranger carrying out research!

The significance of these three themes will become more apparent in the next section, in which I shall look in more detail at research into parental control.

SUMMARY OF SECTION 2

- Early research on styles of parenting identified two dimensions of parental behaviour, parental warmth and control, which appeared to affect children in significant ways.

- More recent research has confirmed that parental styles combine aspects of emotional relationships and control.

- Baumrind identified three styles of parenting: permissive, authoritarian and authoritative. Authoritative parenting, combining high warmth, responsiveness and communication with firm control, led to the most positive developmental outcomes for children and adolescents.

- Nevertheless, there are a number of limitations to Baumrind's studies which make it difficult to generalize about 'optimal' styles of parenting.

3 PARENTAL CONTROL

Implicit in the 'conflict' mode of socialization outlined by Schaffer in Reading B is the notion that parents – or, more generally, adults – need to direct children's behaviour into certain, socially approved, paths so that, increasingly, children come to take control of their own behaviour. They do this, according to the conflict model, by internalizing the standards and expectations which form the basis of whatever the adults are attempting to instil. How far can research clarify this process? Does it confirm or contradict the conflict model?

It is clear that some degree of parental control is necessary for socialization. As I pointed out earlier, socialization is a process of mutual influence between parents and children, but parents usually have more control in these interactions than children. This issue of control is one which most parents have to deal with sooner or later. It is also one on which a lot of early socialization research has focused (stemming from the work by Sears *et al.,* 1957).

Schaffer (1984) points out that there are situations in which a parent has to take the lead, and that parents have goals for the child with which the child has to comply. For instance, a parent may stop a fight between two siblings, insist on a particular bedtime, or want to teach the child certain social rules, such as turn-taking or table manners. All these aspects of parental behaviour are referred to as 'parental control'.

Observational studies of 3 to 5 year olds and mothers' accounts of bringing up children of this age show that issues of compliance and conflict are very salient. Mothers expect children to become more socially competent around this age. For instance, they expect children to use words rather than to gesture or point at things, to obey family rules, to work at tasks, to say 'please' and 'thank you', and to hold conversations (White and Woollett, 1992). Tizard and Hughes (1984) found that confrontations between mothers and children over these issues were quite common (see Research Summary 1).

> ### RESEARCH SUMMARY 1
> ### PARENTAL CONTROL: A NATURALISTIC STUDY
>
> Barbara Tizard and Martin Hughes recorded the conversations of British mothers and their 4-year-old daughters in their own homes. About 14 per cent of their conversations were concerned with control. The two topics most likely to trigger conflicts concerned damage and waste (for example, 'Be careful you don't break it', 'Don't spill it!'), and manners (saying 'please' and 'thank you', table manners). The number of disputes observed in families varied. In some families between one third to a half of the conversations contained at least one dispute, whereas in others less than 5 per cent did. Disputes seemed to occur more frequently in families of lower socio-economic status than they did in families of higher socio-economic status.
>
> In about 60 per cent of the disputes observed, Tizard and Hughes found that mothers gave explanations to their children about why the dispute was taking place. All mothers sometimes justified their demands or their refusal to comply with their children's requests. This suggests that conflict or dispute can provide children with an opportunity for learning about social rules; it is not just about control.
>
> (Tizard and Hughes, 1984)

ACTIVITY 4

Allow about 10 minutes

MOTHER–DAUGHTER EXCHANGES

Read the following extracts of mother–daughter exchanges and ask yourself which mother deals with her child's request most successfully.

(a) Penny (C) and her mother (M) have been playing a card game, but when it ends, Penny wants to play another game.

    C: I said, what are you going to play with? Mummy?

    M: Don't want to play with anything. I, I should do some cooking really.

    C: No.

    M: Get the dinner ready.

    C: No.

Penny's mother complies.

(b) Sally's mother is cooking. Sally (C) calls for her mother (M) to come up because she wants her to do something for her.

    M: I will in a minute, I'll do the pastry first.

    C: Now!

    M: Sally! Don't tell me what to do.

    C: I want to beat you.

    M: You're getting too cheeky and you're going to get a smack.

(Walkerdine and Lucey, 1989, pp. 76 and 130)

Now ask yourself whether the demands the children are making are 'reasonable'. Is your response to this question different from your response at the beginning of this activity?

Note that in both extracts the child is trying to manipulate the mother into doing what the child wants. As Valerie Walkerdine and Helen Lucey (1989) point out, mothers like Penny's, who comply with their children's demands (however unreasonable), are often seen as more 'sensitive' than mothers like Sally's.

'Sensitive' mothering has been described as a very 'middle-class' notion (Walkerdine and Lucey, 1989, White and Woollett, 1992). Furthermore, it may also be a very western concept. In other cultures, as you will see in Section 4, the child is supposed to learn to be sensitive to the needs of adults. While agreeing that children should be treated with sensitivity and respect, some psychologists question whether mothers need to be unfailingly patient and responsive or be involved in constant teaching.

Walkerdine and Lucey (1989) argue that discord exists in all homes, but because 'middle-class' mothers tend to ignore their children's violent emotions, or rationalize them, while 'working–class' mothers are more likely to confront them, discord and consequent *autocratic* behaviour patterns are more 'visible' in the 'working-class' homes. They suggest the strategy of reasoning with children may teach children that rational debate is important for resolving disputes. This is at the cost, however, of letting children learn how to express the strong, sometimes irrational, feelings and emotions they have for their mothers. Always dealing rationally with children, as if they were equal partners, may 'reduce children's opportunities to express and handle resistance, anger or aggression' (White and Woollett, 1992, p. 168). Children's emotional development is explored in more detail in Chapter 4.

Also, the so-called 'autocratic' strategies that some mothers use make sense when we take into account their social context, particularly in terms of the time and resources available (Whiting and Pope Edwards, 1988; Walkerdine and Lucey, 1989). All parents are likely to be sensitive at some times and lack patience at others.

> Mothers trying to clear up toys, prepare a meal and deal simultaneously with the demands of three children under 5 may use power assertive techniques (e.g. 'clear those toys up now because I say so'). On another occasion, the same but less harassed mother may be prepared to negotiate with the children (e.g. 'OK, you can just finish that game and then you must clear up'). Mothers in different social circumstances, who have help with their children or a separate playroom, may not experience the same pressures and may, as a result, employ psychological strategies more frequently.
>
> (White and Woollett, 1992, p. 47)

This quotation highlights two issues we have already come across, (a) consistency: mothers may use different styles at different times, depending on the situation, and (b) social context: the impact of external factors such as housing or the availability of help with child care. Consideration of different social contexts shows us that what is seen as an 'optimal' style in one context may not be possible or appropriate in another.

Is control always accompanied by conflict? A different type of study of control techniques, which offers an answer to this question, was carried out in Britain by Schaffer and Crook (1978). Unlike Baumrind, they were interested in ongoing behaviour, not long-term consequences. In Schaffer and Crook's study, control techniques refer to all the behaviours used by one person to change another's behaviour, and include all communications designed to guide, direct, shape and influence behaviour (see Research Summary 2).

RESEARCH SUMMARY 2
PARENTAL CONTROL : A LABORATORY STUDY

Rudolph Schaffer and Charles Crook video-recorded two groups of mothers (one with 15-month-old children, the other with 24-month-old children) in a laboratory playroom equipped with a large number of toys. The mothers were instructed to make sure that their child played with as many toys as possible and not just one or two. They were asked to intervene actively in order to direct the child's play.

Analysis of the mothers' speech showed that nearly half of all their verbal utterances, for both age groups, were control oriented, that is, attempts to change the course of the child's behaviour. These occurred, on average, once every nine seconds. However, the type of control exerted by the mothers was not 'autocratic'; very few prohibitive statements were found. When the mothers wanted to stop a particular activity, they relied more on distraction than on a direct negative command. Mothers also timed their interventions carefully, usually waiting until the child's attention was focused on a toy before requesting the child to do something with it and they adjusted the type of control to the child's age. For instance, they used a lot more non-verbal devices with the younger children, moving toys within their range, or presenting them to them.

(Schaffer and Crook, 1978)

Schaffer and Crook's study shows that control is not just about 'discipline', about dealing with disputes, exerting authority and 'checking' unacceptable behaviour. Far from being conflict-ridden, these mother–child interactions were harmonious, even though half of the mothers' utterances were coded as ones designed to regulate the children's behaviour. Of course, this may have something to do with the age of the children, the agreeable task (playing with toys) and the context (in which mothers were able to concentrate all their attention on their children).

A subsequent study looked at parent–child interactions in the home using a free-play situation (McLaughlin, 1983). Observations included fathers as well as mothers, and sampled a wider age range of children from 1 year old to 3 years 6 months.

The results of McLaughlin's study were very similar to those of Schaffer and Crook. Again, a significant proportion of parental verbal utterances had a control function, especially in the youngest group (30 per cent of utterances). Non-verbal devices accompanying verbal controls were frequent, especially when directing attention (they were found in 90 per cent of the mothers' and 87 per cent of the fathers' utterances). On the whole, mothers' and fathers' behaviours with children of these ages were remarkably alike. The main difference was that fathers were more likely to use direct commands, and they demanded action as opposed to attention from children. Both parents directed their children's behaviour 'by subtle and harmonious means' (Schaffer, 1984, p. 174).

Although none of these researchers directly related child characteristics to parental styles, it is interesting to note that the type of parental behaviours that gained compliance in a harmonious way are very similar to those Baumrind associates with 'authoritative' styles of parenting (for example, those which are warm, responsive to the child, child-centred, and so on).

The overall picture that emerges from studies of this type is that parents use a wide variety of techniques to gain compliance, and that control is not necessarily accompanied by conflict. Indeed, it may be more appropriate to think of these parenting processes in other terms altogether – for example, Kaye (1982) speaks of the way parents 'frame' their young children's behaviour, while Bruner (1978) describes these processes in terms of 'scaffolding'. The studies reviewed here indicate that socialization is not always related to conflict and discipline. Rather, as Schaffer argues, attempts at socialization are a:

> constant theme in parent–child encounters of all kinds – a theme which expresses the adult's vision of the child's developmental progression and which is designed to help the child along that progression. Socialization attempts may be a more prominent feature of certain kinds of situation in which parents have a very specific aim in mind with which the child is expected to conform; however, they occur in even the most playful and relaxed encounters and are thus part of the very act of interpersonal communication between parent and child.

> (Schaffer, 1984, pp. 174–5)

I shall turn to the study of socialization in other cultures in Section 4.

SUMMARY OF SECTION 3

- A degree of parental control is necessary for socialization. Parents use of control may vary across situations. The degree of control considered optimal may differ across different social groups.
- Control and conflict are not synonymous. Studies have found that parents use a variety of control techniques and modify their behaviour to suit children's age and capacities.

4 SOCIALIZATION ACROSS CULTURES

Many early studies of the effects of socialization practices seemed to presume a culture-free individual. The contribution of the particular culture, which the parents and children (and very often the researcher) were a part of, was largely unacknowledged. Very often socialization practices were judged (either explicitly or implicitly) against taken-for-granted normative standards about childhood, child development and child rearing. In some cases the assumption seemed to be that if only parents were taught the 'correct' child-rearing techniques then they would produce socially competent children.

Adopting a cultural perspective on the family and socialization is important because it helps us avoid the 'ethnocentric fallacy' (Maccoby and Martin, 1983); that is, that what any one culture considers to be optimal child-rearing practices (for example, firm control with clearly explained reasons embedded in a climate of warmth: the authoritative style discussed in Section 2) will also be optimal for every other culture. Authoritative styles of socialization may well be optimal for cultures which value independence and self-regulation, but in cultures in which external social constraints and dependence on the community or tribe are important, obedience is often regarded as more desirable. For example, Robert LeVine drew attention to the importance of obedience among the groups he studied in Africa to illustrate how parental behaviour that may be 'autocratic' by western standards is adaptive within other socio-economic and cultural contexts.

> In the African and other non-Western contexts which we have studied ethnographically, the parental conception of socialization as obedience training seems to be maintained by a variety of factors. One of these is the immediate utility of child labour in the domestic production unit. Obedient and responsible children can contribute directly to food and craft production and food processing by participating in cultivation, herding, fishing, pot making, basket weaving, carrying water and implements, or more indirectly by baby tending and other domestic work that frees their elders for subsistence activity. Children are frequently inducted into these activities between the ages of 3 and 6, thereafter taking on heavier, more complex, and more responsible tasks. However important child labour might be in the subsistence adaptation of some of these groups, its contingent relationship to parental beliefs and values can be exaggerated. Parents in these groups want a great deal from their children, but they are also concerned about their futures as adults and they want to see child behaviour shaped in a direction that will be beneficial to the child in the long run. In a relatively stable agricultural society, these two considerations coincide. The obedient child whose labour is used is simultaneously being inducted into the occupational role that he or she will perform for self-maintenance as an adult. But even where child labour is no longer used in domestic food production to any great

degree, as among the urban Yoruba of western Nigeria, the parental emphasis on obedience remains strong.
(LeVine, 1974, p. 236)

The first attempts to understand childhood as the product of cultural context owed much to the influence of anthropology (see Das Gupta, 1994). An early classic study that took this approach was the 'six cultures study' organized by Beatrice and John Whiting.

4.1 The six cultures study

Starting in the 1950s, the Whitings led a team of anthropologists whose task was to observe child-rearing patterns in local communities located in six countries: India, Japan, Kenya, Mexico, North America and the Philippines (Whiting and Whiting, 1975). The communities studied varied along a number of dimensions: economic development, cultural beliefs, living arrangements and social complexity. Later, Beatrice Whiting and Caroline Pope Edwards headed another team which extended the study, adding six more groups (Whiting and Pope Edwards, 1988). In total, more than 500 children and families were observed by 17 anthropologists of both sexes, who themselves represented several different theoretical orientations.

Before considering the extent of the cultural variation found by these researchers, let us first establish that, at least at a very general level, there were certain universal features of parenting. These universal features can be summarized in terms of parental goals and parental behaviour.

Parental goals and behaviour

From an analysis of the detailed observations and standardized coding schemes used by all their co-workers, Whiting and Pope Edwards (1988) concluded that mothers in all the cultures studied shared five goals:

- *survival*: looking after the physical wellbeing of the child (nutrition, medical attention, protection from harm);
- *attachment*: relieving fear and anxiety by offering emotional comfort;
- *basic health*: for example, ensuring the learning of sphincter control and hygiene;
- *social behaviour*: ensuring the learning of culturally approved forms of etiquette;
- *learning*: introducing children to the skills necessary for survival and social acceptance.

In addition, Whiting and Pope Edwards identified four universal categories of maternal behaviour associated with achieving these goals:

- *nurturant:* caregiving, help, attention and support;
- *training*: teaching children skills, social behaviour and hygiene;
- *control:* correction, reprimands, threats, punishment;
- *sociability:* talking, laughing, joking, exchanging information with children, or by moving closer to them or using other gestures to indicate positive feelings.

These are, of course, only very broad categories of parental behaviour. In order to gain a better understanding of the extent and significance of variations in parental goals and behaviour we need to look more closely at the way the behaviour of parents and the experience of children are shaped by a combination of economic and cultural factors.

I have already offered one example, Robert LeVine's analysis of obedience-training amongst parents in Africa. His study was, incidentally, part of the research co-ordinated by the Whitings. Whiting and Pope Edwards found that differences in maternal behaviour were also influenced by factors such as household composition, mother's workload, support networks and beliefs about children, as Research Summary 3 illustrates.

RESEARCH SUMMARY 3
WORKING PATTERNS AND MATERNAL BELIEF SYSTEMS

In the following extract, Whiting and Pope Edwards (1988) describe the influences on maternal beliefs and behaviour in different communities.

In analyzing the cultural differences in maternal behaviour, two variables appear to be particularly important: the mother's workload and her beliefs about the nature of the child and what factors determine the course of development ... Mothers who must carry water from wells, streams, or town taps, who must gather fuel for rudimentary hearth cooking, and who must grind their own flour on stones have the heaviest workloads in terms of household tasks. Women who are responsible for preparing the soil and for planting, weeding, and harvesting the food for their families have the heaviest workloads outside the house.

Maternal behaviour is influenced by the culturally shared value placed on children. In societies where children are valued both for their present help with work and their future support in times of conflict and old age, and where infant mortality is high, mothers do not attempt to prevent pregnancy and are honoured for giving birth to many children ...

Maternal behaviour is also influenced by beliefs about the nature of a child and the parent's ability and responsibility for shaping the child's character. What are the shared beliefs about the capabilities of a child? Which characteristics are believed to be inherited or 'God-given', and which are believed to be responsive to teaching, thus requiring proper socialization? At one extreme are the Indian mothers of Khalapur and Bhubaneswar, and at the other are the American mothers of Orchard Town ... In accordance with the caste system of traditional India, the former believed that a child's character was pre-ordained – his fate written on his brow – and there was little that could be done to shape a child's personality or behaviour. Parents saw their roles as physical caretakers, with the major responsibility of ensuring that the child survived to live out his preordained life course. In contrast, mothers in a community such as Orchard Town, New England, believed that their infant was a bundle of potentialities and that it was the task of the mother to assess these potentialities and to direct the training of the child so as to maximize them.

(Whiting and Pope Edwards, 1988, pp. 90–1)

In what ways do such different cultural conditions and beliefs about children influence child development? Cole and Cole (1989) used the Whitings' data to draw comparisons between children in Orchard Town, USA and Nyasongo, Kenya. The different contexts in which the two groups lived are described in Research Summary 4.

RESEARCH SUMMARY 4
COMMUNITY STRUCTURES AND THE EXPERIENCE OF CHILDREN: COMPARING KENYA AND USA

At the time they were studied (1950s), the Gusii of Western Kenya were an agricultural community. Women worked mainly on the farm, whilst the men, who had once been herders, sometimes took waged jobs. The Gusii lived in extended families headed by a grandfather and many Gusii men had more than one wife. Each wife had her own house. The preferred pattern was for the husband to sleep in a separate house. Because they worked on the farm, the Gusii mothers were often separated from their infants, and relied on the older siblings and elderly family members for child care. By the age of 3 or 4 years children were expected to help their mothers with simple household tasks, and by the age of 7 they were making significant economic contributions to their family, including caring for younger siblings.

By contrast, in Orchard Town, most of the men were wage-earners who lived in nuclear households. A few mothers had part-time jobs outside the home but the majority worked in the home caring for their husbands and children. The American children spent more time with adults than the Gusii children, and were rarely separated from their mothers in the early years. They attended school where they were supervised by teachers and were rarely asked to help with household chores or any other type of work. However, they often asked for their parent's help for their own activities.

(Cole and Cole, 1989)

In making these comparisons, Cole and Cole illustrated that the behaviours children develop are closely linked to their family situation. The Whitings' data (Whiting and Whiting, 1975) showed that in Gusii society children became more nurturant and responsible (offering help and support to others) from an early age. By 3 to 5 years of age they were already expected to contribute to their family and there was a marked emphasis on interdependency within the family. By contrast, the American children were less 'responsible', perhaps because, as Cole and Cole suggest, their chores were less related to their family's economic welfare, and may even have seemed arbitrary. The American children were described as dependent–dominant (marked by seeking help and attention); they grew up in a more individualistic context where, rather than helping others, 'they competed with them for good grades and were encouraged to think of themselves as individuals, rather than as members of a group' (Cole and Cole, 1989, p. 381).

Although they differ in emphasis, these three cross-cultural examples share a common framework of understanding about the way in which parental beliefs and behaviour and children's development are shaped both by immediate situational demands (living circumstances, survival needs, family structure and so on) as well as wider influences (economics, politics, religions and so on). Bear in mind, though, that the fieldwork for these studies was carried out several decades ago, and that these communities have subsequently been subject to considerable change, especially the effects of modernization through universal schooling.

4.2 Parental expectations of children

The work by Nsamenang and Lamb (1993) discussed below is a good deal more recent. Their research involved an interview-based study of parents' perceptions of the value and role of children in the family and society and their expectations of behaviour and development. It was carried out among the Nso of north-west Cameroon (west Africa). Nsamenang and Lamb constructed a Parent Interview Guide (PIG), translated into Lamnso (the Nso language) and nearly 400 Nso men and women who were either parents or grandparents were interviewed. The interviewees were drawn from both rural and urban settings. Items on the PIG included questions on why parents wanted children, their expectations of children, and the desirable and undesirable characteristics of children.

ACTIVITY 5

Allow about 10 minutes

THE VALUE OF HAVING CHILDREN

This activity will help you reflect on cultural variation in child-rearing expectations and practices. Answer the following questions based on your own experience, and then compare your responses with those of the Nso parents given in Table 4 at the end of this chapter (p. 126).

(a) Why do people want children? What is the value of having children?

(b) What expectations do you think people have for their children?

(c) What qualities do you think are desirable and undesirable in children?

Comment

If you look at Table 4 you can see that the emphasis of Nso answers to the first question is on the children's utility as members of the family – that is, the practical contributions they can make in the context of respect and obedience to parents. This is reflected in the characteristics they view as desirable – honesty, hard work, service to parents and so on. It is also interesting to note that 'good progress in school' has become an important expectation of Nso children, reflecting the impact of modernization, schooling and the shift from a subsistence to a wage-based economy.

Although good progress in school is probably one of a number of attributes now shared with western parents, my guess is that in many respects your answers to the questions in Activity 5 will have been very different from those of the Nso. When Lois Hoffman and colleagues (1987) asked parents in eight countries about the value of children, very few parents in the USA (the country sharing most cultural similarity with Britain) referred to their practical or economic value. Instead, they emphasized more 'psychological' values, notably the mutual affection of close attachment (66 per cent), the stimulation and fun associated with a young child (60 per cent), and the sense of personal fulfilment involved in becoming a parent (35 per cent). When Hoffman *et al.* asked American parents about the characteristics they wanted to see in their children, they emphasized 'becoming a good person' (46 per cent) and 'being independent and self-reliant' (25 per cent). These American views are very different from the role of children and the responsibilities of parents as suggested by the Nso responses. Indeed, some of the qualities thought undesirable by the Nso are the very ones that western parents often view as important (notably playfulness and inquisitiveness).

To understand Nso views on parenting we have to take account of their circumstances, which make socialization to these goals appropriate. For the Nso baby, adult expectations are made clear soon after birth. They are told whom they resemble, what their names will be, and what sorts of adults they are expected to become. Socialization is not the sole responsibility of parents or other adults but is also the responsibility of older siblings and peers. The child does not 'belong' simply to his or her biological parents but to the whole tribe or community. Social competence is learnt as much through interaction with peers and siblings as by observation and imitation of adults, with little or no direct instruction.

The Nso child is under the control of all those superior in status (older siblings, peers and adults, including parents). Adults admonish children when they behave inappropriately (for example, by being disobedient), usually using a proverb or verbal abuse. Sometimes punishment takes the form of withdrawal of privileges. Nsamenang and Lamb note that among the Nso, children accept that parents have the right to punish them and 'deal with them' as the parents see fit, since they believe that 'my father punishes me to correct my behaviour; my mother rebukes me because I am wrong'. Maxims such as 'if a person is trained strictly then a person becomes a good person' and 'to beat a child is not to hate it' justify the strictness of parents (Nsamenang and Lamb, 1993, p. 437).

To summarize the discussion so far, a consideration of socialization practices in different cultures serves to 'illustrate the importance of culturally organized contexts for individual development [and] show how differences in life circumstances produce variations in basic economic activities and family life, influencing the way parents treat their children, which in turn affects the children's development' (Cole and Cole, 1989, p. 380). Adopting such a viewpoint helps us to avoid the ethnocentric fallacy highlighted by Maccoby and Martin (1983) at the beginning of this section.

4.3 Transactional theory in cross-cultural perspective

The studies discussed in this section enable us to see western-based studies of parenting styles in a much broader perspective. Judgements about which approaches are most 'desirable' or 'effective' have to be seen as reflecting a particular cultural context of parental behaviour and values. Nonetheless, these studies still share one of the limitations of the early studies of socializaton described in Section 2: they still presume that socialization is, for the most part, a unidirectional process, from parent to child.

In this section I want to illustrate the value of a transactional perspective (as discussed in Chapter 2, Section 4, and also referred to earlier in this chapter) in making sense of cross-cultural differences in social development. I shall concentrate on the same themes discussed in Chapter 2, Section 4, notably the interrelations between individual differences in children's temperament and variations in the demands of their environment.

As a starting point refer back to Chapter 2, Figure 5. There, Martin Woodhead drew on the concept of 'goodness of fit' to describe the interaction between child and environmental characteristics. According to this view, adaptive psychological and social functioning does not arise simply from either the characteristics of the child or the demands of the context in which the child finds itself. Rather, it is the 'goodness of fit' that is important. Children whose characteristics best fit their contexts are the ones most likely to receive positive parenting and show evidence of the most adaptive behavioural and cognitive development. Children who do not fit the context into which they are born, however, are more likely to experience 'more negative incidences of parenting and, therefore, show alternative developmental outcomes' (Lerner, 1993, p. 106).

It is possible to enrich this model by being more precise about what constitutes 'environmental contexts'. Lerner (1993) has distinguished three elements of context:

- the attitudes, expectations or stereotypes about children's character-istics, 'needs' and development that are held by parents and other caregivers;

- the behaviour and other attributes of parents and others to whom the child must relate;
- the physical characteristics of the settings in which children are growing up.

Cross-cultural comparisons are important, as they allow us to see how patterns of environmental context interact with individual differences in temperament to shape the course of development. Lerner illustrates this point by reference to the work of Super and Harkness (1981).

Super and Harkness compared infants in the rural farming community of the Kokwet, in Kenya, with those in suburban families in Boston, USA, using both interview data and data based on naturalistic observation.

First, Super and Harkness established that the characteristics of infant temperament that had been identified in American samples (notably by Thomas and Chess, 1977; see Stevenson and Oates, 1994) were recognized by Kokwet mothers in their own babies. In other words, like American babies, Kokwet babies varied in terms of the rhythmicity or regularity of their biological functions (sleeping, eating, elimination and so on), mood, adaptability to new situations and intensity of reactions.

However, these temperamental characteristics were being expressed within a markedly different environmental context or *niche* by American and Kokwet babies.

For instance, in many Boston homes the physical space was changed before the arrival of a new baby (a separate room was decorated for the infant). Moreover, while the baby was based at home, most members of the family were out during the day. There was generally only one person at home with the baby at any one time (the mother or childminder). By contrast, no separate rooms were prepared for the Kokwet infants in their sample, who spent the first months of life with the mother and were usually in close physical contact with her. Such close physical contact was not at all characteristic of the Bostonians. In addition, the Kokwet mothers were rarely alone with their infant: there were at least five other people in the house during the day.

In the Boston sample, time schedules were very important – the needs of the baby were only some of the many demands on the caregiver's time. Consequently, feeding, sleeping and other infant activities were often carefully planned. By contrast, in Kokwet the baby slept and nursed at the mother's breast virtually at will, since at most the mother was only a short distance away. When the mother needed a break or had to do something else there was always another caregiver at hand, notably an older sister (6 or 7 years of age) who took increasing responsibility for daily care from around 3 to 4 months.

There were at least two developmental consequences of these cultural differences. First, although they were similar to begin with, the sleeping patterns of Kokwet and Boston infants became very different by 4 months of age – the Boston infants sleeping for about eight hours at night on average, while the Kokwet infants continued to wake briefly and nurse.

Second, variations in infant temperament were treated differently in the two samples. Boston mothers viewed characteristics like low rhythmicity, low adaptability and negative mood as undesirable and as presenting immediate and potentially long-term problems. Kokwet mothers, however, were not really concerned by these characteristics and did not view them as being indicators of long-term problems. In other words 'goodness of fit' applied very differently in the two cultures:

> ... a temperamental disposition toward regularity and 'chunking' has different significance in Kokwet and Boston, as does disposition towards adaptability to the styles of multiple care-takers. A mismatch in either case provides a nucleus around which behaviour problems develop. Night waking by a 1-year-old can severely stress American parents whose own daytime lives are rigidly scheduled; in Kokwet, night waking is normal and not particularly stressful. However, the Kipsigis baby who will not be comforted by anyone but the mother, who will refuse to quiet on the back of a sister, drives the Kipsigis mother to despair. Most mothers in our American sample did not use supplementary caretakers to a significant degree in the first year and did not confront this aspect of adaptability as a serious problem.

(Super and Harkness, 1981, pp. 81–2)

Applying the concept of 'goodness of fit' enables us to see clearly how the *same* temperamental characteristics have different impacts as a consequence of being situated in different contexts. 'Goodness of fit' is helpful in describing the transactional relationship between infant and caregiver at a particular point in time; but for a complete transactional account we would need to look at these processes over a longer time period. For example, if a 3-month-old infant presents sleeping difficulties to American parents, how does the stress and fatigue experienced by the parents modify their behaviour towards the child and towards each other, and with what longer-term repercussions for the way the child is perceived and treated? Or, if a Kokwet child is seen as 'unreasonably' clinging at 3 months, how does this alter the mother's ability to work in the fields or on domestic tasks, and with what repercussions for the child's wider social experience?

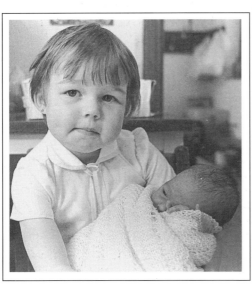

This discussion of the 'goodness of fit' concept shows that in trying to understand the importance of families for development it is not enough to study single influences (such as parental styles). As discussed earlier, children are not simply influenced by their parents, they also influence their parents. Parental behaviour is also influenced by the experiences parents have 'at work and in their communities, while the society of which the community is a part, both shapes and is shaped by its members' (Cole and Cole, 1989, p. 378).

SUMMARY OF SECTION 4

- Cross-cultural studies of socialization practices have found a number of similarities as well as differences across cultures. Mothers everywhere seem to share certain basic goals. However, they differ in their beliefs about the nature of children, and in the types of behaviour they want children to acquire.

- Differences in cultural contexts and parental beliefs, needs and expectations significantly influence parental strategies and child outcomes. Definitions of positive developmental outcomes may also vary across cultures.

- The social and physical contexts in which families are embedded also impact on parent–child relationships. The 'goodness of fit' between an individual and their environment influences developmental outcomes.

---

5 MULTIPLE INFLUENCES IN INTERPERSONAL RELATIONSHIPS

In this chapter I have presented a picture of socialization which highlights the limitations of some of the research into the way parents influence children's development. In Sections 2 and 3 I argued that linear models of influence are inadequate, and that a more interactional or transactional model is required. I also questioned the, often unstated, mono-cultural context of socialization, and suggested that a transactional account of the socialization process is more appropriate. In this final section I want to extend the picture of socialization further by looking at the impact of other family relationships on development.

The research reviewed so far has concentrated mostly on dyadic relationships, and this reflects the focus of much of the work on socialization. Most families, however, do not consist of two members, they consist of many members, each influencing all the others, as illustrated in Figure 2.

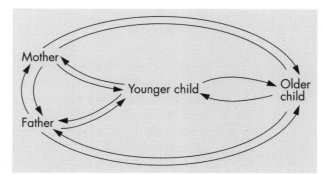

FIGURE 2 Multiple interactions within a family (White and Woollett, 1992).

Activity 6 offers you a chance to think about multiple interactions in more depth.

ACTIVITY 6

Allow about 20 minutes

RELATIONSHIPS AND DEVELOPMENT

1 Read the following description of Jasmine's family.

At 18 months Jasmine lives with her mother, father and brother. Mother returned to work part-time when Jasmine was 6 months old, and Jasmine has come to know her childminder well. The same childminder also looks after her brother. Paternal grandparents live abroad so she does not know them well. However, she is very close to her aunt and her maternal grandmother, who moved into the same street after the death of her maternal grandfather.

2 Take a blank sheet of paper and put Jasmine's name in the centre. Think about the most important relationships in Jasmine's life at 18 months of age. These will probably include the core members of the family plus others who have become involved with the child's day-to-day care (for example, her childminder). Write the names and roles of these individuals in a circle around Jasmine's name.

3 Each individual (by definition) is closely connected with the child, so indicate this with arrows (as in Figure 4 on page 125). Next, think about the relationships within this circle of individuals. Use arrows to indicate which you consider to be the most important relationships, or any other significant characteristics of the relationship. Do not attempt to include all the relationships; if you do your diagram will become very complex – although you should note that there is a lesson to be learned from this complexity!

4 Next, think about the relationships between these various key figures in the child's life. Are they all living under one roof? Are some relationships more intimate than others? Are there different kinds of relationships involved (for example, marital, father–daughter, mother–childminder, and so on)?

5 Now read the following description of Jasmine's family relationships at 6 years of age. Take another sheet of paper and repeat steps 2, 3 and 4 of this activity. As you do so, note any new relationships that need to be added (for example, a newborn sibling, a friend or a teacher) as well as former relationships that have changed or ceased to exist. As before, indicate the relationship patterns that link these individuals with the child, and also patterns between these individuals.

At 6 years, Jasmine is increasingly spending time with her school friends, and she has a very good relationship with her teacher. Since she was 18 months, there have been some important changes in her family relationships. When she was 3 her mother gave birth to another girl. Then, when she was 4½, her parents split up. Father moved away, so Jasmine only sees him about once a fortnight. At around the same time, Jasmine's aunt got married, so she sees much less of her than she used to. Left on her own, grandmother has moved in

> with Jasmine, her mother, brother and sister, to help look
> after the children, so mother can get a full-time job.

Now compare your diagram with Figures 4 and 5 at the end of this
chapter.

Beyond the dyad

Activity 6 is designed to illustrate the complexity of the relationship
patterns within which children's development is embedded, but which
psychological research is only just beginning to take into account (Hinde
and Stevenson-Hinde, 1988).

First, as discussed in Chapter 1, Section 4, young children may form
multiple attachment relationships within (and in some cases outside)
their family. Each is likely to make a significant (and probably
different) contribution to their development.

Second, these attachment relationships do not exist in a vacuum. Each
of a child's attachment figures will have a relationship (of greater or
lesser significance) with the other figures in the child's life. Most
importantly, the character of these relationships *amongst* family
members will have implications for the child. As Gable *et al.* (1992, p.
277) suggest, we need to put the 'pieces of the family system together'.
They suggest that one way to do this is to study the *interrelationship*
between the different family relationships.

In other words, we need to move beyond the study of mother–child
dyads to acknowledge the polyadic relationships in the child's life. This
point can be illustrated by recognizing the complexity in the
relationships between just three family members, known as a 'triadic
relationship'.

Using Activity 6 as an example, let us think about Jasmine at 18
months, her father and her brother. This comprises three sets of
relationships: father–son, father–daughter and brother–sister. Imagine
that Jasmine's father has an easy-going relationship with his daughter,
whom he perceives as a 'little angel', but a more conflictual relationship
with his son, whom he perceives as 'too demanding'. This is likely to
have repercussions for the quality of the relationship that Jasmine
develops with her brother, and the quality of their relationship will feed
back into the relationship they have with their father, separately and
together. There are no clear patterns of cause and effect here — we are
dealing with *multiple, cyclical transactional* processes (as discussed in
Chapter 2, Section 4).

Finally, as Jasmine's case shows, the relationship patterns within
families are not static; they change all the time, as each individual
grows older, as circumstances change, as new relationships form, and
former relationships are weakened within the family life-cycle. In the
example in Activity 6, two notable changes affected Jasmine: the birth
of a sibling and her parents' divorce. For the rest of this chapter I shall
use these two themes to illustrate some of the research that is trying to
take account of triadic and polyadic systems of family relationships.

5.1 Marital discord, separation, divorce and remarriage

In Chapter 2, Section 3, Martin Woodhead noted that a poor marital relationship was one of the risk factors associated with the development of disturbed behaviour. This provides an illustration of a triadic pattern of influence, specifically in the way disharmony and strained and distorted relationships between parents can have an impact on their children.

At the outset, it needs to be made clear that this is a notoriously difficult topic to study. For a start we are not just dealing with one event or process in family relationships, but with a wide range of factors. Divorce marks a legal event, but the psychological processes are more enduring. Their significance will depend on antecedent events (for example, the extent of parental conflict and strife), the reasons for the incompatibility or conflict, concurrent events (for example, how the process of separation is managed, the economic resources and social support available to individual parents and their children), and subsequent events (for example, the circumstances of the custodial parent, prospects for remarriage, and so on).

An influential attempt to disentangle the impact of separation and divorce from the impact of subsequent single parenting/remarriage is described in Research Summary 5.

Hetherington *et al.*'s studies draw attention to the way in which parental separation and divorce is part of a long-term process, a succession of family changes, each of which affects boys and girls in various ways. It is particularly valuable in showing that the processes of remarriage and family reconstruction, establishing relationships with step-parents, step-children and so on, can be just as difficult for children as coping with the initial breakdown in their parents' relationship and a subsequent separation or divorce.

> I felt pretty jealous. I mean after you've had your dad to yourself for a while and then somebody else comes in and your parent shows their love for them rather than you, you get very jealous, and I got very jealous. I hated it. (*Liza*)

> I felt she was abandoning me. But I think if someone had talked to me properly it would have been better, but she just treated me as a very, very awkward child. She was giving her love somewhere else and that's what got me. (*Annie*)

> I like her being here … We asked her what we should call her and she said we could either call her mum or we could call her by her name, Julie. I call her mum … Guess what her nickname is? It's Stepsy. (*Nicky*)

> (McCredie and Horrox, 1985, pp. 44, 45 and 51)

Other researchers have argued that divorce and family changes are not in themselves necessarily the most significant variables affecting

> ## RESEARCH SUMMARY 5
> ## THE EFFECTS OF DIVORCE ON CHILDREN'S PLAY
> ## AND SOCIAL INTERACTIONS
>
> In the USA, Hetherington *et al.* (1979) looked at the effects of divorce on the play and social interaction of 48 children from reasonably affluent families who lived with their mothers. The children were all about 4 years old at the beginning of the study, and were studied for up to 2 years after the divorce. The control group were children of the same age from intact families.
>
> Initially, all the divorce-group children were judged to be more anxious, guilty and apathetic than the control-group children. In the first year of the study, their play appeared less mature, both intellectually and socially, and their social interactions were immature and ineffective. The behaviour of these children was also assessed as being more negative, dependent, attention-seeking and aggressive than that of the control group. However, these immature patterns of behaviour (in play, social behaviour and interactions with other children) slowly disappeared in the girls in the divorce group. Two years after the divorce, there was no difference between the girls in this group and the control children. For boys, however, immature play patterns and behaviour problems persisted into the second year, although in a less extreme form. Two years after the divorce, these boys were found to be unpopular with other boys and to have difficulties in gaining access to play groups.
>
> Hetherington and her colleagues followed up the children again six years after the divorce (Hetherington *et al.*, 1982). The sex differences found in the previous study persisted. In families where the mother had not remarried, girls were no different in psychological adjustment from girls in intact families. Boys, however, were more aggressive and less socially competent than controls in intact families.
>
> Remarriage changed the picture quite a lot. When the mother had been remarried for less than two years, children of both sexes displayed more behavioural problems than the control children. When the remarriage was over two years old, a sex difference emerged again, but in the opposite direction to their previous findings. Boys now showed no difference when compared with their controls, but girls were less well adjusted. However, girls in these families were better adjusted than girls in families where the remarriage was less than two years old.
>
> (Hetherington *et al.*, 1979; 1982)

children. Rather it is the level of parental conflict and family discord that may or may not be associated with these changes.

One of the first to identify parental discord as a critical variable was Michael Rutter. As part of his re-assessment of Bowlby's concept of 'maternal deprivation' (Rutter, 1981) he argued that it is important to distinguish different forms of deprivation associated with different patterns of child outcome. He identified three distinct categories of deprivation – 'privation', 'disruption' and 'distortion' – and presented evidence that boys were at much greater risk of becoming delinquent if they experienced distorted family relationships, with a lot of conflict and unhappiness, than if they experienced a disruption of maternal care *per se* (this argument was developed in Chapter 1, Section 2).

More recent research has confirmed a link between parental discord and behaviour problems, although weaknesses in research design have made it difficult to draw clear-cut conclusions (Gable *et al.*, 1992; Rutter and Giller, 1983). I would like to concentrate in particular on a longitudinal study carried out in New Zealand which appears to demonstrate convincingly a relationship between the long-term effects of family discord in childhood and the risk of offending in adolescence. Note that this evidence is also highly relevant to the discussion of risk factors in the development of conduct disorder in Chapter 2, Section 2.

Fergusson *et al.* (1992) identified a cohort of 1,265 infants which was studied at birth, at 4 months, and at annual intervals up to the age of 13 years. Among the many analyses performed on this data, I shall focus on just one. Fergusson *et al.* categorized their data on children's family experiences during the first ten years of life according to two broad family variables:

- family change (based on the number of separations, reconciliations and other changes);
- parental discord (based on evidence of arguments between parents, reports of assault, sexual and other relationship difficulties).

They then looked at the association between these family variables and child behaviour outcomes (measured in terms of the risk of offending at 13 years). Their results are summarized in Table 3.

The results were striking. There was a strong, statistically significant, link between family change, parental discord and later risk of offending, which remained strong even after controlling for such potentially confounding variables as maternal education, maternal age, family socio-economic status, social position and ethnicity. In other words, the impact of family change and discord on risk of offending applied to children growing up in a wide range of social circumstances.

As a general rule, Fergusson *et al.* found that the more children were exposed to family change and parental discord, the higher the risk of offending. However, there were some complexities which it is important to take into account. First, parental discord appeared to be a much more powerful predictor of later problems than family change. 'Family change' did not, in itself, increase the risk of offending. The impact of this variable appeared to be in placing children experiencing discord under additional family stress.

Second, not all children exposed to parental discord became offenders. According to the transactional model elaborated earlier in this chapter and in Chapter 2, Section 4, child vulnerability variables interacted with family discord variables in determining the impact of discord. It will not surprise you to learn that:

(a) children with a history of behaviour problems before the onset of family problems were more at risk of becoming offenders; and

(b) while both boys and girls were affected by discord, boys were the more vulnerable group, 84.9 per cent presenting problems when exposed to high levels of discord, compared with 63.2 per cent of girls.

TABLE 3 Rates of offending at 11 to 13 years of age by family change and parental discord.

Measure	N[a]	Rate of offending	Significance [b]
Family change			
Number of parental separations			
0	543	24.7	
1	95	49.5	$X^2 = 36.9$
2	43	41.9	$p < 0.001$
3+	28	57.1	
Number of parental reconciliations			
0	645	28.1	$X^2 = 17.8$
1	43	55.8	$p < 0.001$
2+	21	47.6	
Total family changes			
0	515	24.1	
1–2	115	46.1	$X^2 = 35.3$
3–4	47	51.1	$p < 0.001$
5+	32	43.8	
Parental discord			
Number of years of parental arguments			
0	494	23.3	
1	105	43.8	$X^2 = 39.3$
2	70	47.1	$p < 0.001$
3+	40	52.5	
Number of years of reports of assault			
0	565	28.1	
1	37	48.7	$X^2 = 27.0$
2+	16	81.3	$p < 0.001$
Sexual problems			
No	522	28.5	$X^2 = 3.0$
Yes	187	35.3	$p < 0.10$

(a)   N refers to the number of children falling into the various categories.

(b) X^2 refers to the statistical test 'Chi Square', and p to the significance level of the test results: $p < 0.001$ is a highly significant finding; $p < 0.10$ is a non-significant result.

Source: Fergusson *et al.*, 1992, p. 1064.

This research provides some of the most clear–cut evidence on the impact of family discord on children. But such research still leaves many questions unanswered, especially questions about the processes of influence through which children are affected by discordant family experiences.

The impact of discord

> Your mind flows if you hear your mum and dad having an argument or a fight. It stays in your head and however hard you try it won't go away, and tends to stop you from working. It disturbs you. It stays in your head.
>
> (McCredie and Horrox, 1985, p. 13)

To help you think about the multiple influences of family discord on family members, take a few minutes to work through the following activity.

ACTIVITY 7

Allow about 10 minutes

PROCESSES OF INFLUENCE

Think about the vulnerable young children in Fergusson *et al.*'s research, growing up in families where there is constant emotional tension, frequent arguments and possibly physical conflict between their parents. In what ways is this going to affect the child? Think about the parents' behaviour towards the child, both when they are relating to the child separately and when they are together. Think also about the child's experience of their parents' behaviour. What impact is the conflict likely to have on the child? What coping strategies might they use? In what ways might they become 'caught-up' in the conflict?

Let us start with the impact on the child of experiencing overt conflict between parents. This may cause distress in the child, who may become anxious, withdrawn or irritable. Equally, the child might begin to imitate their parents' behaviour in their play or in conflict with a sibling.

A second, more indirect process, is also likely to have an effect. The conflict between parents can modify their relationship to their child in numerous ways. Either or both parents may become pre-occupied with their relationship difficulties, which means they are less available to the child. The emotions associated with their marital difficulties may spill over into their parenting role – for example, through depression or through anger redirected towards the child. There is also likely to be less consistency between parents in their treatment of the child (setting limits, discipline and so on). The parents are likely to seek opportunities for relating separately to the child, or when they are together, routine parenting tasks are likely to become further sources of tension, with the child caught in the middle, possibly colluded with by one parent or scapegoated by either or both parents.

A third process likely to be operating concerns the coping strategies adopted by the child, who may, for example:

*   misbehave in order to attract attention or to distract parents away from conflict;
*   become protective of a 'weaker' parent, while behaving defiantly towards the other parent;
*   play off one parent against another, capitalizing on mutual mistrust and disagreement to serve the child's self-interest.

The present discussion of the impact of parental discord on children does not take into account individual differences in child vulnerability. Nor does it acknowledge that many parents faced with marital difficulties are acutely aware of the potential impact on their children, and separately or jointly take steps to minimize the consequences. While admitting these limitations, I have two reasons for discussing these issues. First, most of the recent research on the impact of divorce on children indicates that the relationship between parents, both pre- and post-divorce, is very important to the child's adjustment, and Gable *et al.* (1992) have suggested that studying the relations between parents, rather than the nature of the break-up *per se,* may be more informative in accounting for children's behaviour problems and adjustment difficulties. Second, research in this area illustrates very clearly the need for developmental psychologists to extend the focus of their research beyond the assumptions of linear causality (parental behaviour to child effects). Children's development takes place in the context of a network of reciprocal relationships, and looking at the effects of parental discord on children illustrates how one set of relationships within a family can influence others.

For a second example of developmental psychologists taking greater account of multiple patterns of influence I shall turn to a normally more welcome family change: the birth of a baby.

5.2 Siblings: investigating triadic relationships

The birth of a sibling is often the first major family change that a young child experiences. It is especially significant for first-born children who will no longer have their parents' undivided attention. Sibling relationships are complex and can change over time; they can be either friendly or hostile, as these two different maternal reports indicate:

*   It's worse now he's on the go. He annoys her. They fight a lot – more than four or five big fights a day, and *every* day. They're very *bad tempered* with each other. He makes her cry such a lot.

*   They rarely fight. If Robin has something, Duncan may take it, but he always gives him something else. Duncan's always been interested in him ... Duncan always holds his hand, walks him up the road. The last month or so they've really played ... And they do comfort each other.

(Dunn and Kendrick, 1982, p. 153)

Chapter 1, Section 4 has already introduced you to the research on this topic by Judy Dunn and her colleagues. In that chapter our interest was in the kind of relationship established between siblings and whether it can best be described as attachment. In this chapter the focus goes beyond this (or any other) dyadic relationship, as Judy Dunn explains:

> It is increasingly evident that to understand fully the development of any one dyadic relationship in the family we should take account of the influences of other family relationships. In the last decade it has been shown, for instance, that the quality of the marital relationship is importantly linked with the course of pregnancy, childbirth and the mother–child relationship in infancy. The birth of a child in turn affects the relationship between husband and wife, and the kind of baby born to a family – in terms of temperament – affects the marital relationship.

(Dunn, 1986, p. 99)

READING

Before going any further, turn to the reading by Judy Dunn at the end of this book and re-read the Introduction and Section 1. You may find it helpful to take notes using the following questions as guidelines.

Why does Dunn think naturalistic observations are important?

What issues associated with conducting such observations does Dunn highlight? Can you think of any others?

How did she tackle these issues?

Why was a longitudinal study important?

What were the questions that she wanted to answer? In what sense do these questions take us beyond the study of mother–child relationships?

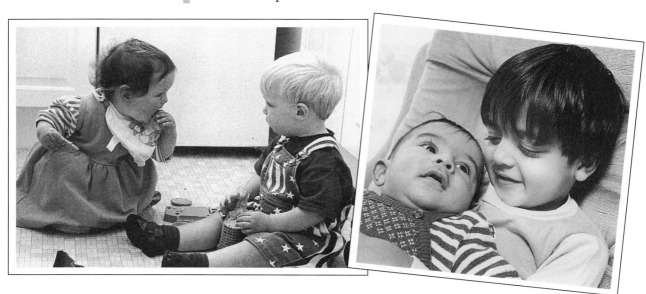

Dunn specifies three questions about relationships in the family. The first is a question about the dyadic relationship between first-born and second-born – in particular, whether the common assumption that children feel jealous of a new baby and display rivalry and behaviour problems is accurate. Dunn and Kendrick's (1982) research suggests that it is not. They found that, in general, first-borns wanted to help care for the baby, to cuddle and play with him or her. Their reactions to the new baby were quite complex and mixed, however, as was discussed in Chapter 1.

Changing patterns of relationships

The birth of a sibling changes the relationships in a family. Fathers may become more involved with the older child while the mother concentrates on the baby. Mothers play less with the older children and give them more responsibility. The focus of conversation changes from the first-born to the new sibling (Dunn and Kendrick, 1982). The birth of a sibling also affects children's behaviour – for instance, over half the first-borns in Dunn and Kendrick's sample displayed increased independence after the birth of a sibling, wanting to dress, feed and go to the toilet on their own.

Dunn and Kendrick also found, however, that the way mothers related to their first-born child influenced the first-born's relationship with the newborn sibling (Figure 3).

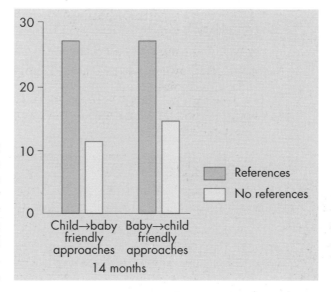

FIGURE 3 Association between mother's reference to baby as a person in the first month, and frequency of sibling-friendly approaches at 14 months (per 1,000 10-second units) (Dunn and Kendrick, 1982, p. 160).

If the mother talked to the first-born about the new baby before the birth, relations between siblings were much friendlier by the time the baby was 14 months old than they were in families where this did not happen (Figure 3). Children who showed more interest in the baby early on (2 to 3 weeks) were also more friendly to siblings at 14 months. Strikingly, their siblings were also significantly more friendly to them than siblings in the rest of the sample (Dunn and Kendrick, 1982).

Another way of approaching these *triadic* influences is to examine how a mother's way of relating to first-born and second-born children alters their relationship with each other. Dunn (1992) reports that there is strong evidence that if mothers treat children differently there is more likely to be hostility in the relationship between siblings. This link seems to be strongest in families under stress, as is shown, for example, in studies of the siblings of cancer patients, or of studies of families after divorce. As before, we have to be careful about presuming that the direction of effects runs from maternal style to sibling relationships. It could be that differences in maternal treatment reflect individual differences in the children (age, gender, temperament and so on) which also shape the character of their relationship.

Indeed, Dunn and Kendrick found that gender is an important factor in sibling relationships. First-born and sibling showed increasingly friendly behaviour towards each other (especially in the 8 to 14-month period) if they were the same sex. These differences were most striking in families with first-born boys. Elder boys were more friendly to a younger brother than to a younger sister.

Individual differences in temperament also contribute to both sibling and parent–child relationships, as the following examples illustrate:

> (a) Sally, an emotionally intense child, who was not very adaptable, reacted with particularly intense protests when her mother became involved with her sister Ruby.
>
> Mother to Ruby (commenting on her playing): Are you enjoying yourself, Ruby?
>
> Sally (shouting crossly): She can't have that any more!
>
> (b) Susan, by contrast, was easy-going, even tempered and adaptable, joining in happily when her mother played with her younger brother Alan, as in this incident where Alan is 'running away'.
>
> Mother to Alan: Bye-bye! Bye-bye!
>
> Susan (joins in by chasing Alan, to his great excitement): I'm going to catch him! I am! I am!
>
> (Dunn and Plomin, 1990, pp. 70–1)

The changing family situation seems to challenge first-born children to try to make sense of their role in the family world. First-borns seem particularly sensitive to interactions between their mother and the new baby, the most common response being 'a protest or a demand for precisely the same attention that the sibling was getting' (Dunn and Plomin, 1990, p. 68). Children sometimes 'mirrored' those actions of the baby that elicited the mother's attention, as is illustrated in the following example:

> Alistair, aged 35 months, watched intently when his mother exclaimed playfully at his younger sister Shirley's muddy hands … Alistair promptly ran to the flower bed and covered his hands with mud, then ran to his mother to show her his dirty hands.
>
> (Dunn and Plomin, 1990, p. 69)

Sensitivity to parent–sibling interactions is not confined to first-born children, simply because the new sibling has usurped their position as 'king of the castle'. In fact, as Dunn and her colleagues found, later children also paid close attention to mother–first-born interactions (Dunn and Plomin, 1990). Children as young as 14 months were 'vigilant monitors' of their mother's relationship with older siblings, particularly when these involved playful games, expressions of emotion and disputes. According to Dunn and her colleagues, children's interest in their mother's relationship with their siblings forms the basis of their social understanding.

Dunn's studies of sibling relationships show that, in general, influences in sibling relationships are reciprocal, with both partners taking responsibility for the relationship. Among the siblings she observed, there was a lot of imitation, with children either doing things together, or copying what the other did. Siblings functioned as teachers, playmates, protectors and adversaries. Older children provide powerful models for younger children, because of similarity of interests and level of competence. Younger children learn patterns of behaviour, language, and ways of relating to others by copying or imitating older siblings. Through conflict and co-operation with their siblings, children learn to understand the feelings, intentions and needs of others.

As children begin to go to school and make friends, the intensity of sibling relationships becomes modified (Dunn, 1984; Dunn and Kendrick, 1982). Most children say they like having siblings because of the help, protection, companionship and affection they receive.

> I like him. He's nicer than anyone. He takes me to school … He's fun to do things with … I'd be lonely without him … and I like everything about him.

(Dunn, 1984, p. 146)

The work of Dunn and her colleagues has played a major role in alerting developmental psychologists to the importance of studying multiple interactions in family settings. As Dunn and Plomin point out:

> The usual view is that it is the direct impact of how a parent relates to a child that influences that child's development. We argue that children are sensitive not only to how their parents relate to them, but also to how their parents relate to their siblings, and that children monitor and respond to that other relationship just as they monitor the relationship between their parents. This is a shift from viewing the child as *child-of-the-parent* to *child-as-family-member* [italics added].

(Dunn and Plomin, 1990, p. 79)

SUMMARY OF SECTION 5

- Children and parents modify and influence each other's behaviour. The physical and psychological characteristics of children can influence parental behaviour.

- Two examples of family change, divorce and the birth of a sibling, illustrate the ways in which changing family relationships impact on children.

- Parental separation and divorce is part of a long-term process that affects boys and girls in different ways.

- Recent research suggests that the impact of parental discord on children is more significant than the impact of family break-up through divorce *per se*.

- A number of factors influence later sibling relationships (for example, whether a mother talks to her first-born about the new baby).

- Individual differences between siblings also affect sibling relationships (for example, temperament).

- Early interest in family interactions marks the beginnings of the growth of social understanding in children.

- Work on the impact of parental discord, divorce and sibling relationships highlights the importance of studying multiple interactions within the family (as opposed to single interactions – for example, parent–child).

6 CONCLUSION

This chapter has been about growing up in the family, and I hope that I have shown that two common assumptions about the influence of families on development are no longer universally acceptable: that is, that the child's role in the developmental process is essentially passive, and that parental values and behaviour have long-term effects. These assumptions reflect the influence of behaviourist and psychoanalytic ideas but, as I have pointed out in this chapter, children make their own contribution to the experiences they have by virtue of their individual characteristics and the types of relationships they construct with their parents and siblings.

Although there are some consistent findings about the effects of parental styles and maternal behaviour on development (albeit in a narrow range of cultures), I have also shown that there are problems in deciding the direction of influence (a child's temperament and behaviour may also affect the parents' responses to that child). Thus a transactional model, one which takes into account the mutual relationships between parents and children, is a more accurate picture of what goes on in families. This theme has been developed throughout this chapter.

Two other themes run through this chapter: the influence of socio-cultural context on development, and the importance of relationships beyond the mother–child dyad. When we look at socialization across cultures, we find similarities as well as differences in maternal behaviour. Differences in cultural values and beliefs about children lead to different socialization practices and produce different behaviours. When we look at relationships within the family as a whole, we see that marital relationships, parent–child relationships and sibling relationships all influence development, as do parent–child–child relationships. A consideration of the concept of 'goodness of fit' allows us to appreciate the complex interaction between parental behaviour, multiple relationships, social context and child characteristics.

Growing up in the same family can entail powerfully different experiences for different children. First, the same parents can behave differently towards different children on those dimensions that are most important (warmth, for example). Second, child characteristics can influence parental behaviour. Third, other sources of influence within the family, such as siblings, also shape development. Influences outside the family that are not shared by siblings (such as peer groups) also affect social and emotional development, as you will see in later chapters.

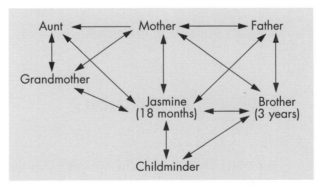

FIGURE 4 Jasmine's key relationships at 18 months.

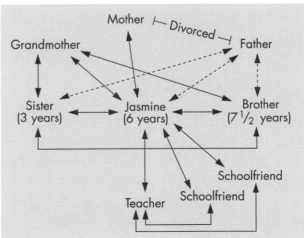

FIGURE 5 Jasmine's key relationships at 6 years.

TABLE 4 Ideas about children among the Nso.

Question	Common reasons	Mentioned by (percentage of sample)
(a) Why do you want children?	to perform domestic chores	56%
	to run errands	30%
	to respect and obey parents	36%
(b) What are your expectations of children?	filial service	27%
	good progress in school	50%
	'success' in life	45%
(c) What are desirable and undesirable characteristics?	*Desirable*	
	display obedience and respect	90%
	filial service	89%
	hard work	91%
	helpfulness	91%
	honesty and intelligence	100%
	Undesirable	
	disobedience and disrespect	93%
	laziness	97%
	fighting	95%
	playfulness	99%
	inquisitiveness	100%

Source: adapted from Nsamenang and Lamb, 1993, p. 434.

FURTHER READING

DUNN, J. (1984) *Sisters and Brothers*, London, Fontana.

SCHAFFER, H. R. (1984) *The Child's Entry into a Social World*, London, Academic Press.

WHITE, D. and WOOLLETT, A. (1992) *Families: a context for development*, London, Falmer Press.

REFERENCES

BAUMRIND, D. (1967) 'Child care practices anteceding three patterns of preschool behaviour', *Genetic Psychology Monographs*, **75**, pp. 43–88.

BAUMRIND, D. (1971) 'Current patterns of parental authority', *Developmental Psychology Monographs*, **1,** pp. 1–103.

BAUMRIND, D. (1972) 'An exploratory study of socialization effects on black children: some black–white comparisons', *Child Development*, **43**, pp. 261–7.

BAUMRIND, D. (1973) 'The development of instrumental competence through socialization' in PICK, A. D. (ed.) *Minnesota Symposium on Child Psychology*, **4,** pp. 3–46, Minneapolis, University of Minnesota Press.

BAUMRIND, D. (1991) 'Effective parenting during the early adolescent transition' in COWAN, P. A. and HETHERINGTON, E. M. (eds) *Family Transitions*, Hillsdale, New Jersey, Lawrence Erlbaum Associates.

BRUNER, J. (1978) 'Learning how to do things with words' in BRUNER, J. and GARTON, A. (eds) *Human Growth and Development*, Oxford, Clarendon Press.

COLE, M. and COLE, S. R. (1989) *The Development of Children*, New York, Scientific American Books, W. H. Freeman & Co.

DAS GUPTA, P. (1994) 'Images of childhood and theories of development' in OATES, J. (ed.) *The Foundations of Child Development*, Oxford, Blackwell/ The Open University (Book 1 of ED209).

DUNN, J. (1984) *Sisters and Brothers*, London, Fontana.

DUNN, J. (1986) 'Growing up in a family world: issues in the study of social development in young children' in RICHARDS, M. and LIGHT, P. (eds) *Children of Social Worlds,* Cambridge, Polity Press.

DUNN, J. (1992) 'Sisters and brothers: current issues in developmental research' in BOER, F. and DUNN, J. (eds) *Children's Sibling Relationships: developmental and clinical issues,* Hillsdale, New Jersey, Lawrence Erlbaum Associates.

DUNN, J. and KENDRICK, C. (1982) *Siblings: love, envy and understanding*, London, Grant McIntyre.

DUNN, J. and PLOMIN, R. (1990) *Separate Lives: why siblings are so different*, New York, Basic Books.

FAMILY POLICY STUDIES CENTRE (1982) *Fact Sheet 1: Families in the Future: Study Commision on the Family*, London, FPSC.

FERGUSSON, D. N., HORWOOD, L. J., and LYNSKEY, M. T. (1992) 'Family change, parental discord and early offending', *Journal of Child Psychology and Psychiatry*, **33**, pp. 1059–75.

GABLE, S., BELSKY, J. and CRNIC, K. (1992) 'Marriage, parenting and child development: progress and prospects', *Journal of Family Psychology*, **5,** pp. 276–94.

GRUSEC, J. and LYTTON, H. (1988) *Social Development*, New York, Springer-Verlag.

HETHERINGTON, E. M., COX, M. J. and COX, R. (1979) 'Play and social interaction in children following divorce', *Journal of Social Issues*, **35**, pp. 26–49.

HETHERINGTON, E. M., COX, M. J. and COX, R. (1982) 'Effects of divorce on parents and children' in LAMB, M. E. (ed.) *Non-Traditional Families: parenting and child development,* Hillsdale, New Jersey, Lawrence Erlbaum Associates.

HETHERINGTON, E. M. and PARKE, R. D. (1993) *Child Psychology: a contemporary viewpoint*, fourth edition, New York, McGraw Hill Inc.

HINDE, R. A. and STEVENSON-HINDE, J. (eds) (1988) *Relationships Within Families*, Oxford, Clarendon Press.

HOFFMAN, L. W. (1987) 'The value of children to parents and child-rearing patterns' in KAGITCIBASI, C. (ed.) *Growth and Progress in Cross-Cultural Psychology*, Berwyn, Swets North America Inc.

KAYE, K. (1982) *The Mental and Social Life of Babies*, London, Methuen.

LERNER, J. V. (1993) 'The influence of child temperamental characteristics on parent behaviour' in LUSTER, T. and OKAGAKI, L. (eds) *Parenting: an ecological perspective*, Hillsdale, New Jersey, Lawence Erlbaum Associates.

LEVINE, R. A. (1974) 'Parental goals: a cross-cultural view' in LEICHTER, H. J. (ed.) *The Family as Educator*, New York, Teachers College Press.

MACCOBY, E. E. (1992) 'The role of parents in the socialization of children: a historical overview', *Developmental Psychology*, **28**, pp. 1006–17.

MACCOBY, E. E. and MARTIN, J. A. (1983) 'Socialization in the context of the family: parent–child interaction' in HETHERINGTON, E. M. (ed.) *Mussen Manual of Child Psychology,* vol. 4, pp. 1–102, New York, Wiley.

MCCREDIE, G. and HORROX, A. (1985) *Voices in the Dark*, London, Unwin Paperback.

MCLAUGHLIN, B. (1983) 'Child compliance to parental control techniques', *Developmental Psychology*, **19**, pp. 667–73.

MILLER, A. (1990) *Banished Knowledge: facing childhood injuries,* London, Virago.

MORGAN, D. H. J. (1988) 'Socialization and family change' in WOODHEAD, M. and MCGRATH, A. (eds) *Family, School and Society*, London, Hodder and Stoughton.

NEWSON, J. and NEWSON, E. (1976) *Seven Years Old in the Home Environment*, London, George Allen and Unwin.

NSAMENANG, A. B. and LAMB, M. E. (1993) 'The acquisition of socio-cognitive competence by Nso children in the Bamenda Grasslands of Northwest Cameroon', *International Journal of Behavioural Development*, **16**, pp. 429–43.

RUTTER, M. (1981) *Maternal Deprivation Reassessed*, second edition, Harmondsworth, Penguin.

RUTTER, M. and GILLER, H. (1983) *Juvenile Delinquency: trends and perspectives*, Harmondsworth, Penguin.

SAMEROFF, A. J. (1991) 'The social context of development' in WOODHEAD, M. and LIGHT, P. (eds) *Becoming a Person*, London, Routledge/The Open University.

SCHAFFER, H. R. (1977) *Mothering,* London, Fontana.

SCHAFFER, H. R. (1984) *The Child's Entry into a Social World*, London, Academic Press.

SCHAFFER, H. R. and CROOK, C. K. (1978) 'The role of the mother in early social development' in MCGURK, H. (ed.) *Issues in Childhood Social Development,* London, Methuen.

SCHNEIDER, B. H. (1993) *Children's Social Competence in Context*, Oxford, Pergamon Press.

SEARS, R. R., MACCOBY, E. E. and LEVIN, H. (1957) *Patterns of Child Rearing*, Evanston, Illinois, Row Peterson.

STEVENSON, J. E. and OATES, J. (1994) 'Infant individuality' in OATES, J. (ed.) *The Foundations of Child Development*, Oxford, Blackwell/The Open University (Book 1 of ED209).

SUPER, C. M. and HARKNESS, S. (1981) 'Figure, ground and gestalt: the cultural context of the active individual' in LERNER, R. M. and BUSCH-ROSSIGNOL, N. A. (eds) *Individuals as Producers of their own Development: a life-span perspective,* New York, Academic Press.

THOMAS, A. and CHESS, S. (1977) *Temperament and Development*, New York, Bruner/Mazel.

TIZARD, B. and HUGHES, M. (1984) *Young Children Talking and Thinking at Home and School*, London, Fontana.

WALKERDINE, V. and LUCEY, H. (1989) *Democracy in the Kitchen: regulating mothers and socialising daughters*, London, Virago.

WHITE, D. and WOOLLETT, A. (1992) *Families: a context for development*, London, Falmer Press.

WHITING, B. and POPE EDWARDS, C. (1988) *Children of Different Worlds: the formation of social behaviour*, Cambridge, Massachusetts, Harvard University Press.

READINGS

Reading A   Edited extracts from 'Socialization and the family: change and diversity'

David H. J. Morgan

Family, School and Society

What is the family?

I have in front of me a travel brochure. On the front is a picture of a sun-soaked beach with a young man and a young woman, together with two children. I have no difficulty in recognising this healthy and happy little group as being a 'family'. How is this?

Partly, I suppose, I know this is a family because I know that the travel agent is selling 'family holidays'. I also know that this is a family because of the way in which the adults and children are grouped; they are close to each other, touching each other, looking at each other. They are not, I understand, a set of random individuals. Most of all, I recognize this group as a family without a moment's hesitation because I 'just know' that it is a family, because I have lived … with such representations from my earliest years.

And yet, perhaps, there is something a little odd about the group. Why, I ask, are the children in their early school years rather than infants … or teenagers …? Where are the grandparents? Already, in considering this particular everyday image … I am contrasting … it with other images that I can bring to mind. Nevertheless, all these images are images of the family.

… My object here is not so much to provide an authoritative definition of '*the* family' but rather to introduce … some of the ways in which uses of the term may vary. Perhaps this flexibility, the fact that we are able to use the word in such a rich variety of contexts, is one of the most important features of family life in contemporary society.

In order to begin to explore this range of meanings and understandings, let us consider a set of distinctions:

1 Ideals/Realities

(a) The family on the travel brochure is clearly presented as a 'happy family' … We know, however, that 'normal' families also have quarrels, misfortunes and tragedies and that many families will experience violence or separation.

(b) The picture is an ideal representation in a second sense. From a whole range of possible family situations, it highlights one, that of a youngish married couple and their school-age children. This represents just one particular stage in the experience of some families, one set of relationships out of a much wider range of possible relationships.

2 Family/Household

A household in sociological writings, is a group of people sharing the same dwelling. They will normally ... share one daily meal together. When we talk of 'families' we are usually talking of a relationship established through parenthood or marriage, however these terms are understood. Households often include family members but they may include others who are not related by either parenthood or marriage; servants or lodgers for example.

More importantly, family relationships extend beyond and between households ... [I]t is likely that each adult [in a particular household] will also have parents, brothers and sisters, etc. who are living in separate, if similar, households.

3 Nuclear/Extended

The group on our travel brochure is sometimes referred to as a 'nuclear family', that is a simple two generational unit consisting of one set of parents and their biological or adopted children. The term 'extended family' refers to those other relationships that extend outwards from this nuclear unit: grandparents, brothers and sisters, aunts, uncles, cousins and so on. This set of people, potentially very large, is sometimes referred to more popularly as 'relatives' or 'kin' although there is nearly always some kind of distinction between those kin whose existence is merely recognized and those between whom there are some kinds of regular relationships and exchanges. Members of an extended family may sometimes share the same household ...

4 Structure and Process

The travel brochure family is literally a snapshot of a family taken at a particular moment of time. But each of these individuals and their relationships with each other, as it were, frozen in time, have a past and a future. In the not too distant past, the married couple had just one child and before that, they simply constituted a couple each of whom had come from different households. Looking into the future we can see the children getting older, leaving the household at different stages and forming their own households.

5 Unity/Diversity

... [S]ome argue that it is possible to talk of 'the British family' (or indeed of *the* family) while others argue for a more diverse picture, based on a variety of family forms. Often, in debates about the nature and future of the family, these differences of approach become confused with our first set of differences, between ideals and realities. Some, therefore, will argue that there is one standard or dominant model of the family (often close to the nuclear based household) and that this is the most desired form of domestic arrangement. Alternatively, others might argue that all different forms of family or household are equally valid and that the nuclear family model should not be privileged over any other chosen form of domestic life. ...

What I hope to have shown up to now is that there are a variety of ways in which the family can be understood, and that we must always be sensitive to the various shades of meaning which come into play whenever the term is being used.

Source: Morgan, D. H. J. (1988) 'Socialization and family change' in Woodhead, M. and McGrath, A. (eds) Family, School and Society, London, Hodder and Stoughton, pp. 28–30.

Reading B　The child's entry into a social world

H. R. Schaffer

The study of socialization

Historically, a number of models of the socialization process have influenced our thinking about child rearing, each based on a particular concept of the nature of children and hence also of the role the parent plays in their development. Of the three principal models …, two need only brief mention: they are of historical interest only in that their inadequacies are now widely recognized. The third remains widely prevalent and deserves rather more discussion.

(a) *Laissez-faire model* The greater the role one ascribes to inherent forces in the child's nature as determinants of development the less weight will be attached to parental influences. Preformationism is the most extreme expression of a belief in inherent forces; its essence is the idea that all basic aspects of an individual's personality are laid down at birth and merely unfold in the course of subsequent development. It follows that the child's caretakers have but a limited part to play: as Rousseau, one of the most articulate proponents of this view, asserted, the only proper role of the environment is to avoid all interference with the processes of self-regulation and spontaneous maturation. The task of parents is thus to provide a maximally permissive atmosphere and thereby allow the child to grow as his nature dictates …

(b) *Clay moulding model* At the other extreme we have a conception of socialization as a clay moulding process: the child, that is, arrives in the world as a formless lump of clay and society, as represented by mothers, fathers, teachers and other such figures, proceeds to mould him into whatever shape it desires … all attempts to understand how socialization comes about must therefore concentrate on the behaviour of the adults with whom the child is in contact. It is their schedules of rewards and punishment, their ways of habit training and the examples which they set that provide an explanation of the final product. Instead of holding a concept of the child as preformed, the child is seen as a purely passive, reactive organism …

Historically this view is usually associated with John Locke, yet the blank slate (*tabula rasa*) to which he likened the newborn child's mind was used by him in a very specific sense only, namely as an argument against the prevailing belief in innate ideas. Children, Locke asserted, have to be provided with mental content; their minds are blank only in the sense that ideas can be derived from experience alone, and experience must be provided by caretakers …

A much more extreme expression of the clay moulding model emerged this century in the writings of J. B. Watson … As he put it: 'The behaviourist finds that the human being at birth is a very lowly piece of unformed protoplasm, ready to be shaped by any family in whose care it is first placed.' Watson's belief in the power of adults to change children's behaviour became the starting point for much of the research in the past few decades that examined child rearing practices from a behaviourist point of view … with its emphasis on training and learning, its faith in the shaping influences of reward and punishment, and its assumption that in reinforcement and association we find the mechanisms to explain the course of child development. Socialization, as Bijou … put it, is simply the product of the individual's reinforcement history.

It has become increasingly evident in recent years that there are many difficulties with such a view. Above all, the concept of the child as a passive recipient of other people's stimulation has had to be abandoned in the face of mounting evidence that children from birth on are capable of themselves exerting influences on their caretakers …

Asymmetry in the power balance between adults and children is, of course, not in question: by definition socialization is an adult-initiated process, the end-point of which is to transform the child into something regarded as desirable by his caretakers. But the manner of bringing this about, its timing and sequence, and the eventual result achieved depend as much on the nature of the child as on that of the adult. Developmental change of any kind cannot be explained in terms of environmental input alone.

(c) *The conflict model* By far the most pervasive view is that which sees socialization in terms of confrontation. Children, it is agreed, are not passive; from the beginning they have wishes and desires of their own which impel them to behave in certain ways. The trouble is that these ways are antithetical to those of society; they bring the child into conflict with his caretakers, whose task is then to compel him to give up his natural preferences and adopt unnatural modes of behaviour regarded as desirable by society.

This view has a long historical tradition behind it. It is based on the doctrine of original sin: the idea that man is conceived and born in sin and that childhood is the crucial period for curbing and eradicating the innate evil in his nature. As Thomas Hobbs, writing in the 17th century, saw it, children come into the world as little savages whose constant aim is to attain power over others, irrespective of the cost … the primary purpose of child rearing is therefore to take the base and negative nature with which the child is endowed and, by virtue of the parent's greater power, to force him into gradually adopting the role of good citizen …

Parents are no longer thus motivated, yet the conflict model of socialization remains prevalent in psychological writings. To a considerable degree this is due to the influence of Freud: he more than any other modern writer propagated the idea of natural man as basically anti-social, as a creature whose instinctual drives are of a selfish, destructive nature and thus incompatible with the conditions of societal living …

Freud's conception of socialization is thus also of a conflict model, addressed to the problem of how the child learns to restrain his inborn anti-social impulses. Various control mechanisms are required, operating both within and outside the child, that make it possible for him to fit into society, though only at the cost of his original nature. Development is thus a painful process, for it requires the resolution of the basic antagonism between the child and his social group. And the picture that emerges of the parent-child relationship is a thoroughly negative one: on the one hand parents are characterised predominantly in terms of prohibitions, commands, threats and exhortations; on the other hand children are painted as aggressive, selfish, fearful and guilt-ridden.

SOURCE: SCHAFFER, H. R. (1984) The Child's Entry into a Social World, *London, Academic Press, pp. 161–5.*

CHAPTER 4 DEVELOPMENTAL PERSPECTIVES ON EMOTION

Martin Woodhead, Peter Barnes, Dorothy Miell and John Oates

CONTENTS

1	**MAKING SENSE OF EMOTIONS**	**136**
2	**EMOTIONS IN INFANCY**	**140**
2.1	Expression of emotion	141
2.2	Recognition of emotion	142
2.3	Early empathy	143
2.4	Socialization and communication	145
2.5	Post-natal depression	149
	Summary of Section 2	150
3	**EMOTIONS, FAMILY RELATIONSHIPS AND SOCIAL UNDERSTANDING**	**151**
3.1	Empathy and self-interest	152
3.2	Talking about emotions	156
	Summary of Section 3	160
4	**UNDERSTANDING EMOTION AND 'THEORY OF MIND'**	**160**
4.1	Children's understanding of beliefs and desires	162
4.2	Understanding complex emotions	166
	Summary of Section 4	167
5	**CONTROLLING EMOTIONS**	**168**
5.1	Showing feelings – hiding feelings	170
5.2	Ways of coping	173
	Summary of Section 5	176
6	**EMOTION AND GENDER**	**176**
7	**CONCLUSION**	**177**
	FURTHER READING	**179**
	REFERENCES	**179**
	READING A: PSYCHOANALYSIS AND EMOTION	**183**
	READING B: HOW CHILDREN MAY REACT TO A MARITAL SEPARATION	**183**
	READING C: GENDER DIFFERENCES IN THE EXPRESSION OF EMOTION	**185**

OBJECTIVES

When you have studied this chapter, you should be able to:

- summarize evidence for the innateness of infant capacities for facial expression and recognition of emotion;
- discuss the development of empathy from early infancy through to the school years, explaining how capacities for empathy can serve self-interest as well as altruism;
- explain the role of early emotional behaviour within caregiver–infant communication by reference to research on post-natal depression;
- outline Judy Dunn's studies of the role of emotionally significant family relationships in the development of children's social understanding;
- outline Paul Harris's research on the growth of perspective-taking abilities within the context of 'theory of mind';
- discuss the significance of language and pretend play for the development of social understanding about emotions;
- apply the concept of socialization to the development of emotion, explaining 'social referencing' and 'display rules', as well as 'coping strategies' that have been identified in the study of children's reactions to trauma;
- give examples of cultural conventions governing the expression of emotion;
- outline evidence for the influence of socialization on gender differences in the experience and expression of emotion.

1 MAKING SENSE OF EMOTIONS

This chapter is about the role that emotions play in development, and especially about how children understand, communicate and regulate the emotions they experience themselves, and recognize in others. As a starting point we ask you to consider what sense you make of children's emotions. This activity will help introduce the themes of the chapter.

ACTIVITY 1

Allow about 30 minutes

EMOTION IN DEVELOPMENT

If you are in regular contact with children, of whatever age, try to recall some occasions where emotions have been significant. They do not have to be highly dramatic examples. Emotions are part of everyday life. Write some brief notes on what strikes you as important and interesting about the role of emotion in those episodes, and/or discuss them with a partner or friend.

Here are a few examples which you could analyse if you have no access to children:

1   I was half an hour late picking up my daughter from nursery. I could see her looking out of the window, obviously worried. When I came through the door she rushed up and wanted a big hug. Next day, she got upset when I dropped her off at nursery again.

2   Lee and James had been happily playing in the paddling pool for some time when they hit on the idea of splashing water at each other. They were having a great time, squealing with delight. Then James went too far and chucked a whole bucket of water over his friend. Lee got really cross, but James seemed to enjoy it more than ever. When I went out there, James claimed it was an accident.

3   It was my birthday yesterday. For the very first time my 10 year old had taken herself to the shops, bought a gift, wrapped it up and presented it to me as I woke up. She was obviously pleased as punch, and I was quite overcome. I don't know which of us was more emotional.

4   I knew there was something the matter the moment he came back from school. He was doing his best to act normal, especially in front of my sister who had just popped in. He tends to bottle up his feelings at the best of times, just like his dad. A bit later on he blurted out about his best friend being seriously ill in hospital. I could see his eyes beginning to fill up, but then he just headed up to his room, to play his music.

Here are some questions to guide your thinking. Do not expect to find straightforward answers in most cases:

• What are 'emotions'? How significant are they within children's lives?

• At what age do children first start to show emotions? Do infants show emotion from birth? How do we know? Do emotions become more or less significant in children's lives as they grow towards maturity? Do outward appearances necessarily represent inner feelings?

• What are emotions for? What function do they serve? Are they about 'letting off steam', communicating with others, or what?

• What do we mean when we say that some people are more 'emotional' than others? Are there differences between individuals, families, and societies in the expression of emotion?

Introductory psychology texts tend to contain, at most, just one chapter devoted to the topic of emotion, with numerous chapters addressing aspects of human cognition: thinking, memory, perception, language, etc. This relative imbalance in treatment may reflect a wider cultural tendency to emphasize the cognitive at the expense of the emotional. As adults our feelings are for the most part regarded as a private or family affair, to be kept under control as much as possible. This is especially true of what are often termed 'negative' emotions. So, the student who becomes tearful in a tutorial because of the stress of preparing for an exam may feel ashamed of this display of weakness. The teacher who loses their temper with a class may regret their behaviour as unprofessional. 'Positive' emotions, such as love and affection or joviality, are more acceptable, but their expression is still regulated by powerful personal and cultural rules.

There are exceptions, of course, when strongly expressed emotions are accepted, and even expected. Obvious examples surround the major life events of birth and death, and there are also ritualized contexts for the expression of feelings, e.g. in religious observances, at a sporting event, or at a party. There are times when public expression of indignation is socially justified (e.g., when someone knocks you off your bike), or joy (on passing an exam) or remorse (for having let down a friend). In general, though, adults in our culture experience emotions as essentially *internal* states, which for the most part are inhibited, contained within boundaries or channelled into 'acceptable' outer expression, except on those occasions when we are 'overwhelmed' by our feelings.

Among children, especially young children, things are very different. Outward displays of sadness and happiness, anger and love, humour and irritability occur much more frequently. Indeed, parents give a lot of attention to these displays, as illustrated by such remarks as, 'There's no need to shout,' 'Big boys don't cry over little things like that,' 'Why are you looking so miserable?', 'Hurt yourself? Come for a cuddle,' and 'Calm down.' It's a matter for debate how far the change from childhood to maturity is about a reduction in felt emotion resulting from the inhibition of feelings, or their redirection and transformation into other forms of expression. Bear in mind that, in one sense, there is an *increase* in emotional expression as children grow older. Maturity permits more varied and subtle forms of emotion than the 'raw' emotions of childhood. For example, adults typically make fine distinctions among such complex feelings as pride, wonder, embarrassment, guilt, exhilaration, envy and sympathy.

Of course, there are enormous individual differences in emotional expressiveness which may be a function of temperament (see Stevenson and Oates, 1994). Some people who appear 'cool' or 'hard' on the surface are also described as 'warm-hearted' or 'soft inside'. In these everyday terms we convey the idea of dissociation between inner feelings and their outer expression. One of the tasks of childhood is to learn about when to show and when to hide one's own feelings, according to cultural, situational, social class and gender rules etc.

Another task of childhood is to learn about emotions in others. Children don't just express their own feelings; they react to the emotions of those around them. Being able to recognize emotions means that children can make sense, for example, of a parent's anger. They soon learn whether it is directed at them, at another member of the family, or is spilling over from a difficult day at work. In this respect the child's own feelings and intelligence are finely tuned to the experiences of those around them.

This applies equally when an adult is distressed; displays of compassion, especially by very young children, can be deeply moving to parents.

Offering day-to-day examples (like those in Activity 1) of the way children recognize and express emotions and how they learn to regulate their feelings is relatively straightforward. Providing an adequate psychological explanation for these emotions is a good deal more problematic. This is hardly surprising in view of the lack of consensus even on how to define 'emotion'. We are dealing with a concept with many different meanings and associations. Some of these have already been illustrated in this discussion. The psychological study of emotion must take account of:

- physiological factors, notably the functioning of the autonomic nervous system in regulating arousal, heart rate, respiration, hunger, sexual activity, etc.;

- experiential characteristics, including the sometimes subtle and other times dramatic shifts in feeling between elation and depression, joy and despair, anger and jollity, love and disgust, etc.;

- behavioural expressions, especially body posture, facial expressions, vocalizations etc.;

- cognitive/attitudinal components, notably the way feelings become intermingled with perceptions, thoughts and values (e.g., in the enjoyment of impressionist painting, the abhorrence of fascist politics, or the amusement of satirical verse);

- control/coping mechanisms, through which emotions are regulated both to protect the individual from painful feelings (by repression, displacement, denial etc.) and to enable them to present a demeanour which is appropriate to their situation/role (e.g., the police officer at an emergency, the host at a party, the debt-collector confronting a defaulter);

- social/moral aspects, when feelings become linked to public standards, ethical issues and normative values, as for 'guilt', 'shame', 'embarrassment', 'pride' etc.;

- cultural rituals whereby the expression of emotion becomes a shared experience (e.g., in religious observances, festivals, mass political rallies, demonstrations);

- pathological issues, notably diagnostic and therapeutic aspects of extreme, over-persistent or maladaptive emotional states, such as depression, manic depression, anxiety states, phobias, obsessions, etc.

In this chapter we do not concentrate on any one dimension of emotion, but favour an approach that integrates the emotional with issues of social and cognitive development. In other words, emotions are embedded in social relations, and they are mediated by cognition. Or, to put it more simply, feelings are shared with others, they are talked about and thought about. Our major focus is on how children make sense of emotions in themselves and in others, in the role of communication and cognition in the way children understand and regulate their feelings; and, conversely, in the role of emotion in motivating children to think and communicate about themselves and their social relationships. The structure of the chapter is broadly developmental, taking the study of facial expressions in infancy as the starting point for asking the question, 'Are emotions innate or learned?'

2 EMOTIONS IN INFANCY

Being able to judge how a very young baby is feeling is a major concern for caregivers. For the most part, such judgements are made with some confidence, but parents have no direct knowledge of their baby's inner state. Their judgements are based instead on the infant's body tone, her activity level, her cries and, especially, her facial expressions. The focus of this section is on the significance of these facial expressions as indicators of babies' emotional state. For example, first smiles are often assumed to mean that the baby is feeling happy, or a wrinkled forehead and screwed-up eyes are taken to indicate pain and distress. Facial expressions are especially important signals in infancy. But even after the development of language, when children are able to express their feelings in words, the look on their face is often taken to be the most reliable indicator of 'true feelings'. One of the earliest investigations of facial expressions was by Charles Darwin, who wrote a book entitled *The Expression of the Emotions in Man and Animals* (1872). Darwin claimed that emotional expression is inborn in two respects. First, he believed that there is a direct, unlearned link between particular inner emotional states and particular outer facial expressions. Secondly, he believed that these same instinctive connections between an infant's inner and outer states enabled the infant to recognize the emotional states expressed by others. We will review recent research on both 'expression' and 'recognition' aspects of Darwin's theory in turn.

How do we recognize a baby's feelings?

2.1 Expression of emotion

Psychologists have made painstaking analyses of the muscular movements involved in facial expressions of emotion elicited in a wide range of situations, for example, a game of peek-a-boo, a vanishing toy, the approach of a stranger, the repeated removal of a tasty biscuit, and receiving a painful inoculation (see Research Summary 1).

RESEARCH SUMMARY 1
INTERPRETING EARLY EXPERIENCE

1 When newborn babies are given a sweet liquid to taste, they respond with a slight parting of the lips, rhythmic licking and sometimes a slight smile. A bitter liquid is met by a mouth which is down at the corners and with repeated pursing of the lips – many of the hallmarks of disgust. Observers (who didn't know which liquid was being tasted) judged that the infants enjoyed the sweet one but disliked the bitter one. The observers could also distinguish degrees of enjoyment/disliking in relation to the relative concentration of the liquids.

(Ganchrow *et al.*, 1983)

2 Video recordings were made of infants aged from 1 to 9 months in situations chosen to generate a variety of emotions – joy, sadness, surprise, anger, disgust. Examples of the babies' expressions were selected and photographed and a sample of college students was asked to look at the photographs and identify the emotions. They performed reasonably well. The most accurately identified emotions were happiness (81 per cent), sadness (72 per cent) and surprise (69 per cent); the least reliably identified were anger (41 per cent) and disgust (37 per cent). Similar findings were obtained from a sample of nurses. From this evidence it seems that infants' expressions of emotion have social validity.

(Izard *et al.*, 1980)

Of course, the early appearance of facial expressions does not prove that these are innate. Darwin's beliefs about the instinctive roots of babies' expressions of emotion are still the subject of controversy. Some argue that the research evidence may reflect a shared cultural communication system into which infants are initiated from a very early age. After all, other research has demonstrated that infants have a remarkable capacity for imitation. They are typically exposed at close range to quite exaggerated facial expressions from their caregivers, and might conceivably have already learned to echo these expressions in their own behaviour (Meltzoff and Moore, 1983).

If this were the case, we might expect to find different patterns of facial expressions of emotion in different societies. However, numerous cross-cultural studies have found, on the contrary, that there is remarkable similarity (Mesquita and Frijda, 1992). One example is given in Research Summary 2.

RESEARCH SUMMARY 2
COMMON EXPRESSIONS OF EMOTION

Paul Ekman visited a very isolated community in New Guinea – the Fore – who had no contact with foreigners and no exposure to films or other representations of people from the 'outside' world. They were told stories in their own language designed to elicit certain emotions (happiness, sadness, anger, disgust, surprise and fear) and then shown photographs of Western children and adults exhibiting that range of emotions. They had no difficulty matching four expressions: happiness (92 per cent), anger (84 per cent), disgust (81 per cent) and sadness (79 per cent). Distinguishing fear from surprise caused more problems. When the Fore themselves were photographed representing expressions suited to particular experiences – positive and negative – they, in turn, were subsequently correctly interpreted by judges in the US, suggesting that there may be a large measure of consistency in facial expressions across even the most contrasting cultures.

(Ekman, 1973)

One of the leading advocates of the biological roots of emotional expression, Eibl-Eibesfeldt (1975), has combined cross-cultural research with studies of other primate species and of blind and deaf babies deprived of normal learning opportunities. He has presented a powerful case in support of Darwin's claim that there is an unlearned link between particular emotional states and particular facial expressions. Even so, we should not underestimate the influence of maturation, learning and socialization, as will become clear later in this section.

2.2 Recognition of emotion

Darwin made a second claim for babies' innate capacities. He said that babies are born with innate abilities to recognize the significance of emotional expressions on the faces of their caregivers. He based his claim on observations of his young son, Doddy. On one occasion, when the boy was just over 6 months old, his nurse pretended to cry. Darwin observed how Doddy's face 'instantly assumed a melancholy expression, with the corners of the mouth strongly depressed' (Darwin, 1872, p. 368). He speculated that since the boy could never have seen a grown-up person cry, 'an innate feeling must have told him that the pretended crying of his nurse expressed grief; and this through the instinct of sympathy excited grief in him' (Darwin, 1872, p. 368).

From a psychological point of view, Doddy's empathy for his nurse is a very considerable achievement. Think for a moment about the processes involved. The infant must be endowed with an innate representation (or schema) which links the visual stimulus in a caregiver's face to the muscular movements that generate the equivalent facial expression in the infant's own face. This is technically known as inter-modal mapping (Meltzoff and Moore, 1983). What is the evidence for such recognition abilities? Research Summary 3 provides some answers.

RESEARCH SUMMARY 3
BABIES' REACTIONS TO FACIAL EXPRESSIONS

Jeannette Haviland and Mary Lelwica asked a group of mothers to display each of three emotions – happiness, sadness and anger – to their 10-week-old babies. They were asked to simulate the appropriate facial expression and use an appropriate tone of voice. The displays were repeated several times. Analysis of video recordings taken of the babies showed that they reacted in distinct ways to each of the displays, but they were not simply copying their mother's expression. They did respond to their mother's happy display with a happy face, but the angry face resulted in either an angry expression or stillness, and the sad display generated an increase in mouthing, chewing and sucking behaviour.

(Haviland and Lelwica, 1987)

Research Summary 3 offers fairly convincing evidence in support of Darwin's claim about infants' recognition abilities, but it also suggests that infants are not necessarily employing the very complex inter-modal skills that would be required for them to imitate accurately their caregivers' emotional expression. An alternative explanation presumes that the infant is sensitively attuned to the emotional signals of its caregiver (which may indicate imminent danger or safe playfulness). These evoke a sympathetic emotional state in the infant and it is the outward expression of the infant's own inner state that is then observed.

2.3 Early empathy

Infants' apparent sensitivity to the emotional state of adults has been viewed as especially significant as the first evidence of emergence of the fundamental human quality of *empathy*, the ability to put yourself into the feeling state of another person and respond appropriately. But children's comforting behaviour can be difficult to interpret.

> When we came home this afternoon, I slipped and fell and came down really whacking my nose. I was in real pain and sat down in J's room, holding and rubbing my nose. J (aged 14 months) was very sympathetic. He acted for me the way I do when he hurts himself. He hugged and patted me and even offered me his blanket that he uses when he's hurt or tired. He seemed very upset, whether for me or because of me.
>
> (Wolf, 1982, quoted in Harris, 1989, p. 30)

The behaviour is clear enough, but this father's final sentence hints at uncertainty over how to interpret his son's behaviour. Is J's emotional expression a reflection of his *own distress* at the incident, or a more *genuine empathy* with his father's pain? There is good reason for being cautious about using the word 'empathy', not least because there is evidence that babies and children show quite distinct patterns of

RESEARCH SUMMARY 4
RESPONSES TO DISTRESS

Carolyn Zahn-Waxler and Marion Radke-Yarrow followed three groups of children aged 10, 15 and 20 months over a nine month period. They trained mothers to record what their children did when someone became distressed. Below a year the children showed a range of responses to distress in others, including crying, hitting out at a parent perceived as having caused the problem, and on occasions offering comfort to a distraught parent. By one year most children offered comfort to a distressed person by patting, hugging or offering a comfort toy (very much as Wolf's son did.) From 18 months, these attempts at comforting were sometimes more elaborate, such as trying to put a sticking-plaster on a wound or covering mother with a blanket. As their language abilities increased, so children began to articulate their concern and offered suggestions about what to do. By 2 years they were responding, on average, on about one-third of the occasions when they witnessed someone in distress, often trying several ways of bringing help and comfort to the other person if their first attempt failed: 'Such precocity on the part of the very young gives one pause. The capabilities for compassion, for various kinds of reaching out to others in a giving sense are viable and effective responses early in life.'
(Yarrow and Waxler, 1975, pp. 78–9)

responding to another's emotion during different phases of development, as an American longitudinal study illustrates (see Research Summary 4).

On the basis of this and other research, it is possible to distinguish some common patterns of reaction in very young children each of which involves progressive levels of empathy:

- 'personal distress' or some other emotional reaction, which shows that the child is affected by the incident;
- 'emotional contagion', where the child displays the same emotion as the other person, apparently in sympathy with their distress;
- 'egocentric empathy', where the child endeavours to comfort by offering the kinds of help *they* find most comforting (e.g., their blanket or doll).

In Sections 3 and 4 of this chapter, we will continue this theme by considering the way slightly older children (aged 2, 3 and 4) employ (and sometimes exploit!) their capacity for empathy, culminating in the point when they have acquired more mature abilities for taking the emotional perspective of another person.

To summarize the argument so far, we have taken Darwin's two claims about innate capacities for emotional expression and recognition as the starting point for reviewing more recent research. This confirms that infants show selective sensitivity to the emotional behaviour of the adults around them, as well as displaying their own emotional state by signals that are readily interpreted by others. When combined with other evidence regarding the newborn's orientation to the sounds, smells and appearance of others, evidence on emotion provides a powerful case for arguing that human infants are innately pre-adapted to engage in social relationships with caregivers on whom their survival, nurturance and learning will depend throughout childhood (Schaffer, 1989).

However, this is only the beginning of the story in two important respects. First, innate rudimentary capacities for recognition and expression of emotion become the building blocks for subsequent learning. We have already described how early responses to emotional distress in others are transformed through children's experiences of relationships as well as processes of maturation and learning. Faced with a parent who is in pain, a 6 month old may show distress and a 3 year old will attempt basic comfort, but a 10 year old is likely also to know how to seek out appropriate help, including dialling 999 if necessary.

The same principle applies to expression of emotion. So far we have discussed emotions in infancy mainly from the child's point of view. We have talked about emotional expression and emotional recognition as if it was only the child who possessed these skills. In practice, of course, parents and indeed other caregivers are sensitively attuned to their children's feelings, as well as feeling and expressing emotions themselves. These processes of mutual expression and recognition are a powerful system of communication, and a powerful context for learning (see Oates, 1994).

2.4 Socialization and communication

ACTIVITY 2

Allow 10 minutes

REACTIONS TO EVERYDAY EVENTS

The aim of this activity is to identify ways in which young children learn through the emotions they are exposed to in their day-to-day lives.

Think about a 1 year old in the care of an adult, going through everyday experiences like feeding, toileting, playing, shopping, spending time with friends, etc. What situations, events or behaviour might provoke an emotional reaction from the caregiver? How might the child learn from these experiences?

In the course of a day, any adult is likely to express a range of emotions with varying degrees of intensity. They might express amusement or irritation when the baby puts its feeding cup on its head, disgust at the smell and mess encountered when changing a nappy, fear of a large dog in the street, happiness when talking with a friend, anger when an older child jumps on the sofa with muddy boots. Some of these expressions of emotions are directed at the child. Many more are directed at other people and events. Whatever the adult's intentions, their child is likely to be monitoring their behaviour closely. Infants' ability to 'read' the

Playing with fire.

emotional expressions of others enables their own reactions to situations to become *socially referenced* in several distinct ways, as Research Summary 5 shows.

Social referencing is only one part of the story. Children don't just monitor adults' emotional reactions as a guide to appropriate feelings about the situations, objects and people they encounter. They are also sensitively attuned to the emotional reactions provoked by their *own* behaviour, including the reactions of others to their own expressions of emotion. For their part, parents monitor, react to and thereby regulate their infants' behaviour and emotional expressions. In short, emotional reactions are at the heart of the communication system that regulates adult–infant transactions.

RESEARCH SUMMARY 5
SOCIAL REFERENCING OF EMOTIONAL REACTIONS

Reactions to objects and situations

Some mothers were asked to introduce their 1-year-old children to a series of new toys and, in each case, to express delight or disgust or neutrality (through silence). Later, the children were observed while playing with these toys. They tended to avoid the one which had been the object of apparent maternal disgust (Hornick *et al.*, 1987). Other research has observed that, when uncertain about an object, or a situation, babies actually look to the caregiver's face, for a guide to the appropriate reaction (Feiring *et al.*, 1984).

Reactions to strangers

The 'strange situation' technique for studying young children's reactions to separation from attachment figures has already been described in Chapter 1. Feinman and Lewis (1983) found that 10-month-old children appeared more at ease in the presence of a stranger where their mother had previously demonstrated positive feelings towards that person, than when they had not.

We will take just one example. Carol Malatesta and Jeannette Haviland (1982) asked 60 mothers to spend time in interactive play with their 3 to 6-month-old infants, while separate cameras recorded the infant's and the mother's face. Table 1 shows how frequently each party displayed emotional expressions during a six minute period.

TABLE 1   Facial expressions of mother–infant pairs during six minutes' interaction.

Expression	Infants' average frequency	Mothers' average frequency
Interest	6	9
Enjoyment	9	23
Surprise	3	8
Sadness	2	1
Anger	7	0
Knit brow	11	2
Discomfort/pain	3	0

Source: adapted from Malatesta and Haviland, 1982, p. 995.

The results for the infants illustrates the wide variety of emotional displays even though only six minutes of interaction were analysed. These facial expressions changed with great frequency (on average, once every eight seconds). By contrast, the mothers showed much greater uniformity of emotional expression, and more positive emotions. (It may be that this was a reaction to being asked to present a relatively public display of mothering. Other more private settings, and other cultures, might yield a different profile of maternal behaviour.)

Although these results may only be true for public displays within one culture, there are still some valuable lessons to be learned about the way mothers regulate their infants' emotional state. Malatesta and Haviland calculated the dependence (or 'contingency') between infants' expressions and mothers' expressions. They report that when infants changed their facial expression, the average response time from mothers was less than half a second. In other words, mothers were monitoring their infants' facial expressions very closely. Further, there were consistent within-dyad patterns of mother–infant responding. For example, some pairs made greater use of brow movements than mouth movements (and vice versa); others engaged in matched patterns of reciprocal smiling, while others were mutually less expressive. When analyses of mother–infant pairs at 6 months old were compared with analyses at 3 months old, there was evidence of increasing convergence of infant and mother expressions. The authors speculated that this increased similarity may be the result of the combined effect of infant imitation and maternal reinforcement. Thirdly, they found a gender difference, whereby boys' expressions tended to be matched by their mothers, whereas girls' expressions tended to produce a wider range of maternal response. They speculated that the mothers may have been

Communicating feelings.

encouraging more expression of emotion in girls than boys, an issue that will be taken up in Section 5. In general, their observations suggest that one of the functions of mothers' responses is to alleviate or dampen down the intensity of their infants' expressive behaviour, especially anger.

Taken together with evidence on social referencing, these results illustrate the earliest stages of socialization of emotional expression. Malatesta *et al.* (1989) have extended their research into emotional expressions to the age of 2, noting that, over time, infant emotions become less changeable and more positive, with the emergence of signs that children are dampening negative emotion (indicated by wrinkled brow, compressed lips, lip biting) concurrently with their mothers' expression of similarly muted feelings. This evidence of early regulation of emotional expressiveness is just the beginning of a long process of acquiring what are known as *display rules*, culturally acquired patterns of intensification, inhibition and masking of emotional states depending on expectations of situations, roles and identities. We will be examining these processes in older children in Section 5.

To conclude this section, we will illustrate the significance of social referencing and socialization by asking how children make sense of emotions within relationships where there are difficulties. Research Summary 6 illustrates how children who have grown up in the context of neglectful, distorted or abusive care may misconstrue conventional display rules.

This example is reminiscent of MacKinnon-Lewis *et al.*'s research on the perceptions of hostility of conduct-disordered boys and their mothers in Chapter 2. Another theme explored in that chapter can also contribute to our understanding of the way disruption to 'normal' patterns of mother–infant interaction can have repercussions for emotional development.

RESEARCH SUMMARY 6
MISCONSTRUING DISPLAY RULES

Camras *et al.* (1983) compared a sample of 5-year-old children who had been physically abused with a sample who had not. The children were told brief stories which involved a child experiencing one of six emotions (happiness, sadness, anger, fear, surprise and disgust), such as 'It is her birthday and she is happy.' They then had to choose from photographs of posed facial expressions the one which matched the emotion in the story.

The abused children found this task more difficult than the control group, making many more inappropriate matchings of situation with emotional expression.

2.5 Post-natal depression

You have already seen in Chapter 2 how babies under the age of 3 months respond in dramatic ways if the normal patterns of communication with their mothers are disrupted (Murray, 1992). When, in a laboratory experiment, mothers assumed an unresponsive, unemotional face (the so-called 'still-face' situation), or when live video communication was disrupted by the introduction of a delay into the link, the babies showed signs that their emotional state was negatively affected by demonstrating higher than usual rates of avoidant eye movements, frowning, mouthing and finger sucking.

Similar disruptions may be a feature of communication between depressed mothers and their infants. This is typically accompanied by lower levels of general activity on the part of the mother, with a reduced amount of 'positive affect' (for example, number of smiles) being shown towards others. Since the mothers become more concerned with themselves there is less space remaining for concern to be shown to their babies. This can be seen in terms of the reduced overall amount of speech directed towards the babies and in the nature of that speech – fewer comments on the babies' activity and experiences, and more 'negative affect' (Murray *et al.*, 1993).

Post-natally depressed mothers are also more likely to rate their own babies' 'affect' more negatively than would another person observing the same behaviour whereas they rate their own behaviour more positively than the same observer would (even though that observer is not aware that the mother is diagnosed as depressed) (Field *et al.*, 1993). Taken together, this suggests that depressed mothers are likely to have a more negative view of their babies' emotional state and this in turn contributes further to the disruption of affective communication between baby and mother.

This evidence highlights once again the limitations of studies of emotion that concentrate mainly on the infant's capacities for expression and recognition of emotion. These are more than matched by the adult's much more developed potential for empathy and for communication. Emotional development is best understood as a process of co-regulation to which both partners bring skills, qualities and expectations, as Colwyn Trevarthen explains:

> Infant communications are better co-ordinated, more regular, more elaborate and more evocative and productive when they are being responded to by a partner who shows positive empathy. This means that the infant is prepared to participate as one actor in a 'dialogic' exchange or 'closure' of feelings that has a certain quality and richness ... The infant is not merely seeking *any* kind of 'contingent' events ... or recurrent forms of stimulation of a given physical intensity or richness. The optimal dyadic patterning of emotions is evidence for a motivation that defines persons as having special conversational and empathic properties and special expressions of feeling. Moreover, the analysis of the behaviours of partners in the 'best' or most organized and co-ordinated engagements shows that infant and adult meet with the same standards of emotion that define 'good' or 'bad' expression and reply, and that is why each is ready to gain immediate emotional support from appropriate responses of the other.

(Trevarthen, 1993, p. 68)

SUMMARY OF SECTION 2

- Psychologists have taken Darwin's claim that basic emotions are innate as the starting point for research on babies' capacities for expression and recognition of emotions.

- Empirical research has shown that infants react with recognizably appropriate expressions which are present from birth but mature during the early months, becoming more focused and differentiated.

- Some cross-cultural and comparative studies confirm that the facial expressions associated with several 'basic' emotions (e.g., happiness, anger, sadness) are recognized universally.

- Young infants are also interested in and responsive to the emotions expressed by others. Recognition abilities are the first step in the development of empathy. Three forms of empathic reaction have been identified, which approximate a developmental sequence ('personal distress', 'emotional contagion' and 'egocentric empathy').

- Early capacities for emotional expression and recognition are the foundation of communication and social learning. Infants learn appropriate emotional reactions to events and people through social referencing. Their own behaviour and their emotional reactions are also regulated through the reactions of their caregiver(s).

- Studies of disrupted adult–infant interactions (as in post-natal depression) illustrate the way feelings are normally co-regulated in a relationship in which both partners share expectations of the pattern of communication.

3 EMOTIONS, FAMILY RELATIONSHIPS AND SOCIAL UNDERSTANDING

In Section 2 we have argued that capacities for emotional expression and recognition are present at birth or shortly after and that they develop within a communication system that co-regulates the behaviour of infant and caregiver. In this section and the next we consider an older age group, from 1 year olds through to 5 and 6 year olds, and ask how their developing skills (especially language and pretend play) influence their understanding and expression of emotion. We will be concentrating on the work of two psychologists in particular: Judy Dunn (whose research you have already met in Chapters 1 and 3) and Paul Harris. Both are interested in how children make sense of emotion, or, more broadly in the role of emotion in the development of social understanding. However, each takes a somewhat different approach to the topic, in both research method and theoretical perspective.

In Section 4 we will describe Paul Harris's experimental studies with pre-school and school-age children. By asking children to interpret the emotional experiences of a variety of story characters, Harris has built up a picture of the growth of perspective-taking abilities entailed in making sense of both simple and more complex emotions. He views children's understanding of emotion as one facet of their cognitive development, and he draws in particular on a research tradition enquiring into how children come to understand what others think and feel, a capacity that is known as 'theory of mind'.

Judy Dunn is also interested in how children understand emotions in social relationships, but she has approached the topic through a series of detailed observational studies of very young children in everyday settings with their parents and siblings. Unlike Harris, she argues that it is through their experience of these emotionally-charged encounters (negotiating their position, offering sympathy, justifying their own and others' actions, protecting self-interest, etc.) that children acquire the capacity for social understanding. We start with Judy Dunn's account of the family processes surrounding children of 1 to 2 years old.

The 'terrible twos' is one way that British and American parents typify this age group, and not without reason. For example, Chapter 2, Section 2 cited a survey of doctors and parents by Jenkins *et al.* (1984) which found that the incidence of 'problems' rose rapidly to peak at around 3 years of age. Judy Dunn has taken a particular interest in the psychological significance of these emotional displays.

READING

Look again at the Reading at the end of this book by Judy Dunn, concentrating on her comments about the significance of emotion in early childhood. Look especially at Sections 2 and 3 of the Reading to remind yourself about how she gathered the data and what she was trying to achieve.

Dunn describes how observations conducted as part of the Cambridge Sibling Study showed children as early as the second year of life engaging in emotionally significant relationships within the family, including with their siblings. From this starting point she designed the first 'study of the beginnings of social understanding'. This study will be our major focus. Briefly, she concludes that the displays of strong emotion that typify the pre-school years are not just an unfortunate by-product of the young child's immaturity. They serve an important function in development, as part of the process that gradually leads to more mature (or at least more socialized) patterns of expression.

3.1 Empathy and self-interest

We have already seen (in Section 2) that very young infants are affected by, show interest in, and eventually display concern for the emotions expressed by others. Dunn's observations also included examples of empathy towards a parent's distress. By the age of 2, children are beginning to offer quite sophisticated verbal expressions of concern. For example, a 28 month old was watching the DIY efforts of his father, who hurt his wrist:

> FATHER: Oooh!
> CHILD: It hurt you, Dad?
> FATHER: No, I just twisted me wrist.
> CHILD TO OBSERVER: He – like that. Boink! Daddy – boink.
> CHILD TO MOTHER: Dad hurt his finger.
> MOTHER: Daddy hurt his finger?
> CHILD: Yes.
> (Dunn, 1988, p. 96)

However, Dunn notes that parents do not often show distress, so opportunities to observe their child's reactions were relatively infrequent in her research. By contrast, expressions of distress by a sibling were very common indeed. These incidents became a major focus for examining the way young children react when a sibling is upset. Dunn found that, by 18 months, most toddlers recognize a range of emotional expressions in their siblings. But their reaction is often far from benign!

ACTIVITY 3
(Allow about 10 minutes)

HOW DO YOUNG CHILDREN RESPOND TO SIBLING DISTRESS?

Study Dunn's data in Figure 1. Within each age group, children's behaviour was coded into five major categories. Frequency rates of responses were further subdivided according to whether the distress had been caused by the child themselves, or was for some other reason.

Start by looking at the reactions of 36 month olds to their siblings' distress. How do they react when they themselves caused the distress? How does this compare with their reaction when there are other reasons for the distress? Next, look at the younger age groups. How far do you discern a similar pattern of response-type depending on the child's role in causing the distress, even amongst 18 months olds?

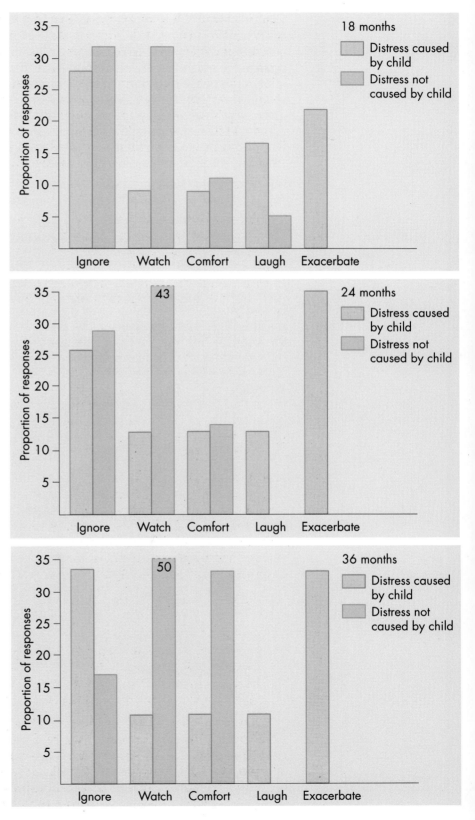

FIGURE 1 Children's reactions to their sibling's distress at three age levels (Dunn, 1988, p. 92).

Figure 1 shows that, where the younger sibling's distress is unrelated to the child's own actions, 'watching' or 'ignoring' is the most common response at 18 months. Watching is still common at 36 months, but ignoring is much less frequent, and instead children are quite likely to offer comfort. By contrast, where children caused the problem themselves, they are quite likely to act in a way that increases the distress or to laugh, even at 18 months. Under these circumstances, age did not encourage greater compassion. Indeed, it made it more likely that children would exacerbate or ignore their sibling's distress. In other words, these children are able

(a)　to recognize the emotional expressions of their sibling;

(b)　to respond in ways which serve to modify (reduce or amplify) their sibling's emotional state;

(c)　to modify their response according to the circumstances.

Dunn's evidence offers an antidote to the image of childhood conveyed by research that concentrates solely on situations that evoke a compassionate response. Children's powers of empathy can be driven by motives of self-interest as well as altruism. Their behaviour towards their sibling appears to be related to their responsibility for the sibling's distress, and this differentiation becomes more marked as they get older. Furthermore, they develop a wide range of strategies to elicit an emotional response from their siblings, commonly known as 'teasing'.

Teasing

Dunn found instances of teasing amongst children as young as 14 months. By 18 months, nearly half of her sample had been observed to tease, and virtually all by 24 months. As the children matured, so their teasing strategies became more elaborate, including taking away a sibling's comfort object, hiding a favourite toy, or taunting them with something they disliked. Dunn describes one particularly sophisticated strategy:

> One child whose sibling had three imaginary friends, named Lily, Allelujah, and Peepee, taunted the sibling by announcing that *she* was the imaginary friend. It was an act that reliably angered the sibling, and an act of considerable intellectual virtuosity for a child of 24 months.
>
> (Dunn, 1988, p. 48)

Although siblings bear the brunt of most young children's teasing, parents may be on the receiving end too, as in the case of an 18 month old who has pulled her mother's hair hard while sitting on her knee:

> MOTHER: Don't pull my hair! Madam! Don't pull hair. No. It's not nice to pull hair, is it?
>
> CHILD: Hair.
>
> MOTHER: Hair, yes, but you mustn't pull it, must you?
>
> CHILD: Yes! (smiles).
>
> MOTHER: No! No!
>
> CHILD: No!
>
> MOTHER: No. No. It's not kind to pull hair, is it?
>
> CHILD: Nice! (smiles).
>
> MOTHER: No, it isn't.
>
> CHILD: Nice!
>
> (Dunn, 1988, pp. 16–17)

Jokes and humour

The relationships of 2 year olds aren't marked only by distress and conflict. Dunn also observed a good deal of humour, smiles and laughter. She was particularly interested in when children began to show amusement at jokes and funny events and to make their own contribution to family fun. One year olds were observed laughing when their mother played the clown, and making their mother laugh by putting their (empty!) potty on their heads. Toileting can be a considerable source of interest and humour to an 18 month old:

> Child sits on potty (fully clothed, not asked to do so), looks at mother.
>
> Child: Poo! (grunts heavily). Poo! (grunts). Poo! (gets up, looks at mother, picks up empty potty and waves it at mother, laughing).
>
> (Dunn, 1988, p. 154)

By 2 years, playing on words start to appear, a delight in using 'forbidden' words (also often associated with bodily functions!), along with mock (and real) insults to siblings (e.g., 'piggyface').

Dunn's interest in these everyday occurrences (teasing, comforting, and joking) is that they demonstrate that young children's understanding extends beyond their own behaviour, experiences and feelings; that they are profoundly interested in and affected by the feelings expressed by their parents and siblings; and that they use this understanding in order to negotiate their position in these key relationships. Furthermore, Dunn argues, the children's experience of their own powerful emotions associated with these relationships may serve an important function in driving them towards social understanding:

> ... the child develops social knowledge *as a family member*. It is not simply that the context of family relationships is one that reveals the child's capabilities. Rather, it may be that the special nature of children's relationships with father, mother, siblings, grandparents, and close friends if they have them ... elicits the development of their ability to understand other people's feelings, intentions, and relationships – and their ability to grasp the nature of authority relations, principles of justice, and so on. What drives children to read and understand their mothers' moods or their siblings' intentions, to comprehend the rules that can be used to get their own way in disputes, or to deflect punishment from themselves to others? It may be the very quality of those relationships that motivates the child to understand the family world – *the emotional power of attachment and rivalry, of dominance, envy, competition, and affection.*
>
> (Dunn, 1988, pp. 72–3, our emphasis)

So, according to Dunn, it is the emotional power of close relationships that drives the child towards social understanding. This process is greatly facilitated by the emergence of language.

3.2 Talking about emotions

By the time children reach the age of 2, they aren't just expressing, recognizing and sharing emotions, and showing empathy through comforting, teasing and making each other laugh. They are also beginning to talk about their feelings and the feelings of others. Many of the examples (above) are strongly language-based not just in the words used but in the emotional power of the delivery of speech. The emergence of speech transforms communication in the family at a time when children are becoming increasingly mobile, relatively more independent and extending their range of social relationships.

As Section 2 made clear, mothers talk to their children about feelings even from earliest infancy. Grimaces and gurgles, cries and calls are named and commented on, encouraged or discouraged – 'You're a grumpy girl today,' 'What a lovely smile,' etc. As feelings become labelled, they become more readily available within the domain of reflective self-consciousness, and they are open to social scrutiny and regulation – 'If you keep on being grumpy, we won't go to the park.'

As the child's capacity for memory, images and abstract thinking matures ... language becomes an increasingly powerful tool for evoking *remote* emotion processes – emotional events that are anticipated and those that have taken place in the past ... Eventually the child who was once capable only of experiencing a given emotion directly as a feeling, becomes capable of labelling or symbolizing that feeling in consciousness, with or without that particular feeling being present.

(Izard and Malatesta, 1987, p. 539)

Once again, we will draw mainly on Judy Dunn's research to illustrate the significance of this shift to verbalization.

In an intensive longitudinal study of six children between 2 and 3 years of age, Dunn noted the sorts of questions they asked about other people. Figure 2 summarizes the data on children's questions about other people, in terms of four categories:

- actions, e.g., 'What's Daddy doing?'
- whereabouts, e.g., 'Where's Jenny gone?'
- inner states, e.g., 'Why's Grandpa cross?'
- application of rules, e.g., 'Why Tom [sibling] not go to bed?'

Notice the marked shift during this twelve month period, from a preoccupation with observables (whereabouts and actions), to an interest in inner states and rules. Dunn argues that the changing focus of children's questions signals their increased appreciation of mental and emotional states in others and the beginnings of their capacity to apply rules, reason about causes and consequences, as well as attribute blame and responsibility, justify their own and others' actions, identify intentions and make excuses.

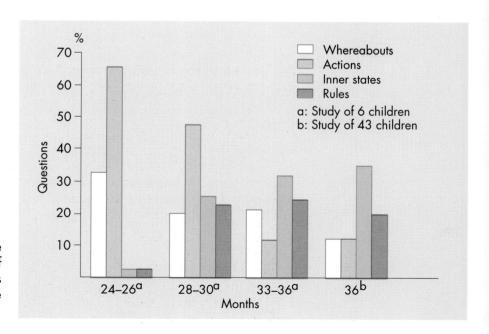

FIGURE 2 The changing focus of children's questions about other people (Dunn, 1988, p. 130).

For example, during their third year children begin to attribute *blame* for incidents; Dunn notes that many children have become adept at drawing their mother's attention to their sibling's behaviour rather than their own, as the cause of the problem. By 3 years old, Dunn found cases of children trying to apportion blame in terms of beliefs about *intentionality*. So, in the following transcript (taken from the Pennsylvania Study of Social Understanding), a 33-month-old girl appeals to her mother after her brother has bitten her. Notice the girl's recognition of the importance of establishing that the transgression was 'on purpose'.

> CHILD: Look what Philip did! He bited me! (crying)
>
> MOTHER: He bit you on the head?
>
> CHILD: Yes.
>
> MOTHER TO SIBLING: Philip is that true?
>
> SIBLING: No.
>
> CHILD TO MOTHER: Yes! On purpose!
>
> MOTHER TO CHILD: He did it on purpose?
>
> CHILD: Yes!
>
> MOTHER TO SIBLING: Come on over Philip.
>
> SIBLING TO MOTHER: I didn't do it on purpose Mom.
>
> CHILD TO MOTHER: Yes he did.
>
> (Dunn, 1991, pp. 101–2)

In short, study of children's use of language in emotionally-charged family situations illustrates:

(a) that they are now able to talk and think about emotions, independently of feeling them;

(b) that they are gaining understanding of the way their own interests, intentions, feelings and behaviour relate to those of their siblings, their parents and others;

(c) that, increasingly, they appreciate that these interpersonal processes are regulated by complex cultural and family rule systems.

Next, Dunn took the argument a stage further, with research designed to test the hypothesis that opportunities for talking about feelings are directly linked to children's social understanding and their behaviour.

Talk, understanding and behaviour

Before Dunn began her research there was already some evidence of a link between 'talk' and 'understanding'. For example, Yarrow and Waxler (1975) found that in families in which the mothers drew their children's attention to the distress they had caused to others in a clear, consistent and insistent way, the children were, at a later time, more concerned and altruistic towards others than children whose mothers did not discuss the cause of distress like this. Similar findings emerged from Dunn and Kendrick's study of how 2 year olds come to terms with the arrival of a new sibling. Mothers' talk about feelings regarding the baby seemed to be significant:

… We found a network of correlations between the frequency of mothers' references to the needs, wants, and feelings of the newborn sibling, their references to the motives and intentions of others, their use of language for complex cognitive purposes and their use of justification for control. Mothers who talked to their 2 year olds with a high frequency of these references were most likely to encourage their firstborn to discuss how the new baby should be cared for, and to take part in this caregiving. They were also more likely to enter into the child's world of pretend by making pretend suggestions and comments than other mothers. One year after the sibling was born, the children from these families in which the mothers had talked to them about the feelings of the new baby were more friendly to the sibling than the children from families in which the mothers had not talked to them in this way – and, most strikingly, the babies themselves were also more friendly to their older siblings.

(Dunn, 1987, pp. 37–8)

In a subsequent study, Dunn and colleagues calculated the number of comments about feeling states made by mothers and siblings during everyday conversations in the home. An example of the type of conversation they analysed is given below:

Child 24 months. Baby sibling is crying after child knocked him (accidentally). Mother comes into room.

CHILD: Poor Thomas.

MOTHER: What?

CHILD: I banged his head.

MOTHER: You banged it?

CHILD: Yes.

MOTHER: Are you going to kiss it?

CHILD: Yes.

MOTHER: Kiss his head.

(Dunn *et al.*, 1987, p. 36)

Differences between families in these types of conversations were striking. In some, mothers pursued conversations concerning feeling states as often as 10 times in an hour, whereas they were much less common in other families. Dunn *et al.* found that children who experienced these types of conversation when they were 18 months old were more likely to talk about their own feelings and those of others when they were 24 months old. This was particularly marked for girls. With children of 18 months, mothers encouraged communication about feelings by girls more than by boys, and by 24 months the girls were found to be talking more about feelings than the boys (further indication of a gender difference that will be taken up in Section 5).

Finally, when Dunn carried out the Pennsylvania study of social understanding, she found that children's conversational experiences in the family (along with pretend play) were linked to their performance on formal assessments of their social understanding. These findings are summarized in the Reading at the end of this book.

SUMMARY OF SECTION 3

- Judy Dunn's naturalistic studies of family interactions during the pre-school years illustrate the central role of emotion in children's development of social understanding.

- Children's perspective-taking abilities serve self-interest as well as empathy. By 3 years there is clear differentiation in the way children respond to a sibling's distress. When they have caused the problem, they are most likely to ignore the distress, or exacerbate it. When there are other reasons for the distress they are most likely to watch or to attempt to give comfort.

- Observations of empathy, teasing, conflict, jokes and humour suggest that it is in emotionally charged family relationships that children gain social understanding.

- Emergence of language transforms communication possibilities. Children use language to question and comment on emotional states, as well as to negotiate family rules, issues of blame and responsibility, intentions and consequences.

- Individual differences in the use of language to talk about feelings appear to be linked to social understanding. Children who have been engaged in conversations and play about relationships and feelings were more likely to succeed in a perspective-taking task.

4 UNDERSTANDING EMOTION AND 'THEORY OF MIND'

Dunn's research concentrated on how social development and emotional understanding is embedded in intimate, emotionally charged family relationships. For Dunn, it is not just that children's developing understanding is revealed to the researcher in the context of family relationships, but that these emotionally charged relationships drive children towards understanding. Evidence of a link between differences in family process and differences in understanding lends support to her argument. However, there is another rather different interpretation of how children reach an understanding of feelings, intentions and behaviour in the family, which views these abilities as an expression of their general cognitive development. For this chapter we will consider one particular aspect of this research tradition, which Dunn refers to in the Reading as 'theory of mind' (see Research Summary 7).

Theory of mind can be used to explain how children come to understand the feelings of others, as Activity 4 is designed to show.

RESEARCH SUMMARY 7
WHAT IS 'THEORY OF MIND'?

In order to function in a complex social world, children must acquire the capacity to represent the mental states and processes of others – to have a sense of how other people think. They must, in effect, develop their own folk psychology or 'theory of mind'. Ironically, recent interest in this originated in work not with humans but with chimpanzees. Premack and Woodruff (1978) argued that the chimpanzees they studied exhibited behaviour that indicated an understanding of the mental states of the human experimenter. Wimmer and Perner (1983) were amongst the first to apply the idea to children, using an experimental procedure that has come to be known as the false-belief paradigm.

Children are told a story using dolls and props to depict the sequence of events (see Figure 3).

From about 4 years of age, children usually have no difficulty with the question 'Where will Sally look for her marble?'. They realize that Sally still believes the marble is where she left it and they understand she will go and search there. Younger children are much more likely to say Sally will look for the marble where it actually is, in Anne's box. Wimmer and Perner argued that this experiment demonstrates that older children come to understand that a person's actions will be based on their beliefs about reality, which are 'true' to them even though the child knows them to be false. In the language of Piagetian theory, these children's judgements are no longer egocentric: they are able to adopt other perspectives than their own. The idea that understanding about other minds is as important to cognitive development as understanding about the properties of the physical world has spawned a large volume of research and theory (e.g., Frye and Moore, 1991). The idea also has important clinical

FIGURE 3 The false-belief paradigm (Frith, 1989, p. 160).

implications, especially for autistic children who have great difficulty with this task and are increasingly being understood as having difficulties constructing a theory of mind (e.g., Frith, 1989).

ACTIVITY 4

Allow about 10 minutes

DESIRES, BELIEFS AND FEELINGS

Imagine that you like chocolate and that you have a friend who doesn't like chocolate. You are an onlooker as your friend unwraps a birthday present of a large box of chocolates. How would you be expecting your friend to react if:

(a) you don't know your friend dislikes chocolate.

(b) you do know your friend dislikes chocolate.

> **Comment**
>
> *Taking account of desires*
>
> In situation (a) you would be likely to expect that your friend would be pleased on the grounds that for you such a present would be highly desirable. However, if you were aware that your friend dislikes chocolates (as in situation b), you would have expected them to be disappointed.
>
> The essential point is that it is not sufficient to apply your own likes and dislikes in order to judge accurately how another person will react to an event. You need to be able to take their perspective – to know what it feels like *from their point of view*.
>
> *Taking account of beliefs*
>
> But understanding a person's desires isn't always sufficient to make a judgement about their reaction to a situation. You also need to take account of their *beliefs*. For example, imagine that the chocolate box didn't contain chocolates at all. You are aware that it had been re-used to protect a delicate glass ornament with which you know your friend will be delighted. How would you expect your friend to react:
>
> (a) when they find a chocolate box beneath the gift wrap; and
>
> (b) when they discover the ornament inside the box?
>
> What skills are entailed in your being able to make these judgements?
>
> Clearly, you would expect your friend to look disappointed at first, and then pleased when they discovered the ornament. To be able to distinguish these two reactions we must be able (like the children making judgements about where Sally will look for her marble) to think beyond our own knowledge about what is in the box and base our judgement on understanding the point of view of our friend, who at first (falsely) believes they are being given an unwanted gift.

4.1 Children's understanding of beliefs and desires

Much research into 'theory of mind' as it applies to emotion has been on how far children can take account of another person's perspective in terms of *desires* (likes and dislikes) and *beliefs* (how they perceive a situation). We will base this discussion mainly around the research of Paul Harris and colleagues at Oxford University. As you start to read about this research note that, whereas Dunn's insights about social understanding are based on observations of real-life family processes, Harris's more cognitive approach is mainly based on asking children to respond to hypothetical stories in experimental settings.

When Harris began his research there was already good evidence that children could make judgements about the emotions that would be felt by other people in a variety of situations. For example, if you tell children as young as 3 or 4 years old stories in which the characters find themselves in situations likely to generate particular emotions – being at a party or getting lost in the woods – and then ask them to select a picture of a face expressing the emotion experienced by the character concerned, they are reasonably good at picking the right one (Borke, 1971). Presented with words describing emotions – happy, excited, surprised, sad, angry, scared – in the context of the start of a story, children of the same age showed some skill at continuing the story so as to explain why that particular emotion was being experienced; about 75 per cent of the continuations were judged to be appropriate (Trabasso *et al.*, 1981). From evidence of this sort, it looks as if children are able to use their own experience of the links between everyday events and their accompanying emotional experiences and generalize this to other situations. But, as we have seen from the chocolate example, basing judgements on one's own beliefs and desires can be unreliable. It is necessary to enter more deeply into the mind of the character in order to understand the likely emotions being experienced. We need to make an imaginative leap into their perspective. Research Summary 8 describes an experiment designed by Harris to test children's ability to take such imaginative leaps.

RESEARCH SUMMARY 8
MAKING ALLOWANCES FOR OTHERS' DESIRES AND BELIEFS

Children aged 4 and 6 were told a story about Ellie the elephant who went for a walk and dreamed about her favourite cola drink that would be waiting for her on her return. But while she was away Mickey the mischievous monkey had emptied the can of cola and refilled it with milk (which Ellie didn't like).

The children were then asked what Ellie's feelings would be when she first got home and saw the can of cola on the table, and then when she had taken a drink from it and discovered that the can contained milk instead. Regardless of age the children were able to take the elephant's *desires* into account – that she would be sad on discovering the trick – but the older children were better at appreciating that initially Ellie's feelings would be based on her mistaken *belief* about what was in the can. By contrast, the younger children typically failed to take account of Ellie's mistaken belief and instead assessed her feelings in terms of what *they* knew about the actual contents in relation to Ellie's preferences.

Harris and his colleagues see this as evidence that these 6 year olds are able to enter into an *imaginative understanding* of another person's (or elephant's) mental state rather than merely basing judgement on memories of how *they* felt in a particular situation. In other words they have developed a capacity for perspective taking or *empathy*.

(Harris *et al.*, 1989)

ACTIVITY 5

Allow about 10 minutes

DEGREES OF EMPATHY

Children's capacities for perspective-taking or empathy have been referred to at various points in this chapter. Review this topic now, in particular summarizing evidence for different expressions of 'empathy' from infancy to middle childhood.

As a guide, start by referring to the discussion in Section 2, especially the distinction between 'personal distress', 'emotional contagion' and 'egocentric empathy'. Next, look at the way children in Dunn's research use empathy to guide self-interest and altruism (Section 3). Finally, try to link these various forms of 'empathy' to the discussion in this section. Would you see the 4 year old in Harris's experiment (Research Summary 8) as displaying 'egocentric empathy', whereas the 6 year olds have attained a more mature capacity for empathy – 'imaginative understanding'?

Harris argues that when a 6 month old shows concern on seeing his caregiver crying (as Darwin's son did), the baby is experiencing some kind of 'emotional contagion' which is quite different from the egocentric empathy of the 2 year old who offers a favourite doll or the 6 year old who can recognize the difference between her own and others' beliefs and desires. To begin with, the understanding of the 6 year old does not necessarily entail any overt emotional expression at all.

> Imaginative understanding does not involve a contagious transmission of mental states from observed to observer. Rather, when you feel embarrassed or proud, I observe this and imagine what emotion I would feel were I in your shoes. As a result, I generate an 'as if' or pretend emotion. Unless I have contributed to or in some way shared your success or discomfiture, I do not feel any genuine pride or embarrassment myself. Similarly, if I am a spectator at tennis, I can appreciate, by an act of imaginative projection, what you perceive as you receive a service. I can imagine myself in your position with the ball coming towards me and, if my imagery is vivid enough, I may even generate, again in an 'as if' mode, some of the sensations that you experience: the effort of trying to reach the ball, the recoil of the racquet, and so forth. I can imagine all of these sensations without actually having them.
>
> (Harris, 1989, p. 53)

In Section 3 we discussed the contribution of dialogue within families to the development of this kind of understanding. But there is another enabling process that gains increasing significance in the lives of young children during the pre-school years – pretend play.

Pretend play and imaginative understanding

Like Judy Dunn and many others, Paul Harris (1989) views children's pretend play as serving a powerful function in the development of social perspective-taking skills. He argues that the capacity for imaginative understanding has four components. Children must have:

(a) self-awareness – being aware of their own mental states;

(b) the capacity for pretence – being able to escape from their own identity into other roles, or make one thing represent something else;

(c) recognition that reality is different from pretence, being able to switch comfortably between make-believe feelings and behaviour to real feelings and behaviour in self and others;

(d) the ability to incorporate a representation of other people's mental states within their own mental state, so that they can imagine someone's feelings, desires and beliefs without necessarily sharing them.

Pretend play is essential to this process, enabling the child to step beyond the boundaries of their own identity into ways of behaving, talking, thinking and feeling that they attribute to others, and to step into places, relationships and events far beyond the here-and-now:

> It allows the child to entertain possible realities and, what is especially important, to entertain the possible realities that other people entertain. It is the key that unlocks the minds of other people and allows the child temporarily to enter into their plans, hopes and fears.
>
> (Harris, 1989, pp. 51–2)

First signs that children are 'pretending' are usually focused on a doll or toy. Gradually children's pretend repertoire grows – a sofa becomes a castle, their sibling becomes a condemned prisoner and the washing basket a ship to explore the high seas. Role-play is particularly important to the processes described by Harris (archetypically doctors and patients, shoppers and shop assistants, etc.), which enable them to enter into a complex network of pretend relationships.

Pretend feelings are at the heart of pretend play, and language is the medium through which they are described and negotiated. Indeed, Dunn (1987) reports that 94 per cent of conversations about feelings between siblings took place within the context of pretend play. This was particularly the case when the relationship between the siblings was warm and friendly. In pretend games with a sibling, children often 'took on' a pretend internal state themselves (such as pain, distress, sleepiness, hunger or sadness), or assigned such a state to their sibling. They also shared a pretend framework with their sibling in which the state was discussed and agreed on by the children together. Within these pretend games the younger children (from about 18 months old) did not just obey their older siblings but contributed their own ideas to the development of the joint fantasy and acted out pretend feeling states, which reveals a relatively sophisticated understanding of their own and others' feelings and experiences. (You can learn more about the significance of pretend play in Chapter 6.)

Returning to the major theme of this section, we have referred to the origins of children's understanding of emotion in emotional contagion, the emergence of egocentric empathy, and subsequently the ability to take account of other perspectives in terms of 'beliefs' and 'desires'. We want to extend this developmental account by asking how children's understanding develops through the school years, especially in relation to more complex emotions.

4.2 Understanding complex emotions

Happiness and sadness can be identified fairly reliably through particular facial expressions. Yet, as we have seen, children's understanding of these feelings requires quite sophisticated perspective-taking. What of more complex emotions such as pride, shame or guilt? What levels of understanding do these emotions entail?

ACTIVITY 6

Allow at most 10 minutes

FEELINGS OF PRIDE AND SHAME

What is entailed in feeling proud about something? Think of some examples and try to extract what is common to them. Then do the same for 'shame'. Write brief notes on your conclusions.

Comment

If I feel proud of something that I've made or written, or something I've done for someone else, or when my children do well in their school exams, it's usually because I feel that I've been responsible in some way for an achievement that has reached some sort of standard. This is more than the experience of happiness in two respects: the sense of personal responsibility and the fact that some externally recognised standard, however ill-defined, is being met. Shame is the negative form of this, but the sense of personal responsibility and the reference to some sort of standard is an integral part of it. These standards are defined socially. Different cultures or groups of people will set different standards of behaviour. In this sense, the context for emotional experience is essentially *socially constructed.*

Harris *et al.* (1987) presented children of different ages with a range of emotion words, some simple like 'happy' and 'sad', others more complex like 'proud', 'guilty', 'relieved' and 'disappointed', and asked them to think up situations that would lead to the experience of those emotions. Their responses were then looked at by judges who had to decide (without knowing) which emotion word was being illustrated through each story. The youngest children, who were 5 years old, produced recognizable accounts of the simpler emotions – 'happy', 'sad', 'angry', i.e. the ones with recognizable facial characteristics – but that was their limit. The 7 year olds, however, came up with situations that the judges recognised as illustrations of more complex emotions, ones which don't have a distinctive facial or behavioural expression, e.g. 'proud', 'jealous',

'grateful', 'worried', 'guilty', 'excited'. By 10 and 14 years, the list included terms like 'relieved' and 'disappointed'.

Other studies have indicated that when the younger children try to demonstrate their understanding of emotions such as 'pride' and 'shame', they typically fail to take into account the ideas of personal responsibility and standards that we have already identified as being essential features. Harris has represented the difference between the 'emotional universe' of the 4 to 5 year old and that of the 7 to 8 year old in the following way:

> The younger child typically sees people as agents who set out to get what they want; if they succeed they are happy and if not, they are sad. The older child sees people as agents who should conform to a normative or moral standard; if they manage to do so, they may feel proud but if they deliberately ignore or defy that standard, they are likely to feel guilty or ashamed.
>
> (Harris, 1989, p. 92)

How does this important development come about? Harris proposes that the child has to 'switch from seeing people simply as agents to seeing them as *observers of their own agency*, observers who assess their responsibility in matching up to normative standards' (Harris, 1989, p. 92, our emphasis), or, to put it into the framework of this section, they have to expand their 'theory of mind' to incorporate another person's standards alongside their beliefs and desires.

SUMMARY OF SECTION 4

- Paul Harris's experimental studies of children's ability to take the perspective of others illustrate the way theories of cognitive development can apply to emotion;

- 'Theory of mind' is the starting point for research designed to assess how far children are able to take account of 'beliefs' and 'desires' in judging how others will react;

- Pretend play is an important context for rehearsing perspective-taking skills and developing capacities for imaginative understanding.

- Among older school-age children, perspective-taking abilities recognize other people as observers and critics of how behaviour matches up to normative standards.

5 CONTROLLING EMOTIONS

Sections 3 and 4 have been mainly concerned with children's recognition of emotional states in others, the way they react in pursuit of self-interest or altruism, and their imaginative abilities to adopt the perspective of others. In this final section, we return to more personal aspects of emotional transactions, namely children's own emotions, how they learn to regulate their expression, hide true feelings, and cope with emotional events. As in previous sections, our emphasis will be on how emotions develop in the context of social relationships, and on how children come to understand these interpersonal processes.

In Section 2 we discussed early socialization of emotional expression. In this section we will extend this discussion into the middle years of childhood, looking at the way children learn to regulate everyday, moment-by-moment feelings, as well as at the way they cope with more enduring, profound emotions, especially associated with family separations.

We begin by asking you to reflect on your own experience of these issues.

ACTIVITY 7

Allow about 15 minutes

'WHENEVER I FEEL AFRAID ... '

Whenever I feel afraid,
I hold my head erect
And whistle a happy tune
So no one will suspect
I'm afraid.

Anna, the governess in Rodgers and Hammerstein's *The King and I*, had a strategy for dealing with the unwelcome emotion of fear.

What can we learn from her example?

(a) Think about situations that have the potential to make you feel afraid. They don't have to be dramatic or life-threatening – everyday situations can be just as instructive.

(b) In each case, to what extent, and in what ways, would you be likely to feel and express that fear?

(c) Are there some situations in which you are more likely to 'whistle happy tunes', 'put on a brave face' or 'adopt a stiff upper lip', and others where you are more likely to give vent to your feelings? (For example, think about a situation where you are responsible for children, or where you are alone in a wood at night.)

(d) There are no easy answers to the next question. If you do follow Anna's example, what happens to the emotions? Are they simply hidden from view? Or is it possible actively to alter our feelings by 'whistling happy tunes' or some other strategy? What are your preferred coping strategies?

(e) Do you think the way you react to fear-provoking situations and how you cope are strategies related to your gender? How do men as opposed to women behave in other situations that might provoke sadness, or anger, or disappointment?

There are considerable individual differences in how much people experience and express emotion. Even so, there are some general lessons, notably that the expression of emotions is strongly regulated by rule systems that govern what is and isn't appropriate to situations. We called these *display rules* in Section 2. Some display rules are widely shared within a society, while others are more personal, such as how we think others present will react to the emotions we display. The capacity to employ display rules to regulate emotional expression grows with age, as the spontaneity and volatility of the infant is displaced by a more measured and stable demeanour.

This isn't just a process of maturation. It is also a product of socialization. In some Western cultures, being able to temper the extremes of emotional experience is seen as a sign of maturity, a virtue if not an imperative, with children from an early age firmly told not to be 'soft', exhorted to 'pull themselves together', chastised for behaving 'over the top' or encouraged to 'think positive' and 'cheer up' because 'things will turn out all right in the end'. Socialization doesn't just inhibit emotional expression, but also channels expression in socially approved ways, and teaches coping strategies for dealing with strong feelings. Cultural groups vary in their tolerance and encouragement of various emotional expressions, and in the coping strategies considered acceptable and appropriate, as the examples in Research Summary 9 illustrate. While there may be universality in the facial expressions that signify particular emotional states (as was claimed in Research Summary 2), whether those states are experienced and expressed is strongly regulated by personal, situational and cultural constraints.

RESEARCH SUMMARY 9
CULTURE AND THE EXPRESSION OF ANGER

- Expressions of violent anger were traditionally discouraged amongst the Utku Eskimos. Hostility was expressed in sulking, silence and withdrawal. The only legitimate outlet for aggression for Utku was towards their dogs.

- Among the Hare Indians of Colville Lake, USA, displays of anger, happiness or jealousy were only approved of when a person was drunk. Not only were these emotions sanctioned by intoxication, they were eagerly observed by onlookers.

- Among the Kaluli of Papua New Guinea, strong expressions of anger are encouraged. When a man has been wronged he may stamp furiously up and down outside his longhouse, shouting out the details of the problem for all to hear, which ensures their sympathetic support.

- Bedouin living in Western Egypt tend to react to bereavement by expressing anger and indignation as much as sadness. This is because sadness is seen as an expression of weakness which can undermine their sense of honour.

(Examples cited in Mesquita and Frijda, 1992)

5.1 Showing feelings – hiding feelings

In Section 2 we reviewed research into the way emotional expressions become regulated within the mother–infant relationship. In this section, we ask when children begin to disguise feelings.

ACTIVITY 8

Allow about 10 minutes

RULES FOR DISPLAYING EMOTION

Go back to Activity 4 on pages 161–2 , where you thought about the example of a friend opening a box of chocolates. We discussed the processes involved in identifying a friend's feelings from knowledge about their beliefs and desires. Now think about this same situation from a slightly different point of view.

Think about your friend's reaction on discovering a chocolate box:

(a) What emotion would you expect a friend to *show on their face:*

    (i) if they were at home, alone?

    (ii) if they were in the presence of the person giving the present?

(b) How would their expressed emotion relate to their real feelings in each case?

(c) Finally, think about what *display rule* is being used in this example.

In this simple example, we expect a difference in reaction according to whether the donor is present. In each case we expect our friend to feel disappointment but they would probably follow the display rule that one shows pleasure and gratitude when receiving a gift. We said they would *probably* follow the display rule, acknowledging that we are dealing with cultural conventions, which differ not only between societies, but within societies according to the particular relationship amongst the people involved (e.g., receiving a retirement gift from an employer versus a birthday gift from a close friend). Psychologists have been interested to find out at what age children begin to be able to use such display rules (Research Summary 10).

In general, the findings of Saarni's study complement those by Cole. Even by the age of 3, children have the capacity to mask their true feelings, although whether they do so will depend on how they interpret the social situation. Note that the transitional behaviour among older boys has much in common with social referencing. In Saarni's studies, the younger children were already nearly twice the age of Cole's girl subjects (i.e. 6), yet many of them (especially boys) were still quite likely to show their feelings of disappointment. As a rule, the older children (especially girls) were more likely to regulate their expression of disappointment, conforming to social expectations of 'mature' behaviour. In other words, this research complements Section 3 in showing how relatively young children master cultural rules that govern interpersonal behaviour in social relationships. But as Section 4 illustrated, there is another way of approaching these issues, which asks not just about children's ability to employ display rules, but about their *understanding* of those rules. Once again, Paul Harris's research effectively illustrates this approach (see Research Summary 11).

RESEARCH SUMMARY 10
CHILDREN'S REACTIONS TO DISAPPOINTMENT

Study 1

Pamela Cole (1986) asked 3 to 4-year-old girls about their preferences among a set of toys. She then presented them with the one that they liked least, wrapped up as a parcel. This was done in two conditions. In one the donor was present when the toy was being unwrapped (analogous to many a birthday party) and in the other the child unwrapped it alone. There was a marked difference in reaction between the two conditions. When they were alone the girls exhibited their disappointment, but when the donor was there with them they concealed the disappointment with a half-smile. So even at 3 years old children appear to be able to monitor their emotional expressions.

On an ethical point, note that after the experiment the children were given the opportunity to exchange their disappointing present for something that they liked.

Also, after the experiment, Cole interviewed the children to find out whether they had any understanding of the rules governing facial expressions in social situations. She wanted to find out whether such young children can consciously and deliberately assume an expression calculated to give a misleading impression of what they actually feel. Or is a simpler explanation in order, that they are following an often reinforced rule of politeness that says that the correct behaviour on receipt of any present is to smile and say 'thank you'? Their responses led her to believe that these 4 year olds were *not* aware of the way that they were using their facial expression either to convey or conceal their feelings.

Study 2

Carolyn Saarni (1984) compared reactions to disappointment amongst an older group of boys and girls (aged between 6 and 10 years of age). She carried out the study in schools and presented it as about children's use of self-help workbooks. Each child was seen twice. *Condition 1*: they were shown the workbooks and video-recorded while completing some sample pages of problems. Then they were offered an attractively wrapped gift containing a drink, sweets and money and invited to return two days later for a second session and a second gift. *Condition 2*: during this second session the same procedure was followed with a different workbook, after which the children were invited to select a wrapped gift from a bag, only this time the gift was a poor quality, uninteresting baby-toy. The video camera recorded the children's facial expressions as they opened the wrapper, after which the investigator explained that the gift must be a mistake and substituted an attractive pack of pens.

On both occasions the donor of the gift (the investigator) was present at the time of opening.

Saarni reported a strong developmental trend in children's reactions to being given a gift. Even in the first (appropriate gift) condition, the older children were much more likely to offer socially approved positive emotional expressions than younger children, and much less likely to offer negative expressions. In the second (disappointing gift) condition, these differences were maintained, but positive responses were virtually eliminated among the younger children. There were two other notable findings. First, there was a gender difference, whereby girls of all ages and in both conditions were more likely than boys to offer a positive response. Second, among the older boys (8–10 years) there was a much higher incidence of 'transitional' responses to the disappointing gift, including a puzzled expression, gaze shifting back and forth between gift and experimenter and so on. Finally, when the children were subsequently asked to give their comments, the older children appeared much more aware of their use of a display rule than the younger ones, offering comments about their disappointment with the gift but 'not wanting to make a fuss about it'.

Whereas Cole and Saarni have investigated the way children actually mask their own emotions, Harris is interested in the way children understand masking in hypothetical stories about other children.

RESEARCH SUMMARY 11
APPEARANCE AND REALITY

Harris *et al.* (1986) presented children of different ages with stories where the characters are involved in either a happy or a sad event but need to hide how they feel. The emotions were not named, so the children had to work them out for themselves. Here are two examples:

* 'Diana is playing a game with her friend. At the end of the game Diana wins and her friend loses. Diana tries to hide how she feels because otherwise her friend won't play any more.'

* 'Diana falls over and hurts herself. She knows that the other children will laugh if she shows how she feels. So she tries to hide how she feels.'

The children were asked two sorts of questions:

* What emotion does the story character *really* feel?
* What emotion *appears* on the character's face?

Harris has conducted several variants of this experiment and the results have been remarkably consistent. He found that 6 year olds and 10 year olds demonstrated that they understood that the characters can really feel sad but appear to be happy (and vice versa), i.e. that the real emotion may be quite different from the emotion displayed; 3 and 4 year olds, however, could not do this. They could usually answer the first question correctly and indicate how the character was really feeling, but they were much less successful at saying what the character's face would reveal. This age-related pattern has been found not only in the UK and the US but also in Japan, suggesting that it may reflect the course of general cognitive development. In drawing this conclusion it is important to make clear that while there may be universality in children's understanding about display rules, their use of particular rules will be strongly influenced by their social/cultural context.

Harris has taken children's understanding of the appearance–reality distinction a stage further, by adding a third question after the stories have been presented:

* How do the other children think that Diana feels?

Their answers showed that 6 year olds realize that other children in the story would be misled into thinking that Diana's expression indicated what she really felt. Thus, these children are demonstrating an ability to handle two different views of the situation simultaneously; the *actual* state of affairs (that Diana is happy/sad) and the state of affairs *as observed by the other children* (that she looks sad/happy). Furthermore, they have to understand the intended relationship between them. This is further evidence of complex perspective-taking abilities, or 'theory of mind' (Gross and Harris, 1988).

To summarize the studies discussed in this section so far:

(a) learning to dissociate true feelings from outward expressions is a usual part of growing up;

(b) children are able to 'mask' their feelings from an early age;

(c) older children are much more likely to mask their feelings than younger children;

(d) the extent of association between felt emotion and expressed emotion is dependent on children's reading of the situation;

(e) children actively search for clues in the situation and the experimenter's face (social referencing), to try to work out the most appropriate reaction (the display rules);

(f) girls are much more likely than boys to try to 'please' the experimenter;

(g) understanding the distinction between feeling and expression appears to be related to cognitive development, whereas particular display rules are more culture-specific.

5.2 Ways of coping

So far, we have reviewed research into the social regulation of relatively transitory feelings evoked in everyday situations. But what of situations that cause more profound and enduring emotional reactions in children? For instance, how do children cope with the trauma of separation or loss of a loved one? If they cope by 'putting on a brave face', 'whistling happy tunes' or just by 'going quiet', what becomes of the sadness, grief and/or anger that they may be feeling? Is it possible to transform an experience by these coping strategies, or do the effects of the emotion linger on?

While there is widespread agreement that early trauma can have continuing effects in children's lives, there is much less consensus about the precise processes through which this happens. One of the most influential theoretical models has been offered by psychoanalysts, and many key concepts from their way of thinking have found their way into everyday language, notably 'regression', 'repression', 'denial', 'defence mechanism', etc.

READING

You should now read Reading A at the end of this chapter, which is an outline of the psychoanalytic view of emotional development.

Psychoanalytic theory has mainly been derived from the insights of working with adult patients in analysis. However, direct studies of children's ways of coping with trauma can also be revealing. We will briefly illustrate this theme through two examples:

(a) coping with family break-up;

(b) going to boarding school.

Family break-up

READING

In Reading B at the end of this chapter, Burgoyne *et al.* discuss some common reactions to separation and divorce. Please read this now. Note that they root their discussion in the concept of attachment and the secure base, and then go on to consider how children deal with conflicting feelings of anger and dependency on their parents. They refer to two ways of coping: redirecting the anger to siblings and peers, and turning it against themselves. (This distinction is analogous to that between externalizing and internalizing expressions of disturbance discussed in Chapter 2.)

Next they discuss regression in young children and displacement activities among teenagers, and the importance of parents acknowledging their children's emotional reactions and giving them an opportunity to express their feelings, especially by talking about them (see Section 3.2).

Homesickness

British traditions in some sections of society of sending children to boarding school from an early age provide a very clear context for studying the way children learn to cope with and conceal 'unacceptable' feelings:

For example, comfort objects can be helpful:

> My Teddy helps me when I cry, it is from home, he's a bit old but I like him, Mummy always tucks us up and we say our prayers. I worry 'cause next year when I am in the big boys' dormitories they take teddies away and I shall be by myself. (Boy, seven)
>
> (Lambert and Milham, 1974 edn, p. 241)

Boarding school is a social setting where there has traditionally been only limited sympathy for outward expressions of distress. In one study of a boys' school, Harris and Guz (1986) asked recent arrivals about whether it is possible to hide feelings of homesickness:

**EXAMPLE 1
IS IT POSSIBLE TO HIDE FEELINGS?**

'If you smile and act cheerful, it doesn't show that you're actually afraid and worried really.' (8 year old)

'Well, you'd have to act cheerfully and try and make friends with everybody.' (8 year old)

'You can hide your feelings easily by day, if they're not too bad, when everyone's watching you, by joining in and by smiling and getting on with other people. But at night when no one is watching you, you can go back to being normal. If you're upset, you're just upset.' (13 year old)

'It is possible but it's quite difficult if you smile all the time. Normally, you can see through a false smile.' (13 year old)

(Harris, 1989, p.162)

These findings are consistent with the experimental work on hiding feelings, described earlier, but the comments from the 13 year olds also hint at a more sophisticated social understanding, through their distinction between 'true' and 'false' expressions of emotion.

When asked how, if at all, negative feelings could be changed, many were sceptical. As one 13 year old put it, 'I don't think that smiling which is a movement of your mouth can help things in your mind' (Harris, 1989, p. 162). They were more positive about two types of strategy. Some advocated trying to change whatever it was that was causing the homesickness, for example by phoning home or making an effort to make friends. More popular, however, was a form of displacement, distracting attention away from the source of the negative feelings by finding lots of things to do. An 8 year old argued that thinking about things other than home helped ' … 'cos it takes your mind off feeling sad. It occupies your mind. I don't think you can think two things at once' (Harris, 1989, p. 163).

> ### SUMMARY OF SECTION 5
>
> - Emotional expression is strongly governed by display rules which children begin to learn from an early age. Inhibition and expression vary between emotions, according to individual differences, situational and role demands, and cultural expectations.
> - Studies of children's reactions to disappointment show that older children are more likely than younger children and girls are more likely than boys to mask their feelings.
> - Although particular display rules vary between cultures, there is general consistency in young children's ability to understand the distinction between 'appearance' and 'feelings' from around the age of 6.
> - Besides moment-by-moment display rules, children learn to regulate more enduring emotions, especially following a separation or loss.

6 EMOTION AND GENDER

For the most part this chapter has been concerned with general principles of emotional development. But in this concluding section we want to draw attention to the profound significance of variations in the socialization experience of particular individuals. These variations can be most clearly illustrated by taking the example of gender, a topic which has already been mentioned at various points in the chapter. The following are significant references:

- Malatesta and Haviland found that mothers appeared to be encouraging different patterns of emotional expression in girls and boys (Section 2).
- Dunn noted that mothers engaged in more conversation about feelings with girls than boys, (Section 3).
- Saarni found girls more likely than boys to mask their feelings of disappointment (Section 5).

These are but a few examples from a very extensive research literature (reviewed by Archer and Lloyd, 1985; Brody and Hall, 1993; Brody, 1993) which shows that there is a consistent relationship between gender and emotion. However, this does not justify the stereotypical image of girls as more 'emotional' than boys (Fischer, 1993). Such stereotypes fail to acknowledge that emotion is not a single state, but a wide variety of states, each of which may be associated with gender in a different way; that it is essential to distinguish emotional experience from emotional expression; and that females and males may adopt different strategies for regulating their own and others' emotions, and use different display rules in various situations which are consistent with their social role in a gender-differentiated family, school and society.

READING

Reading C is the conclusion to a comprehensive review of this literature. Brody not only links evidence of gender differences to wider issues of social role, but also offers a model of the socialization of these gender-differentiated expressions of emotion, drawing on a transactional model with which you are already familiar from Chapters 2 and 3. Please read this now.

In the next chapter, gender is a major theme in the study of the development of a sense of self.

7 CONCLUSION

In this chapter we have emphasized interrelationships between emotion, cognition and social development. We have argued that the newborn infant's capacities for expressing and recognizing emotional states soon become regulated within early relationships. Social referencing enables the baby to associate emotional reactions with objects, people and situations, as well as their own behaviour and emotions being modified according to the emotional reactions of caregivers.

From the start, young children show capacities for empathy, but their social perspective-taking abilities are greatly extended during the pre-school years, as they negotiate their position in family relationships, offer sympathy, tease and joke. Emerging capacities for language and pretend play extend the possibilities for talking about, thinking about and imagining emotional events affecting themselves and others, which may be remote in space and time. By about 6 years, most children are able to make judgements which take account of another person's perspective, in terms of both desires and beliefs; by about 8 years they are also taking account of their standards.

These capacities for recognizing, understanding and empathizing with emotional reactions in others develop in tandem with children's mastery of display rules governing the expression of emotions. Pre-school children are already capable of masking their true feelings, but it is only later that they become fully self-conscious about this distinction between inner emotion and outer expression in themselves and others. Learning to present situation-appropriate emotions is essential for functioning in everyday social situations. But children also adopt strategies for coping with enduring and painful emotions, for example those associated with separation and loss.

Finally, many of these themes have general applicability, but it is also important to take account of cultural, situational and personal variables that affect emotion. We have taken the example of gender in order briefly to illustrate the transactional processes of socialization that can produce diversity in the experiences, expression and understanding of emotion. Gender will also be a major topic of Chapter 5.

FURTHER READING

DUNN, J. (1988) *The Beginnings of Social Understanding*, Oxford, Basil Blackwell.

HARRIS, P. (1989) *Children and Emotion,* Oxford, Basil Blackwell.

LEWIS, M. and HAVILAND, J. M. (eds) (1993) *Handbook of Emotions*, New York, Guilford Press.

SAARNI, C. and HARRIS, P. L. (1989) *Children's Understanding of Emotion,* Cambridge, Cambridge University Press.

REFERENCES

ARCHER, J. and LLOYD, B. (1985) *Sex and Gender*, Cambridge, Cambridge University Press.

BORKE, H. (1971) 'Interpersonal perception of young children: egocentrism or empathy?', *Developmental Psychology*, **5**, pp. 163–9.

BRODY, L. R. (1993) 'On understanding gender differences in the expression of emotion' in ABLON, S., BROWN, D., KHANTZIAN, E. and MACK, J. (eds) *Human Feelings: explorations in affect development and meaning*, New York, Analytic Press.

BRODY, L. R. and HALL, J. A. (1993) 'Gender and emotion' in LEWIS, M. and HAVILAND, J. M. (eds) *Handbook of Emotions*, New York, Guilford Press.

CAMRAS, L. A., GROW, J. G. and RIBORDY, S. C. (1983) 'Recognition of emotional expression by abused children', *Journal of Clinical and Child Psychology*, **12**(3), pp. 325–8.

COLE, P. (1986) 'Children's spontaneous control of facial expression', *Child Development,* **57**, pp. 1309–21.

DARWIN, C. (1872) *The Expression of the Emotions in Man and Animals*, London, Murray.

DUNN, J. (1987) 'Understanding feelings: the early stages' in BRUNER, J. and HASTE, H. (eds) *Making Sense: the child's construction of the world*, London, Methuen.

DUNN, J. (1988) *The Beginnings of Social Understanding*, Oxford, Basil Blackwell.

DUNN, J. (1991) 'Young children's understanding of other people: evidence from observations within the family' in FRYE, D. and MOORE, C. (eds) *Children's Theories of Mind*, Hillsdale (NJ), Lawrence Erlbaum.

DUNN, J., BRETHERTON, I. and MUNN, P. (1987) 'Conversations about feeling states between mothers and their young children', *Developmental Psychology*, **23**, pp. 1–8.

EIBL-EIBESFELDT, I. (1975, 2nd edn) *Ethology: the biology of behaviour*, New York, Holt, Rinehart and Winston.

EKMAN, P. (1973) 'Cross-cultural studies of facial expression' in EKMAN, P. (ed.) *Darwin and Facial Expression*, New York, Academic Press.

FEINMAN, S. and LEWIS, M. (1983) 'Social referencing and second order effects in 10-month-old infants', *Child Development*, **54**, pp. 878–87.

FEIRING, C., LEWIS, M. and STARR, M. D. (1984) 'Indirect effects and infants' reaction to strangers', *Developmental Psychology*, **20**, pp. 485–91.

FIELD, T., MORROW, C. and ADELSTEIN, D. (1993) 'Depressed mothers' perceptions of infant behaviour', *Infant Behaviour and Development*, **16**, pp. 99–108.

FISCHER, A. H. (1993) 'Sex differences in emotionality: fact or stereotype?' *Feminism and Psychology*, **3**, pp. 303–18.

FRITH, U. (1989) *Autism: explaining the enigma*, Oxford, Blackwell.

FRYE, D. and MOORE, C. (eds) (1991) *Children's Theories of Mind*, Hillsdale (NJ), Lawrence Erlbaum.

GANCHROW, J. R., STEINER, J. E. and DAHER, M. (1983) 'Neonatal facial expressions in response to different quantities and intensities of gustatory stimuli', *Infant Behaviour and Development*, **6,** pp. 473–84.

GROSS, D and HARRIS, P. L. (1988) 'Understanding false beliefs about emotion', *International Journal of Behavioural Development*, **11**, pp. 475–88.

HARRIS, P. (1989) *Children and Emotion,* Oxford, Basil Blackwell.

HARRIS, P. L., DONNELLY, K., GUZ, G. R. and PITT-WATSON, R. (1986) 'Children's understanding of distinction between real and apparent emotion', *Child Development*, **57**, pp. 895–909.

HARRIS, P. L., and GUZ, G. R. (1986) 'Models of emotion: how boys report their emotional reactions upon entering an English boarding school', unpublished paper, Oxford, University of Oxford, Department of Experimental Psychology.

HARRIS, P. L., JOHNSON, C. N., HUTTON, D., ANDREWS, G. and COOKE, T. (1989) 'Young children's theory of mind and emotion', *Cognition and Emotion,* **3**, pp. 379–400.

HARRIS, P. L., OLTHOF, T., MEERUM TERWOGT, M. and HARDMAN, C. E. (1987) 'Children's knowledge of the situations that provoke emotion', *International Journal of Behavioural Development*, **10**, pp. 319–44.

HAVILAND, J. M. and LELWICA, M. (1987) 'The induced affect response: 10-week-old infants' responses to three emotional expressions', *Developmental Psychology,* **23**, pp. 97–104.

HORNICK, R., RISENHOOVER, N. and GUNNAR, M. (1987) 'The effects of maternal positive, neutral and negative affective communications on infant responses to new toys', *Child Development*, **58**, pp. 937–44.

IZARD, C. E., HEUBNER, R. R., RISSER, D., McGINNES, G. C., and DOUGHERTY, L. M. (1980) 'The young infant's ability to produce discrete emotion expressions', *Developmental Psychology*, **16**, pp. 132–40.

IZARD, C. E., and MALATESTA, C. Z. (1987) 'Perspectives on emotional development: differential emotions theory of early emotional development' in OSOFSKY, J. (ed.) (2nd edn) *Handbook of Infant Development*, New York, Wiley.

JENKINS, S., OWEN, C., BAX, M. and HART, H. (1984) 'Continuities of common behaviour problems in pre-school children', *Journal of Child Psychology and Psychiatry*, **25**, pp. 75–89.

LAMBERT, R. and MILHAM, S. (1968) *The Hothouse Society*, London, Weidenfeld and Nicholson (published by Penguin Books, 1974).

MacKINNON-LEWIS, C., LAMB, M. E., ARBUCKLE, B., BARADARAN, L. P. and VOLLING, B. L. (1992) 'The relationship between biased maternal and filial attributions and the aggresiveness of their interactions', *Development and Psychopathology*, **4**, pp. 403–15.

MALATESTA, C. Z. and HAVILAND, J. M. (1982) 'Learning display rules: the socialization of emotion expression in infancy', *Child Development*, **53**, pp. 991–1003.

MALATESTA, C. Z., CULVER, C., TESMAN, J. and SHEPARD, B. (1989) 'The development of emotion expressions in the first two years of life', *Monographs of the Society for Research in Child Development*, **50**, pp. 1–2.

MELTZOFF, A. N. and MOORE, M. K. (1983) 'Newborn infants imitate adult facial gestures', *Child Development*, **54**, pp. 702–19.

MESQUITA, B. and FRIJDA, N. H. (1992) 'Cultural variations in emotions: a review', *Psychological Bulletin*, **112**, pp. 179–204.

MURRAY, L. (1992) 'The impact of post-natal depression on infant development', *Journal of Child Psychology and Psychiatry*, **33**, pp. 543–61.

MURRAY, L., KEMPTON, C., WOOLGAR, M. and HOOPER, R. (1993) 'Depressed mothers' speech to their infants and its relation to infant gender and cognitive development', *Journal of Child Psychology and Psychiatry*, **34** (7), pp. 1083–1102.

OATES, J. (1994) 'First relationships' in OATES, J. (ed.) *The Foundations of Child Development*, Oxford, Blackwell/The Open University (Book 1 of ED209).

PREMACK, D. and WOODRUFF, G. (1978) 'Does the chimpanzee have a theory of mind?', *The Behavioural and Brain Sciences*, **7**, pp. 515–26.

SAARNI, C. (1984) 'An observational study of children's attempts to monitor their expressive behaviour', *Child Development*, **55**, pp. 1504–13.

SCHAFFER, R. (1989) 'Early social development' in WOODHEAD, M., CARR, R. and LIGHT, P. (eds) *Becoming a Person*, London, Routledge/The Open University.

STEVENSON, J. and OATES, J. (1994) 'Infant individuality' in OATES, J. (ed.) *The Foundations of Child Development*, Oxford, Blackwell/The Open University (Book 1 of ED 209).

TRABASSO, T., STEIN, N. L. and JOHNSON, L. R. (1981) 'Children's knowledge of events: a causal analysis of story structure' in BOWER, G. (ed.) *Learning and Motivation*, vol. 15, New York, Academic Press.

TREVARTHEN, C. (1993) 'The function of emotions in early infant communication and development' in NADEL, J. and CAMAIONI, L. (eds) *New Perspectives in Early Communicative Development*, London, Routledge.

WIMMER, H. and PERNER, J. (1983) 'Beliefs about beliefs: representations and constraining function of wrong beliefs in young children's understanding of deception', *Cognition,* **13**, pp. 103–28.

WOLF, D. (1982) 'Understanding others: a longitudinal case study of the concept of independent agency' in FORMAN, G. E. (ed.) *Action and Thought*, New York, Academic Press.

YARROW, M. R. and WAXLER, C. Z. (1975) 'The emergence and functions of prosocial behaviour in young children', paper presented at the Society for Research in Child Development meeting, Denver.

READINGS

Reading A   Psychoanalysis and emotional development

John Oates

The psychoanalytic view of emotional development, as proposed by Freud, is that the emotions we consciously experience may often have their roots in inner conflicts that have been repressed because of the unacceptability of the wishes that underlie them. According to the theory, these unconscious wishes (*id*) arise from primary 'drives': needs for physical satisfaction and pleasure. In development, the child internalizes the prohibition that the parent(s) place on certain ways of satisfying these needs and this 'internalized parent' forms the child's *superego*, or conscience. The repression of primary desires by the superego becomes largely unconscious, and as a result a person only experiences consciously secondary feelings and wishes which, according to the theory, have only a symbolic relation to their original source. The ego, our conscious, experiencing self, is thus defended against unacceptable feelings and desires: they are denied consciousness. Also, according to the theory, in development these conflicts arise in turn in the areas of oral, anal and genital pleasure-seeking. Unresolved difficulties arising from parental prohibitions, for example in premature weaning, may result in particular sorts of regressive behaviours: when a child is upset, for example, sucking the thumb may represent symbolically a regression to a way of satisfying oral needs from an earlier age.

Modern psychoanalytic theory, notably the theory of object relations (see Chapter 5 of this volume and Oates, 1994) has extended the Freudian idea of primary drives to include a need to relate, and the internalization of the parent(s) as superego into the building up of 'inner working models' of ways of forming attachments to others (see Chapter 1). Traumatic separation from or loss of an early attachment figure impacts on the development of these inner working models, affecting the child's later ability to attach to others and, in turn, on their capacities to be a parent themselves.

Source: Specially written for this chapter.

Reading B   How children may react to a marital separation

Jacqueline Burgoyne, Roger Ormrod and Martin Richards

One of the first signs that children may be affected by an impending or actual separation is their fear of being left alone. In younger children this may take the form of clinging and perhaps insisting on having the bedroom light on at night as they used to when younger. Similarly, a child who has previously settled easily at bedtime may begin to demand endless drinks and stories or perhaps that a parent should sit with them until they are asleep. Children who have formerly gone to school or nursery quite happily may refuse to be left at the school gate or protest at the whole idea of going. They may stay in bed and defeat all attempts to get them dressed. Many parents have described being in a shop or other public place with their child. The child turns round, cannot immediately see the parent and goes into a blind panic believing that they have been abandoned.

Behaviour of this kind by the child is a clear indication that he or she is anxious that their remaining parent may disappear, an understandable fear if you consider marital separation from a child's point of view. Young children generally believe that social relationships, especially those with their parents and other family members, are everlasting. These people are the constant feature in a child's life and the base from which a child looks out to the rest of the world. Separation and divorce are deeply disturbing because they demonstrate to a child that social relationships can end, even those as fundamental as the ones they have with their own parents or the bond between their parents …

It is important to remember that children do not choose a parental separation; rather, it is imposed on them. To make it worse, it is imposed by the very people on whom a child depends most and to whom they look for protection of their interests. This adds to a child's sense of abandonment and disturbing feelings of powerlessness. This can make a child angry, sad and depressed. Many of us get angry when others do things to us which we don't want and are against our interests but the feelings are likely to be especially strong when we know the other person is aware that their actions will hurt us. So it is for many children. But anger for a child is more complicated because it may be accompanied by the fear that to be angry with one or both parents may drive them away. So the anger may become a dangerous feeling which must be hidden. More simply, there may also be a conflict between feelings of love and anger for a parent. Anger may lead a child to feel guilty for having bad feelings about their parent.

If anger is too threatening to express directly, it may be transferred to a safer target. In some families, brothers and sisters become particularly quarrelsome and cross with each other or anger may be displaced on to friends at school. Observation in schools suggests that children may become aggressive and demanding with their peers. This, of course, may drive their friends away so a child may feel even more abandoned and unloved. For others, anger is turned inwards and the child becomes depressed. Thus, many children endure a phase of depressed sadness as their parents separate.

In the upheaval of divorce, children may return, or regress, to earlier patterns of behaviour that they had already given up as they got older. A child once dry at night may begin bedwetting again for a period. Young children who drink from a cup may demand a bottle or talk in baby language. These kinds of regressive behaviour are usually short lived and interpretations of their cause vary. Some see them as bids for attention while others interpret the return to an earlier phase of behaviour as an attempt by the child to evoke the calmer and more secure relationships with the parents and within the family which characterized the period before separation was considered …

For older children there may be a tendency to cope with what is happening at home by throwing themselves into activities outside. Some may choose school for this, so teachers, instead of seeing a change towards demanding and aggressive behaviour and perhaps a lack of interest in school work, may notice that a child is suddenly investing almost all his or her energies in school activities and may be quite reluctant to go home at the end of the day. For teenagers, boyfriends and girlfriends

may seem much more attractive and reassuring than warring parents or depressed parents who seem totally preoccupied with their own problems. There is some evidence to suggest that children who have experienced a parental divorce are likely to get into sexual relationships and perhaps marriage at a slightly earlier age. Where older children are unhappy at home, getting married as early as possible may be seen as a means of escape …

The overt distress of children when their parents separate and eventually divorce that we have described is generally short lived. It may last for a matter of months or a year and then gradually subside. The time this takes depends very much on what happens after the divorce and the quality of the children's relationship with *both* parents. Broadly speaking, the better their relationship with their parents, the less marked the distress will be and the shorter its duration. However, there are other factors involved: boys for instance tend to be more disturbed than girls. As most children live with their mothers after divorce, so boys are more likely to lose a close relationship with their same-sex parent. But this cannot be the whole story, as boys also seem to be the more disturbed by conflict between parents who are still living together. It is also possible that boys who are distressed are less likely than girls to receive support from peers and adults in situations like school …

Some recently divorced parents do not consider that their children are showing any signs of distress or disturbance at all. As we have already pointed out, children vary a great deal and in some circumstances their lives may not be greatly affected by their parents' separation. However, it is not unnatural that parents tend to minimize their children's problems especially if they feel that their own actions may be part of the cause. If a child does not show any obvious signs of disturbance, it may be that they are given few opportunities to express their feelings. Clinical experience suggests that in the longer term it is better that such feelings are expressed and it may be important to provide a child with a situation or a person with whom they feel safe enough to air their feelings and anxieties more freely.

SOURCE: BURGOYNE, J., ORMROD, R. and RICHARDS, M. (1987) *Divorce Matters, Harmondsworth, Penguin Books, pp. 124–8.*

Reading C Gender differences in the expression of emotion

Leslie R. Brody

The data on gender differences in emotional expressiveness indicate that females are more intensely verbally and facially expressive of a wide variety of emotions than are males. Males are more intensely emotionally expressive through actions and behaviors than are females. Sex differences in the intensity of verbal emotional expressivity are especially marked for emotions that are adaptive for stereotyped gender roles. Thus, females express more intense fear and hurt, related to stereotypic feminine vulnerability; more intense warmth and guilt, related to stereotypic feminine social bonding; and more intense shame and embarrassment, related to low status and power. The few emotions that are in some contexts expressed verbally more by males than by females are related to stereotypic male gender roles, including differentiation and competition (e.g., anger and pride).

I have suggested that gender differences are multidetermined and may be a function of gender differences in the affect socialization process, including parent, peer, and teacher socialization influences, as well as the language socialization process. A transactional developmental model (that is, reciprocal dyadic or systems interactions that vary over time) may well account for early gender differences in the affect socialization of boys versus girls. Such a model views development as a series of bidirectional influences over time between an individual (with innate temperamental and other constitutional response tendencies) and that individual's context (including parents, teachers, socioeconomic status). Each part (or partner) in the series of interactions reciprocally influences and changes other parts. Using such a model to understand early affect socialization, I have posited the following series of transactions. First, because neonatal boys may have more intense affective expressions than do neonatal girls, boys' 'expressions may be easier for caretakers to match than girls'. Girls may have to learn to amplify the intensity and clarity of their emotional expressions in order to convey their feelings, because their early facial expressions are more muted. Further, caretakers may enter a relationship with their newborns with a set of gender-role differentiated expectations that may differentially influence their interaction patterns with their sons and with their daughters. As a result of both their differing expectations for sons versus daughters, as well as in response to the early temperamental differences between their sons and their daughters, parents may emphasize emotions when interacting with their daughters, while de-emphasizing, or attempting to contain, emotions in their sons.

Taking the model one step further, girls' early language facility may also influence parents to talk to them about a wide variety of feeling states (with the exceptions of anger and disgust) from a very early age. Girls may therefore enter later peer relationships more prepared to articulate emotions; boys enter later peer relationships more prepared to mute their feelings. The quality of boys' peer relationships seems to further minimize the expression of feelings, with the exception of those feelings that are adaptive for the hierarchical, competitive games found to be characteristic of boys' play, such as anger and disgust. Such gender differences in the quality of peer relationships would further influence as well as be influenced by other socialization differences (e.g. teachers and the media) to affect gender differences in emotional functioning.

To summarize, it may well be that gender differences in emotion socialization result from a complex series of interactions between early subtle neuropsychological, genetic and hormonal differences between boys and girls (especially the propensity for expressive language), which reciprocally affect the quality of caretaker and peer affective responsivity. Gender differences in peer and caretaker socialization are influenced not only by innate response and temperamental tendencies but also by expectations about gender roles. Eventually, females and males learn to use emotions and affect language differently, which may lead them to become differentially accountable to others as well as differentially aware of their own feeling states.

SOURCE: ABLON, S., BROWN, D. KHANTZIAN, E. and MACK, J. (eds) (1993) Human Feelings: explorations in affect development and meaning, New York, Analytic Press, pp. 113–16.

CHAPTER 5 DEVELOPING A SENSE OF SELF

Dorothy Miell

CONTENTS

1	**INTRODUCTION**	**188**
2	**AN EMERGING SENSE OF SELF: EARLY DEVELOPMENTS**	**192**
2.1	First steps: establishing that I exist	192
2.2	Later developments: social categories	194
2.3	In conclusion	198
	Summary of Section 2	199
3	**SELF-ESTEEM**	**199**
3.1	Measuring self-esteem	200
3.2	Developing a sense of self and self-esteem	204
	Summary of Section 3	206
4	**GENDER IDENTITY**	**206**
4.1	Gender in everyday interaction	207
4.2	Gender stability and constancy	208
4.3	Learning gender appropriate behaviour	213
	Summary of Section 4	220
5	**REFLECTING ON THE SELF: SELF-DESCRIPTIONS AND SELF-ESTEEM**	**221**
5.1	Describing the self	222
6	**CONCLUSION**	**224**
	FURTHER READING	**225**
	REFERENCES	**225**
	READING: GENDER SCHEMA THEORY	**228**

OBJECTIVES

When you have studied this chapter, you should be able to:

1 describe the distinction between the *existential* and *categorical* self and give an account of the infant's early development in these two areas;

2 describe the influences on a child's level of self-esteem and discuss the difficulties involved in measuring it;

3 discuss some of the factors which affect children's development of gender identity, considering the influence of both internal psychological and wider interpersonal and social processes;

4 describe the developments in children's self-description and appreciate the way in which these can be seen to reflect the continuing attempt to make sense of the self.

1 INTRODUCTION

What is the 'self' and how do we study its development? These are important questions for developmental psychologists but they are not easy ones to answer. While each of us may have an intuitive sense of a 'self', it is not easy to convey to others. Some aspects of it may stay constant for many years, but others may change rapidly. There may be big differences between what we feel we are and what we wish or hope to be, and also what *we* think we are and what we feel *others* think we are. We are also, at least some of the time, aware of being evaluated by others (and of evaluating them). This chapter will attempt to tease out some of the many aspects of the development of the self, using and discussing a range of research studies and theories to do so.

Before turning to these, however, let's hear from some children and young people about themselves – about their sense of self – as they answer the question, 'Who am I?' They are all attempting to express what they see as important aspects of themselves, their distinguishing features, that which makes them unique. The descriptions they offer cover a number of the issues which this chapter will be covering in more detail.

ACTIVITY 1

Allow about 20 minutes

IDENTIFYING FEATURES OF SELF-DESCRIPTIONS

Look through the self-descriptions opposite and try to identify some of the things they have in common. What themes can you identify and which features in them strike you as potentially useful for comparing descriptions? You might, for example, consider the balance between the parts of the descriptions which deal with physical abilities or activities and those which deal with more psychological aspects of the self – such as feelings, thoughts and hopes. You might also consider the number and type of references made to other people, and whether these are to adults or to other children. We will return to your notes at various points in the chapter and particularly descriptions in Section 5.

EXAMPLE 1
SELF-DESCRIPTION

1 [*Dictated description*] Emily is a sister and I am big. I got toes and a belly button (are you allowed to say that?). I've got a head, eyes, mouth, elbow, finger, ear. I draw. I write, 'cause I do write, don't I? I do gluing at school, I do. I go to see my teachers. I go outside to play with all the toys and the bikes and when it's time to go in, we all walk into nursery. I eat a lot. I walk. I go to PE and I go on the climbing frame – it's not like Linda's. And I go to the 'sembly [assembly], but I always eat my lunch up. I always go outside to play in our garden. I sit on chairs. I play with my toys. Can I knit or can I do sewing? … I sew. I can talk numbers [count]. And we always have a wash. I brush my teeth. I always hoover up. Just very one more … I wash my face and I sit down to listen to books. *(Emily, aged 4 years 9 months)*

2 My name is Mary. I am a girl. I am 6 years old. I have long hair, it is brown. I started Brownies a few days ago. I would like another girl to be my friend. A girl with long brown hair the same length as mine. I like a lot of jewellery. I like horses. I like dressing up. I like drawing. I like my best teddy bear. He is called Andy Pandy, and I had him since I was a baby. *(Mary, aged 6 years 8 months)*

3 I am a girl. I am seven years old. I am Indian and Malaysian. I like playing football with Matthew. I like doing work because it is nice to learn things. I like reading and making models of cartoon characters. My hobby is badges. I get a lot of things that I need. I love playing schools, it is my favourite game because I can teach children how to do things. *(Malini, aged 7 years)*

4 My name is Jenny and I have a long plait. I am 9 and I have one sister called Anna. If I had £100 I would give it to starving people. My hobbies are swimming and collecting owls. *(Jenny, aged 9 years)*

5 Hello I'm Luke. I live in the countryside so I often like going on adventures. I love insects and I love my family and friends. Often I can be a bit mean. I like reading but my handwriting's scruffy and I'm not very good at grama [*sic*]. *(Luke, aged 10 years)*.

6 I am a 13-year-old boy called James. I enjoy playing sport, in particular cricket, tennis and hockey. I also quite like to walk and cycle and I like to relax with a good fantasy or sci-fi book or listen to some music. I occasionally listen to something quiet and classical, but I prefer rock or grunge. I follow a football team heavily and I listen to any match or buy any books on the subject. I tend to take life as it comes rather than plan ahead which makes me a bit disorganized – as my teachers keep telling me! I like to learn Spanish and French and I like to do my best at *most* subjects at school. I am quite committed at things when I want to be and I am really enjoying my Duke of Edinburgh award. Overall I tend to be happy, but at times I can get frustrated with my teachers and parents, and get depressed. I have one very close best friend and a few other good friends. I would like to become a journalist, or perhaps a cricketer. *(James, aged 13 years)*

7 Scott and Greg are my friends. I want to phone them tonight about swimming next Wednesday. I get someone to help me use the phone. I wish school was open. I go there to see my friends … At school I like drama best. Now I enjoy maths and science more than humanities and English. My friends do trampolining and dance with me … Each night I talk about tomorrow. The arrangements are important to me so I ask until I understand. On Monday, Tuesday and Wednesday I take my brother to school. He sits on my lap in the wheelchair. I put his shoes in the bag at school and get his trainers … I really like my school uniform. I need to know who will do my hair in the morning. It is important to look nice. Sometimes I ask for my earrings. I wore my nicest clothes and dangly earrings at the school disco. My friends all came to see me.

People matter to me. Gil and Linsey help me at school. Sometimes mum and dad come instead. I like going out and having visits from friends. I enjoy my food, my listening, and swimming, but I like being with people best. *(Samantha, aged about 14 years, quoted in Atkinson and Williams, 1990, p. 66)*

8 Over the last few years my personality has changed drastically, mostly due to pressures from my peers to conform, although I am happier with my new 'image' than I was before. However I now feel the need to find my true personality, if this is possible, and to define myself. It is difficult not to do this by fitting into a stereotype, as I see many people doing, where the way they dress, their way of talking and even their values are defined by something as immaterial as their taste in music. I think quite deeply about my personality. From talking to my friends I think I am fairly unusual in this. Most people seem to take the way they are for granted whereas I see myself as having to work at myself to find a state in which I am happy. I worry a lot about what people think of me so it is important to me to be complimented. *(Anna, aged 16 years)*

Developing a sense of self is often seen in Western cultures as the long process of becoming a self-aware individual – becoming aware, for example, of what you look like, your gender, what makes you happy and sad, what roles you play (all themes raised in the self-descriptions in Example 1) – all the things which delineate you as an individual. This is a long and complex process. As the psychologist Eleanor Maccoby has pointed out, developing a sense of self is not accomplished quickly:

> If we ask, 'Do infants have or do they not have a sense of self?' we are asking the wrong question. A sense of self is not achieved in a single step; it is not something that is either present or absent; it develops by degrees and is a product of more and more complex understandings. We might more reasonably ask how the understanding of self grows and changes through a lifetime, and how far a given child has progressed along the path to a mature concept of self.
>
> (Maccoby, 1980, p. 251)

It also involves *judgements* of features of yourself (again apparent in Example 1): how you *feel* about your physical appearance, your abilities and roles – often referred to as a sense of *self-worth* or *self-esteem*. Such issues are the concern of this chapter. While they all relate to individual personal development, this chapter will emphasize the contribution of children's *social* interactions and relationships. As we saw in Chapter 3, relationships within the family in particular have an enormous impact on children, and these relationships are as influential for children's developing sense of self as they are for their emotional, social or moral development.

Before we continue, we need to pause to consider the model of the self that has been built up so far. I have implied that everyone experiences the gradual development of a sense of an autonomous, unique and reflexive self, of a private inner world distinct from other people's. This may ring true to you, but should we assume that this 'primacy of the individual' is a universal experience – or might other people and cultures have a different view of the relationship between the individual and society at large? Anthropologists have argued that this emphasis on the uniqueness of the individual is a Western cultural view. Geertz (1984) describes how other cultures, notably the Javanese and Balinese, have very different views. For these people, the distinction between the individual and society is blurred, with the individual being seen as simply part of a whole, rather than as special and distinct. Rather than stressing uniqueness and separateness, overt displays of personal expression are considered vulgar and uncivilized. Instead, the individual is defined by his or her social status and relationship with others. The ideal is for a person to blend in with others, to avoid disrupting smooth social life by being unpredictable, distinctive or, from our perspective, 'individual'. In Bali, it is the social position that someone occupies which defines who they are, and care is taken to behave in a manner that is appropriate for that position; individuals are not important *as individuals*, but as part of a social whole:

All Balinese receive what might be called birth order names. There are four of these, 'firstborn', 'secondborn', 'thirdborn', 'fourthborn', after which they recycle, so that the fifthborn child is called again 'firstborn', the sixth, 'secondborn', and so on. Further, these names are bestowed independently of the fates of the children. Dead children, even stillborn ones, count, so that in fact, in this still high-birthrate, high-mortality society, the names don't really tell you anything very reliable about the birth-order relations of concrete individuals. The birth order naming system does not identify individuals as individuals, nor is it intended to; what it does is to suggest that, for all procreating couples, births form a circular succession of 'firsts', 'seconds', 'thirds' and 'fourths', an endless four stage replication of an imperishable form. Physically men appear and disappear as the ephemera they are, but socially the acting figures remain eternally the same as new 'firsts', 'seconds', and so on, emerging from the timeless world of the gods to replace those who dying, dissolve once more into it.

(Geertz, 1984, pp. 129–30, quoted in Open University, 1991, p. 71)

Roles and social status are important parts of the Western definition of the self (see the number of references to these in Example 1; such as 'Indian', 'sister', 'Brownie', 'football fan', 'teacher' and 'friend'), but they are seen as only *parts* of a more global self. While many theorists have incorporated social roles into their accounts of how the self is formed (as we will see in the next sections), the private inner world is often seen as the more basic, more central part of the self than the face we show to the outer social world. In talking about the self, Westerners are more concerned to distinguish themselves from others and stress what makes them unique, rather than emphasizing what they share with society in general.

The important thing to take away from this brief discussion is that ideas about individuality are not universal, but instead are culturally bound:

Some answers to questions seem so obvious, they appear to be so natural, that they seem beyond reasoning and conceptualization, simply the way things are. From a Western perspective autonomy, self-control, uniqueness, separateness and mastery over the world seem like facts of nature – just the way people are by nature. It is hard to treat this view as an assumption, an idea, a theory, a representation which so firmly structures the way we understand ourselves that it seems as though we must always have thought in this way.

(Open University, 1991, p. 72)

To consider, even briefly, the different ways in which other cultures view the self helps us to put our taken-for-granted views into perspective, to see them as theories, as assumptions. While we will be discussing the Western view of the self in the rest of this chapter, it is worth bearing in mind the *constructed* nature of this concept, rather than assuming it is a natural and universal way of conceptualizing the nature of the individual.

SUMMARY OF SECTION 1

- Western ideas of the self are fundamentally concerned with establishing features which mark the person out from others and emphasize the role of a private inner life.

- Some other cultures are more concerned to emphasize those aspects that make a person part of society, such as roles and relationships to others.

- Our views of what constitutes a self are assumptions or theories which are culturally developed and not universal experiences.

2 AN EMERGING SENSE OF SELF: EARLY DEVELOPMENTS

As we saw earlier, Maccoby pointed out that a sense of self develops by degrees. This process can usefully be thought of in terms of the gradual emergence and elaboration of two somewhat separate features: the *self as a subject* of experience and the *self as an object* of knowledge. This distinction is quite a difficult one to grasp, and has continued to be a subject of debate and discussion amongst psychologists since its introduction by William James in 1892. In this section and the next, we will explore the theoretical background to these two aspects of the self and consider their implications for the developing child's understanding of him or herself and, indeed, of the selves of other people.

2.1 First steps: establishing that I exist

A child's first step on the road to self-understanding and the establishment of a personal identity can be seen as the recognition that she exists. William James labelled this self the 'I', or the self-as-subject, now often referred to as the 'existential self' (Lewis, 1990). James gave it four elements:

(a) an awareness of one's own agency (i.e., one's power to act) in life events;

(b) an awareness of the uniqueness of one's own experience, of one's distinctiveness from other people;

(c) an awareness of the continuity of one's identity;

(d) an awareness of one's own awareness, the element of reflexiveness.

We can see the gradual emergence of these features as the infant explores her world and interacts with caregivers. Particularly striking is the infant's development of an understanding of herself as having power, of being an *agent* in the environment; that is, of being able to cause things to happen and control objects. A contemporary of James,

Charles Cooley, was a sociologist concerned with personal development and he also discussed this aspect of the self, suggesting that a sense of self

> ... appears to be associated chiefly with ideas of the exercise of power, of being a cause ... The first definite thoughts that a child associates with self-feeling are probably those of his earliest endeavours to control visible objects – his limbs, his playthings, his bottle and the like. Then he attempts to control the actions of the persons about him, and so his circle of power and self-feeling widens without interruption to the most complex of mature ambition.
>
> (Cooley, 1902, pp. 145–6, quoted in Dunn, 1988, pp. 176–7)

The infant learns that when she closes her eyes the world goes dark, when she lets go of something it drops, when she touches a toy it moves, when she cries or smiles someone responds to her. In this way a sense of agency emerges and is consolidated.

Many parents spend a lot of time, particularly in the early months, imitating the infant's behaviour, vocalizations and expressions. This is another powerful source of information for infants, not only about their particular relationship with their parents, but also about the effects they can have on the world around them generally. The young child's liking for imitation can be seen in a study described in Research Summary 1 below.

RESEARCH SUMMARY 1
LIKING FOR IMITATION

In Meltzoff's (1990) study, 14-month-old children were individually seated at a table opposite two adults. The child and the two adults all had an identical toy, and whenever the child moved or manipulated it one of the adults copied the child's actions exactly whilst the other adult did something different with it. The infants smiled and looked more and for longer at the adult who imitated them, thereby indicating that they preferred this imitation.

The same amusement with and liking for imitation is also apparent in the behaviour of the young siblings observed at home in Dunn and Kendrick's study:

> Joyce (8 months) vocalizes while playing. Warren looks at her, she looks at him; mutual gaze. Warren 'imitates' her vocalization. Joyce repeats her vocalization. Both laugh.
>
> (Dunn and Kendrick, 1982, p. 141)

Since young children appear very interested in and attracted to imitation and similar behaviours, perhaps this is why they enjoy looking in mirrors, where they detect not just similar but *identical* behaviour to their own, through the movements they can see there which are contingent (meaning 'dependent') upon their own movements. Such contingency has important lessons for the infant, learnt from the fact that what they *do* in front of the mirror and what they *see* in it are the same. Lewis and Brooks-Gunn (1979) suggest that this contingency of movement is a powerful cue for the infant's emerging sense of the self as an independent agent – that it is the self that is 'making things happen'. As Harter (1983) suggests,

> … an appreciation of this contingency exemplifies an important developmental step in the differentiation of self from other, since the infant learns that 'other people do not produce behaviour sequences identical to theirs and that only a reflective image of themselves does' (Lewis and Brooks-Gunn, 1979, p. 200). The infant comes to learn, then, that a reflection is not another person but is the 'self', the product of one's own actions.
>
> (Harter, 1983, p. 280)

This is not to say that infants *recognize* the reflection as their own image (this is a later development which is discussed further below), but they do seem to appreciate that they are making the reflection move, that they are causing it to happen, and that they are different from other people, as although these others can imitate the infant's behaviour, they cannot produce the *identical* movements in the same way as the mirror does. These achievements represent the first two aspects of James' definition of the self-as-subject which was given on p. 192. We can see continuing developments in children's understanding of themselves as agents in their battles to get attention at a busy family meal table and attempts to co-operate with others in play. Dunn (1988) points out that it is in such day-to-day relationships and interactions that the child's understanding of his or her self emerges.

Empirical investigations of the self-as-subject are, however, rather scarce. This could in part be due to the difficulties in defining the various features of the self-as-subject in order to define it – indeed William James himself 'despaired of ever studying the "I" in an empirical and nonspeculative way' (Damon and Hart, 1988, p. viii). Even if young infants *can* reflect on these experiences, they certainly cannot articulate this aspect of the self directly.

2.2 Later developments: social categories

A second step in the development of a full sense of self can be seen as the acquisition and elaboration of what James (1892) called the 'me', or the self-as-object, and which is now often referred to as the 'categorical self' (Lewis, 1990). This aspect of the self concerns the qualities or characteristics that define a person, such as gender, name, size, and relationship to others. Once a child has gained a certain level of self-awareness (of the existential self), she begins to place herself – and to be placed by others – in a whole series of such categories which go on to play such an important role in defining her uniquely as 'herself'.

Since James put forward this distinction between the 'I' and the 'me', others have developed and elaborated it, and particularly the understanding of the 'me' – the categorical self. This has been seen by many to be the aspect of the self which is most influenced by social factors, since it is made up of social roles (such as student, brother, colleague) and of characteristics which derive their meaning from comparison or interaction with other people (such as trustworthiness, shyness, sporting ability). As a result, emphasizing the importance of the social context in self-development has been an important feature of the work of many theorists in this area.

From the early days of the study of child development, writers have emphasized the role of the social context. Baldwin, for example, at the end of the nineteenth century believed that the development of understanding of the self parallels the growth of understanding of others and stressed the need for interaction with others to allow this development to take place, particularly, he believed, through imitation: 'My sense of myself grows by imitation of you, and my sense of yourself grows in terms of my sense of myself' (Baldwin, 1897, p. 7).

The looking-glass self

While we might question the *central* role Baldwin gave to imitation, Cooley and G. H. Mead further developed the suggestion of the close connection between an understanding of self and others. Cooley believed that we build up our sense of self from the reactions of others to us and how we believe they view us. Cooley called this the 'looking-glass self', since it is as if other people provide a 'social mirror', and we come to see ourselves as we are reflected in them. Mead was one of the founders of the *'symbolic interactionist'* school of thought which emphasized the importance of language and interaction. He saw the self and the social world as inextricably bound together: 'The self is essentially a social structure, and it arises in social experience ... it is impossible to conceive of a self arising outside of social experience' (Mead, 1934, p. 135). He believed that through their use of language, their games and their play, young children begin to take the perspectives of other people towards themselves, and, in so doing, become capable of reflecting on themselves.

So, for Baldwin, Cooley and Mead, the child cannot develop a sense of self without the chance to interact with others in order to begin to understand how these others view the world, including how they view the child.

Other major developmental theorists have also stressed the interplay of the personal and social development of the child. Piaget, often criticised for not paying enough heed to the role of the social context in children's cognitive development, did in fact believe that the social context was crucial for children in presenting them, amongst other things, with challenges to their own view of things. In *Judgement and Reasoning*, he explains, 'We are all constantly hatching an enormous number of false ideas, conceits, utopias, mystical explanations, suspicions and megalomaniac fantasies, which disappear when brought into contact with other people'. The social need to share the thoughts of others and to communicate our own effectively is at the 'root of our need for verification. Proof is the outcome of argument' (Piaget, 1928, 1976, p. 204). For Piaget, the goal of development is to overcome egocentricity, which can only be achieved through co-operation with others. Children do not learn by observing others nor do others impose their ideas on them. Instead, he believed that children develop through coping with and trying to grasp how best to make interpersonal relationships work (a point which will be developed further in the following chapter).

From such analyses by theorists, it is clear that without being part of a community a child could not develop a sense of self in the Western sense. Most explicitly in Mead's work, we see that children develop concepts of themselves as they learn to communicate and interact with those around them.

He suggests that others provide us with a perspective on ourselves and on the world around us that we cannot obtain alone. The importance of this interplay of social experience with personal and emotional development can be illustrated by briefly examining the rare cases of children who have suffered extreme social deprivation early in life and by looking at the effects of this deprivation on the development of their sense of self, their emotions and their ability to interact with others. These children are called *feral* or wild children, since some were found abandoned in the wild, having had to fend for themselves for several years. Other cases report children who have been kept isolated from more than minimal human contact in attics or cellars (see Rymer, 1993, for a fascinating discussion of the case of Genie, kept locked in an attic for several years).

Perhaps the most famous case of a feral child was Victor, the 'wild boy of Aveyron', found living in a wood in France in 1800. It emerged that he was about 12 years old, but no details of his earlier years were ever fully established.

It is clear from contemporary accounts that Victor had a very limited understanding of the world about him when he was first found. He was obviously skilled at survival in the wild, being able to gather and store food and keep away from danger, but he had no real ability to reason, to engage in human interaction, or to think about himself in an abstract way. Even after intensive training, some of these abilities never fully developed. At the time it was suggested that these problems were largely the result of his lack of social experience during his formative years: 'The mind of a man deprived of the commerce of others is so little exercised, so little cultivated, that he thinks only in the measure that he is obliged to by exterior objects. *The greatest source of ideas among men is their human interactions*' (Itard, the doctor who adopted and studied Victor, quoted in Lane, 1977, p. 38; my emphasis).

Victor lacked the social experience that Mead saw as all-important. He had managed to establish many of the features of the existential self (except the capacity for reflexiveness) but had very few if any of the elements of the categorical self. He could not recognize himself in a mirror, and apparently had no sense of his psychological characteristics or of social roles. He had not been able to develop the capacity to reflect on himself as he did not have others around him whose behaviour he could observe, or who could give him feedback about his own behaviour and characteristics. We must be cautious about the conclusions we draw from this account, particularly since so little is known about Victor *before* he lived in the wild; he may have been abandoned *because* he was unresponsive socially or a slow developer. However, the case does suggest that his isolation had profound effects, and that the presence of others can be an important factor in a child's developing a complete sense of self.

Around their second birthday, many children display visual self-recognition (an aspect of knowledge of the self-as-object or categorical self), when they see themselves in a mirror or in a photograph. As Lewis and Brooks-Gunn (1979) have shown, some form of self-recognition can be observed from about the age of 15 months. In a series of studies, they observed how often young children touched their noses during a control period playing in front of a mirror. Then they dabbed some rouge on the children's noses (during a 'routine nose wipe' by the mother) and counted how often they touched their noses when they again played in front of a mirror. Lewis and Brooks-Gunn reasoned that if the children knew what they usually looked like, they would be surprised by the unusual red mark on their noses and would explore it by touching their

own nose. However, this early self-recognition is not stable, since Lewis and Brooks-Gunn showed that children of 15 to 18 months are generally not able to recognize themselves if other cues (such as movements corresponding to their own) are absent. Lewis and Brooks-Gunn investigated this by showing the infants a still photograph of themselves and video images of themselves filmed on a previous occasion. In each case the researchers looked for signs of recognition from the toddler. As Lewis and Brooks-Gunn argue, 'it is the ability to recognize and respond to self *independent* of contingency which represents the important developmental milestone in self-recognition' (Lewis and Brooks-Gunn, 1979, p. 218). A full appreciation of what the self looks like develops fairly gradually from this age, until the children have an awareness of what their own features look like, even when their image is no longer contingent on their current movements or expressions.

Perhaps the most graphic expressions of self-awareness in the young child can be seen in the displays of rage and aggression which are most common, certainly in Western societies, from 18 months to 3 years of age, when the infant is already displaying an increasing awareness of the self through the use of the words 'me' and, particularly in this context, 'mine'. Cooley, in his early writings on self development, had stressed the importance of such struggles over possession:

> [For Cooley] … the self-sense is not discovered in quiet reflection, but in the course of vigorous effort, especially when that effort brings the individual into rivalry with other persons … The sense of self arises in connection with active striving in the face of obstacles.
>
> (Turner, 1968, p. 99)

In a longitudinal study of groups of three or four children over the course of their second year Bronson (1975) found that the *intensity* of the frustration and anger in their disagreements increased sharply. Often, the children's disagreements involved a struggle over a toy that none of them was playing with before or after the tug-of-war was over! The children seemed to be disputing possession itself rather than wanting to play with the toy. The link between the sense of 'self' and of 'ownership' may be less marked in other cultures where sole possession of objects is less emphasized, but such struggles are a notable feature of childhood in western societies.

2.3 In conclusion

Between the ages of two and three, most children are developing a more elaborated understanding of their basic characteristics (e.g. their appearance and their name) and their experiences and actions. They also know quite a lot about their environment, including the members of their family, their home, toys and pets. Dunn's work with young children interacting with siblings and parents in their own homes (described in the Reading at the end of this book) has given us many examples of what young children understand about themselves and their social world and has suggested that it is in these everyday interactions that they acquire this understanding.

Although these examples show that children's understanding of themselves and others makes tremendous strides in the two to three years after birth, it is still limited. They have a considerable amount to learn about themselves and about how other people think and feel before they can become fully competent members of the social world.

We began this chapter with a quotation from Maccoby which emphasized this gradual and complex path of development. We will now move on to examine some of the processes involved in acquiring more complex understandings in the years up to adolescence. The sometimes radical shifts in a young person's sense of self during adolescence are discussed in Chapter 7.

> **SUMMARY OF SECTION 2**
>
> - The self can be divided into two aspects, the existential and the categorical.
> - The existential self (also referred to as the 'I' or the *self-as-subject*) involves an awareness of being distinct from others, of having the power to act on the world and of continuity, and the ability to reflect on this awareness. It is a very difficult area to investigate empirically.
> - The categorical self (also referred to as the 'me' or the *self-as-object*) involves a recognition of the physical characteristics of the self, as well as an understanding of various other characteristics, such as gender, name and a growing range of social roles.
> - Developments in these two areas occur rapidly during the second and third years of life, in the context of social interactions and relationships. The developments may be dependent on these factors.

3 SELF-ESTEEM

The categorical self, as we have seen, is the aspect of the self which is composed of a number of characteristics describing the person, grouped under categories such as relationship to others, sporting ability, temperament, social roles etc. Looking back at the self-descriptions in Example 1, we can see that such descriptions are often not value-free, however, but usually involve some degree of evaluation, or expressions of self-worth, related to the presence (or absence) of a particular characteristic.

ACTIVITY 2

Allow about 10 minutes

EVALUATIONS OF THE SELF

Go back to the self-descriptions in Example 1 (p. 189) and list any statements which refer to the categorical self. Once you have this list, examine the way in which each characteristic is described and note down any evaluations made of it (e.g., *'good at* schoolwork'). Where possible, you should also think about whether the evaluation appears to be derived from the views of others (such as 'my parents think I am … ') or whether they are more personal judgements about abilities and worth (such as 'I'm not happy with the way I …'). This is not always easy to distinguish, but it is worth looking for and making notes on if you can. In some cases, a comment may be phrased as a self-evaluation but it has been derived from reflecting on evaluations made indirectly by others, or from comparisons made with others. The confusion here can tell us a lot about the extent of the 'meshing' between the self and others in this area, and reinforces the points made in the previous section about the vital role played by the social world in this 'private' world of the self.

In this section we will be exploring further this aspect of self development – the way in which a child develops a sense of self-worth, or, as it is most commonly called, a sense of self-esteem. Before we turn to a discussion of how this develops in a child, however, it is important to consider the difficulties which have been faced by those psychologists who have attempted to measure children's self-esteem.

3.1 Measuring self-esteem

Despite us all having an intuitive notion of what we mean by self-esteem, psychologists have found it extremely difficult to define and to assess. The definitions offered by researchers are often rather general – as you can see in the example below from Coopersmith's extensive study of children's self-esteem:

> By self-esteem we refer to the evaluation which the individual makes and customarily maintains with regard to himself; it expresses an attitude of approval or disapproval, and indicates the extent to which the individual believes himself to be capable, significant, successful, and worthy.
>
> (Coopersmith, 1967, p. 5, quoted in Harter, 1983, p. 321)

As Harter comments on this and other similar definitions:

> Given the generality of such a conceptual definition, it is difficult to imagine how one might arrive at a precise *operational* definition of self-esteem. This problem has not stood in the way of efforts to assess this psychological commodity, however.
>
> (Harter, 1983, p. 321)

We will now look at some of these efforts to assess self-esteem, before looking in more detail at some discussion of how children's sense of self-esteem develops.

One of the first and most extensive studies of self-esteem in children was conducted by Coopersmith in 1967. He investigated the origins and stability of self-esteem and its relation to personality, concentrating mainly on children aged 10 and 11. Coopersmith developed a questionnaire (called the Self-Esteem Inventory) which used 58 statements adapted from an adult scale. Children were asked to indicate whether statements such as 'I'm pretty sure of myself', 'I'm popular with kids my own age' and 'My parents understand me' were 'like me' or 'unlike me'. The statements covered how children saw themselves with regard to peers, parents, school and personal interests. He found that scores in all of these areas were very closely related, so he felt confident in deriving an overall, or global, self-esteem score by combining scores from each area.

The inventory was not, however, very well received by self-esteem researchers. There were a number of problems with its construction, for instance with the wording of the questions. They were phrased in such a way that, of the two possible responses, one is rather more socially desirable and acceptable than the other (at least for people in a Western culture). As a result, children may be tempted to respond with these socially desirable responses (e.g., 'I'm easy to like', 'I'm popular with kids my own age') even where these are not a true reflection of their feelings about themselves.

Since Coopersmith did this research, a number of questions have been raised about the best way of measuring self-esteem. Is this global measure sensitive enough to the possibly different levels of self-esteem that children may experience about different aspects of their lives? It is possible to imagine that a child could feel very competent in her work at school and yet not evaluate herself highly in sports, or in relationships with peers. A global measure of the sort that Coopersmith derived from the true/false answers to his inventory may 'gloss over' such differences, giving the child with high scores in some areas and low scores in others an average level of overall self-esteem. As a result of these types of questions being raised about global measures, there has been a move towards measuring the different aspects, or domains, of self-esteem separately (Harter, 1988).

Harter's Self-Perception Profile for Children (see Example 2 overleaf) taps five specific domains in children by asking six questions on each domain. These domains are:

(a) Scholastic competence. How able the child feels in schoolwork.
(b) Athletic competence. How competent the child feels in sports and games.
(c) Social acceptance. How popular the child feels with peers.
(d) Behavioural conduct. The extent to which the child feels he or she behaves appropriately and acceptably.
(e) Physical appearance. How good-looking the child feels, and how much he or she likes various physical characteristics.

For each item, the child is read a statement about two groups of children, one which felt or did one thing, and the other which felt or did the opposite. The child is asked to say which group of others she feels most like (see example below). This design is an attempt to overcome the social desirability effect of other scales, since the child is choosing to be like *some* children, regardless of which choice she makes. Having chosen which group of children she is most like, the child can then make a further choice, saying whether the statement is 'really' or only 'sort of' like her. Harter feels this is easier for children than making a true/false choice on each item.

For children under eight years, Harter has devised a pictorial version of the Self-Perception Profile which consists of two pictures for each item, one showing a competent child and the other a less competent child (see Figure 1 overleaf). The child chooses which picture is most like him or herself and then touches a large circle (to indicate 'a lot like self') or a small circle ('a little like self') underneath the picture to record his or her answer.

EXAMPLE 2
SOME ITEMS FROM HARTER'S SELF-PERCEPTION PROFILE FOR CHILDREN

(The numbers in the boxes represent the scores which would be given for responses in those boxes. These numbers would not be printed on the questionnaires which the children completed.)

The children answering the questionnaire have to decide which of the two sets of children described in each item they are more like, and then tick in a box to say whether that is 'really' or 'sort of' true of them.

Really true for me	Sort of true for me				Sort of true for me	Really true for me
1	2	Some kids have *trouble* figuring out the answers in school	BUT	Other kids almost *always* can figure out the answers	3	4
4	3	Some kids do very *well* at all kinds of sports	BUT	Others *don't* feel that they are very good when it comes to sports	2	1
4	3	Some kids are popular with others their age	BUT	Other kids are *not* very popular	2	1
1	2	Some kids usually get into *trouble* because of the things they do	BUT	Other kids usually *don't* do things that get them in trouble	3	4
1	2	Some kids wish their physical appearance was *different*	BUT	Other kids *like* their physical appearance the way it is	3	4

FIGURE 1 Pictures from Harter's Self-Perception Profile for younger children (Vasta *et al.*, 1992, p. 487).

Using the written or the pictorial version of the questionnaire, a profile of a child's self-esteem in each of the five domains of the self can be constructed from their scores. As you can see from the examples in Figure 2, levels of self-esteem can vary across domains, which reinforces Harter's view that it is important to look at the domains separately rather than combining them to obtain a global measure, since the children obviously feel very different about the various aspects of their lives.

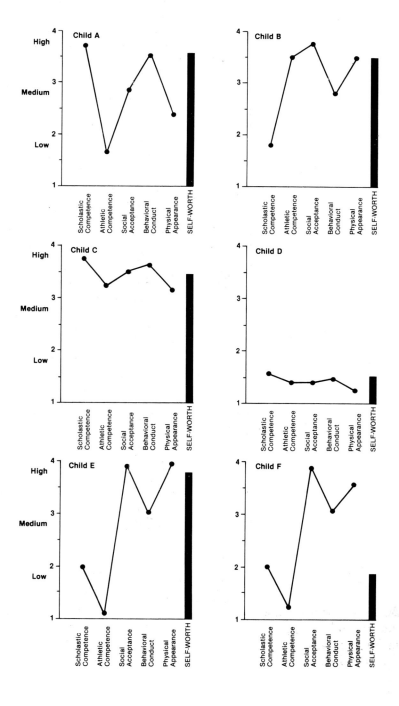

FIGURE 2 Sample self-perception profiles (Yawkey and Johnson, 1988, p. 66).

Separating the different domains of self-esteem does not imply that children do not have a feeling for their overall self-esteem at all, but Harter would argue that this should be measured separately, rather than being derived from an average score. She included six items in the Self-Perception Profile which assessed this overall feeling of self-worth, such as the choice between 'Some kids like the kind of person that they are BUT other kids often wish they are someone else'. As you can see from Figure 2, even when the scores in each of the other five domains are rather similar (e.g. Child E and Child F), their feelings of overall self-worth could be very different (this will be discussed further). This seems to confirm that the feeling of overall self-worth is not simply an amalgam of the scores in other domains, but is determined separately. We will now turn to an examination of these different aspects of self-esteem in more detail.

3.2 Developing a sense of self and self-esteem

What might be the factors which influence the development of this overall sense of self-esteem? William James suggested that 'internal' psychological factors were the most important, rather than the social pressures suggested by some later theorists. James believed that our evaluation of our achievements and competence was the main factor determining our sense of self-esteem, particularly our achievements in areas where success is important to us. A child who is anxious to succeed at sport, for example, would have a high level of self-esteem if she did well at sport, but low self-esteem if her performance in sport was poor, even if the child was very successful academically or socially. As James himself put it,

> We have the paradox of a man shamed to death because he is only the second pugilist or the second oarsman in the world. That he is able to beat the whole population of the globe minus one is nothing; he has pitted himself to beat that one, and as long as he doesn't do that nothing else counts ... Yonder puny fellow, however, whom everyone can beat, suffers no chagrin about it, for he has long ago abandoned the attempt to 'carry that line' ... With no attempt there can be no failure, with no failure, no humiliation.

(James, 1896, p. 310, quoted in Maccoby, 1980, p. 272)

To estimate the importance of this factor in determining children's overall feeling of self-esteem, Harter asked a group of children to say how important each of the domains in the self-perception profile were to them (i.e., scholastic, athletic, social, etc.). The differences in ratings of importance made by different children were revealing. For example, looking back at Child E and Child F in Figure 2 (p. 203), you can see that, despite having the same scores in each of the five domains of the profile, their self-worth scores were very different. When their ratings for the importance to them of each of these domains are examined, clear differences emerge. Child E had similar scores for her perceived competence in a domain and for its importance to her, so that she saw popularity and appearance as most important to her (the areas in which she was performing well) and schoolwork and sports as not very or not at all important (the areas in which she was performing least well). So Child E sees herself as doing well in the areas that are important to her.

Child F in Figure 2, by contrast, sees his schoolwork (in which he is performing poorly) to be very important, and sports also to be quite important (where he is performing even less well). He is anxious to do well in areas in which he is currently not succeeding, and cannot discount them as less important. This could explain why he has lower self-esteem scores than Child E, despite similar assessments of competence across the various domains.

Harter found this same pattern of a strong link between performance in an area judged to be important and overall self-esteem in large numbers of children, suggesting that the match between our aspirations and performance is one important factor in determining self-esteem, as James had suggested.

Cooley's work on the looking-glass self (referred to in Section 2, page 9) suggested another factor that might influence children's overall feeling of self-esteem; the regard in which they are held by 'significant others', the people whose opinions matter to the children. Harter (1986) extended her original Self-Perception Profile by assessing the extent to which the children felt accepted and supported by parents and peers. She found a high correlation between the overall self-esteem scores of children and the extent to which they felt supported and held in high regard by others such as parents and peers. Over time, children are likely to change the people to whom they look for support – someone who is significant for a young child may not retain that significance as the child grows older. Rosenberg (1979) asked children how much they cared about what a variety of people thought about them, including parents, classmates, teachers, siblings and friends. He found that younger children relied heavily on adults for evaluations of themselves, a finding consistent with the literature on moral development which follows Piaget's observations of children's understanding of rules and of adult authority. Older children began to place more weight on the judgements of their peers, with adolescents caring most about what their best friends thought of them. For many, particular aspects of what they see themselves to be assume huge importance:

> The first time the doubt that I belonged to this particular planet struck me, was a glorious, calm, blue-skied day when I was twelve years old. Lying flat on my back in the garden, staring at the sky, I was thinking about growing up. Until that moment I think I had somehow believed that when I grew up I would become 'normal', i.e. without a disability. 'Normal' then meant to me, 'like my big sister', pretty, rebellious, going out with boys, doing wonderful, naughty things with them, leaving school and getting a job, leaving home, getting married and having children. That momentous day I suddenly realised that my life was not going to be like that at all. I was going to be just the same as I had always

been – very small, funnily shaped, unable to walk. It seemed at that moment that the sky cracked. My vision expanded wildly. My simply black and white world exploded into vivid colours which dazzled and frightened me in a way in which I had never been frightened before. Everything took on an ominous hue. At that point I saw life, especially with regard to other women, as a huge competition, and I believed that I was just not equipped to cope.

(Micheline Mason, who now sees her differences as something to be proud of, in Campling, 1981, p. 24)

The importance of dealing with problems surrounding self-esteem in schools has been stressed by many education theorists. Murray White (1990) describes the benefits of the 'circletime' approach, in which children discuss positive views of others and how to deal with personal and interpersonal difficulties. White sees this as an effective way of raising self-esteem, stressing as it does positive feedback from both the teacher *and* the peer group.

The following chapter looks at how children develop their sense of morality beyond a personal concern with their own thoughts and behaviour, and examines the way in which children gradually discover more general societal rules about how they and others should behave.

> **SUMMARY OF SECTION 3**
> - Self-esteem has proved difficult to measure, but Harter has developed a questionnaire which taps five domains of a child's self-esteem.
> - The degree of match between children's aspirations and performance in a domain is important in determining feelings of self-esteem.
> - Another important factor determining self-esteem is the respect given to the child by significant others such as parents, teachers and peers.

4 GENDER IDENTITY

An appreciation of one's gender is an important aspect of a developing sense of identity. For children, knowing that they are boys or girls may be one of the first categories to which they assign themselves in developing their sense of categorical self, as they are constantly hearing themselves referred to with gender labels, such as 'good boy' or 'clever girl'. By the age of 2, children can often identify themselves as girls or boys, and this remains an important category for them, as you will have noticed in the number of mentions of gender given in Example 1. How do children come to know they are boys or girls, and when and how do they learn what is 'appropriate' behaviour for their gender? This section explores these questions, beginning with a discussion of the way in which gender is discussed in everyday interactions in British families.

4.1 Gender in everyday interaction

In Dunn and Kendrick's 1982 study of siblings, the researchers found references to gender in many everyday conversations between the children and their parents, particularly after the arrival of the new baby in the family. Dunn and Kendrick suggested that the presence of the baby, and discussions about the baby between the mother and elder child, often led the children to make remarks which categorized both themselves and the baby in terms of characteristics such as age, size and good/bad behaviour and that these discussions helped the older children to develop their sense of identity.

Some of these discussions began with comments being made about physical differences between the child and the baby, such as of size and physical abilities. Where gender was different, this provided a clear topic of conversation:

Brendan F and mother:
CHILD: Done a wee-wee.
MOTHER: Yes, she has.
CHILD: Hasn't got a widdly.
MOTHER: No she hasn't, has she?
CHILD: Hasn't

(Dunn and Kendrick, 1982, p. 65)

In many observations the children seemed to be very clear about gender identity even when they were not verbally advanced:

[Warren D, aged 26 months] throwing comic book at baby
MOTHER: You giving Joyce your comic, are you?
CHILD: No
MOTHER: Are you a monkey?
CHILD: No. Me not monkey. Me boy. Joyce girl. Joyce baby.
MOTHER: Is she?
CHILD: Joyce baby.

(Dunn and Kendrick, 1982, p. 111)

In some cases, the children played with and joked about gender categories, as in the following example where Sally is talking to her father.

CHILD (playing with her teddy, to father):   Teddy's a man
FATHER: What are you?
CHILD: You're a boy.
FATHER: Yeah. What are you?
CHILD: A menace.
FATHER: Yeah, a menace. Apart from that are you a boy or a girl?
CHILD: Boy (laughs).

FATHER:　Are you? What's Trevor?
CHILD:　A girl (laughs).
FATHER:　You're silly.

(Dunn and Kendrick, 1982, pp. 110–11)

Dunn and Kendrick interpret the type of playing with the concept of gender seen in these and many others of their observations as evidence of the confidence with which these children are applying self categories such as gender to themselves. The same confidence was also seen in the 'enthusiasm and adroitness' which the children employed in their pretend games, in which various dimensions of the self such as gender, size and age were manipulated and changed as readily as their dressing-up clothes (Dunn and Kendrick, 1982, p. 112).

From examples such as these, typical of Dunn and Kendrick's observations, it can be seen that young children discuss gender quite naturally in everyday interactions and seem to have a good working definition of their own and others' gender identities at around the age of two. But it is also clear that this sense of identity is by no means a fully developed concept; for example, some children think that anyone with short hair is a boy, or that boys can grow up to be mummies. But a basic sense of gender identity seems to be in place at an early age, and in this section of the chapter we will be considering how this develops and continues to be elaborated, and how it fits into the child's growing sense of his or her identity.

4.2 Gender stability and constancy

ACTIVITY 3

Allow about 5 minutes

EXPLORING DEVELOPING IDEAS ABOUT GENDER

How do you think children between the ages of two and six would answer the questions below? If possible, ask a child *you know well* who is around this age to answer the questions for you (you will need to allow more time for this activity if you are asking a child to answer the questions). Think about what you expect he or she might say, and the understanding this reveals, before you ask the child. Think about the type of understanding which is required to answer each question.

Please do not try asking a child you do not know well, and do not approach any child without the prior approval of his or her parents.

(a)　Are you a boy or girl?

(b)　When you're ten, will you be a boy or a girl?

(c)　When you're grown up, will you be a man or a woman?

(d)　If you have children when you grow up, will you be a daddy or a mummy?

[In the following two questions, refer to the gender opposite the child's own.]

(e)　If you put on a girl's/boy's clothes, could you be a girl/boy?

(f)　If you wanted to, could you be a daddy/mummy when you grow up?

Comment

These questions assess different aspects of gender identity, which are typically acquired gradually over the first six or seven years of life. A young child of around three, for example, will probably only be able to answer some of these questions correctly (as we will see below) and there seems to be a pattern in the sequence in which a fuller understanding develops. The developmental pattern in the acquisition of aspects of gender is discussed in the rest of this section.

The ability to understand that gender remains constant throughout life does not seem to emerge as early as the ability to label oneself as a girl or boy. Researchers in the cognitive development tradition have examined this by asking children such questions as those used in the above activity, and have found that most children answered the questions assessing the *stability* of gender accurately, by the age of four.

The answers children gave to questions (b), (c), (d) and (f) in Activity 3 will have given you some data on this. Did you find that children of about 4 years of age and older seemed to have a sense that gender was stable?

A further important step in the development of gender identity can be seen to occur when the child gains an understanding of gender *constancy*, that is, an understanding that people stay the same gender even when they change their appearance, for instance by wearing different clothes or altering their hair length. Some researchers have argued that the child understands this at a later age than gender stability, since an appreciation that something remains the same despite a change in appearance is conceptually difficult. Piaget suggested that the conservation of mass, weight and number is not typically observed in children until the age of about 5 or 6, and a parallel can be drawn with the conservation of gender, where children may not understand that a boy with long hair is still a boy until a year or so after they understand that they themselves will remain the same gender throughout their life.

Question (e) in Activity 3 addressed this issue. What responses did you get from the children when you asked this question? Did the children who could answer the gender stability questions (b, c, d, and f) seem still to have difficulty with the one assessing gender constancy?

Kohlberg (1966) adopted this approach to gender identity development, which was grounded in Piaget's theory of cognitive development, and emphasized children's active attempts to understand and interpret their gender identity. Proponents of this cognitive model view the child as developing through distinct stages of understanding in interaction with the environment. The first stage is to recognize oneself as a boy or a girl, followed by an understanding of gender stability and then, finally, of gender constancy. In each stage, there is a qualitatively different organization of the world, such that a child's gender-role concepts represent developing ways of viewing and understanding the differences between the sexes. Kohlberg and Zigler suggest that

> The child's basic sex-role identity is largely the result of a self-categorization as a male or a female made early in development ... The reality judgement, 'I really am and will always be a boy', or, 'I really am and will always be a girl' are judgements with a regular course of age development relatively independent of the vicissitudes of social labelling and reinforcement.
>
> (Kohlberg and Zigler, 1967, p. 103)

The cognitive developmentalists, therefore, believe that the child understands that the world is divided into two genders and that he or she belongs to one of these, and makes an early self-categorization by the age of about 2. Once this has been achieved, the theory suggests that children will seek out and value behaviours and attributes that link them to the same-sex others in the world. Young children should, then, be able to differentiate between males and females and to describe accurately the typical attributes of each gender. A study which investigated whether young children could do this was carried out by Kuhn *et al.* (1978) and is described in Research Summary 2.

However, it is unclear whether the development of these views is dependent solely on the child's realization of his or her gender identity and his or her own construction of appropriate behaviour for that gender (as the cognitive developmental theory would predict). It could also be

---

RESEARCH SUMMARY 2
GENDER STEREOTYPES IN 2 AND 3 YEAR OLDS

Kuhn *et al.* asked 72 children to pick out which of two dolls (a boy and girl doll) would be more likely to say each of a series of statements associated with stereotypical gender roles. The statements were grouped into ones about traits ('I'm strong'), activities ('I like to play with trains'), and future roles ('When I grow up, I'll fly an airplane').

The researchers found that the children attributed only some of the statements equally to the boy or girl doll, and these were the statements that were affectively neutral (such as 'I like to play ball'). Generally, they chose to attribute statements to the doll of the same sex as themselves which were positively valued (such as, for boys, 'When I grow up, I'll be a doctor', and for girls, 'I never like to fight') and to attribute negative statements to the opposite sex doll (such as boys saying the girl doll said, 'I'm slow', and girls saying the boy doll said, 'I am mean').

Kuhn *et al.* believe these results support Kohlberg's cognitive developmental theory which suggests that children label themselves as male or female, identify males and females in the world around them and are motivated to value, associate with and be like the people of the same gender. As Kuhn *et al.* say, 'The present data can be interpreted as supportive of Kohlberg's position in the sense of demonstrating that the basic gender-identity attainment is associated with affectively related processes of same-sex valuation and opposite sex devaluation' (Kuhn *et al.*, 1978, p. 449).

argued that young children's beliefs and behaviour are more influenced by social expectations, conveyed, for instance, by their parents' remarks and judgements. As Henshall and McGuire (1986) put it, the cognitive developmentalists' view:

> ... fails to acknowledge the true nature of the social context in which children are developing and neatly diverts psychologists' attention from the possible effects of this context by locating the aspects of the situation worthy of attention firmly inside the child's head. It is possible, however, to maintain a cognitive approach without ignoring the true complexity of the social environment about which children are learning. Children are developing in an environment in which behaviour has meaning and intention, and they are learning not only *what* people do but *why* they do it.
>
> (Henshall and McGuire, 1986, p. 149)

We need to re-emphasize the *social context* in which gender is discussed and referred to if we are to make sense of the importance of gender to children. As Henshall and McGuire suggest, not only are children given guidance on their general behaviour, but they are also given explanations based on gender as a defining category. Dunn and Kendrick (1982), for example, have commented on how often the parents in their observational study picked up on remarks made by the children in their study about gender, and in particular how eager the parents were to correct confusion over gender terms (a tendency not apparent for other errors in the children's conversations). This can be seen in the following extract from a conversation between Marvin and his mother about his baby sister:

CHILD: ... (inaudible) boy.

MOTHER: She's not a boy. She's a little girl.

CHILD: Is she?

MOTHER: You're a little boy.

CHILD: Is she a girl?

MOTHER: Yes, a little girl.

CHILD: A little girl.

CHILD (to baby):   You messy. Messy.

MOTHER: She's a messy eater 'cause she's only a baby.

CHILD: Hallo, little fellow.

MOTHER: She's not a fellow.

CHILD: She a little girl. A little girl.

MOTHER: Yes, she's a little girl.

CHILD: Brenda good girl, aren't she?

MOTHER: Yes, and you're a good boy.

CHILD: Yes, Brenda good boy.

MOTHER: No, Brenda's a good *girl*.

CHILD: Brenda Ann, isn't she?

MOTHER: Mm. Brenda Ann ...

(Dunn and Kendrick, 1982, pp. 65–6)

Children do not acquire a sense of the social importance of gender only through such direct 'teaching', however. As was discussed in Chapter 3, socialization involves both active teaching *and* more indirect learning through observation. In the extract below from a mother's diary about her daughter, we can see that young Anneli has picked up messages from observing the behaviour and speech of others which suggest that, for example, being a boy is linked with a number of particular behaviours (such as knocking in nails) and being a girl means having considerably less power in relationships.

> At breakfast today Anneli (aged two and a half) talks about making a mess with food on the table and mentions that Felix does this. When I explain that Felix is smaller than she is, almost still a baby really (two months younger in fact) and that's why he can't eat properly yet, she says. 'But Felix is bigger than me, and Schorschi (one month younger) is as well.'
>
> I say, 'No, they're both smaller than you' to which she replies, 'No, they're boys and boys are bigger than me.'
>
> I'm shocked by this statement, since to Anneli being bigger means being able to do things and allowed to do them. I ask her who told her this. She says it was Barbara, Felix's mother. I don't believe this and can only imagine that she had misunderstood one mother saying to another that boys were bigger in size and interpreted this in terms of her expectations of life. Another of those ominous atmospheric items that help give boys an advantage and teach girls to respect the male and give them that insidious, lifelong inferiority complex.
>
> In the afternoon she's sitting in the lavatory chattering to herself. She says, 'Schorschi is a boy and I'm a girl.'
>
> I ask, 'What's Daddy?'
>
> She: 'A boy.'
>
> I: 'And what's Mummy?'
>
> She: 'A boy'. I laugh.
>
> When she comes back into the living room she says, 'Everybody's a boy. I'm the only girl.' She seems to have internalized a hierarchy in which the person on the bottom rung has to be a girl; all the others are boys.
>
> Later she's hammering nails with her little wooden mallet. She really enjoys it and I encourage her. Then she says, 'Just like Daddy.' I feel peeved because she's seen me knock in nails. But it can't have been enough.
>
> (from Marianne Grabrucker's diary of her daughter's first three years, *There's a Good Girl* (1988). Quoted in *New Internationalist*, February 1993, p. 15)

In instances such as this, children can be seen not only to be attempting to construct their own views on gender differences and gender appropriate behaviour but also as picking up the messages within their own culture about what it means to be a boy or a girl, to be masculine or feminine, and these messages can override their own direct experience.

Whiting and Edwards (1988) have examined the ways in which young children in different parts of the world become fully integrated into their culture and develop an understanding of the rules for behaviour considered appropriate by that culture. A very important part of this process is gender socialization, through which children become aware of the behaviour considered appropriate for girls and boys. Whiting and Edwards' extensive study was reported in Chapter 3 in the context of a discussion of the effects of maternal style on children's behaviour.

One important part of their study was the finding that children in many parts of the world understand at an early age the differential power of men and women in their society, just as in the quotation above from Anneli there were glimpses of her ideas about girls' and women's lack of power. Whiting and Edwards point to the struggles engaged in by 'yard boys' with their mothers, where these 7 to 10 year olds try to dominate their mothers and get away from their authority by leaving the home as much as possible, choosing same-sex playmates and refusing tasks which they see as 'women's work'. They found these conflicts particularly in Northern India, where, 'as the young boy becomes aware of his identity and the power of males, he tries out his relative power with his mother, who has been, along with all the other adult women in the courtyard, the person who has hand fed him and bathed him since he was born' (p. 237).

The next section looks in more detail at the influences of the various 'messages' about appropriate gender behaviour and characteristics which children receive, directly and indirectly, as they grow up.

4.3 Learning gender appropriate behaviour

Psychodynamic explanations

Theorists from several perspectives within psychology have suggested different means by which children come to appreciate what behaviour is deemed by their culture to be appropriate for them as girls or boys. The psychodynamic tradition, developed from Freud's work which mapped out stages in psychosexual development, has stressed the importance of the child *identifying* with the same-sex parent in the development of a clear sense of gender identity. In his theory of psychosexual development, Freud emphasized the role of very powerful instinctual urges, such as the sexual instinct, which drive the child to seek pleasurable experiences. These (unconscious) urges may well be socially inappropriate and lead the child to develop means of repressing them or diverting the energy in more acceptable directions. Freud suggested, for example, that around the age of 4, children overcome their anxiety about their (inappropriate) desire for their opposite-sex parent by identifying with the parent of the same sex. They aspire to the behaviours and characteristics of this parent and as a result adopt the culturally approved models of masculinity or femininity.

This brief description might seem to imply that the process of identification will be basically the same for girls and boys, but in fact Freud gave a much fuller account of this process in boys (where the task is to resolve the 'Oedipus complex' – the consequences of the boy's desire for his mother) and saw girls' experience as simply a mirror image of that of boys. More recently, object-relations theorists working within the psychodynamic tradition have attempted to give a fuller account of the process through which girls acquire their gender identity (e.g., Chodorow, 1978). These theorists place a much greater emphasis on the role played by close relationships in development than did Freud, who had emphasized biological urges or 'drives'. Object-relations theory suggests that the quality of early relationships, particularly with the mother (since she is usually the main caretaker), establishes a pattern for future close relationships, a template for how to relate to other people. Girls do not have to break away from this 'template' as they grow up; their model of relating is based on a woman like themselves and they come to see femininity and closeness in relationships as inextricably bound together. However, to develop as men, boys have to distance themselves from the model offered by their mothers and as a result masculinity becomes defined in terms of a lack of closeness in relationships, a distancing from that close and nurturing model offered by the mother.

Social learning theories

Identification is also seen as a key process in gender identity development by the social learning theorists who, although they had their roots in behaviourism, saw the importance of going beyond observable behaviour and simple reinforcement to explain such aspects of development.

> ... social learning theorists have operationalized identification by means of the modelling process. They have made this the cornerstone of their theory and have submitted it to extensive experimentation with the purpose of specifying more precisely how, when, and why it operates. Bandura, one of the main proponents of social learning theory, acknowledges that identification involves the acquisition of complex behaviours and motive systems, whereas imitation involves only the reproduction of discrete responses, but he consider them essentially the same process ... Identification-imitation develops through observational learning, not through reinforcement, and Bandura recognizes that motivation and self-regulation, that is, cognitive processes, play a crucial role in it.
>
> (Grusec and Lytton, 1988, p. 188)

A third theoretical approach to the development of a gender identity is that proposed by Sandra Bem in what is called gender schema theory. This contains features of both the cognitive developmental approach to the child's developing understanding of gender, described earlier, and the social learning accounts.

READING

You should now read the account given by Bem of her gender schema theory in the reading at the end of this chapter. It lays out the basic tenets of the theory and explains the common features that exist between this theory and the cognitive developmental and social learning theories. As you read Bem's account, you should consider the way in which she emphasizes children's 'internal' world of cognitive development as well as the influence of the social world around them.

The importance to Bem and social learning theorists of children's observation of the people around them (particularly parents) for the development of their views on gender appropriate behaviour is clear. One aspect of adults' behaviour, the way in which they respond differently to boys and girls, has received a good deal of research attention. Adults often buy boys and girls different toys, such as construction toys for boys and dolls for girls, but even when they buy children unisex or cross-sex toys, the *way* they interact with their children playing with these toys may still be different. They may be more enthusiastic when they join in play with same-sex toys, especially if the child is the same sex as themselves (since they can remember how such play is conducted from their own childhood) – thus unconsciously modelling what they see as gender appropriate behaviour.

Some cultures make more marked or more deliberate distinctions between how boys and girls are treated. Whiting and Edwards studied children's socialization in many parts of the world, including the ways in which gender is marked. As you read the extract below, you should consider the points of similarity to and difference from your own culture – perhaps in the clothing and attitudes to children helping with adult work.

> … One of the most obvious symbols of gender in all societies is the style of clothing of males and females. One of the ways in which mothers can accentuate differences is by making a distinction in the clothes, hairstyles, and adornments of girls and boys … For example, in Juxtlahuaca [Mexico] the ears of little girls are pierced during the first few weeks of life, and all females wear earrings. Young female knee children already have miniature *rebozas* (shawls), and little boys wear their *sombreros* with pride …
>
> … Some of the 4- and 5-year-olds who have earned the privilege of wearing more elaborate clothing, especially the girls, are obviously proud of their new gender-typed clothing. The Juxtlahuacan and North Indian girls seem to enjoy learning to manage *rebozas* and the miniature saris. Subsaharan girls like to try on the head scarves that women wear. The Juxtlahuacan boys constantly check the condition of their large hats, which they like to wear all the time. Tairan girls are proud of the

underpants they may now wear, often exposing them with bravado to their age mates. Orchard Town girls compare notes about their Sunday School and party-going apparel …

The division of labor by gender in the adult world that exists in all societies is also obvious to observant children. When it is possible, some of the parents in our samples call attention to the adult division of labor by assigning different types of chores to girls and boys …

In many societies in the world, the care of large animals is the task that is considered masculine, and young boys can participate in this work beginning at age 4 or 5. In Tarong the care and use of the carabao (water buffalo) are considered to be in the domain of men, and all three of the 4- and 5-year-old boys in the sample were observed watering and grazing carabao. No girls were observed caring for these animals.

(Whiting and Edwards, 1988, pp. 219–25)

In Western societies, many parents are attempting to raise their children in a way which makes fewer such distinctions between girls and boys, and, particularly, between what are appropriate behaviours and aspirations for boys and girls. However, this is not an easy task given the images and messages passed on to children through the media from wider society, and indeed the pressure from peers who may have different views and parents with different approaches to the gender socialization of their children.

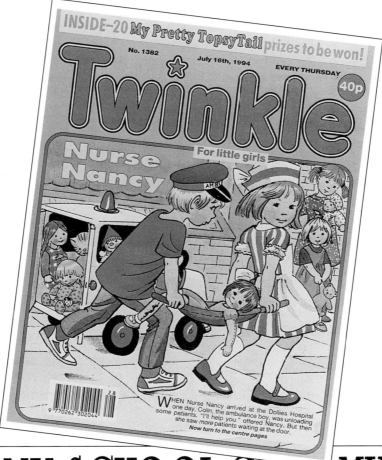

ACTIVITY 4

Allow about 1 hour

MEDIA IMAGES

Gather together some current children's books, comics and/or videos of children's TV programmes, including cartoon programmes. Look at how boys and girls are presented in these different sources, focusing on: the typical behaviours they each engage in (aggression, nurturance, problem-solving, conformity, physically exertive behaviour); what roles they take (central character, secondary character or minor character); perhaps also the type of language they use. If you have access to some old children's books or comics, you could compare the types of behaviours and language used by boys and girls in those.

You might also like to look at adverts between children's TV programmes for a set period (a good time to choose is in the morning at weekends). Note down the numbers of girls and boys shown, the activities they are engaged in, and the products they are promoting.

Are there any differences between the images of boys and girls presented by these various sources? If you found such differences, where were they most marked – in the behaviours, roles, appearance or language of the male and female characters? Were there differences in how the different sources portrayed girls and boys? Were there examples which deliberately tried to avoid or confront gender stereotypes (such as Babette Cole's *Prince Cinders* book)? How might you go about investigating the issue of gender stereotypes in the media in more detail? Try to come up with one or two further research ideas.

Comment

This activity is designed to highlight the types of images children are exposed to in their everyday lives and to give some concrete examples for our discussion of social messages of appropriate behaviour for girls and boys.

This is obviously not a reliable study of media images of gender stereotypes. If you want to go further, you should look at Durkin, 1985, for a review of more thorough research. Durkin's book might also give you some ideas for future research. The book *Frogs and Snails and Feminist Tales* by Davies (1989) is also useful, since it reports research examining young children's reactions to deliberately non-traditionally stereotypical characters in children's books.

Despite the preponderance of stereotypical views of gender roles in material targeted at children, some parents have tried to socialize their children in a non-sexist way. A study of their efforts was carried out by Statham (1986) and is reported in Research summary 3 (overleaf).

Sandra Bem (1983), in an extension of her work on gender schema theory (explained in the reading), has suggested that such attempts to counteract gender stereotypes in society are unlikely to be successful as they do not place enough emphasis on giving children alternative ways

> ## RESEARCH SUMMARY 3
> ## NON-SEXIST CHILDRAISING
>
> Statham interviewed parents who were trying to raise their children in a non-sexist way. The parents reported that they tried to provide their children with non-sexist toys, clothes, and books. In general, the parents of boys expressed less concern over the role of toys and clothes in perpetuating traditional stereotypes than the parents of girls. Statham suggested that this was perhaps because, in modern Western societies, making girls aware of sex-role stereotypes allows them to seek greater equality, whereas making boys aware of these stereotypes requires them to forgo some of their privileges.
>
> As one father put it:
>
> 'I tend to see what you'd do with a boy as making him more able to accept the feminine in himself and believe in it and not suppress it. I tend not to see it as opening up many more options in society for a boy, by being more feminine.'
>
> (John Noble, in Statham, 1986, p. 92)
>
> Although parents' aims for their sons and daughters were similar – that they should be independent *and* caring, sensitive *and* adventurous, able to develop their potential in feminine *and* masculine areas – the way in which parents *could* socialize their children was very much influenced by the society in which they lived. In particular, the parents felt it was less acceptable for a boy to develop non-traditional sex roles than for a girl. Although parents felt there were such limitations to non-sexist childrearing, all the parents in Statham's study were very committed to it and hoped that by changing their children's attitudes they would contribute to wider social change.

of organizing and assimilating gender-related information. She suggests that children not only need to be made aware of individual differences between people (to counter arguments such as 'all girls like playing with dolls' with 'Susan next door doesn't like dolls, but your cousin Peter does'), but also need to appreciate cultural relativism – that 'different people believe different things'. This allows children to accept that the contradictory beliefs frequently co-exist, so that, for example, the rules and values of their family may be different from those of the family next door, but both are valid. It also teaches them that cultural messages reflect the beliefs of the person or people who created the messages, and explaining this to them can help 'frame' stories such as traditional fairy tales in such a way that the messages contained in them about men and women are seen as constructions, not as facts.

Bem goes further, however, claiming that it is not enough for parents wishing to raise non-sexist children to imply that all ideas about gender are equally valid. Instead, she suggests that children need to be given a 'sexism schema' in order to oppose 'the gender-related constraints that those with a gender schema will inevitably seek to impose' (Bem, 1983, p. 615). She cites an example of a developing sexism schema from her own daughter's reaction to Norma Klein's book, *Girls Can Be Anything*.

One of the characters is Adam Sobel, who insists that 'girls are always nurses and boys are always doctors' and that 'girls can't be pilots ... they have to be stewardesses'. After reading this book, our daughter, then aged four, spontaneously began to label with contempt anyone who voiced stereotypical beliefs about gender an 'Adam Sobel'. Adam Sobel thus became for her the nucleus of an evolving sexism schema, a schema that enables her now to perceive – and also to become morally outraged by and to oppose – whatever sex discrimination she meets in daily life.

(Bem, 1983, p. 615)

Ending on this discussion of attempts to raise children in a non-sexist way pulls out several of the key themes in this section. The importance of several different levels of influence on children's gender development is clear. We have looked at internal, cognitive processes in children's development, as well as interpersonal influences (for example in family discussions when playing with particular toys or reading together) and wider social influences about what is considered appropriate for males and females. Different views about appropriate behaviour can be found not only across cultures, but also within a culture, with different emphases being put on the importance of conforming to traditional views of appropriate behaviour.

SUMMARY OF SECTION 4

- The social and cultural aspects of gender are of great importance to a child's developing sense of (categorical) self and in defining appropriate behaviour for boys and girls.

- Children seem to have a good working definition of their own gender by the age of two, correctly labelling themselves as a girl or boy, but it is not until later that they understand that gender is a stable concept. Finally, children gain an understanding of gender constancy.

- Freud's view of gender identity development stresses the influence of instinctual urges, played out in interaction between the child and parents. Some of his followers have departed from this view, particularly from his account of girls' development, and have suggested that more emphasis should be placed on the child's early relationships and the process of separation from the mother.

- Social learning theory suggests that gender-role learning occurs through the imitation of models. Parental reaction to the child's behaviour and other models of male and female behaviour are therefore important influences on the child's developing sense of gender identity.

- Attempts to raise children in a non-sexist way have encountered some difficulties, often as a result of societal pressures to conform. However, Bem's work on gender schemas suggests ways in which children can be encouraged to challenge such pressures.

5 REFLECTING ON THE SELF: SELF-DESCRIPTIONS AND SELF-ESTEEM

We have been looking at gender as an example of the categorical self (Section 2). As was discussed there, many of the categories a child comes to label herself with seem to be very dependent on the people around her. For example, in order to categorize herself as 'shy', 'clever', 'feminine' or even 'tall', she has to either compare herself with other people (on a physical level, e.g., height, or on more abstract levels), or consider their evaluations of her. She will find that some categories are actually *defined* socially (such as 'shy') and could not be assessed independently at all, but depend on others assigning a label based on cultural views of appropriate or 'normal' behaviour. Gender is a particularly strong example of this, as we have seen in Section 4: cultural expectations of what it is appropriate for a girl or boy to do can have a very strong impact on the child's developing personal identity.

A study by Bannister and Agnew confirmed the importance of these two sources of information about the self – other people's assessments, and comparisons of one's own abilities and actions with those of others (see Research summary 4).

In this final section of the chapter we will be considering further how children use this contrast between self and other(s) to develop an increasingly complex understanding of themselves. In the theoretical framework discussed earlier in Sections 1 and 2, we saw how Mead and others viewed developments in self-understanding as clearly located in a social context. The child understands more about herself as she learns about the characteristics of people around her and as she in turn discovers the way these others view her. This section looks at the way in which children's self-descriptions change as they become more able to

---

**RESEARCH SUMMARY 4
BECOMING AWARE OF THE SELF**

Bannister and Agnew asked adults to recall how they had first become aware of themselves as individuals when they were children. The adults mentioned such events as:

- being able to see someone who could not see them,
- doing something their mother would not know about until she was told,
- becoming aware of differences between their own possessions and those of others,
- being mocked by an adult for not being able to perform a task.

Common to all the instances recalled was the contrast between self and others that came either through a judgement made by others or through comparisons with them.

(Bannister and Agnew, 1977)

take account of the information about themselves available from others and how they evaluate themselves and develop a sense of self-worth and self-esteem.

5.1 Describing the self

In part of their study, Bannister and Agnew (1977) examined how children come to see themselves as individuals, as *psychologically* separate from others (see Research summary 5). This can be seen as an extension of the process discussed in Section 2 whereby infants come to see themselves as *physically* distinct from others.

Bannister and Agnew suggested that these results supported their view that children become gradually better able to distinguish themselves psychologically from others as they get older. Children do not just become, in a global sense, more able to distinguish themselves as individuals, they actually seem to think about themselves in different *ways* as they get older. When Bannister and Agnew asked the children *how* they knew whether a statement was one they had made themselves, it was apparent that the younger children were using different types of strategies to identify their own statements from those used by the older children. The younger children said they remembered that they had made a statement, or chose it as one of theirs if, for example, they typically enjoyed the activity being spoken about. Older children judged the *psychological appropriateness* of a statement and the logical possibility of it applying to them. This supported evidence from Bannister and Agnew's direct questioning of the children about how they were alike and different from other children: the younger children typically focused on physical features, activities and behaviours, whereas the older children mentioned more psychological characteristics.

This progression from physical to psychological descriptions of the self has been found in other studies of children's self-descriptions. In one study, Rosenberg (1979) interviewed 10–18 year olds about themselves, asking questions such as how they were seen by themselves and others, how they would like to be and how they differed from other children.

RESEARCH SUMMARY 5
TALKING ABOUT THE SELF

Bannister and Agnew put together groups of six children aged between 5 and 9 years old and asked them questions about their favourite activities, friends, teachers, other adults and themselves. Each of the statements was then re-recorded in a random order with a single adult's voice, omitting clues as to the identity of the speaker. Four months later, the children were asked to listen to the tape of the adult speaking, and to identify the statements which they themselves had made in the original discussion. The 5 year olds correctly identified only 40 per cent of their own statements, but the 9 year olds were more accurate – they were correct in 60 per cent of cases.

Rosenberg categorized the responses to these and other questions and looked at the proportion of responses falling into each category across the age range of children. Harter's review of this and other similar studies describes Rosenberg's results:

> The younger children ... describe a world of behavior, objective facts, overt achievements, manifested preferences, possessions, physical attributes, and membership categories ... the child's self-descriptors are limited to characteristics that could potentially be described by others.
>
> With development comes the emergence and increasing use of dispositions and traits to define the self ...
>
> The earliest trait descriptions tend to focus on qualities of character (brave, honest), emotional characteristics (happy, cheerful), and emotional control (don't get into fights or lose my temper). With increasing age, there is greater emphasis on *interpersonal* traits, for example, friendly, outgoing, shy, sociable, well-liked, kind, considerate, traits that include being attracted to others, being attractive to others, and possessing interpersonal virtues ...
>
> The oldest subjects in Rosenberg's sample, extending to age 18, typically described themselves in terms of their 'psychological interior', a world of emotions, attitudes, wishes and secrets. The self-reflective gaze is turned inward toward the private and invisible ...
>
> (Harter, 1983, p. 299)

ACTIVITY 5
Allow about 35 minutes

DEVELOPMENTAL SEQUENCES IN SELF-DESCRIPTIONS

Allow about 20 minutes initially, and a further 10 to 15 minutes to elicit each self-description.

Go back to the self-descriptions in Example 1 (p. 189) and consider them in terms of the developmental sequence which Rosenberg suggested. Look at the elements you drew out of the self-descriptions for Activity 1 (e.g., extent of reference to other people, psychological versus physical descriptions of the self, extent of evaluation of the self). What are the differences between the children's self-descriptions on these types of dimensions?

If you are able to ask some other children to talk about themselves, collect more examples of these types of self-descriptions (first asking permission from the children's parents). Try to elicit self-descriptions from children from a range of ages. It is helpful to ask children to try to come up with answers to a question such as 'Who am I?', rather than asking them to just give an open-ended description of themselves. This is particularly true for younger children who might find the idea of describing themselves quite difficult.

One you have elicited some self-descriptions, compare them with those at the beginning of the chapter and with Rosenberg's suggested developmental sequence.

Recently the study of accounts such as the ones in Example 1 has led to the suggestion that the self only in fact exists in such narratives – these are not descriptions of some inner 'real' self, but are constructions which change across time and in different situations. These ideas about narrative have their roots in philosophy and the humanities, but they are increasingly being drawn on by psychologists such as Bruner (1986) to emphasize that the self is not to be regarded as 'a thing', but as situated *within discourse*, within the communication between people (either directly or through means such as autobiographies). 'The self, after all, is not a thing; it is not a substance, a material entity that we can somehow grab hold of and place before our very eyes' (Freeman, 1993, p. 8).

From this view, the children providing the self-descriptions in Example 1 were involved in *creating a self* as they gave their accounts – they were putting their thoughts and experiences into a coherent narrative for their audience, and may have created a different version for a different audience. Studying such attempts to make sense of ourselves and create narratives of our life has become an important area within social and developmental psychology, emphasizing the importance of the continuing creation and re-creation of our 'self' throughout our lives, through interaction and relationship with others. From this view, we never arrive at a point where we can say our self is 'established', since other versions will develop with each new discussion or reflection upon new experiences.

6 CONCLUSION

Children become more sophisticated in their understanding of themselves as they acquire more complex understandings of how other people think and also as they begin to take more account of how they themselves are perceived and evaluated by others. The complex interplay between children's developing understanding of the self and of others is discussed further in an article by Harter (1983). She draws on the distinction made by Mead and James between the 'I' and the 'me' (introduced in Section 2 above) to suggest how the child moves from observing others to being able to reflect on the self as seen by others – the 'I' evaluating the 'me'.

As we reach the end of this chapter, it is appropriate to return to the self-descriptions in Example 1 and to the distinction between the 'I' and the 'me'. Many of the concepts and processes we have been examining are linked together and linked in turn to the subject matter of the other chapters in this book. The ways in which children construct a view of themselves are inextricably bound up with their developing understanding of other people around them and of the web of relationships in which they live. Their feelings of self-worth are not only cognitive constructions but also social and emotional. While the focus of this chapter has been on what seems to be an entirely personal feature (the development of a sense of self) it should be clear that it is essential to study this within a social, cognitive *and* emotional context.

FURTHER READING

DUNN, J. (1988) *The Beginnings of Social Understanding*, Oxford, Blackwell.

HARTER, S. (1988) 'The determinants and mediational role of global self-worth in children' in EISENBERG, N. (ed.) *Contemporary Topics in Developmental Psychology*, New York, Wiley-Interscience.

LEWIS, M. and BROOKS-GUNN, J. (1979) *Social Cognition and the Acquisition of Self*, New York, Plenum.

MACCOBY, E. E. (1990) 'Gender and relationships. A developmental account', *American Psychologist*, **45**, pp. 513–20.

RYMER, R. (1993) *Genie*, Harmondsworth, Penguin Books.

STATHAM, J. (1986) *Daughters and Sons: experiences of non-sexist childraising*, Oxford, Basil Blackwell Ltd.

REFERENCES

ATKINSON, D. and WILLIAMS, F. (eds) (1990) *'Know Me As I Am'. An anthology of prose, poetry and art by people with learning difficulties*, London, Hodder and Stoughton/The Open University.

BALDWIN, J. M. (1897) *Social and Ethical Interpretations in Mental Development*, New York, Macmillan.

BANNISTER, D. and AGNEW, J. (1977) 'The child's construing of self' in COLE, J. (ed.) *Nebraska Symposium on Motivation*, Lincoln, University of Nebraska Press.

BEM, S. (1983) 'Gender schema theory: a cognitive account of sex typing', *Psychological Review*, **88** (4), pp. 354–64.

BRONSON, W. C. (1975) 'Developments in behaviour with age mates during the second year of life' in LEWIS, M. and ROSENBLUM, L. A. (eds) *The Origins of Behaviour: friendship and peer relations*, New York.

BRUNER, J. (1986) *Actual Minds: possible worlds*, Cambridge (Mass.), Harvard University Press

CHODOROW, N. (1978) *The Reproduction of Mothering,* London, University of California Press.

COOLEY, C.H. (1902) *Human Nature and the Social Order*, New York, Scribner.

COOPERSMITH, S. (1967) *The Antecedents of Self-esteem*, San Francisco, Freeman.

DAMON, W. and HART, D. (1988) *Self Understanding in Childhood and Adolescence*, Cambridge, Cambridge University Press.

DAVIES, B. (1989) *Frogs and Snails and Feminist Tales*, Sydney, Allen and Unwin.

DUNN, J. (1988) *The Beginnings of Social Understanding*, Oxford, Blackwell.

DUNN, J. and KENDRICK, C. (1982) *Siblings: love, envy and understanding*, Cambridge (Mass.), Harvard University Press.

DURKIN, K. (1985) *Television, Sex Roles and Children*, Milton Keynes, Open University Press.

FREEMAN, M. (1993) *Rewriting the Self: history, memory and narrative*, London, Routledge.

GEERTZ, C. (1984) 'From the natives' point of view. On the nature of anthropological understanding' in SCHWEDER, R. and LEVINE, R. A. (eds) *Culture Theory: essays on mind, self, emotion*, Cambridge, Cambridge University Press.

GRABRUCKER, M. (1988) *There's a Good Girl*, London, The Women's Press.

GRUSEK, J. E. and LYTTON, H. (1988) *Social Development. History, theory and research*, New York, Springer-Verlag.

HARTER, S. (1983) 'Developmental perspectives on the self-system' in MUSSEN, P. H. (ed.) *Handbook of Child Psychology*, vol. 4, New York, Wiley.

HARTER, S. (1986) 'Processes underlying the construction, maintenance and enhancement of the self-concept in children' in SULS, J. and GREENWALD, A. G. (eds) *Psychological Perspectives on the Self*, vol. 3, Hillsdale (New Jersey), Lawrence Erlbaum.

HARTER, S. (1988) 'The determinations and mediational role of global self-worth in children' in EISENBERG, N. (ed.) *Contemporary Topics in Developmental Psychology*, New York, Wiley-Interscience.

HENSHALL, C. and McGUIRE, J. (1986) 'Gender development' in RICHARDS, M. and LIGHT, P.(eds), *Children of Social Worlds*, Cambridge, Polity Press.

JAMES, W. (1892) *Psychology; the briefer course*, New York (published in 1961 by Harper and Row).

KOHLBERG, L. (1966) 'A cognitive developmental analysis of children's sex-role concepts and attitudes' in MACCOBY, E. (ed.) *The Development of Sex Differences*, Stanford (Calif.), Stanford University Press.

KOHLBERG, L. and ZIGLER, E. (1967) 'The impact of cognitive maturity on the development of sex-role attitudes in the years 4 to 18', *Genetic Psychology Monographs*, **75**, pp. 89–165.

KUHN, D., NASH, S. and BRUCKEN, L. (1978) 'Sex role concepts of two and three year olds', *Child Development*, **49**, pp. 445–51.

LAMB, M. E. (1977) 'The development of parental preferences in the first two years of life', *Sex Roles*, **3**, pp. 495–7.

LANE, H. (1977) *The Wild Boy of Aveyron*, Cambridge (Mass.), Harvard University Press.

LEWIS, M. (1990) 'Social knowledge and social development', *Merrill-Palmer Quarterly*, **36**, pp. 93–116.

LEWIS, M. and BROOKS-GUNN, J. (1979) *Social Cognition and the Acquisition of Self*, New York, Plenum Press.

MACCOBY, E. (1980) *Social Development, Psychological Growth and the Parent–Child Relationship*, New York, Harcourt Brace Jovanovich.

MEAD, G. H. (1934) *Mind, Self and Society*, Chicago, University of Chicago Press.

THE OPEN UNIVERSITY (1991) D103 *Society and Social Science: a foundation course*, Block 5 *Identities and Interaction*, Unit 20 *Social Identity*, Milton Keynes, The Open University.

PIAGET, J. (1976) *Judgement and Reasoning in the Child*, New York, Harcourt Brace Jovanovich (first published 1928).

ROSENBERG, M. (1979) *Conceiving the Self*, New York, Basic Books.

RYMER, R. (1993) *Genie*, Harmondsworth, Penguin Books.

SELMAN, R. (1980) *The Growth of Interpersonal Understanding*, New York, Academic Press.

STATHAM, J. (1986) *Daughters and Sons: experiences of non-sexist childraising*, Oxford, Basil Blackwell Ltd.

TURNER, R. H. (1968) 'The self-conception in social interaction' in GORDON, C. and GERGEN, K. J. (eds) *The Self in Social Interaction*, vol. 1, New York, Wiley.

VASTA, R., HAITH, M. and MILLER, S. (1992) *Child Psychology: the modern science*, New York, Wiley.

WHITE, D. and WOOLLETT, A. (1992) *Families: a context for development*, London, Falmer Press.

WHITING, B., and EDWARDS, C. (1988) *Children of Different Worlds: the formation of social behaviour*, Cambridge (Mass.), Harvard University Press.

YAWKEY, T. and JOHNSON, J. (1988) *Integrative Processes and Socialization*, Hove, Lawrence Erlbaum Associates.

READING

Gender schema theory

Sandra Bem

Gender schema theory proposes that sex typing derives in large measure from gender-schematic processing, from a generalized readiness on the part of the child to encode and to organize information – including information about the self-according to the culture's definitions of maleness and femaleness. Like cognitive-developmental theory, then, gender schema theory proposes that sex typing is mediated by the child's own cognitive processing. However, gender schema theory further proposes that gender-schematic processing is itself derived from the sex-differentiated practices of the social community. Thus, like social learning theory, gender schema theory assumes that sex typing is a learned phenomenon and, hence, that it is neither inevitable nor unmodifiable ...

Gender-schematic processing

Gender schema theory begins with the observation that the developing child invariably learns his or her society's cultural definitions of femaleness and maleness. In most societies, these definitions comprise a diverse and sprawling network of sex-linked associations encompassing not only those features directly related to female and male persons – such as anatomy, reproductive function, division of labour, and personality attributes – but also features more remotely or metaphorically related to sex, such as the angularity or roundness of an abstract shape and the periodicity of the moon. Indeed, no other dichotomy in human experience appears to have as many entities linked to it as does the distinction between female and male.

But there is more. Gender schema theory proposes that, in addition to learning such content-specific information about gender, the child also learns to invoke this heterogeneous network of sex-related associations in order to evaluate and assimilate new information. The child in short, learns to encode and to organize information in terms of an evolving gender schema.

A schema is a cognitive structure, a network of associations that organizes and guides an individual's perception. A schema functions as an anticipatory structure, a readiness to search for and to assimilate incoming information in schema-relevant terms. Schematic information processing is thus highly selective and enables the individual to impose structure and meaning onto a vast array of incoming stimuli. More specifically, schematic information processing entails a readiness to sort information into categories on the basis of some particular dimension, despite the existence of other dimensions that could serve equally well in this regard. Gender-schematic processing in particular thus involves spontaneously sorting attributes and behaviours into masculine and feminine categories or 'equivalence classes', regardless of their differences on a variety of dimensions unrelated to gender, for example, spontaneously placing items like 'tender' and 'nightingale' into a feminine category and items like 'assertive' and 'eagle' into a masculine category.

Like schema theories generally, gender schema theory thus construes perception as a constructive process in which the interaction between incoming information and individual's pre-existing schema determines what is perceived.

What gender schema theory proposes, then, is that the phenomenon of sex typing derives, in part, from gender-schematic processing, from an individual's generalized readiness to process information on the basis of the sex-linked associations that constitute the gender schema. Specifically, the theory proposes that sex typing results, in part, from the assimilation of the self-concept itself to the gender schema. As children learn the contents of their society's gender schema, they learn which attributes are to be linked with their own sex and, hence, with themselves. This does not simply entail learning the defined relationship between each sex and each dimension or attribute – that boys are to be strong and girls weak, for example – but involves the deeper lesson that the dimensions themselves are differentially applicable to the two sexes. Thus the strong-weak dimension itself is absent from the schema to be applied to girls just as the dimension of nurturance is implicitly omitted from the schema to be applied to boys. Adults in the child's world rarely notice or remark upon how strong a little girl is becoming or how nurturant a little boy is becoming, despite their readiness to note precisely these attributes in the 'appropriate' sex. The child learns to apply this same schematic selectivity to the self, to choose from among the many possible dimensions of human personality only that subset defined as applicable to his or her own sex and thereby eligible for organizing the diverse contents of the self-concept. Thus do children's self-concepts become sex typed, and thus do the two sexes become, in their own eyes, not only different in degree, but different in kind.

Simultaneously, the child also learns to evaluate his or her adequacy as a person according to the gender schema, to match his or her preferences, behaviours, and personal attributes against the prototypes stored within it. The gender schema becomes a prescriptive standard or guide, and self-esteem becomes its hostage. Here, then, enters an internalized motivational factor that prompts an individual to regulate his or her behaviour so that it conforms to cultural definitions of femaleness and maleness. Thus do cultural myths become self-fulfilling prophecies, and thus, according to gender schema theory, do we arrive at the phenomenon known as sex typing.

Source: Bem, S.L. (1983) 'Gender schema theory and its implications for child development: raising gender-schematic children in a gender-schematic society', Signs: Journal of Women in Culture and Society, *8(4), pp. 598–616.*

Dorothy Faulkner

CONTENTS

1	**INTRODUCTION**	**232**
1.1	Play: categories and definitions	233
	Summary of Section 1	238
2	**THEORETICAL ACCOUNTS OF PLAY**	**239**
2.1	Piaget's theory	239
2.2	Vygotsky's theory	241
2.3	Mead's theory	242
	Summary of Section 2	245
3	**PLAY AND THE DEVELOPMENT OF SOCIAL UNDERSTANDING IN YOUNG CHILDREN**	**246**
3.1	The development of social perspective-taking skills	247
3.2	The development of social competence	249
3.3	Explanations and models	252
	Summary of Section 3	254
4	**THE CONTENT OF PLAY**	**254**
4.1	Socio-dramatic play	255
4.2	Gender and cultural identity	257
4.3	Scripts and socio-dramatic play	259
4.4	Thematic fantasy play	260
4.5	Playing at society	263
	Summary of Section 4	264
5	**PLAY AND GAMES IN MIDDLE CHILDHOOD**	**265**
5.1	Researching playground behaviour	267
5.2	Play and moral development	272
5.3	Criticisms of Piaget's theory of moral development	274
	Summary of Section 5	276
6	**CONCLUSION**	**276**
	COMMENTS ON ACTIVITIES	**278**
	FURTHER READING	**278**
	REFERENCES	**279**
	READING A: TYPES OF PLAY	**283**
	READING B: STAGES IN THE DEVELOPMENT OF THE SELF	**284**
	READING C: MRS COMPHRET – AN IMAGINARY COMPANION	**285**

OBJECTIVES

When you have studied this chapter, you should be able to:

1 compare and contrast the different functions of play suggested by the theories of Piaget, Vygotsky and Mead and evaluate the status of these theories in the light of research evidence;

2 outline research on socio-dramatic play and explain how this is related to the development of social competence;

3 discuss the evidence that children reveal their knowledge about society through play, and also claims that play acts as an anticipatory socialization device;

4 outline the significance of thematic fantasy play for children's personal and emotional development;

5 discuss alternative explanations of the role of playground games and peer interaction in social and moral development;

6 explain how research on children's early experiences within the family might modify claims about the importance of play for social development.

1 INTRODUCTION

Granting that childhood is playhood, how do we adults generally relate to this fact? We *ignore* it. We forget all about it – because play, to us, is a waste of time. Hence we erect a large city school with many rooms and expensive apparatus for teaching; but more often than not, all we offer to the play instinct is a small concrete space.

(Neill, 1962, p. 68)

In 1920 A. S. Neill and his wife founded a residential school called Summerhill where children did not sit at desks all day, where they were free to play or to engage in lessons and classroom activities as they wished. Neill wanted to create a learning environment which genuinely fitted the needs of children, rather than one based on adult conceptions of what children ought to be like and of what they want to learn. He believed that play, particularly 'fantasy' play, was of the greatest importance for children's social, intellectual and moral development.

Neill, of course, was not the only educationist to recognize the importance of play for children's development. In western Europe, what Peter Smith (1988) terms the 'play ethos' steadily grew in importance during the early part of the twentieth century. In the UK, this was led by pioneers of nursery education such as Susan Isaacs and Margaret McMillan, whose child- and play-centred philosophies were inspired by the nineteenth-century educational theorists Froebel in Germany and

Dewey in the US (see Bruce, 1991, for a detailed history). Susan Isaacs was so convinced of the value of play that she claimed that 'play indeed is the child's work, and the means by which he or she develops' (Isaacs, 1929). Her philosophy and writings continue to influence nursery education in the UK to the present day.

While most developmental psychologists would also agree that play is important for children's development, especially during the early years, Peter Smith (1994) points out that there is still insufficient firm, empirical evidence on the benefits of play for children's social and cognitive development. The view that play is important for development is still controversial and many teachers and parents are uncomfortable with the idea that play should have a place in the school curriculum, particularly after children have started their formal education.

Much of the research on play has concentrated on the question of whether or not it has an important role in *cognitive* development (e.g. Hutt *et al.,* 1989; Sylva *et al.,* 1980). This chapter, however, will examine the claim that play is important for *social* development, and will look at what the study of play and peer interaction can tell us about socialization and the development of social competence in early and middle childhood (that is, between the ages of 2 and about 10). As far as the question of whether children need to play in order to develop socially is concerned, three positions seem possible:

- play has a major causal role in development. Young children learn as much, or more, about social skills and interpersonal relationships through play as they do from other types of social interaction;

- play has its place in development, but other types of social experience have equally important causative roles in the development of children's social understanding;

- play itself is of little consequence for social development, it merely allows children to practise and consolidate the social skills they have already acquired through other means.

In this chapter I shall present evidence which supports the first two of these positions, and you will have to make up your own mind as to which of the two you find more convincing, based on your reading of this and other chapters in this book. I hope the evidence here will convince you that the third position is untenable.

1.1 Play: categories and definitions

One of the earliest studies of children's social participation in play was carried out in the US by Mildred Parten in 1932. She observed 2- to 5-year-old children's play at their nursery school when they were allowed to play by themselves without adult guidance or intervention. She identified four categories of play which differed in terms of the amount of social participation the children engaged in during these free play sessions: solitary independent play; parallel activity; associative play; and co-operative play. Parten's definition of these categories is given in Research Summary 1.

RESEARCH SUMMARY 1
PARTEN'S PLAY CATEGORIES

Solitary independent play: The child plays alone and independently with toys that are different from those used by the children within speaking distance and makes no effort to get close to other children. He pursues his own activity without reference to what others are doing.

Parallel activity: The child plays independently, but the activity he chooses naturally brings him among other children. He plays with toys that are like those which the children around him are using but he plays with the toys as he sees fit, and does not try to influence or modify the activity of the children near him. He plays *beside* rather than *with* the other children. There is no attempt to control the coming or going of the children in the group.

Associative play: The child plays with other children. The conversation concerns the common activity; there is a borrowing or loaning of play material; following one another with trains or wagons; mild attempts to control which children may or may not play in the group. All the members engage in similar if not identical activity; there is no division of labour, and no organization of the activity of several individuals around any material goal or product. The children do not subordinate their individual interests to that of the group, instead each child acts as he wishes. By his conversation with the other children one can tell that his interest is primarily in his associations, not in his activity. [...]

Co-operative or organized supplementary play: The child plays in a group that is organized for the purpose of making some material product, or striving to attain some competitive goal, or of dramatizing situations of adult and group life, or of playing formal games. There is a marked sense of belonging or of not belonging to the group. The control of the group situation is in the hands of one or two of the group members who direct the activity of the others. The goal as well as the method of attaining it necessitates a division of labour, taking of different roles by the various group members and the organization of activity so that the efforts of one child are supplemented by those of another.

(Parten, 1932/33, pp. 243–69, cited in Irwin and Bushnell, 1980, pp. 169–270)

As well as discriminating between these four different types of play activity, Parten's observations also showed that there was a developmental sequence to children's behaviour. The younger children were more often to be observed in solitary or parallel play situations, whereas the 4 and 5 year olds spent more time in associative or co-operative play. Although her observational system was devised as long ago as 1932, it is still frequently used by researchers interested in the development of children's social participation in play (e.g. Sylva *et al.*, 1980), and the categories she came up with have proved to be extremely reliable.

Here I shall concentrate on describing research which has looked at play and games involving social participation between pairs or groups of

children rather than solitary, parallel or associative play, as the main focus of the chapter is on an examination of how children's developing social skills affect their understanding of themselves and others.

Chapter 5 has already introduced you to psychological perspectives on the development of children's concept of self. One of the things I shall concentrate on in this chapter is the function of play and games in the development of the self. I shall also look at what the form and content of children's collaborative play and games at different ages can tell us about their conceptions of the social world and the social rules and conventions by which it is organized.

As I pointed out at the beginning of this introduction, psychologists are still divided as to whether the experience of play is a causal factor in children's social development. If it is, then one might expect that the social skills of children who (for whatever reason) have limited opportunities to play with other children will be different from those of children who have plenty of such opportunities. If, on the other hand, play is just one of a number of different experiences which allows children to develop further social skills and concepts acquired through other types of interactions, then children who have limited play experiences will not necessarily be disadvantaged in terms of their social development. You should bear these two perspectives in mind as you read this chapter.

But what do we mean by 'play'? Parten's categories describe different levels of social participation in play, but they do not really tell us much about what children *do* when they are playing, or what different types of play experiences mean to children. When I asked my own daughters, aged 8 and 6, why they thought it was important for children to play, they said that you play because it's enjoyable and because it makes you happy. The older one said that you could make friends through play, and that you could learn new games. The younger one said that when you 'pretended' you could be different people, and play at doing grown-up things. When I asked them about 'playtime' at school they gave me a fairly detailed account of how their school playground was organized in terms of the games that were played and how the space was divided up between the younger and older children and the boys and girls.

For my two children, then, play is about friendship, enjoyment, pretending and playing games. When psychologists have attempted to categorize the forms and functions of play, however, the picture has not always been so clear cut. Reading A outlines some of the distinctions which psychologists have drawn up as a result of their observations of play.

READING

In Reading A, Peter Smith, a leading expert on children's play, describes various categories of behaviour which come under the heading of play. In this chapter we will be concentrating on 'symbolic play', 'role-play', 'socio-dramatic play', and 'play with rules', and you should make careful note of the descriptions of these, and of Smith's discussion of the developmental skills associated with each. The particular terms which Smith has chosen to describe different types of play are not the only ones in current use. In the case of what he describes as 'role-play' and 'socio-dramatic play' in particular, a variety of other terms such as 'fantasy play', 'pretend play', and 'imaginative play' are also used.

ACTIVITY 1

Allow about 20 minutes

PLAYING WITH DEFINITIONS

The following observations and transcripts of conversations are all examples of children playing. First, decide which of Smith's categories of play the examples fit best (if they do), then identify some of the social skills you think the children in the examples may be learning.

(a) In the following extract Johnathan and Genevive (both aged 4) enact a 'birth fantasy':

    J: Pretend I was inside your stomach.

    G: You got out of my stomach and you popped out. You were just a little baby. Pop!

    J: Pop!

    G: And you went 'Waa…waa…waa'.

    J: And you did 'Moo-ma, moo-ma'.

    G: Oh stay that way little baby, you'd better.

    J: Naa, naa, naa. Let me get out of your stomach.

    G: And you can't get on the stomach, You're pulling, you're pulling my stomach apart, little bubba, bubba.

    J: Bubba, bubba, bubba ba, ba, bubba, ba, ba.

    G: [Laughs and giggles] Wait! Stop! You're wiggling around [Laughing]!

(Gottman, 1986, p. 166)

(b) The following extract is an example of the many detailed observations that the Swiss psychologist, Jean Piaget, made of his own children's play. In this observation, Piaget describes his eldest daughter, Jaqueline, playing with her dolls and bricks:

> From about 5 [years] 6 [months] onwards, Jaqueline spent her time organizing scenes dealing with families, education, weddings etc., with her dolls, but also making houses, gardens and often furniture. At 6 [years] 5 [months], using interlocking bricks and rods she built a big house, a stable and a woodshed, surrounded by a garden, with paths and avenues. Her dolls continually walked about and held conversations but she also

took care that the material constructions should be exact and true to life.

(Piaget, 1951, p. 137)

(c) This extract describes Iona Opie's observations of the play of some 8 year olds in a school playground:

> Where the grass joins the tarmac a dust-bowl has slowly been growing ... A crowd of boys – at least ten – were hurling toy cars and lorries along the tarmac towards this cavity. The idea, I was assured was 'to make it go along into the hole without toppling over'; but the enjoyment of the game seemed to derive from the speed and wildness of the throwing, and the quick retrieval of the vehicle after it had (as it usually had) landed on its back. As a boy positioned his car he shouted, 'Out of the way, I'm having a go. Watch this then!' As he hurled the car he screamed, 'Neeow!' A boy who had no car was making do with a lozenge tin; it had a much more stable shape than a car, and was in fact very much the shape of the Formula One racing cars, which are very wide.

(Opie, 1993, pp. 82–3)

(d) In this final extract, from the same playground, some 11 year olds are playing with marbles, and one girl is describing their play to Iona Opie:

> A friend came and opened the lid of the marbles tin. She routed about with a finger. 'Where is it? Where is the big bull-bearian?' 'It's inside,' said the first girl. 'Shall I go and fetch it?' She went and fetched a large scratched ball-bearing from her classroom and gave it to the other. 'She's going to play it for me,' she said, and resumed her role as mentor.
>
> 'This game, you see, they're playing eight coloured fourers for a blue see-through' [types of marbles] ... 'No drags!' said one player. 'That means you mustn't push it along with your finger,' said the girl. Someone called 'Aims away!' '"Aims away"? Well it's like having a point, almost, having an "Aims away". Say I had the last marble in the hole and I had an "Aims away", I would have won the game.' 'What's the other thing they're shouting, "on the line"?' 'That's if your marble stops on the edge of the hole. You have to chuck it out – I mean you have to send it right away.' The game was over, the blue see-through had been won.

(Opie, 1993, p. 27)

Comment

Examples (a) and (c) both describe children engaged in types of role-play. The first is an example of *socio-dramatic play* as it involves two children jointly constructing a play scenario and its accompanying dialogue. This type of play is also called *fantasy play*. The play described in (c), however, would not really count as 'socio-dramatic play' even though quite a large group of boys are playing together. The boy described is possibly playing the role of a racing driver, but there is nothing particularly social in the way he is playing; 'Out of the way, I'm having a go', he says, and one can imagine him pushing the other boys aside without waiting his turn. This extract also provides an example of a boy pretending that a lozenge tin is a car. In Piagetian terms his play would be categorized as *symbolic*.

In example (b) Jaqueline's play would be categorized as both *role - play* and also as *constructive play*. As Jaqueline is playing by herself, however, her play is *solitary* rather than *social*, although it does possibly have a *social theme*, as she appears to be pretending that her dolls symbolize the people who live in the house and garden that she has constructed.

Finally, extract (d) is an example of children playing a *game with rules*. This type of play is clearly social, but it has several qualities which distinguish it from socio-dramatic play. First, the game of marbles is played for high stakes, 'eight coloured fourers for a blue see-through'. There is a definite element of competitiveness to the children's play, unlike in the first example where Genevive and Johnathan are jointly engaged in *co-operative* play. Secondly, games with marbles have well defined rules which need to be understood by all the children involved and which stay the same from one game to the next. The younger children playing out their birth fantasy are inventing their own rules about who says what, and how the game should be played as they go along. Should they construct their play around a similar theme again, it would probably take quite a different form. By contrast, the game of marbles has a clearly defined set of rules, a definite goal and an end point, features which seem lacking in the younger children's play.

The preceding discussion and Activity 1 have centred on the definition of various types of play, and the degree to which children's involvement in play may be described as social or solitary. The next section looks at three major theories which have been put forward to explain the role of play in development.

SUMMARY OF SECTION 1

- There is disagreement among psychologists and others on the question of whether play is important for social development.
- Parten's work shows that throughout infancy and early childhood the nature and amount of social participation in play changes. Initially play is solitary or parallel, and later becomes more social and co-operative.
- Psychologists distinguish between several types of *social* play including symbolic play, role-play, socio-dramatic play, fantasy play, and play with rules.

2 THEORETICAL ACCOUNTS OF PLAY

2.1 Piaget's theory

As in other areas of child development, investigations of the function of play in development have been heavily influenced by the theories of the Swiss psychologist Jean Piaget (1896–1980). Piaget based his theory partly on detailed observations of his own three children (see Activity 1 for an example), and partly on observations and interviews with children from schools in Geneva, where he lived and worked for most of his long career. His account of the development of children's play is closely tied to his description of the stages of intellectual growth which children move through, from infancy to early adolescence (Piaget, 1951). It is also linked to his theory of moral development which describes how children come to understand the function of rules and sanctions through the games they play (Piaget, 1932, and see Section 5, this chapter). Piaget's writings on play and games have provided the theoretical framework for much of the later work in this particular area.

Piaget proposed that two activities, play and imitation, were important for development during infancy and early childhood. He maintained that while both activities were equally significant, play was a product of *assimilation,* whereas imitation was a product of *accommodation* (Oates, 1995, Chapter 1). Piaget recognized that when children play they do so primarily for the enjoyment it gives them, rather than anything else. The goal of imitation, by contrast, is not enjoyment; here the child is copying another person's action in order to understand the nature of that action.

Piaget saw children's play as developing in three main stages: the *mastery stage*, the *play stage* and the *game stage*. Table 1 shows how these stages relate to the first three of Piaget's four stages of intellectual development. Piaget (1951) proposed that the play stage is necessary for the development of symbolic representation, which in turn is a prerequisite for genuine interaction and the creation of shared meaning between individuals. He maintained, however, that during the play stage children's thinking is egocentric. So, although preoperational children can construct quite elaborate pretend play sequences, and act out particular roles, they find it difficult to take part in co-operative play as this requires them to exercise *social perspective-taking* skills.

Social perspective-taking skills, or the ability to put oneself in another's shoes and see things from their point of view, are necessary if children are to play together in a co-operative fashion. In order to avoid disputes and quarrels children need to negotiate and agree on what they want to play at, who should do what, and so on.

These skills are especially important when children start to play more organized, rule-based games such as board games and team sports. When taking part in this kind of game children have to accept the fact

TABLE 1   Piaget's play stages

'Play' stage and approximate ages	Piagetian operational stage	Type of play
Mastery stage 1 and 2 year olds	*Sensorimotor stage*	Solitary play which involves the repetition, practice and mastery of behaviours which infants and toddlers have acquired through imitation.
Play stage 3 to 6 year olds	*Preoperational stage (egocentric phase)*	Children begin to use objects and actions symbolically in their pretend play but initially do not play together as they are egocentric. Play is either solitary or parallel. Towards the end of this stage egocentrism begins to wane.
Game stage 7 year olds and older	*Concrete operational stage*	Children cease to be egocentric and start to play together in a co-operative way. They begin to gain the intellectual and linguistic sophistication to engage in social perspective taking and also to understand the rules of games.

that rules cannot be changed unilaterally to suit their own individual needs. They can only be changed by a process of mutual consent and agreement. If, as Piaget claimed, preoperational children lack social perspective-taking skills then this would explain why much of their play is solitary or parallel.

Contrary to Piaget's original observations, however, later studies have shown that children are capable of playing together in a genuinely social fashion from a very early age (e.g. Dunn, 1988; Fein, 1984). These studies are discussed in more detail in the next section. If you look back at the description of 4-year-old Johnathan and Genevive's play in Activity 1(a), for example, you can see that the socio-dramatic scenario they are constructing demands much mutual co-operation and social perspective taking. Observations such as this call into question the whole notion of egocentrism, and are one of the reasons why it has been severely criticized in recent years (e.g. Cox, 1991; Dunn, 1988).

Also, as research on the development of children's *theory of mind* (discussed in Chapter 4) has shown, from the age of about 3, children begin to appreciate that other people may have feelings, beliefs, desires and intentions which are different from their own. This suggests that while children's social perspective-taking skills may not be fully developed during the preoperational phase, their play and the ways in which they interact with other people show that they are not egocentric.

What stands out from Piaget's account is that he regarded play as a manifestation of the thought processes of individual children. Indeed, he explicitly states that 'make-believe play is the most important manifestation of "symbolic thought" in the child' (Piaget, 1951, p. 169). His main concern was with the development of symbolic representation rather than with an examination of the social function of play. With the exception of his later work on children's understanding of games and abstract concepts such as justice and fairness related to playing games, most of his observations were of young children playing alone.

2.2 Vygotsky's theory

The Soviet psychologist Lev Vygotsky (1896–1934), a contemporary of Piaget, has also had a seminal influence on theories of child development. Unlike Piaget, he did not discuss play extensively in his writing, but he did see it as having a major role in children's development:

> Play creates a zone of proximal development of the child. In play a child always behaves beyond his average age, above his daily behaviour; in play it is as though he were a head taller than himself. As in the focus of a magnifying glass, play contains all developmental tendencies in a condensed form and is itself a major source of development.
>
> (Vygotsky, 1978, p. 102)

The concept of the *zone of proximal development* (or ZPD) is central to Vygotsky's development theory. He maintained that a distinction ought to be made between a child's *actual* developmental level and his or her *potential* developmental level. A child's actual developmental level is the level at which he or she demonstrates understanding and the ability to use ideas and concepts competently without help or assistance from another person. When children are operating within their ZPD (their potential developmental level), they can work with more advanced ideas and concepts, provided they are receiving the support of someone who already has a more sophisticated grasp of the relevant concepts.

The concept of the ZPD is more usually employed in connection with learning and cognitive development (see, for example, Wood, 1988). It is interesting, therefore, that Vygotsky saw play between children as creating a zone in which their performance is in advance of their actual developmental level. In order to understand how play can do this it is useful to think of the ZPD as a sort of inter-psychological, social space in which children can explore new knowledge and ideas through conversation and other forms of interaction.

Unlike Piaget, who held that children discovered new ideas and concepts for themselves through their interactions with the environment, Vygotsky claimed that children are introduced to new knowledge and different perspectives on old knowledge through speech and conversation with other children and adults. Knowledge and ideas initially expressed overtly through language and social interactions gradually become internalized to form part of an individual child's system of mental representations. Thus, according to Vygotsky, inter-psychological *relations* become inter-psychological *mental functions* through the zone of proximal development.

How does this relate to play and social development? Vygotsky maintained that when they play children are learning how to use psychological tools, such as the particular rules and conventions which govern effective discourse and social interaction. This shows in the way they use language and behaviour quite unlike that of their normal everyday interactions as they act out and experiment with different roles in their socio-dramatic play. The following description of children's play in Malawi is an illustration of this:

> A perennial amusement among Ngoni boys of five to seven was playing at law courts. They sat around in traditional style with a 'chief' and his elders facing the court, the plaintiffs and defendants presenting their case, and the counsellors conducting proceedings and cross-examining witnesses. In their high, squeaky voices the little boys imitated their fathers whom they had seen in the courts, and they gave judgements, imposing heavy penalties, and keeping order in the court with ferocious severity.
>
> (Read, cited in Leacock, 1976, p. 468)

At one level these young boys are simply imitating the ways in which other people speak and behave in order to help their mini-drama along. Vygotsky would argue, however, that play of this kind is providing children with an important mental support system that allows them to think and act in new ways (Cole and Cole, 1989). This example from Malawi also illustrates how social and cultural knowledge is transmitted through play.

2.3 Mead's theory

The writings of the American philosopher George Herbert Mead (1863–1931) have been extremely influential in developing the symbolic interactionist perspective within social psychology (Mead, 1934). As you saw in Chapter 5, this perspective emphasizes the importance of language and social interaction for the development of the self. Mead maintained, however, that children also acquire a sense of who they are through play.

Mead has much in common with Vygotsky, whose theory has also been influential in informing the thinking of the symbolic interactionist school, though Mead puts more emphasis on explaining the development of the self. The concept of 'self' is extremely important in Mead's theoretical framework. Bernard Meltzer summarizes his position thus:

> In referring to the human being as having a self, Mead simply means that such an individual may act socially towards himself, just as toward others. He may praise, blame, or encourage himself; he may become disgusted with himself, may seek to punish himself, and so forth. Thus the human being may become the object of his own actions. The self is formed in the same way as other objects – through the 'definitions' made by others.
>
> (Meltzer, 1967, pp. 9–10)

Mead maintained that children do not develop a mature sense of self until they have learnt to take on the role of the other. He claimed that the experience of role-play and pretence in early childhood was vital for the development of the self. Mead described three major stages in the development of the self, the preparatory stage, the play stage, and the game stage. These are described in Reading B. It is important to realize that although both Mead's and Piaget's 'play' and 'game' stages have the same names, the two theorists described the developmental functions of each stage in very different ways.

READING

In Reading B Bernard Meltzer describes Mead's stages, and explains the relationship between the development of the self and the changing nature of children's role-play at different ages.

Research Summary 2 contains some young girls' descriptions of the characteristics of various stable friendship groups which formed in their school playground every break-time. They provide a nice illustration of what Mead meant when he proposed that in order to develop a sense of the 'generalized other' the child must abstract and internalize a composite role that typifies ideals and expectations which members of the group hold in common.

RESEARCH SUMMARY 2
GOODIES, JOKERS AND GANGS

The descriptions below are taken from Andrew Pollard's longitudinal study of 8- to 12-year-old children's perspectives on school life. Working in one school over a two year period, Pollard identified three 'types' of friendship group, Goodies, Jokers and Gangs – labels chosen to typify the prevailing ethos. Each type had a well-defined sense of identity which determined how its members behaved, and how they felt about themselves in relation to their peers and teachers.

Gill: We like playing with a ball and skipping and playing out in the playground. We like to talk and have a good laugh. Sometimes we play chasing with the boys or watching them playing football.

Tina: I have a good group of friends when I don't fall out with them. Katherine is always falling out with me and going off with Carly. If that happens, like, she has pinched my friend, then Carly's a fat cow. When I'm friends with Susan, just because I'm small for my age, she always pushes me around and blames me for things, but Lucy, if we are friends and we play hitting one another it's good fun. But if I hit her too hard she will not play at all. She can be a baby sometimes.

Linda: We call our club the Lion Club and it's very successful. We are all friends in it. We are honest and fair. We all have nicknames for being in the club, mine is 'Rory', Caroline's is 'Little Boots', Mandy's is 'Shelly' and Kirsty's is 'Thackey'. Our's is a friendly group, we never fall out, or if we do it's only because of silly things.

(Pollard, 1987, pp. 170, 173, 168)

ACTIVITY 2

Allow about 10 minutes

IDENTIFYING THE 'GENERALIZED OTHER'

Together with Reading B, this activity should help you understand Mead's notion of the 'generalized other'. It should not be too difficult to identify which girl belongs to a 'Goodie', 'Joker' or 'Gang' group from the extracts in Research Summary 2. The extracts also provide clues about the set of standpoints which are common to each group, which have allowed these girls to develop a sense of the 'generalized other'.

You should read the extracts again and then identify (a) which group each girl appears to belong to; (b) what the standpoints are of the three groups, and (c) features of the girls' descriptions which illustrate Mead's notion of the 'generalized other'.

Comment on this activity is given at the end of the chapter.

I have included Pollard's study as an example of research which has attempted to validate aspects of Mead's theory, particularly those related to the function of games and friendships in the development of children's sense of self. In the following section, I shall describe other studies which have drawn on Mead's theory in order to investigate the function of socio-dramatic role-play in early childhood.

Piaget, Vygotsky and Mead have all had a profound influence on the ways in which psychologists have studied play and social development. The following sections describe some of the research on children's play, games and friendships which have developed these theories further.

SUMMARY OF SECTION 2

- For Piaget, play and games reveal the stage of development a child has reached in terms of symbolic understanding and, later, abstract reasoning. Their function is to allow children to assimilate, master, and experiment with the boundaries and limitations of newly acquired concepts and behaviours. According to this theory, play does not itself lead to development.

- The concept of egocentricity has been critically examined. More recent research indicates that, contrary to Piagetian theory, preoperational children do have social perspective-taking skills.

- Vygotsky's theory claims that play contributes to children's development in two main ways. First, it creates a zone of proximal development which allows children to acquire sophisticated psychological tools, such as conversational skills. Secondly, in play, children begin to work out the meaning and significance of the many mysterious (to children) cultural and social practices to which they are exposed as members of a particular society or group.

- According to Mead, role-play is important for the development of self in early childhood. In later childhood, participation in team games and the experience of belonging to various social groups allows children to develop a sense of themselves as social beings through the concept of the generalized other.

3 PLAY AND THE DEVELOPMENT OF SOCIAL UNDERSTANDING IN YOUNG CHILDREN

3.1 The development of social perspective-taking skills

Mead was first and foremost a philosopher rather than a psychologist and he made no attempt to try and gather empirical evidence for his theories. More recently, however, psychologists working within the symbolic interactionist framework have attempted to validate his theories. Andrew Pollard's research, which was outlined in the previous section, is one example of how Mead's theory can be applied to the study of peer relationships and identity formation in school-aged children. In a similar vein, the work of the American psychologist Greta Fein provides an example of how Mead's conceptual framework can be applied to understanding the play of pre-school children. Fein has carried out a number of studies which examine the contribution of socio-dramatic play to the acquisition of social perspective-taking skills and self development in young children. One of these studies is described in Research Summary 3.

RESEARCH SUMMARY 3
THE SELF-BUILDING POTENTIAL OF PRETEND PLAY

In order to look at the development of young children's perspective taking, Fein videotaped 2- to 4-year-old children's play sequences. Each child in the study was filmed for fifteen minutes on four different occasions with four different play partners of the same age. From her analysis of these play sequences Fein was able to describe four levels in the development of young children's perspective-taking skills:

Level 1 – *Self in pretend activities*
Children do not take on roles but do engage in pretence, e.g. 'I'm pretending to make cakes'.

Level 2 – *Generic role transformation*
Child pretends to be someone else carrying out an activity typical to the role, e.g. 'I'm pretending to be a mummy making cakes'.

Level 3 – *Generic role with complementarity*
Child takes on a role which involves interacting with a 'complementary other', e.g. 'I'm pretending to be a busy Mummy making cakes with my little boy'.

Level 4 – *Generic role with complementarity and reversibility*
Child constantly switches from pretending to be the mother to being the child helping to make cakes and vice versa.

(Fein, 1984)

Fein conducted a number of detailed observational investigations of young children's role-play and socio-dramatic play (Fein, 1984). Her research shows that between the ages of 2 and 4 years children's socio-dramatic play becomes increasingly sophisticated. She argues that this indicates that their concept of self is also developing over this period in much the way that Mead's theory would predict:

> Two processes contribute to the self building potential of play. One is overt role *playing* (i.e., the behavioural responses and the stimuli they provide to the player). In a sense, the child observes himself in the role of another. The other process is the covert role *taking* that accompanies the overt behaviour. Psychologically, the role-playing child is organizing the attitudes and perspectives of the others whose role responses are being produced. However, the self is always at the centre of these encounters, interpreting the social meaning of the relationships being enacted.
>
> (Fein, 1984, p. 126)

Fein found that children's pretend play sequences became more complex in terms of the roles children invented for themselves, and also that children's social perspective-taking skills developed considerably between the ages of 2 and 4. Research Summary 3 gives descriptions of four increasingly sophisticated levels of role-taking skills. Note, however, that these levels describe individual children's play rather than what happens when two or more children play together. The following example is an extract from a play sequence recorded by Fein, in which Peter and Michael – both aged 3½ – are playing a game involving a 'dracula monster' and a 'monster-vanishing hero', and are using toy blocks as substitute weapons:

P: (Swings hat in air, approaches M) 'You be dracula.'

M: 'Okay' (Gets up, extends arms in front of him) 'Grrow!'

P: (Points block at M) 'Pow!'

M: (Falls down)

P: (Approaches, points block at M) 'Pow!'

M: (Stirs slightly while lying down)

P: (Starts to put block in pocket)

M: (Starts to get up)

P: (Points block at M) 'Pow!'

M: (Falls down)

P: (Puts block in pocket)

M: (Gets up) 'Now you be dracula.'

P: 'Wait … I gotta put my cowboy hat on first.' (Puts hat on, approaches M)

M: (Points block at P) 'Pow!'

P: (Falls down)

M: (Points block at P) 'Pow, pow, pow, pow!' (Puts block in pocket) 'You're dead.' (Leaves)

P: 'Hey, aahh!' (Gets up) 'Ahh, ahh!'

M: (Points block at P)

P: (Approaches M)

M: 'Prsh, prsh, prsh, prsh, prsh!'

M: (Pushes P down, places block in pocket)

P: (Falls down) (Gets up) 'Now you be dracula.'

M: (Gets toy from shelf) 'No, I ... pow, pow, pow!' (Points toy at P)

P: 'You be dracula.'

M: (Pushes P)

P: 'Be you like you?'

M: 'No, you be dracula, and you say wow, and I push you down, and I shoot you.' (Approaches P with block extended in front of him)

P: 'The hell you shoot me. No.' (Pushes M's arm) 'You ...'

M: 'All right.' (Lies down)

P: (Points block at M) 'Pow!'

M: (Stirs slightly)

P: (Puts block in pocket, puts hat on head)

M: (Gets up, points block at P) 'Pow, pow, pow!'

P: (Points block at M) 'Pow!' (Pushes M with block and arms extended in front of him)

M: (Pushes P with arms and block extended in front of him)

P: 'Pow, pow!'

M: (Falls down)

P: (Puts block in pocket).

(Fein, 1984, pp. 136–7)

To a casual observer, this play sequence might simply look like two little boys rushing around pretending to shoot at each other. Note how, at the beginning of the sequence, however, there is quite a bit of negotiation around who is to be Dracula, and who is to be the hero. The children also instruct each other on how to behave and what to say in their respective roles. This is an example of what Fein and Mead mean when they claim that, through play, children develop the ability to acknowledge and understand the perspectives of others as well as their own. Fein's interpretation of the overt play roles, covert role-taking skills and perspectives taken by each child in this play sequence are shown in Figure 1.

Contrary to Piaget's description of the play of pre-school children, Fein's research clearly shows that in *socio-dramatic play* situations, young children's behaviour cannot be described as egocentric, though in certain *non-play* situations it may be decidedly so.

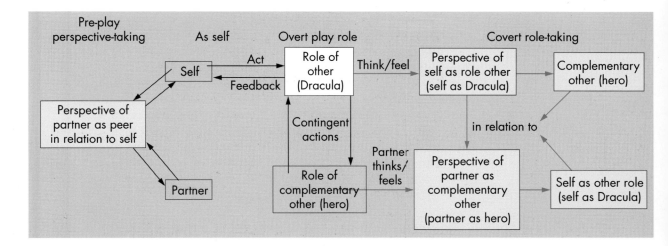

FIGURE 1 Social pretence: role complementarity and the perspective of others.
Source: Fein, 1984, p. 129.

As Vygotsky suggests, socio-dramatic play may provide a zone of proximal development which allows them to transcend this type of egocentric behaviour.

3.2 The development of social competence

While there is now considerable evidence that socio-dramatic play of the kind described above allows children to develop their social perspective-taking skills, social competence involves a range of other skills as well. Two important aspects of social competence are the ability to adjust social behaviour to different social contexts and the ability to take into account the particular characteristics of one's social partner, such as age and gender (Brownell, 1990). Skills such as sharing, co-operation, negotiation and the ability to display and control one's behaviour and emotions all contribute to social competence. Several researchers have suggested that socio-dramatic and fantasy play may contribute to the development of the skills and behaviours which underlie social competence (e.g. Smilansky, 1968). As social competence is a complex construct, however, it cannot be measured in any simple way. Psychologists who have investigated the relationship between socio-dramatic play and the development of social competence have tended to use research designs which assess several areas of competence individually.

Canadian researchers Jennifer Connolly and Anna-Beth Doyle (1984) investigated whether the amount and complexity of fantasy play was related to social competence in 3- to 5-year-old children. They used several measures to assess children's social competence, including teacher ratings of children's popularity with their peers; their observed ability to comply with classroom rules; observations of the length of time each child spent in social interaction; observations of the amount of attention-seeking behaviour; competitive behaviour; expressions of friendliness; and affective (mood) behaviour.

Before measuring their social competence, however, Connolly and Doyle looked at how long and how often each child engages in fantasy play, and also at the type of pretence and role-play they engaged in. They found that the amount and complexity of children's fantasy play were significantly correlated with four measures of social competence: teacher rating of social skill; peer popularity; affective role-taking ability; and amount of positive social activity (e.g. expressions of friendship, invitations to play and amount of conversation). Another important finding was that these four measures were not statistically related to children's age, gender or intellectual competence, nor were they related to the amount and complexity of the other types of play they observed.

ACTIVITY 3

Allow about 5 minutes

THE RELATIONSHIP BETWEEN FANTASY PLAY AND SOCIAL COMPETENCE

What do Connolly and Doyle's findings tell us about the nature of the relationship between fantasy play and the development of social competence?

Comment on this activity is given at the end of the chapter.

The youngest children in Connolly and Doyle's study were 3 years old. Other evidence suggests that the hypothesized relationship between socio-dramatic play, fantasy play, and the development of social competence also holds for younger children. For example, in a study involving detailed longitudinal observations and assessment of over 300 children, Carollee Howes (1983) found that 2 to 3 year olds who spent a large proportion of their day engaged in co-operative socio-dramatic play during their time in day care, were rated by their teachers as being more socially competent than children who spent less time playing in this way.

Howes' study, however, presents us with a problem: socially competent children were found to spend more time in socio-dramatic play than less competent children, but the former were rated by their teachers as having already been more socially competent than the latter when they first started at nursery school. It cannot be argued, therefore, that the socio-dramatic play experiences available to them in their day care were directly responsible for their more advanced social skills. So where do these skills come from?

Judy Dunn's research suggests an answer. She found that children as young as 18 months engage in socio-dramatic pretence with their older brothers and sisters (see Research Summary 4).

The findings of the Cambridge Sibling Study (discussed in more detail in the reading at the end of this book) highlight the importance of studying young children's social development in the natural context of everyday interactions within the family. It clearly shows that under some circumstances children begin to develop the capacity for engaging

RESEARCH SUMMARY 4
JOINT PRETEND PLAY IN SIBLINGS

Forty-three families took part in Judy Dunn and Penny Munn's Cambridge Sibling Study (Dunn, 1988). Detailed observations of sibling interactions were carried out when the second-born child in each family was aged 18, 24, and 36 months. Among other things, the observers noted the number of times the children engaged in joint pretend play which had a clear element of fantasy or make-believe in it. Dunn describes such play as 'The ability to share a pretend framework with another person, to carry out pretend actions in co-ordination with that other; [and] enacting the part of another person or thing, with the incorporation of another person into a reciprocal role' (Dunn, 1988, p. 117).

Older siblings directed their younger brothers and sisters in joint pretend play episodes and gave them instructions about what to say and how to behave when they were in their pretend roles. At 18 months, 15 per cent of the younger siblings in the study were playing in this way with their brothers and sisters. By the time they were aged 24 months, 80 per cent of younger siblings were observed in joint pretend play and over a third of these younger children clearly understood that they were taking on a different identity during the play episode.

in joint pretend play at a very early age. More importantly, this study has provided further insights into some of the processes underlying the development of social competence in young children.

For example, Dunn has shown that older siblings give specific role-playing instructions and directions to younger siblings and this helps them make appropriate and relevant contributions to the play. Instruction seems to be welcomed in the context of joint pretend play but young children are much less tolerant of this kind of help in other contexts. Joint pretend play and co-operative behaviour between siblings were most frequently observed in families where there was a friendly affectionate relationship between siblings. It was much less frequent in families where sibling relationships were less harmonious. This suggests that sibling instruction is not the only process contributing to the development of young children's role-playing ability. Other factors in the child's environment must also contribute to the development of social perspective taking, otherwise how would first-born and only children acquire this ability? Chapter 4 (Section 2) gives examples of research which show that children also learn about other people's actions, intentions, feelings and motivations by monitoring their emotional states. This research indicates that socio-dramatic and fantasy play experiences are not the only ways in which children begin to develop their social perspective-taking skills and sense of themselves in relation to others. In early infancy they acquire these insights by observing other people's emotional reactions to objects and events in their environment and by noting how others respond to and regulate their own behaviour and expressions of emotion. Later on, discussion of their own and other people's feelings becomes important. In the Reading *Studying relationships and social understanding* at the end of this book, Dunn points out that:

> A variety of different processes were implicated in the development of social understanding, including not only frequent engagement in pretend play with a sibling, but discourse processes such as participation in talk about why people behave in the way they do …

As social competence appears to be related to so many facets of children's development, perhaps we should not be too surprised that it is difficult to establish a simple causal relationship between socio-dramatic play and social competence.

3.3 Explanations and models

Studies such as those of Connolly and Doyle, Howes and Dunn show that there is a lot of individual variation between children of the same age in terms of their social competence. One reason for this is that the social experience of any one child is unique to that child. Even within the same family, siblings may experience widely different types of social experience. As Dunn's studies have shown, not all children enjoy friendly relationships with their siblings; not all children come from families where behaviours and feelings are freely commented on and discussed; and not all children have the opportunity to meet and play with other children on a regular basis in nurseries and play groups.

The research discussed in Chapter 3 shows that styles of parenting and family experiences are certainly not uniform across children.

The picture becomes even more complicated in the light of evidence that children exhibit different levels of social skill depending on the age of the other child they are playing with. Celia Brownell has shown that 2 year olds adjust the content and complexity of their social behaviour to match the age of their play partners. When their partner was a younger child, their social behaviour was less complex than when they were playing with a child of the same age. The ability to adapt one's social behaviour appropriately to the social context is an important aspect of social competence. If children as young as 2 can modify their social behaviours according to the age of their play partners, and if there is wide variation between children of the same age in terms of their social skills, then it becomes difficult to maintain the view that social development proceeds stage-by-stage. It is also difficult to argue that particular types of play are uniquely associated with each stage.

Norman Denzin (1972, 1975) recognized that stage-like models, such as those of Mead and Piaget, could not account for individual differences in the development of children's social understanding and the development of the self. He argued that these models do not take into account the fact that differences in the nature and quality of early social experience mean that, at any one age, children are likely to display contrasting levels of social competence, and understanding of the self. Denzin recommended that in order to disentangle the complex relationships between play, role-taking ability and social competence, researchers should compare groups of children of different *interactional* age (i.e. level of social competence), rather than comparing groups of children of different chronological age.

Like Fein, Denzin belongs to the symbolic interactionist school. His own studies on the relationship between role-taking ability and the development of the self have shown that, as Mead originally suggested, self development takes place in a sequential or stage-like fashion. They also demonstrated that this sequence is not tied to any one age range; it is contingent on the character of the child's early symbolic and interactional experience.

Finally, Denzin's research revealed that situational constraints also affected children's role-taking ability. When exposed to new social contexts and unfamiliar play partners, children may revert to less mature forms of social behaviours than they demonstrate with familiar others. This has clear implications for research methodology. Denzin recommended that in order to unravel the complex factors influencing the effects of different kinds of interactional experience (including play) on children's personal and social development, observational studies of children in everyday contexts were needed, which looked at the range and variety of individual children's social behaviours over extended time periods. As this section has shown, many of Denzin's original insights have been confirmed by more recent studies.

> ## SUMMARY OF SECTION 3
>
> - Several studies have shown that between the ages of 2 and 4, socio-dramatic play shows increasing sophistication as children develop the ability to integrate a variety of roles and perspectives into their play sequences.
> - According to symbolic interactionist models of social development, this increase in perspective-taking skills is closely related to the development of the self and increases in children's social competence.
> - Social competence is a complex construct which can only be assessed by measuring a number of different but related social skills and behaviours.
> - Social skills such as the ability to adjust one's social behaviour and interactional style to different social contexts and play partners have been shown to be important for the development of social competence.
> - It is difficult to argue that there is a direct causal link between the amount and complexity of socio-dramatic or fantasy play experience and the development of children's social competence. A number of other types of family, emotional and linguistic experiences are also implicated in the development of social competence.
> - Similarly, as same-aged children are likely to be very different in terms of their interactional age as a result of the diversity of individual family circumstances and opportunities for social interaction, stage-like models relating play stages to the development of social competence are inadequate.

4   THE CONTENT OF PLAY

In this section I shall introduce some of the research on the content of socio-dramatic and fantasy play and show how it has helped psychologists understand some of the processes which underlie the development of children's understanding of themselves and their social world. Furth and Kane (1992) maintain that 'whatever else they may play at, children pretending always "play society" '. They go on to argue that it is possible to gain an understanding of the ways in which children think about society through their play.

ACTIVITY 4
Allow about 5 minutes

THE *KAPENTA* GAME

In terms of Furth and Kane's assertion that children always 'play society', what does the following 12-year-old girl's account of a popular Zambian children's game suggest to you?

In this game, people sell *kapenta* [dried fish]. One person in the game is Nsenga and the other Bemba [two of the many national groups in Zambia]. The Bemba sells the *kapenta*, saying, 'I am selling *kapenta*.' The Nsenga asks the Bemba what he is selling in Nsenga. The Bemba misunderstands, and a fight starts due to the misunderstanding of the languages. Someone who knows both languages comes to intervene in a fight between the two and explains what each one has said to the other.

(Leacock, 1976, p. 471)

Comment

Eleanor Leacock carried out observations of children's play in Zambia. Like Furth and Kane she believed that play reflected the 'consciously patterned ways in which children relate to, and experiment with, their social and physical environment and their own abilities' (p. 466). In her discussion of this particular game she comments that the children who were playing it came from a large African city where all the children were very used to hearing and interpreting a variety of closely related tribal languages. The extract shows not only that children were very adept at this, but also that they had a sophisticated understanding of what happens when language differences result in a breakdown of communication, and also of ways in which such a breakdown can be repaired. It also shows that the children understand that good communication is essential for the success of important economic transactions.

The game of kapenta has a certain ritualistic feel to it, and it was always played according to the same formula. Later on in this section I shall discuss research which shows that European and American children also adopt certain formulae or 'scripts' in their socio-dramatic play.

4.1 Socio-dramatic play

Activity 1 introduced you to various different types of play, including socio-dramatic play. Although their use of the terms is somewhat inconsistent, many psychologists make a further distinction between socio-dramatic play and thematic fantasy play (e.g. Smilansky, 1968). Socio-dramatic play involves pretend activities which are based on domestic scenarios, such as putting baby to bed, going to tea at

a friend's house, shopping, cooking and the like. This type of play may also reflect real life experiences outside the home, such as going to the doctor, visiting the zoo, or attending a wedding. Thematic fantasy play, by contrast, is based on fictional narratives and imaginary events, and can be observed whenever children create imaginary worlds for themselves and their toys, or when they act out the plots of stories in books, films and television programmes. The following sections discuss some of the research which has investigated the forms and functions of these two different types of play in children's development.

There have been many studies of socio-dramatic play in young children as it is an ideal context in which to observe changes in cognitive, linguistic and social development. It is actively encouraged in nursery and pre-school settings as it is known to promote children's language and communication skills, and in Western societies a vast toy industry services its needs.

ACTIVITY 5

Allow about 40 minutes

TOYS AND SOCIO-DRAMATIC PLAY

This activity is designed to illustrate the kinds of play activities we as a society seem to encourage in our children, and to think about the sorts of messages about society that children can receive from them.

If you have access to any catalogues from mail order outlets, toy manufacturers, toy shops, or the like, look through the pages advertising children's toys and list those that appear designed to promote socio-dramatic play or thematic fantasy play. Ignore toys which are clearly educational, board games, and things like swings, slides and art and craft materials. Next, divide your list into toys which, in your view, are specifically geared towards girls and those geared towards boys. What do you notice about these lists?

Comment

It is likely that your first list will contain examples of toys such as dolls with their buggies, baths, feeding bottles, etc., play houses and domestic play items such as tea sets, cooking utensils, cookers, and vacuum cleaners; doctors and nurses sets; policemen's helmets; and models of fire-stations, garages, zoos and the like. What did you notice about your list for boys and girls? When I carried out this exercise I was struck by the fact that girls' toys are much more geared to 'domestic' socio-dramatic play, while boys' toys are more geared towards thematic fantasy play. Boys can choose space-stations, pirate ships, cowboy outfits, monster masks and the like.

4.2 Gender and cultural identity

Of course there is no real reason why girls shouldn't abandon their Barbie dolls, toy supermarket checkouts and nurses outfits in favour of the space-stations and the like. Indeed many children do, but if you have the kind of catalogue which also shows children playing with the toys you will see that it shows girls playing with the girls' toys, and boys with the boys' toys (unless your catalogue was from the Early Learning Centre, for example). These images of nicely dressed, smiling children deliver powerful messages to juvenile consumers. I don't think it is really necessary to labour the point that, for toy manufacturers at least, boys and girls are expected to play in very different ways.

As was pointed out in Chapter 5, some parents of young children strongly object to the explicit gender bias of many toys and the messages about gender-appropriate roles and activities directed at children through the media. Even when these parents try to avoid exposing their children to these messages, however, inevitably most children do become aware of them sooner or later. From her cross-cultural study of children's play, Feitelson drew the conclusion that 'The style of play in any one society was by no means a random occurrence but was closely linked to its social makeup and the role of young children in it' (cited in Curry and Arnaud, 1984, p. 283).

The previous section outlined the social interactionist position that socio-dramatic play is fundamental for the development of the child's self identity, and also for the development of understanding of the rules of social interaction. In Chapter 5 it was pointed out that developing a sense of gender identity is important for the development of one's sense of self. Another important aspect of the self is one's sense of cultural and social identity. One can begin to appreciate, therefore, that toys, and the types of play activities they encourage, might have a powerful influence on children's developing identities.

In common with other psychologists working within the symbolic interactionist tradition, Gregory Stone (1981) suggests that dramatic play functions as an 'anticipatory socialization' device. By this he means that through socio-dramatic play children prepare themselves for the types of roles they may be called upon to adopt as adults. Reviewing some of the many studies of gender differences in children's play, Stone claims that available evidence suggests that in westernized societies socio-dramatic play involving domestic themes is more characteristic of girls than it is of boys, and that boys are more likely than girls to act out thematic fantasies. He suggests that 'the dramatic play of children in our society may function more to prepare little girls for adulthood than little boys' (Stone, 1981, p. 263). Descriptions of children's play in other societies, however, indicate that *both* boys and girls engage in play which appears to function as an anticipatory socialization device. The example of the Ngoni boys given in Section 2 shows how these children were rehearsing the male roles and judicial customs of their society in their mock courts of law.

The cross-cultural studies of Nancy Curry and Sarah Arnaud (1984) provide further evidence that socio-dramatic play has an anticipatory socialization function, not only in terms of the development of gender identity but also in terms of the development of children's cultural identity (see Research Summary 5).

Curry and Arnaud found that while children's play had many things in common in the different cultures they studied, it also reflected the types

---

RESEARCH SUMMARY 5
CROSS-CULTURAL PERSPECTIVES ON SOCIO-DRAMATIC PLAY

Curry and Arnaud compared the play of children in five different North American cultures: Appalachian children from West Virginia; Mexican Americans in Texas; southern Black children in Texas; Native American Indians in Montana; and city children of mixed socio-economic background in Western Pennsylvania. They analysed films of these groups of children's dramatic play and observed that in all cultures children acted out the following common themes:

- Nurturance and domestic play based on food preparation and feeding;
- Family relationships and roles such as mother–baby interactions and the roles of fathers and siblings;
- Representations of the children's physical and human environment using blocks and miniature life toys;
- Relationships between medical personnel and patients;
- Play based on aggressive themes and frightening happenings involving monsters, accidents and the like.

of environment they came from, and the roles of the adults in that environment:

> There were also clear differences in play styles, emphases and cultural content ... The children in the five groups also built quite different representations of their surroundings (e.g. coal mines, farms, corrals, super highways, cities and rural villages) and enacted different adult occupations related to their own experiences (e.g. animal auctioneers and butchers, miners, rural medical clinic personnel, Native American dancers).
>
> (Curry and Arnaud, 1984, p. 283)

They also found that when children were playing with toys which were particularly relevant to their own culture, children appeared more involved, and played for longer than when they were playing with other types of toys. This is an example of how children adopt culturally-determined themes and roles in their play. As I mentioned at the beginning of this section, Furth and Kane (1992) argue that detailed analysis of these themes can reveal what children understand about social and economic institutions, and the various roles, including gender roles, of salient people in their society.

4.3 Scripts and socio-dramatic play

The American psychologist Jaqueline Sachs and her colleagues (Sachs *et al.*, 1985) claim that improvement in children's ability to create and sustain roles and themes in their play is related to two factors: (a) children's knowledge of 'scripted events' and (b) children's communicative competence.

Scripted events are organized sequences of actions which 'involve people in purposeful activities ... acting on objects and interacting with each other to achieve some result' (Nelson, 1986, p. 11). For example a 'restaurant script' might include sitting down at a table, studying a menu, ordering food, eating the food and paying the bill. A 'mother and baby script' might include feeding the baby, bathing baby, changing nappies and getting the baby ready for bed.

Research on the development of script knowledge (e.g. Nelson, 1986) has shown that children acquire many such scripts through repeated experience of observing and taking part in common everyday sequences of activities. Over time children's script knowledge becomes more elaborate as they become more familiar with the details of such events. In order to use script knowledge in their play, however, children also have to be able to convey their ideas to each other, negotiate shared meanings, reach agreement about roles, and decide what is to be done in the play.

William Corsaro (1986) has shown that the language and discourse used by children in socio-dramatic play is distinctly different from the language they use in fantasy theme play. When children are acting out socio-dramatic scripts the dialogues they create tend to be based on

> ## RESEARCH SUMMARY 6
> ## PLAYING DOCTORS AND PATIENTS
>
> Jaqueline Sachs and her colleagues observed and recorded the spontaneous play of 18 pairs of 2- to 5-year-old children of the same age and sex. The children were left alone together for up to half an hour in a playroom containing a variety of objects suggesting a doctor theme, such as a first aid box, stethoscope, syringe and bandages. Dolls, hats, and other toys were also provided.
>
> The pairs of 2 year olds rarely played out medical themes with the toys and they had frequent disagreements with each other. The 3-year-old pairs played at being doctors briefly before switching to other themes when they ran out of ideas, or could not agree on how to use the toys. Only the 5 year olds played out extended doctor/patient themes and knew what all the 'medical equipment' was used for. Their more complete knowledge about doctor situations provided them with a means of structuring their play. This in turn allowed them to create longer and more sustained play episodes.

routine exchanges which echo the content and style of real-life exchanges between adults engaged in similar activities. These routine exchanges are essentially identical each time children decide to play out a particular script. By contrast, the dialogues children create for their fantasy theme play are much more creative and flexible and are likely to change from one occasion to the next, even though the theme of the play might be the same. One play episode based on the theme of monsters and heroes, such as the Dracula theme described in Section 3, may be completely different from the next, even though it is the same children who are developing the theme.

4.4 Thematic fantasy play

Play, imagination and fears

The American psychologists Dorothy and Jerome Singer (1990) have studied children's pretend play for the light it can shed on the development of children's imagination. They make the interesting claim that the distinction between socio-dramatic pretend play and thematic fantasy play echoes the distinction Bruner (1986) makes between two different modes of thinking, the paradigmatic mode, and the narrative mode. According to Bruner, paradigmatic thought is logical, sequential and analytical. It involves the kind of thought processes people carry out when they attempt to order, categorize and make sense of experience. Narrative thought is more creative and expressionistic, and is involved in day-dreaming and the construction of real or imagined events. Singer and Singer suggest that the content of socio-dramatic and thematic fantasy play reflects these two different modes of thought and they argue that the two types of play have different functions in terms of the development of children's imagination and thought processes.

As I pointed out earlier, research on the development of script knowledge in young children has shown that scripts function to organize children's internal memory representations of common everyday experiences and events (Nelson, 1986). When children draw on these stored representations to help them structure their socio-dramatic play, Singer and Singer claim that their thinking is paradigmatic. By contrast, children's fantasy play is often highly original and imaginative, and involves narrative modes of thought. In their fantasy play children cast themselves as heroes and villains and act out scenes and events they can never have experienced at first hand, such as going to the moon. Singer and Singer also found that stories and television programmes often provide inspiration for thematic fantasy play, although children adapt the characters and plots to suit the mood of the moment.

They also claim that observations of children's fantasy play can provide insights into their internal perspectives on the self–other relationship. This is a key concept of the psychoanalytic theory of object-relations (see Oates, 1995, Chapter 7, which informs certain play therapy techniques). Psychiatrists and analysts working within this tradition, such as Melanie Klein (1932), Margaret Lowenfeld (1979) and Donald Winnicott (1971), believe that children's play can be an unconscious expression of attachment relationships formed in early infancy. They maintain that play has an important role in emotional development as it gives children the opportunity to suspend reality and explore potentially threatening and/or traumatic experiences in the controlled and relatively safe context of imagination, pretence and fantasy.

READING

Reading C is taken from American child psychotherapist Frances Wickes' book, *The Inner World of Childhood,* which was first published in 1927. Frances Wickes was interested in discovering what children's fantasy play and the imaginary companions they invented for themselves could reveal about their emotional life. She regarded play and imagination as a window into the child's unconscious, and maintained that through play children were unconsciously attempting to come to grips with fundamental emotional issues and problems related to relationships within the child's family.

The reading describes an imaginary character, Mrs Comphret, invented by two sisters, and includes Wickes' interpretation of the meaning that Mrs Comphret had in the emotional life of one of the sisters. It is an example of how child therapists interpret children's fantasy play in terms of what it appears to reveal about unconscious family tensions. It is up to you to decide whether you find Wickes' interpretation of Mrs Comphret's role in the child's fantasy convincing or not.

Other psychologists such as Corsaro (1986) have also shown that analyses of thematic fantasy play can reveal some of the wider, extra-familial sources of tension in children's emotional lives. From his observations of

RESEARCH SUMMARY 7
LOST AND FOUND IN THE SAND BOX

The following is an extract of one of Corsaro's (1986) videotaped observations of nursery children's fantasy play. Four children, A, MH, M, and H are playing with small toy horses in the sand box. *Lost–found* is the underlying theme of their play.

Transcription	*Description*
1. A – MH: Help, Help! I'm off in the forest	A has three horses and moves them at the end of the sandbox some distance from M and H, who have placed their animals in the sand pile (hideout) A moves one horse up and down as she calls for help
2. M – A: Come in here	M is referring to the hideout.
3. H – A: In here ·	
4. M – A: Come in here! Come here!	
5. A – M: I can't!	
6. M – A: Come in this …	
7. A – M: I'm lost!	
8. M – A: OK	M reaches over and takes A's horse from her hand and puts it in the sand pile.
9. A – MH: My friends, they'll get burnt	
10. A – MH: I'm cold! Freezing!	A now moves her horse up and down near the sand pile.
11. M – A: Stay in here	M take A's horse and puts is in the hideout.
12. A – M: I'm freezing too! I'm freezing too!	A picks up the third horse.
13. M – A: Get in here!	M takes third horse from A and places in the hideout.
14. A – M: Let me	
15. M – A: Get in here	All animals are now in the hideout. M taps the top of the pile. A pats top of the pile
16. A – MH: Warm!	A pats top of the pile
17. H – MA: It's starting to rain! O-O-O-Oh!	H sprinkles sand on top of the pile.

(Corsaro, 1986, pp. 92–3)

nursery school children he was able to show that three major themes recurred time and again in their spontaneous fantasy play. These themes were: lost–found, danger–rescue, and death–rebirth. Wickes, who was a Jungian psychotherapist, would argue that these are basic human, or archetypal themes, which unconsciously preoccupy all people in all cultures throughout their lives.

According to Corsaro, play like that described in Research Summary 7 has two very important functions. First, it facilitates the development of interpersonal skills and a sense of trust and mutual support between children. Secondly, it allows children to gain control over their fears and anxieties by sharing them with other children and developing mutual coping strategies.

> Overall it is clear that in spontaneous fantasy play the children cooperatively construct fantasy events in which they communally share the tensions associated with such fears as being lost, encountering danger, and thinking about death and dying. In these same play events the children also share the relief of these tensions in the enactment and resolution of the fantasy episodes. In this way the children gain *control* over their fears and uncertainties and at the same time *communally share* this sense of control and the resolution of the tension generated in the spontaneous fantasy play.
>
> (Corsaro, 1986, pp. 93–4, original emphases)

Corsaro argues that this communal sharing of fears and anxieties makes a key contribution to the development of the kinds of interpersonal skills and coping strategies that children will need later in life. Corsaro's detailed analysis of the specific language devices children use in their joint development of their play themes provides evidence of the kinds of interpersonal skills that are being developed. These skills allow them to participate in the peer culture which revolves around fantasy play.

4.5 Playing at society

To close this section, I would like to return to Furth and Kane's point made at the beginning, which was that children's pretend play reveals their 'societal knowledge'. This is defined as that 'framework of shared presuppositions, values, traditions, customs, [and] norms' which children need to develop in order to understand the society and culture to which they belong (Furth and Kane, 1992, p. 153). They base the claim that when children engage in pretend play they 'always play society', on their analyses of play episodes such as the one described in Research Summary 8.

Furth and Kane argue that the story created by Annie, Beth and Celia through their play has a social-historical content which shows that they understand about traditions and customs such as royal ceremonies, privilege, power and status, the value of property and the rules and rituals surrounding these issues. They derived these insights into the children's societal knowledge, not so much from the play itself, but from the conversations which took place between the children as they argued

RESEARCH SUMMARY 8
GETTING READY FOR THE ROYAL BALL

As part of a larger study investigating children's play, Furth and Kane made an hour-long video of Annie (5 years 11 months), Beth (5 years 2 months) and Celia (4 years 9 months) as they developed their play around the theme of getting ready to go to a Royal Ball. The children were given access to the props and costumes provided in the dramatic play corner of their classroom, but were free to devise their own theme.

'The play began with Annie's proposal to *get things ready for tomorrow night's ball*. After 19 minutes into the play – choosing clothes, laying them out, making plans and preparing for bed – Annie and Beth were joined by Celia[...] who had come in early from the playground. During the next 30 minutes, further preparations were made, *good night* wishes exchanged and costumes put on for the Royal Ball. Finally, in the last 8 minutes, aware that other students were returning, the three girls hastened the concluding events of proceeding to the ball, meeting the prince and becoming queens, towards which the entire play was a preamble.'

(Furth and Kane, 1992, p. 154)

and negotiated about the theme of the play, the props they needed to use and the roles they were each to play. Like Corsaro, they maintain that children are developing a sophisticated range of interpersonal skills and social competencies as they attempt to manage their play and reach consensus on the form it is going to take.

In this section I have outlined some of the research which suggests that socio-dramatic and thematic fantasy play is important for young children's personal, emotional and social development in early childhood. The next section discusses the contribution research on playground games has made to our understanding of socialization and societal knowledge during middle childhood.

SUMMARY OF SECTION 4

- Investigations of the content and themes of children's play can tell us about their developing social knowledge and also about their emotional fears and anxieties.

- Psychologists make a distinction between socio-dramatic play and thematic fantasy play.

- Evidence suggests that socio-dramatic play is script-based and promotes children's language and communication skills and is important for the establishment of gender and cultural identity.

- Thematic fantasy play develops children's creative imagination, and also allows them to play out, and come to terms, with important emotional tensions and themes. It can also reveal what children understand about power, status and ritual in their society.

5 PLAY AND GAMES IN MIDDLE CHILDHOOD

So far in this chapter, all the examples of children's play have been of young children playing together in pairs or small groups of three or four. As I explained in Section 1, this is characteristic of the play of younger children. In societies where children attend school they begin to play together in larger groups, and informal and team games begin to assume importance. The location and context of their play changes too. Children play in school playgrounds, the street and play spaces near their homes. Play and social interactions are no longer confined to the home, or to places where children are taken to play, such as nursery and day-care centres. Finally, although adults may keep a watchful eye on older children's play and games, they rarely intervene and their presence is much less evident than with younger children.

Piaget (1932) believed that the ways in which children of different ages interpreted the rules of games revealed their understanding of various moral concepts such as fairness and justice. He carried out observations of working-class Genevan children of different ages playing with marbles, and a version of hide-and-seek called 'îlet'. From these observations and from asking children about their games, Piaget formulated a theory of moral development. This will be described in more detail below. Like his account of the development of play (described in Section 2), Piaget's theory of moral development builds on his theory of intellectual development.

Like Piaget, Mead also believed that the experience of playing team games was a vital aspect of children's socialization during the middle childhood years. Reading B outlined Mead's theory that during middle childhood children acquire a concept of the 'generalized other' which allows them to develop a more sophisticated sense of self and an understanding of the dynamics of interpersonal relationships.

In this section I shall describe some of the research on children's games and playground activities during the middle childhood years. There is now a substantial literature on the subject, most of which is British or American. Just as in previous sections I questioned the view that play experiences are solely responsible for various aspects of social development in early childhood, here I shall question the view that participating in games is the most important type of activity leading to social development in middle childhood.

ACTIVITY 6

Allow about 10 minutes

PERSONAL IMPRESSIONS OF THE PLAYGROUND

Before you read any further, take a few minutes to try and remember your own playground experiences when you were at primary school.

Who did you play with?

Where did you play?

Can you remember any games you used to play?

What else did you do in the playground?

Did you enjoy playtimes?

If you have children, you could ask them about their playground experiences.

Comment

When I asked my older daughter, Katie (8 years), about her school playground, she was able to produce a very detailed account, not only about who she played with, but also about who children in other classes played with as well. She and her contemporaries were 'into' skipping and clapping games. The chasing game, 'Tig', was also popular. She and her friends also made up pretend games which centred on riding-stables, ponies, and a great deal of wishful thinking. The boys, I was told, played football and 'kiss-chase' where they chased the girls. Her school playground is officially divided into several areas which allow younger and older children their own play spaces (see Figure 2). Katie also described several informal 'territories' where only certain children are allowed to go, such as an area at the side of the playground where the older girls congregate to chat to their friends. As a quick reliability check on the accuracy of Katie's account, I later asked Jenny (aged 6) about her experiences in the playground. Her account was essentially the same as her sister's.

Katie clearly has a detailed and exhaustive knowledge of what goes on in her school playground at break-times which indicates how important these experiences are to her. Not all of her experiences are happy ones; she is continually falling in and out of friendships and teasing and fighting worry her, as she hasn't quite learnt how to retaliate. Like most other UK children, Katie spends approximately one hour out of her six hour school day in the playground. Over the weeks and years this amounts to a significant proportion of time. Many psychologists are interested in studying children's playground behaviour to see what it can reveal about children's personal and social development. I shall describe some typical studies in the following section.

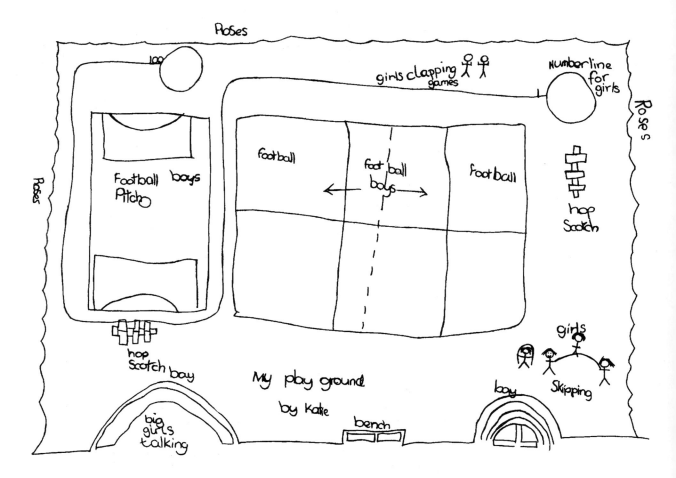

FIGURE 2 Map of Katie's playground

5.1 Researching playground behaviour

The cultural life of the playground

It is not as easy to investigate the play of older children as it is to study that of younger children. Most school playgrounds are large and noisy, and give the appearance of there being large numbers of children roaming about in a fairly disorganized fashion. This makes it difficult to carry out observational studies unless one is prepared to carry out observations over several weeks or even months. Both the British psychologist Andy Sluckin and the folklorist Iona Opie have spent considerable amounts of time visiting particular playgrounds on a regular basis in order to document the games, jokes, rhymes, social rituals and friendships that are part and parcel of children's everyday experience.

Sluckin's and Opie's own accounts of their methods are given in Research Summary 9. As you can see, both methods would be classed as ethnographic.

There is a basic difference between Sluckin's and Opie's method of collecting data about children's playground activities in that Sluckin's

> ### RESEARCH SUMMARY 9
> ### OBSERVING THE PLAYGROUND
>
> I started going down to the playground in the spring of 1960, and in January 1970 began the regular weekly visits that continued until November 1983. My notes gradually became less note-like, and more like a narrative account of what one person could see and overhear and be told directly during the fifteen eventful minutes of morning playtime. I learned to submerge myself as far as possible in the milling throng. I wrote down in home-made shorthand the children's descriptions, comments, and opinions exactly as they expressed them, and their stories and jokes exactly as they told them. Then I hurried home to set it all down before my own impression of the experience had faded.
> (Opie, 1993, p. vii)
>
> Children are inevitably interested in a strange man talking into a pocket dictaphone and walking round their playground, but they are not nearly so self conscious as adults. Over a period of three years, I attended roughly six months of playtimes in a single Oxford first school and later followed up some of the children who went to a nearby middle school. At first I collected basic information such as who was doing what with whom. This led to a catalogue of activities. Later, I collected episodes of potential or actual conflicts, trying to note as far as possible exactly what the children did and said to each other. I followed up my observations by talking individually to every child about playtime.
> (Sluckin, 1987, p. 152)

approach is more systematic, but as you can see, both researchers spent years documenting playground life in order to understand its significance for children.

Iona and Peter Opie were primarily interested in how playground 'lore' is transmitted from one generation of children to the next. Their research since the 1950s has documented children's games, rhymes, jokes and stories in playgrounds up and down Britain. They found that although local dialect variations existed for some of the rhymes and games, and different generations of children had incorporated topical references into their games and stories, there were remarkable similarities between the games and jokes told in one part of the country and those told in other parts. This led them to propose that playground culture is unique to children and that it is one from which adults are excluded. Opie (1993) suggests that children use this culture to escape from the tensions and anxieties of the real world of school and the wider adult society.

By contrast, Sluckin's research led him to propose that playgrounds represent a kind of social microcosm which mirrors the relationships and social institutions of the adult society to which children belong. First, his evidence showed that the games and interactions which took place in the playground were actually highly structured. For example,

dominance hierarchies existed which determined who could initiate games and make up rules and who could join in with games. Secondly, he noted that 'the means or processes by which children and adults manage their worlds are remarkably similar' (Sluckin, 1987, p. 150). Like adults, children make and break rules and promises, negotiate contracts and bargains, and use tried and trusted verbal formulae, phrases and ritual exchanges in order to regulate their social interactions. Observations such as these led him to conclude that the playground provides children with an important preparation for adult life. This is an example of the view (discussed in Section 3) that children's play and games act as *anticipatory socialization* devices.

Whether one regards the playground culture as one which is unique to children or not, both these studies show that while games are important to children, other aspects of playground behaviour are also highly significant. Games themselves clearly generate high levels of discussion and interaction about how they should be played, who can join in and whether or not the rules are fair. So also do other types of verbal exchange, however, such as joking, teasing, and ritual insults. It may well be the case that these are just as important to children's social development as interactions centred on games.

Playgrounds as problem areas

Peter Blatchford, another British psychologist who has carried out research into children's playground behaviour, has dubbed as 'romantic' both the view that playground lore and activities represent a unique children's culture and the view that they represent adult society in microcosm (Blatchford, 1994). He argues that both these views concentrate on the positive, idealistic side of children's playground experiences and ignore the more negative, 'problem' aspects such as the aggression, bullying and often bitter struggles for power and resources that occur. However, even this negative side of playground life may be seen from some perspectives as being a useful preparation for adult life:

> As models of power, games serve to prepare children for expected life experiences ... In games children learn all those necessary arts of trickery, deception, harassment, divination and foul play that their teachers won't teach them but are most important in successful human relationships in marriage, business and war.
>
> (Sutton-Smith, 1973, quoted in Sluckin, 1987, p. 163)

If one regards such things as trickery, deception, harassment etc. as necessary survival strategies which allow children to cope with bullying and aggression, then perhaps Sutton-Smith was making a valid point. Learning how to manage conflict and aggression is an important aspect of children's social development.

What evidence is there that children's behaviour in the playground is problematic? It is important to remember that behaviour which might be seen as negative and problematic by adults, is not necessarily seen in the same light by children. For example, what appears to adults to be real fighting may only be *play* fighting. Recent investigations of playground behaviour have shown that teachers and playground supervisors intervene to prevent play fighting and rough and tumble play in much the same way as they intervene in real fights (see Blatchford and Sharpe, 1994). Some researchers argue that to investigate the significance of playground experiences for children it is necessary to use self-report data and actually to ask them what they feel about playtime. As part of a longitudinal study of children's educational progress, Peter Blatchford and colleagues from the London University Institute of Education have investigated how children's perspectives on the playground change as they move through junior school and into secondary school.

RESEARCH SUMMARY 10
CHILDREN'S PERSPECTIVES ON THE PLAYGROUND

Over 300 children in 33 inner London primary schools were questioned in the Institute of Education Study. In the initial phase both 7 and 11 year olds were interviewed about their schools; school work; break-time; teasing and fighting. All children were interviewed individually and the interviewers used structured interview schedules which contained a mix of closed and open questions. For example, children were asked to give three reasons why they liked and did not like break-time. They were also asked to describe three activities or games they played at break-time, and were asked to judge how much they enjoyed playtime according to a five-point scale. Children from the first phase of the study were interviewed again once they reached the age of 16.

(Blatchford, Creeser and Mooney, 1990; Blatchford, 1994).

The study described in Research Summary 10 showed that, on the whole, most children reported that they enjoy going out to play games and socialize with their friends at break-time. Quite a sizeable minority, mostly girls, however, reported that they did not like being made to go out in bad weather, and that they did not like the bullying, fighting, and teasing that took place. The most popular games amongst the younger children were soccer, chasing games and other ball games. With the exception of soccer, the 16 year olds did not play games at break-time, preferring instead to spend the time talking to their friends. Blatchford comments that

> During the course of their secondary school years (11–16 years) children seem to have forgotten the games and lost the incentive to play … By 16 years the culture is more obviously a youth culture, with social life and friendships more independent of particular activities.

(Blatchford, 1994, p. 10)

Like Sluckin and the Opies, Blatchford came to the conclusion that for children of all ages there is a separate, child-governed break-time culture in the playground from which adults are for the most part excluded. This culture is not always a benign one; racist and sexist teasing and fighting are known to occur (e.g. Kelly, 1994). It is nevertheless extremely important to children, as it allows them freedom from adults. Without adult intervention children have to learn how to regulate playground games and space, and also how to manage teasing and bullying. In doing so, Blatchford argues, they are beginning to develop 'a sophisticated set of social understandings'.

What is striking about this and other studies is that there seems to be a reasonably clear consensus of opinion that playground experience helps children develop important social skills. Even so, other studies have shown that the incidence of bullying and aggression in the playground is sufficiently widespread to cause serious concern (e.g. Whitney and Smith, 1993). Because of this, many psychologists and educators do not now believe that, left to their own devices, children will necessarily develop socially acceptable behaviours in the playground. In Britain this has led to a number of initiatives to try and improve the quality of playground life, either by changing the physical environment to make it more attractive, or by teaching children particular social skills and strategies for dealing with aggression and conflict (see for example Blatchford and Sharpe, 1994).

As both observational and interview studies confirm that children create their own culture in the playground, an important message for programmes designed to improve the playground climate is that interventions are unlikely to be successful unless they take children's views and knowledge of this culture into account. Interventions imposed by adults from without are likely to fail.

This section, so far, has outlined some of the ways in which psychologists have tried to make sense of the importance of playtime in terms of children's social development. As I mentioned earlier, however, Piaget made an even stronger claim about the benefits of playing games for children's development. He claimed that the experience of playing games was necessary for children's moral development. This claim will be discussed next.

5.2 Play and moral development

Central to Piaget's ideas about moral development is the assumption that whenever people come together to form a group, then it is necessary for them to devise a set of social and moral rules in order to regulate the conduct of the group and of the individuals in it. According to Piaget, rules are necessary for the existence of any group, for without them, there can be no genuine co-operation and sense of group identity.

Piaget argued that games are important for moral development because they help children to develop an understanding of how rules function; where they come from; whether they can be changed; the consequences of changing the rules; and so on. He claimed that children generalize their experience of using rules in the context of games to the regulation of behaviour in other contexts. Piaget also recognized, however, that there is a distinction between the practice of moral rules (moral behaviour) and being able to explain those rules (moral understanding). His observations of Genevan children playing games of marbles showed that although they clearly abided by sets of rules, children younger than 10 years of age were not able to explain why rules were necessary, where rules came from or how they could be changed. This led him to propose that moral behaviour and moral understanding develop in identifiable stages, according to two separate but parallel sequences: a practical sequence and a verbal sequence.

ACTIVITY 7

Allow about 5 minutes

AGES AND STAGES IN MORAL DEVELOPMENT

So as to understand the difference between children's explanations of rules and their behaviour when actually playing games, compare Piaget's descriptions of the practical and verbal stages described in Research Summary 11. In what ways does children's behaviour contradict what they say about rules?

Comment

A major contradiction between what children say and what they do occurs during the years between 5 and 9. Piaget found that at this age, children *say* that rules cannot be changed as they are laid down by people in authority. When they play together, however, they frequently make up rules to suit their own needs, and while the rules may be in place for the duration of a particular game, the next time it is played its rules may change.

RESEARCH SUMMARY 11
STAGES AND SEQUENCES OF MORAL DEVELOPMENT

Practical stages

0–3 years.   Children do not play games; behaviour is regulated entirely by child's own needs.

3–6 years.   Children play with each other but do not follow common rules. They are more interested in developing their own skills than in winning the game.

7–10 years.   Children play and try to win games but the rules they follow may be arbitrary and made up on the spot.

11–13 years.   Playing with the rules and seeing what happens when you change them becomes more interesting than playing a game in order to win.

Verbal stages

3–4 years.   Children attach no precise meaning to rules; their description of a rule changes each time they tell it.

5–9 years.   Children think that rules are permanent and unchangeable as they are made up by adults who must be respected and obeyed.

10+ years.   Children understand that rules are invented by people and are based on mutual co-operation and respect. They are not imposed by external authority and can be changed by mutual negotiation.

The descriptions of the ages and stages of moral development given in Research Summary 11 also show that, as far as Piaget was concerned, moral development was effectively complete around the age of 12 to 13 years. According to Piaget, by the time they have reached early adolescence children have moved from a morality based on the idea of *adult constraint*, where rules are imposed by powerful moral authority figures such as parents and teachers, to one founded on the idea of *mutual respect,* where rules are negotiated between people, rather than imposed from outside. Piaget argued that the process of negotiating rules with peers was vital in producing this movement.

This is because he believed that relationships between peers are based on equality rather than power. The equal status of peers allows differences in perspectives to be aired and resolved in a non-threatening climate, and helps children to realize both the limitations of their own views and to accept the legitimacy of other people's views. Where relationships are based on inequality, however, the more powerful person in the relationship may attempt to impose his or her version of the rules on the weaker member, even when these rules are not necessarily fair or just.

5.3 Criticisms of Piaget's theory of moral development

Piaget's assumptions that moral development is complete by about 12 years of age, and that children move from a constraint-based morality to one based on mutual respect, have both been challenged. Subsequent theories of moral development recognize that our ideas about morality continue to develop and change throughout adolescence and adulthood (e.g. Kohlberg, 1984). Research has also shown that some people never achieve the transition from a constraint-based morality to one based on mutual respect.

There are many reasons why this might be the case. Even Piaget recognized that his theory of moral development was not necessarily universal, and that the distinction between constraint and respect simply might not be relevant in some cultures. Where moral rules are derived from sacred texts, for example, children's moral behaviour becomes *more* constraint-based as they grow older and are expected to learn the practice and observance of traditional rules handed down through the generations (e.g. Schweder *et al.*, 1990).

Also, research on children's peer relationships in the playground shows that it is simply not the case that these relationships are always based on equality and mutual respect. In any one group of children there will be differences in the power and status of its various members. Also, as Pollard's (1987) work on playground gangs has shown, there are differences between gangs in terms of status, power and moral and behavioural codes (see the discussion in Section 2). Similarly, in the playgrounds he studied, Andy Sluckin found that children establish pecking orders and dominance hierarchies which allowed certain 'powerful' children to direct and control younger and weaker children's access to games, play spaces and resources.

Other research on peer relationships has shown that children can be classified according to whether they are 'agenda setters', 'responders' or 'isolates' (Haslett and Bowen, 1989). Agenda setters initiate games and dominate the play of other children. These children tend to have good interpersonal and role-taking skills, and are also good communicators. Responders join in with games and help maintain the action, but do not themselves initiate or propose changes to the games. Isolates are children with poor interpersonal skills who do not react appropriately to other children's invitations to join in their games. These children may try to impose their own rules on an already established game and may react aggressively when other children refuse to accept these rules.

Frequently, inequalities of power and status are based not so much on superior physical or social skills and access to resources but on perceived differences between children such as social class, gender and race. As Elinor Kelly points out:

> Playgrounds are sites for social learning – of the negative as well as the positive in human relationships … if pupils are engaged in social learning, then we can be sure that they are dealing with differences

of social class, gender, race, physical and intellectual abilities; how to decide what is acceptable and unacceptable in the behaviour of others; how to deal with those who 'do not fit in'. If left to their own devices, they often order their world into hierarchical patterns of domination, subordination and marginality.

In such a context racism and sexism can thrive.

(Kelly, 1994, p. 64)

Such observed inequalities between children in terms of power and status seem more congruent with the 'problem' view of the playground than with the 'romantic' view. It could be argued that, in failing to recognize this aspect of children's peer relationships, Piaget himself had a rather romantic view of children.

Finally, although Piaget recognized the importance of parents and other adults in providing moral guidance to children during the early years of childhood, more recent evidence suggests that he underestimated the nature and extent of parental influence in shaping children's moral development. Chapter 3 describes different parenting styles and their effects on children's socialization. Research on the long-term effects of different parental styles of socialization on the development of children's ·social competence is still in its infancy. Nevertheless, interesting findings are beginning to emerge which suggest that children's social competence and peer status are related to differences in parenting styles.

Phil Erwin, a British psychologist who has carried out research into children's and adults' friendships, comments that:

> In general terms, the social orientations implicit within caregiver–child and child–peer interactions do appear to be related. Caregivers regularly offering toys to their child produce children who in turn are more likely to offer toys to their peers ... In similar vein, aggressive children are often reflecting their learning experiences, in the family or wider social world. Rejecting parents using frequent prohibitions and controlling behaviour have been consistently associated with aggressiveness in their children, as have high levels of physical punishment. Clearly parents are, wittingly or unwittingly, acting as models for their child.
>
> (Erwin, 1993, p. 88)

Research by the American psychologists Delia and Applegate (1990) has shown that different maternal styles of communication and discipline are related to the ways in which children interact with their peers. The children of mothers who adopt an authoritative disciplinary style and who encourage their children to reflect on the consequences of their own actions, are more likely to develop styles of communication based on co-operation and mutual respect, than are the children of mothers who adopt a more authoritarian style of discipline.

Children do not come into the playground on their first day of school with neutral behaviours and expectations. Their general level of sociability and manner of interacting with other children will have been affected by the models and experiences provided by their parents, siblings, and early childhood playmates. This in turn will affect whether they are popular or unpopular and the type of experiences they have in the playground. Some children, but not all, will enjoy good relations with their peers. For these children, play and games are likely to provide an important context in which they can further develop their social skills and ideas about morality along the lines Piaget suggested. Other children, as Chapter 2 shows, may not be so fortunate.

SUMMARY OF SECTION 5

- Piaget claimed that children's moral development is promoted through peer interaction centred around games with rules. He proposed that children's ideas about morality are initially based on notions of adult-imposed constraint. With time, however, they develop an appreciation of a morality based on mutual respect and co-operation.
- Some research on playground behaviour suggests that a culture unique to children exists in the playground. An alternative view is that the culture of the playground mirrors that of adult society and thus prepares children for adult life.
- Both of these views have been classified as 'romantic', and can be contrasted with the 'problem' view which emphasizes the effects on children of more negative playground behaviours, such as teasing, bullying and aggression.
- A view is beginning to emerge that moral development does not always proceed in the manner suggested by Piaget and is influenced just as much by children's early experiences in the family as it is by their later interactions with peers.

6 CONCLUSION

At the beginning of this chapter I set out to persuade you that play is important for social development. I have presented evidence which shows that role-play in early childhood helps children develop a sense of self. It also fosters their social perspective-taking skills and social competencies. The chapter has discussed research on the nature and function of socio-dramatic play and thematic fantasy play. These types of play seem to be instrumental in promoting a sense of gender and cultural identity. They may also help children come to terms with unexpressed fears and anxieties about their environment and their own personal relationships. Finally, the chapter discussed the relationship between playground games and children's developing sense of personal morality. One argument is that children's experience of regulating their own playground culture prepares them for adult life. Games are part of this culture and introduce children to the necessity for having rules to ensure fair play.

Throughout the chapter, however, I have pointed to other areas of development which may equally affect children's social understanding and their subsequent development. It is clear from research described in previous chapters that the family and the discourse that occurs between carers and children is initially at least as influential as play with peers. Once children enter full-time schooling, however, play with peers begins to exert a significant effect on their personal, social and moral development. The next chapter describes how the peer culture assumes even greater importance for the further development of young people's personal identity during adolescence.

COMMENTS ON ACTIVITIES

ACTIVITY 2   IDENTIFYING THE 'GENERALIZED OTHER'

In his description of the characteristics of the Goodies, Jokers and Gangs, Pollard notes that the 'Good' groups had a positive attitude towards themselves and to their teachers. They conformed to the school rules, and were quiet and studious. The Lion Club identify themselves as a group with high moral standards, and the fact that everybody in it has a nickname suggests that its members all have well-defined roles. The 'Jokers' (Gill's group) also have a positive attitude towards school and each other, but also like to have a laugh and muck about. Tina belongs to a 'Gang'. Relationships within the gang do not seem to be based on a coherent sense of group identity, but more on changing patterns of like and dislike. It is interesting that while both Linda and Gill refer to themselves as 'we', which reflects their identification with their respective groups, Tina refers to herself as 'I'. Does Tina have a less well developed sense of the 'generalized other' than either Gill or Linda?

ACTIVITY 3   THE RELATIONSHIP BETWEEN FANTASY PLAY AND SOCIAL COMPETENCE

As Connolly and Doyle found significant correlations between four measures of social competence and fantasy play, this suggests that experience of fantasy play is indeed related to the development of social competence. Establishing correlations does not allow one to infer that experience of fantasy play, rather than any other sort of play experience, leads directly to enhanced social competence. That the relationship might well be a causal one, however, is supported by their finding that these four measures were not correlated with measures of other types of play.

FURTHER READING

BLATCHFORD, P. and SHARPE, S. (eds) (1994) *Break Time and the School*, London, Routledge.

DUNN, J. (1993) *Young Children's Close Relationships: beyond attachment*, London, Sage.

ERWIN, P. (1993) *Friendship and Peer Relations in Children*, Chichester, Wiley.

SINGER, D. G. and SINGER, J. L. (1990) *The House of Make-believe: children's play and the developing imagination*, Cambridge, Mass., Harvard University Press.

GOLDSTEIN, J. (ed.) (1994) *Toys, Play and Child Development*, Cambridge, Cambridge University Press.

REFERENCES

BLATCHFORD, P. (1994) 'Pupil perceptions of breaktime and implications for breaktime improvements: evidence from England', paper presented to the *Annual Meeting of the American Research Association,* New Orleans, April.

BLATCHFORD, P., CREESER, R. and MOONEY, A. (1990) 'Playground games and play time: the children's view', *Educational Research,* **32,** pp. 163–74.

BLATCHFORD, P. and SHARPE, S. (eds) (1994) *Break-time and the School,* London, Routledge.

BROWNELL, C. (1990) 'Peer social skills in toddlers: competencies and constraints illustrated by same-age and mixed-age interaction', *Child Development,* **61,** pp. 838–48.

BRUCE, T. (1991) *Time to Play in Early Childhood Education*, London, Hodder and Stoughton.

BRUNER, J. (1986) *Actual Minds, Possible Worlds*, Cambridge (Mass.), Harvard University Press.

COLE, M. and COLE, S. R. (1989) *The Development of Children*, New York, Scientific American Books.

CONNOLLY, J. A. and DOYLE, A.-B. (1984) 'Relation of social fantasy play to social competence in preschoolers', *Developmental Psychology,* **20,** pp. 797–806.

CORSARO, W. (1986) 'Discourse processes within peer culture: from a constructivist to an interpretative approach to childhood socialization', *Sociological Studies of Child Development*, **1**, pp. 81–101.

COX, M. (1991) *The Child's Point of View*, Hemel Hempstead, Harvester Wheatsheaf.

CURRY, N. E. and ARNAUD, S. H. (1984) 'Play in developmental pre-school settings' in YAWKEY, T. D. and PELLEGRINI, A. (eds) *Child's Play: developmental and applied*, Hillsdale (N. J.), Lawrence Erlbaum Associates.

DELIA, J. G. and APPLEGATE, J. L. (1990),'From cognition to communication to cognition to communication', paper presented at the *Fifth International Conference on Personal Relationships,* Oxford, July.

DENZIN, N. (1972) 'The genesis of self in early childhood', *Sociological Quarterly,* **13**, pp. 291–314.

DENZIN, N. (1975) 'Play, games and interaction: the contexts of childhood socialization', *Sociological Quarterly*, **16**, pp. 458–78.

DUNN, J. (1988) *The Beginnings of Social Understanding,* Oxford, Basil Blackwell.

ERWIN, P. (1993) *Friendship and Peer Relations in Children,* Chichester, Wiley.

FEIN, G. G. (1984) 'The self-building potential of pretend play or "I got a fish, all by myself" ' in YAWKEY, T. D. and PELLEGRINI, A. D. (eds) *Child's Play: developmental and applied*, Hillsdale (N. J.), Lawrence Erlbaum Associates.

FURTH, H. G. and KANE, S. R. (1992) 'Children constructing society: a new perspective on children at play' in MCGURK, H. (ed.) *Childhood Social Development: contemporary perspectives,* London, Lawrence Erlbaum Associates.

GOTTMAN, J. (1986) 'The world of co-ordinated play: same- and cross-sex friendship in young children' in GOTTMAN, J. M. and PARKER, J. G. (eds) *Conversations of Friends: speculations on affective development*, Cambridge, Cambridge University Press.

HASLETT, B. and BOWEN, S. P. (1989) 'Children's strategies in initiating contact with peers' in NUSSBAUM, J. G. (ed.) *Life-span Communication: normative processes*, Hillsdale (N. J.), Lawrence Erlbaum Associates.

HOWES, C. (1983) 'Peer interaction of young children', *Monographs of the Society for Research in Child Development,* No. 217, **53**(1), Chicago, University of Chicago Press.

HUTT, S. J., TYLER, S., HUTT, C. and CHRISTOPHERSON, H. (1989) *Play, Exploration and Learning: a natural history of the pre-school*, London, Routledge.

IRWIN, D. M. and BUSHNELL, M. M. (1980) *Observational Strategies for Child Study*, New York, Holt, Rinehart and Winston.

ISAACS, S. (1929) *The Nursery Years*, London, Routledge and Kegan Paul.

KELLY, E. (1994) 'Racism and sexism in the playground' in BLATCHFORD, P. and SHARP, S. (eds) *Break-time and the School*, London, Routledge.

KLEIN, M. (1932) *The Psychoanalysis of Children,* London, Hogarth Press.

KOHLBERG, L. (1984) *The Psychology of Moral Development*, San Francisco, Harper and Row.

LEACOCK, E. (1976) 'At play in African villages' in BRUNER, J. S., JOLLY, A. and SYLVA, K. (eds) *Play: its role in development and evolution,* Harmondsworth, Penguin.

LOWENFELD, M. (1979) *The World Technique*, London, Allen and Unwin.

MEAD, G. H. (1934) *Mind, Self and Society,* Chicago, University of Chicago Press.

MELTZER, B. N. (1967) 'Mead's social psychology' in MANIS, J. G. and MELTZER, B. N. (eds) *Symbolic Interaction: a reader in social psychology,* Boston, Allyn and Bacon.

NEILL, A. S. (1962) *Summerhill*, Harmondsworth, Penguin.

NELSON, K. (1986) *Event Knowledge: structure and function in development,* Hillsdale (N. J.), Lawrence Erlbaum Associates.

OATES, J. (ed.) (1995) *The Foundations of Child Development*, Oxford, Blackwell/The Open University (Book 1 of ED209).

OPIE, I. (1993) *The People in the Playground,* Oxford, Oxford University Press.

OPIE, I. and OPIE, P. (1969) *Children's Games in Street and Playground*, London, Oxford University Press.

PARTEN, M. (1932/33) 'Social participation among pre-school children', *Journal of Abnormal and Social Psychology*, **27,** pp. 243–69.

PIAGET, J. (1932) *The Moral Judgement of the Child*, London, Routledge and Kegan Paul.

PIAGET, J. (1951) *Play Dreams and Imitation in Childhood,* London, Routledge and Kegan Paul.

POLLARD, A. (1987) 'Goodies, jokers and gangs' in POLLARD, A. (ed.) *Children and their Primary Schools*, Lewes, Falmer.

SACHS, J., GOLDMAN, J. and CHAILLE, C. (1985) 'Narratives in preschoolers' sociodramatic play: the role of knowledge and communicative competence' in GALDA, L. and PELLEGRINI, A. D. (eds) *Play, Language and Stories: the development of children's literate behaviour*, Norwood (N.J.), Ablex Publishing Corporation.

SCHWEDER, R. A., MAHAPATRA, M. and MILLER J. A. (1990) 'Culture and Moral Development' in STIGLER, J. W. SCHWEDER, R. A. and HURT, G. (eds) *Cultural Psychology: essays on comparative human development,* Cambridge, Cambridge University Press.

SINGER, D. and SINGER, J. (1990) *The House of Make Believe: children's play and the developing imagination*, Cambridge (Mass.), Harvard University Press.

SLUCKIN, A. (1987) 'The culture of the primary school playground' in POLLARD, A. (ed.) *Children and their Primary Schools*, Lewes, Falmer.

SMILANSKY, S. (1968) *The Effects of Sociodramatic Play on Disadvantaged Pre-school Children*, New York, Wiley.

SMITH, P. K. (1988) 'Children's play and its role in early development: a re-evaluation of the "play ethos" ' in PELLEGRINI, A. D. (ed.) *Psychological Bases for Early Education,* Chichester, Wiley.

SMITH, P. K. (1994) 'Play and the uses of play' in MOYLES, J. (ed.) *The Excellence of Play*, Buckingham, Open University Press.

STONE, G. P. (1981) 'The play of little children' in STONE, G. P. and FABERMAN, H. A. (eds) *Social Psychology through Symbolic Interaction*, New York, Wiley.

SYLVA, K., ROY, C. and PAINTER, M. (1980) *Childwatching at Playgroup and Nursery School*, London, Grant McIntyre.

VYGOTSKY, L. (1978) *Mind in Society: the development of higher psychological processes,* Cambridge, Mass., Harvard University Press.

WHITNEY, I. and SMITH, P. K. (1993) 'A survey of the nature and extent of bullying in junior/middle and secondary schools', *Educational Research*, **35**, pp. 3–25.

WICKES, F. G. (1927/1978) *The Inner World of Childhood: a study in analytical psychology*, Boston, Sigo Press.

WINNICOTT, D. (1971) *Therapeutic Consultations in Child Psychiatry*, London, Hogarth Press.

WOOD, D. (1988) *How Children Think and Learn,* Oxford, Basil Blackwell.

READINGS

Reading A Types of play

Peter K. Smith

Play is very characteristic of children in the age range two to six years. This is the major developmental period for symbolic play. Piaget (1951) distinguished between *'practice play'*, *'symbolic play'* and *'games with rules'*. Practice play includes the sensorimotor and exploratory play of the young infant – especially six months to two years; symbolic play the pretend, fantasy and socio-dramatic play of the pre-school and early infant school child, from about two or three to six years; games with rules characterize the activities of children from six or seven years onwards.

Much of the play of the pre-school child will be *symbolic*. Children pretend that an action or object has some meaning other than its usual, real-life meaning; for example if a child rotates his arms, goes 'poop-poop', and gives out pieces of paper, he is pretending to turn a steering-wheel, sound a horn and give out bus tickets. If these actions are sufficiently well-integrated, we can say that the child is in *'role play'* (in this case, pretending to be a bus driver). If two or more children are engaged in role play together, this is *'socio-dramatic play'*. Such forms of play, according to Piaget, appear to increase with age, then decline through the three to seven year age period.

Piaget's scheme was changed slightly and augmented by Smilansky (1968). She added a category of *'constructive play'*, in which objects are manipulated to construct or create something. Many teachers do indeed regard such constructive activities as play. Piaget (1951), however, believed that 'constructive games ... occupy ... a position halfway between play and intelligent work, or between play and imitation', stating this because he thought that the goal-directed nature of constructive activities meant it was 'accommodative' – the child adapting his/her behaviour to fit reality – whereas symbolic play was 'assimilative' – adapting reality to fit the child's own wishes.

Certain kinds of play do not fit well into the schemes of either Piaget or Smilansky. For example, *physical activity play* (running, climbing, sliding, swinging and other gross muscular play) and *rough-and-tumble play* (playful fighting, wrestling and chasing) are very characteristic of young children, especially in outdoor play areas. But they are not constructive, and they are not necessarily symbolic. These kinds of play have been somewhat neglected by psychologists and educationalists, who have paid most attention to constructive play and symbolic play, especially in discussions of nursery and infant school curricula.

Play behaviour is one useful way in which the child can acquire developmental skills — social, intellectual, creative, physical. First, much play is social. Socio-dramatic play and rough-and-tumble play necessarily involve coordination of activities with one or more play partners. Such forms of play can form a primary mode of social interaction at this age range (including gender identity). This is less true of constructive play, which can, but need not, be social. Most forms of play occur naturally between like-aged children, but play can also foster child–adult relationships if the adult engages in a play activity with the child.

Second, many theorists claim that play has intellectual benefits. Socio-dramatic play may foster language and role-taking skills, while constructive play may encourage cognitive development and concept formation. Such aspects of cognitive development may overlap with, though are not identical to, school-based criteria of academic achievement.

Many theorists and practitioners believe that play experience is the optimal way of enhancing creativity and imagination. This is because children have the freedom to try out new ideas in play and can express themselves in their own way, especially in socio-dramatic and fantasy play where they can invent roles and develop a story as their imagination leads them. Finally, much play is physically active. Constructive play may practise fine motor skills, while gross physical play and rough-and-tumble play can provide whole-body exercise and motor coordination.

References

PIAGET, J. (1951) *Play Dreams and Imitation in Childhood*, London, Routledge and Kegan Paul.

SMILANSKY, S. (1968) *The Effects of Sociodramatic Play on Disadvantaged Pre-school Children*, New York, Wiley.

SOURCE: SMITH, P. K. (1994), 'Play and the uses of play' in MOYLES, J. (ed.) The Excellence of Play, *Buckingham, Open University Press, pp. 15–17.*

Reading B   Stages in the development of the self

Bernard N. Meltzer

Genesis of the self. The relationship between role-playing and various stages in the development of the self is described below:

1   *Preparatory Stage.* (Not explicitly named by Mead, but inferable from various fragmentary essays.)

     This stage is one of meaningless imitation by the infant (for example, 'reading' the newspaper). The child does certain things that others near it do without any understanding of what he is doing. Such imitation, however, implies that the child is incipiently taking the roles of those around it, i.e., is on the verge of putting itself in the position of others and acting like them.

2   *Play Stage.* In this stage the actual playing of roles occurs. The child plays mother, teacher, storekeeper, postman, streetcar conductor, Mr Jones, etc. What is of central importance in such play-acting is that it places the child in the position where it is able to act back toward itself in such roles as 'mother' or 'teacher'. In this stage, then, the child first begins to form a self, that is, to direct activity toward itself – and it does so by taking the roles of others. This is clearly indicated by use of the third person in referring to oneself instead of the first person: 'John wants…', 'John is a bad boy'.

However, in this stage the young child's configuration of roles is unstable; the child passes from one role to another in unorganized, inconsistent fashion. He has, as yet, no unitary standpoint from which to view himself and hence, he has no unified conception of himself. In other words the child forms a number of separate discrete objects of itself, depending on the roles in which it acts toward itself.

3   *Game Stage.* This is the 'completing' stage of the self. In time, the child finds himself in situations wherein he must take a number of roles simultaneously. That is, he must respond to the expectations of several people at the same time. This sort of situation is exemplified by the game of baseball – to use Mead's own illustration. Each player must visualize the intentions and expectations of several other players. In such situations the child must take the roles of groups of individuals [...] over [and above] particular roles. The child becomes enabled to do this by abstracting a 'composite' role out of the concrete roles of particular persons. In the course of his association with others, then, he builds up a *generalized other*, a generalized role or standpoint from which he views himself and his behaviour. This generalized other represents, then, the set of standpoints which are common to the group.

SOURCE: MELTZER, B. N. (1967) 'Mead's social psychology' in MANIS, J. G. and MELTZER, B. N. (eds) Symbolic Interaction: a reader in social psychology, Boston, Allyn and Bacon, pp. 10–11.

Reading C   Mrs Comphret – an imaginary companion
Frances G. Wickes

Mrs Comphret lived on the cellar stairs. She was short and plump and comfortable, and she was always smiling. She wore a little black bonnet tied in a neat bow under her chin. It had a jet ornament that stood up in front and tinkled as she walked or nodded. Sometimes she sat out on the cellar door in the sun and smiled. When the days were warm the cellar doors were opened and my sister and I played on the cellar stairs with Mrs Comphret. She did not talk much but was just comfortable and smiling and slow and quiet. We liked to feel her there. I never went to school or anywhere without stopping to talk to Mrs Comphret, or if we were in a great hurry at least we whispered good-bye. [...]

One day a neighbor died. There was a funeral, a 'finneral' we children called it. We were very much impressed with the solemnity and hush. It was not very real to us except as an impressive bit of drama, but in that way it seemed very mysterious and important. Then one day Mrs Comphret died and had a 'finneral'. It was strange to have her go but she never came back. I knew she never would.

Whimsical, quaintly charming as this fantasy is, we find that it has a deeper meaning. When we come to study its reason for being, its relation to the actual life of this particular child, we find that it was called into existence because of a psychological need.

This child felt the lack of certain things in her relationship with her mother. The mother was, like Mrs Comphret, a small woman, but there was no plump restfulness, no quiet smile. Instead she was alert, quick, dominating. The next thing to be done must be done at once. It did not matter where the development of an important game might be, it was time right now to go out or to wash one's hands, or to put one's things away. Something was building in the child's world, perhaps was nearing completion. It was intensely, absorbingly important, but it must be swept away, demolished, because 'we were going down to the store,' or 'supper was ready'. Her mother's voice was quick, charged with nervous energy, immensely disturbing. It broke in upon play or fantasy with irritating persistency. She always intended to be very fond of her mother but before she quite accomplished it the voice would break in upon something very important and then she would be angry and very far away.

She 'adored' her father. He was slow and quiet. If they were going anywhere he would come in ahead of time and say, 'We'll be going in half an hour. You might begin to get washed up in fifteen minutes or so.' Or, 'Ten minutes more to bedtime.' With Mother everything had to be done in a hurry, toys picked up anyhow and at once. The child, too, was high-strung. Her mother's jangling nerves set hers jangling to the same discords. Her father's quiet soothed her. He was a farmer and she loved to tramp the fields after him, wearing boy's shoes, passionately pretending that she was a boy. But after all she was also very much of a girl and loved girl's things. She like dancing school and liked to be admired by boys. Very early she had a special boy whom she liked to consider quite her own. As she grew older the intense love for her father increased. She and her mother made conscious attempts at establishing a relationship, but they could never reach across those intangible barriers.

Mrs Comphret was the personification of the things she had wanted in a mother and had not found. Gradually, as the relationship with her father had grown more satisfying, that need had grown less insistent. Mrs Comphret, quiet, restful, slow and smiling, died and had her 'finneral.'

Source: Wickes, F. G. (1927/1978) The Inner World of Childhood: a study in analytical psychology, Boston, Sigo Press, pp. 156–8.

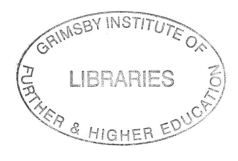

Peter Barnes

CONTENTS

	OBJECTIVES	**288**
1	**INTRODUCTION**	**288**
1.1	Cognitive development	289
1.2	Variability as a rule	290
1.3	Lessons from history	291
1.4	G. Stanley Hall and the discovery of 'adolescence'	292
1.5	A personal perspective on adolescence	293
	Summary of Section 1	295
2	**PUBERTY AND ITS PSYCHOLOGICAL IMPLICATIONS**	**295**
2.1	Physical change	295
2.2	Implications of the timing of maturity	298
	Summary of Section 2	301
3	**ADOLESCENCE AS AN IDENTITY CRISIS?**	**301**
3.1	The influence of psychoanalysis	302
3.2	Erik Erikson's view of identity	302
3.3	Research on identity formation	306
3.4	A question of time and place	310
3.5	A role for intervention in identity development?	313
	Summary of Section 3	314
4	**CRISIS? WHAT CRISIS?**	**314**
4.1	An empirical approach	315
4.2	Evidence from the Isle of Wight study	315
4.3	Evidence from the NCDS	316
4.4	Inner turmoil?	318
4.5	Depression	319
4.6	Coleman's focal theory	319
4.7	Criticisms of focal theory	322
	Summary of Section 4	323
5	**ADOLESCENCE AND FAMILY RELATIONSHIPS**	**323**
	Summary of Section 5	326
6	**CONCLUSION**	**326**
	Answers to Activity 4	326
	FURTHER READING	**327**
	REFERENCES	**327**
	READING A: ADOLESCENCE	**330**
	READING B: EMANCIPATION	**331**

OBJECTIVES

When you have studied this chapter, you should be able to:

1 give an account of the physical changes that occur at adolescence and their possible implications for psychological development;

2 describe and evaluate Erikson's view of adolescence and its significance in the formation of identity, and give a critical account of research that has been carried out on this subject;

3 evaluate the representation of adolescence as a stage marked by storm and stress in the light of evidence from epidemiological studies;

4 describe and evaluate Coleman's focal theory of adolescence;

5 identify ways in which family processes may accommodate the developments of the adolescent period.

1 INTRODUCTION

The previous chapters of this book have mostly been concerned with development during early and middle childhood. In this final chapter it is the later, adolescent stage that is the focus of attention.

It is possible to represent and interpret adolescence as a stage of development in a variety of ways. The following description by two historians of childhood offers one account of its significant features.

> Adolescence is, among other things, an organized set of expectations closely tied to the structure of adult society. It stands out from the other stages of human development as a period of preparation rather than fulfillment. Infancy is cherished in its own right; childhood and adulthood are seen as noble enterprises; [...] But adolescence is a phase of imminence that is not quite imminent enough, of emergent adult biology that is not yet completely coordinated with adult roles, of hopes that are not yet seasoned by contact with adult reality, and of peer culture and society that mimic those of adults but are without adult ambitions or responsibilities. Adolescents are in a state of preparing themselves for adulthood by experimenting, studying, resisting, or playing.
>
> (Modell and Goodman, 1990, p. 93)

This brief account identifies some important features. The first is that adolescence is defined both *biologically* and *culturally*. In terms of biology, profound physical changes take place during the teen years, in particular, puberty. In terms of culture, societies define the expectations, tasks and roles for this period of life. You may not agree with all of the contrasts that Modell and Goodman highlight but the sense of transition and preparation are widely shared. This sense is well matched by the title of the book from which the quote comes: *At the Threshold*.

In some cultures the biological changes are themselves a signal for a change in status in the community; puberty is acknowledged as a *rite of passage*, marked by public ceremonial. In Example 1 you can read of one such ceremony for boys as practised earlier in the twentieth century by the Mano of Liberia.

EXAMPLE 1
RITE OF PASSAGE IN LIBERIA

The boys went through a ceremonial 'death'. In the old days they were apparently run through with a spear and tossed over the curtain. Onlookers heard a thud as he was supposed to hit the ground inside, dead. Actually, the boy was protected by a chunk of plantain stalk tied on under his clothes. Into this the spear was thrust. A bladder of chicken's blood at the right spot was punctured and spilled to make it all very realistic to other boys and women who could not resist the desire to see their sons, perhaps for the last time. Inside the fence *sa yi ge* (a ritual personage) and two assistants, all masked, caught the boys in mid-air, and dropped a heavy dummy to complete the delusion. The boys were actually unharmed and were quickly carried away into the deep forest.

(Harley, 1941; cited in Brooks-Gunn and Reiter, 1990, p. 36)

Although puberty is acknowledged as a significant event in modern societies it has much less clearly defined social repercussions. Children remain at school and continue, for the most part, in the care of their parents throughout their mid-teen years and may remain financially reliant on them for longer still. As Modell and Goodman (1990) point out, it is the structure and expectations of adult society that set the framework of a more protracted transition from the dependence of childhood to the relative autonomy of adulthood. One reflection of this is the ages at which young people are deemed legally competent to take on particular 'adult' responsibilities such as: marriage; casting a vote; watching certain films; driving a motorcycle, car or lorry; and engaging in a homosexual relationship. Adolescence, then, may well be an experience extended over time and this can result in some difficulties of definition when the activities and characteristics of quite different age groups are labelled with the single term; for this reason some researchers distinguish between 'early', 'middle' and 'late' adolescence.

1.1 Cognitive development

From the psychologists' point of view, biological and cultural factors are not the only significant features associated with adolescence. There are important cognitive changes, too, including an increasing self-consciousness and social understanding which enables young people to think and reason about themselves, their world and their relationships.

Piaget, in his influential theory of cognitive development, pointed to the age of 12 years or thereabouts as the time when children begin to move from the stage of *concrete operations* into the fourth and final stage of *formal operations*. This stage is characterized by the appearance of the ability to produce and explore hypotheses and to think about what *might* happen rather than being constrained by the here and now. Further features of this adolescent thinking are, supposedly, that it can accommodate more than one dimension; it can regard knowledge as being relative rather than absolute; and it can incorporate self-reflection and self-awareness (Keating, 1990).

Although research has shown that children younger than 12 demonstrate these features of 'adolescent' thinking under certain conditions, and although by no means all adolescents – or adults for that matter – use them in appropriate situations, there does appear to be a qualitative shift in the modes of thinking they spontaneously employ. And this underlies developments in other areas of adolescents' lives, too:

> Issues that have never or rarely been considered by the adolescent will take on enlarged significance and meaning. Topics of identity, society, existence, religion, justice, morality, friendship, and so on, are examined in detail and are contemplated with high emotion as well as increased cognitive capacity. The spark for such consideration is not purely cognitive, of course; there are many lines of development converging with special significance for the adolescent. But at least some of the motivation for this stretching and breaking of old limits is probably cognitive in the purest sense: '*Cogito ergo sum.*' ['I think, therefore I am.'] In addition, the cognitive skills that can be applied to the task are much sharper, which makes the enterprise all the more exciting and attractive.
>
> (Keating, 1980, p. 215)

1.2 Variability as a rule

Biology, culture and psychology each have their part to play in defining adolescence. Yet in the end we should not expect to find a precise set of parameters for this essentially unstable concept. Issues of variability reverberate through much of the research into adolescence. Three senses of variability need to be taken into account.

First, experiences of adolescence – and, indeed, childhood generally – are specific to the social context of growing up for a particular generation (Elder *et al.*, 1993). If you were to travel back in time, stopping at regular intervals to observe the context of adolescents' lives, you would undoubtedly be struck by contrasts in such features as:

- family experiences – shaped by the incidence of divorce; single-parent families; step-families; changing parental roles (mothers working outside the home, fathers absent because of war or present because of unemployment or early retirement); the generational composition of households (the presence of grandparents); size of family (the number of siblings);

- education and training – standards of education attained; the extent of school careers; opportunities for further and higher education; the availability of apprenticeships and vocational training;
- employment prospects – the availability of work, types of work; conditions of employment; benefit systems to accommodate the absence of work opportunities;
- attitudes towards sexual activity – the availability of reliable birth control methods; HIV infection and AIDS; attitudes toward homosexual relationships;
- the significance of religious belief and observance;
- dominant issues of the day – war and peace, the environment.

Secondly, within any generation there is marked variability in the experience of adolescence as related to gender, social class and ethnic background.

Thirdly, despite trends towards the globalization of child development, for example through the provision of basic schooling, there remain large variations around the world in the extent to which childhood and adolescence is 'protected' as a period of life. In many countries children are expected and required to take 'adult' responsibilities from a very early age, for example labouring in plantations and workshops, and caring for younger siblings.

These sources of variation make any simplistic conception of the 'nature of adolescence' untenable. This caution applies not only to societal expectations about adolescent behaviour: it applies especially to concepts of adolescence implicit in psychological theorizing. One major criticism of theories of adolescence is that they tend to be based on experience in particular cultures, in particular social groups, at particular points in time. Whether or not this is avoidable, the implications of it have to be taken into account. Further, they tend to reflect the beliefs about adolescence of the adult community of which the theorist is a member. In terms of drawing lessons from this literature, it becomes important to distinguish generalizable principles from context-specific features. This theme will become clearer as we turn to the history of the psychological study of adolescence.

1.3 Lessons from history

Although the presence of 'adolescents' and the notion of 'adolescence' is very much part and parcel of our experience and vocabulary today, this has not always been so. Indeed, although the word 'adolescence' (or its equivalent in other languages) existed, it was not widely used before the 19th century. Historians of childhood (e.g. Aries, 1962; Kett, 1977) have illustrated how, in western societies, economic and social factors have helped to place different constructions on stages of human development. So, in the relatively stable agrarian societies of the 16th and 17th centuries children were treated in certain respects as miniature adults, being socialized into adult roles, including work, from an early age. The transition to adulthood was achieved with little evidence of personal crisis or psychological trauma; adolescence was not seen as a socially significant or psychologically complex period in the way that it is today.

For that to come about required, among other things, the existence of communities of young people of a similar age, sharing similar experiences and expectations, and isolated to some degree from the adult world. A significant change in that direction began in the 19th century with the advent of the industrial revolution in Europe and North America and the consequent migration to the towns. In the closing stages of the century, legislation to do with education and child labour had the increasing effect of removing children from the labour market and postponing the onset of adult economic life. One consequence was that 'youths' – mostly male – became more conspicuous and were regarded increasingly as a social problem.

1.4 G. Stanley Hall and the discovery of 'adolescence'

Within this changing social context the emerging discipline of psychology, and in particular the 'Child Study' movement, played its part in constructing a concept of adolescence as a stage of development. The American psychologist G. Stanley Hall was particularly influential, and his wide-ranging, two-volume study *Adolescence: its psychology, and its relations to anthropology, sex, crime, religion and education*, published in 1904, set the tone as to what were the important features of this stage. Drawing on ideas from theology, medicine and science, Hall portrayed adolescence as a period of transition and as a process of becoming. He was particularly influenced by the idea of *recapitulation* – that the development of each individual corresponds to the development of the human race throughout its history. So, the stages of infancy, childhood and adolescence were regarded in terms of a progression from animal-like primitivism through periods of savagery, culminating in the civilized state of adulthood. Hall typified adolescence as a period of turmoil, of *storm and stress*:

> It is the age of natural inebriation without the need of intoxicants, which made Plato define youth as spiritual drunkenness. It is a natural impulse to experience hot and perfervid [glowing] psychic states, and it is characterized by emotionalism. We see here the instability and fluctuations now so characteristic. The emotions develop by contrast and reaction into the opposite.
>
> (Hall, 1904, vol. 2, pp. 74–5; quoted by Coleman, 1974, p. 12)

These views played an influential part in a move away from seeing the newly emergent youth as being troublesome, to regarding them instead as vulnerable and in need of help (Modell and Goodman, 1990). In Section 4 we will examine in more detail one descendant of this view of adolescence as a time of storm and stress, and review more recent research that has increasingly challenged it. For now, the point to note is that it grew out of a particular constellation of social and economic circumstances and was informed by contemporary ideas from science, religion and, indeed, literature.

Though the circumstances may have changed along with the sources of influential ideas, more recent accounts also emphasize the respects in which adolescence comes to be demarcated as a stage in development. As the psychiatrist Michael Rutter has observed:

> Adolescence was not discovered in the sense that anyone studied the behaviour of young people and noted its distinctive character. Rather, the teenage years came to constitute an age period of interest and concern and it was decided that adolescence, in the psychosocial sense, *should* be a universal experience. [...]
>
> Adolescence is recognized and treated as a distinct stage of development because the coincidence of extended education and early sexual maturation have meant a prolonged phase of physical maturity associated with economic and psychosocial dependence; because many of the widely held psychological theories specify that adolescence *should* be different; because commercial interests demanded a youth culture; and because schools and colleges have ensured that large numbers of young people are kept together in an age-segregated social group. To that extent, psychosocial adolescence is created by society and has no necessary connection with the developmental process.
>
> (Rutter, 1979, pp. 6, 7)

1.5 A personal perspective on adolescence

ACTIVITY 1

Allow about 40 minutes

RECOLLECTIONS OF ADOLESCENCE

One feature of the adolescent years – as distinct from earlier childhood – is that it is a time that most people can recall and describe quite vividly. And this process may be further assisted by reference to personal diaries and letters, as well as photographs, scrapbooks and other memorabilia.

The purpose of this activity is to ground your reading of the remainder of the chapter in a personal account of what adolescence means for you and to which you can relate the depictions of it that appear in the research literature.

Spend some time noting down and reflecting on your recollections of your own experience of adolescence. You are already aware of the flexibility of the definition in terms of chronological age. You may want to focus on a time when you were 'in the thick of it'; or you may decide to compare and contrast two different points across a longer time frame.

The following prompts may help you with the task. If you find that some provoke strong feelings, consider what these feelings are about – but if you find yourself strongly affected, move on.

Note that this exercise could involve you in a fair amount of time if it engages your interest. You could also extend its scope by talking about the issues it raises with others currently experiencing adolescence and to those who can recall it from the perspective of a generation different to your own. Further sources of comparison are books and magazines where adolescence is depicted; have these undergone change over time? For present purposes, however, be aware that a time allowance has been put on this activity in the context of your study of this chapter.

- How would you describe the relationship you had with your parents? Did it change in significant ways? How, if at all, did it differ with your mother and your father?
- Did the nature of your friendships with your peers – both male and female – change? In what ways?

- Did your behaviour and habits change in a marked way? Did this cause concern to adults, particularly your parents?
- Did you become introspective and moody?
- Did you become anti social? If so, what form did this take?
- To what extent do you see your adolescence as being shaped by the time and place in which you experienced it – the attitudes and expectations of those around you? Who were your idols and role models? What books and films had a particular impact on you?
- Did the physical changes of puberty have a particular significance for you?
- What changes in your feelings about yourself were associated with your sexual development?
- Do you see your adolescence as a passing phase that you 'grew out of' without its leaving any lasting impression, or do you see it as having had an identifiable and continuing effect upon you as a developing person? Try to describe that impression.

The outcomes of Activity 1 are personal ones. Keep in mind your response to the questions about puberty and feelings about sexual development as you move on to the next section which considers the nature and timing of the biological changes that constitute puberty and reflects on their possible psychological impact.

> ### SUMMARY OF SECTION 1
>
> - Adolescence as a stage in development is characterized in part by biological change but is, in significant respects, a cultural construct.
> - The experience of adolescence at any one time is bound up with the prevailing social context; this encourages caution in making generalizations over time and between places.
> - The development in cognitive abilities during adolescence has implications for some of the tasks of personal and social development.
> - G. S. Hall's early representation of adolescence as a time of storm and stress set the tone for much subsequent enquiry.

2 PUBERTY AND ITS PSYCHOLOGICAL IMPLICATIONS

2.1 Physical change

Whatever cultural overlay may be applied to the adolescent stage, its one unquestioned feature is the major physical changes that take place in the human body; growth speeds up and the body's character alters. There is an accelerated increase in height and weight and, notably in boys, an increase in physical strength and endurance. There are profound changes in the *primary sexual characteristics* as the reproductive organs grow and become fully functional. There are changes, too, in the *secondary sexual characteristics*: breast development, the growth of body hair, and deepening of the voice, particularly in boys. In girls the first menstruation (menarche) is regarded as a significant sign of the start of puberty.

Personal experience tells us that the age of onset and the duration of these physical changes varies from individual to individual. An extensive, systematic account of the nature and timing of such changes during childhood and adolescence has been provided by James Tanner and his colleagues who recorded the physical characteristics of large samples of children of different ages, in the UK and elsewhere (Tanner, 1989). From these data it is possible to establish both the normal (i.e. average) progress of development and the variation in age at which different developments first take place and are concluded. It is also possible to compare the growth of boys and girls.

ACTIVITY 2

Allow about 5 minutes

COMPARING BOYS AND GIRLS

Look at Figure 1 which shows for (a) girls and (b) boys the course of different pubertal processes at adolescence. The data are based on European and North American samples. On each of the horizontal bars is marked the average age of onset and the average age of completion.

Note down what strikes you as significant about the information contained in these diagrams. Look, in particular, at the contrast between girls and boys.

Comment

Three important points emerge. The first is that girls mature earlier than boys. For example, the average onset of the height spurt for girls is around 10.5 years, whereas for boys it is about two years later. The second is that, in general, the pubertal processes are spread over a long time. Breast growth, for example, takes place on average over a four-year time span. And the third is that, for both sexes, there is a considerable spread of ages around the average figures. So, while the mean age of menarche in this sample was about 13 years, the range ran from about 10 to 16.5.

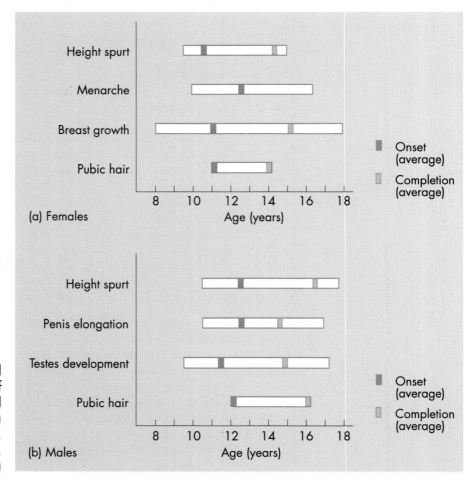

FIGURE 1 The normal range and average age of development of sexual characteristics in (a) females and (b) males. (Adapted from Tanner, 1973, p. 4.)

What accounts for these variations in ages of onset? A number of different factors are involved. Among pairs of identical twins, for example, the average age difference for menarche is less than 3 months, whereas for sisters it is 13 months and for unrelated girls 19 months (Tanner, 1962); this suggests a genetic influence. Environmental factors can also play a part and, of these, standards of nutrition and general health appear to be particularly significant. This goes some way to explaining differences between children from different social class backgrounds and different countries. It also helps to explain what is termed the *secular trend*: the fact that, over the last 150 years or so since systematic records began to be kept, children have grown faster and further, and matured earlier.

One well-documented example of the secular trend is the average age of menarche in different countries (see Figure 2). The data indicate a reduction from about 16 years in the mid 19th century to about 13 years in the 1960s, at a rate of approximately 4 months per decade. The nutrition/health-care explanation is supported by evidence which indicates that the average age of menarche is higher where people are living under conditions of material deprivation; also the rate of reduction slows down during times such as wars when nutritional standards are adversely affected. Obviously there has to be a biological lower limit to the age of menarche and there is some evidence from Figure 2 of a levelling-off in the figures during the 1960s.

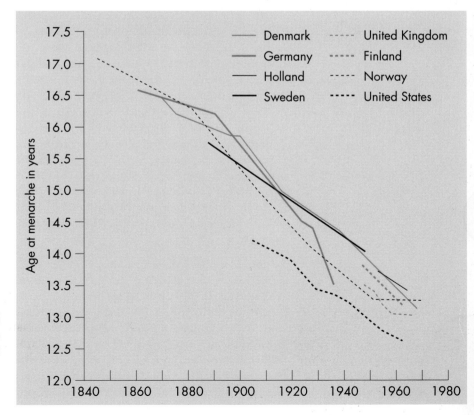

FIGURE 2 Secular trend in the age of menarche between 1860 and 1970 in eight countries. (Adapted from Tanner, 1973, p. 43.)

2.2 Implications of the timing of maturity

These physical transformations are considerable. What is their impact on psychological development? For example, how do individuals perceive these bodily changes and incorporate them into their self-concepts? The development of identity requires both a sense of self-consistency – that you remain the same person over time – and a knowledge of how you appear to others; at a time of considerable bodily changes both of these are put under strain.

Adolescents tend to be both sensitive to and critical of their changing physical self; idealized standards of attractiveness are readily available on television and in magazines, and the perceptions of the peer group are likely to be influential, too. Those who see themselves as deviating from these standards may well suffer impaired self-concepts. In one US study where adolescents were asked what they did and did not like about themselves, those in the earlier stages of adolescence were more likely to describe themselves in terms of physical characteristics, and those characteristics figured high in the list of dislikes (Simmons and Rosenberg, 1975).

What are the implications for those who mature either early or late; does it affect their self-perception and social relationships? Jean Brooks-Gunn, a leading researcher in this field, has summarized a number of research studies – mostly from the US – which indicate trends that differ for boys and girls (Brooks-Gunn and Reiter, 1990). There is evidence to suggest that boys who mature early have an advantage over those who mature late in areas of self-esteem, popularity and school life. Some of this may be attributable to the value the culture tends to place on physical strength, sports and generally 'macho' behaviour. By contrast, the implications for early maturing girls tend to be more negative: they are more likely to exhibit eating problems, to come into conflict with their parents and teachers, to have poor body images, and to begin to smoke, drink alcohol and have sexual intercourse earlier. It is suggested that some of these features may be a consequence of the girls' friendship patterns; being more mature in certain respects they spend more time in the company of older peers and become socialized into their ways. By the same token, girls and boys who mature late are likely to be at a disadvantage in a wide range of areas of development when compared with their peers whose maturation has conformed to the norm.

In considering evidence of this kind it is important to be aware of the significance of society's expectations and values in influencing how early maturation is perceived. The point can be illustrated by looking at weight and dieting. A US study found that girls who matured early were more likely to have eating problems that lasted throughout adolescence than did those who matured on-time or late (Brooks-Gunn and Warren, 1985). Brooks-Gunn and Warren draw links between three observations: body build is associated with popularity; in the culture in which the study was conducted being thin is perceived as a desirable condition by most adolescent girls; and early maturers are somewhat heavier than average. Hence, there is a tendency for early maturing girls to have a less positive body image and to be more concerned with dieting.

In another US study, Maryse Richards and colleagues measured the level of satisfaction with their weight expressed by nearly three hundred 11- to 13-year-old boys and girls (Richards *et al.*, 1990). These ratings were then related to whether the participants were themselves underweight, of average weight or overweight (see Figure 3).

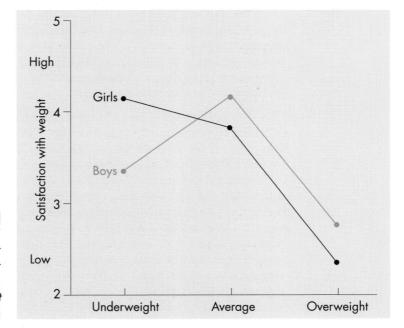

FIGURE 3 Male and female adolescents' satisfaction with their weight in relation to their own weight category. (Adapted from Richards *et al.*, 1990, p. 317.)

ACTIVITY 3

Allow about 5 minutes

INTERPRETING WEIGHTY DATA

Study Figure 3 and note down your interpretation of the data. How might these results be interpreted in the light of what you have just been reading?

For both sexes the lowest levels of satisfaction were expressed by those who were overweight. But whereas it was the boys of average weight who were the most satisfied, for girls the highest levels of satisfaction were expressed by those who were underweight. This seems to fit the picture that emerges from Brooks-Gunn's research and what has already been noted about the physique favoured by boys. However, there was a further dimension to Richards *et al.*'s study. These adolescents came from two different communities (which Richards labelled Northshore and Westside) and an interesting contrast appeared when the data for the two were analysed separately. In both communities being overweight was associated with low satisfaction ratings but only in one, Northshore, was being underweight associated with high satisfaction by the girls. In Westside the ratings for the underweight and those of average weight were the same. Why? Richards noted a difference between the two communities which seemed to be significant:

adolescents in Westside were more likely to take part in after-school activities, particularly sports, and the data indicated a relationship between feeling satisfied with sports and feeling satisfied with their weight and their bodies. Richards suggests that 'the community differences in satisfaction reflect community values that are probably transmitted through school policies and practices, as well as through the attitudes of the youngsters, families, and peer groups' (Richards *et al.*, 1990, p. 319). Drawing on other research in this area she further suggests that the positive relationship between exercise and fitness on the one hand and self-esteem and bodily satisfaction on the other might operate in one or more of three ways: that exercise helps bring about weight reduction and a firmer, trimmer body; that it helps create a sense of mastery and competence; and that 'mood elevation' results from participation in the activity itself.

This study offers an important message which can be generalized. Specifically, when considering the implications of the physical changes that occur at adolescence for other aspects of development – and particularly self-image and self-esteem – it is necessary to be aware that the relationships are not fixed. They may vary both between cultures and within the same culture, depending on what value is placed on particular physical characteristics. The more general point is that *context* plays an important part in perceptions of the self and this should encourage caution in how we treat findings from research; what may be true for one sample of adolescents in a particular setting is not necessarily true elsewhere. Likewise, relationships can vary over time; what was associated with high prestige by one generation may not be regarded in the same way by another. A visit to any art gallery will quickly confirm how images of what constitutes a desirable and positively regarded figure appear to have varied considerably throughout history.

A final question to ask in this section: are these sorts of relationships between physical maturity and personal feelings and behaviour transitory or do they have longer-term implications? An American study (Mussen and Jones, 1957) investigated a group of boys who were among the slowest 20 per cent in terms of physical maturity. Adults judged them more negatively in a number of respects: they were less attractive, less socially mature, and more restless, talkative and bossy. Their peers likewise judged them as being less popular and few of them were leaders. The boys themselves showed more feelings of inadequacy, negative self-perceptions, feelings of rejection and persistent dependency needs. When the sample was followed up at the age of 33 a majority continued to exhibit difficulties in personal adjustment (Jones, 1957). Even if the values placed on the particular manifestations of physical development have changed since this study was carried out, it raises the possibility that, for some at least, the perception of physical maturity and the personal values attributed to it can have lasting effects.

The relationship between physical characteristics, self-image and self-esteem is but part of the establishment of identity. It is to this broader issue that we now turn.

SUMMARY OF SECTION 2

- There is considerable variation in the age of onset and rate of development of puberty.
- Physical changes associated with puberty are related to changing self-perceptions and self-esteem.
- The nature of these relationships is variable and appears to be linked to the values society attributes to particular physiques at a given time.

3 ADOLESCENCE AS AN IDENTITY CRISIS?

Fifteen years old! This was indeed the most memorable day of my life, for on that evening I began to think about myself, and my thoughts were strange and unhappy thoughts to me – what I was, what I was in the world for, what I wanted, what destiny was going to make of me! ... It was the first time such questions had come to me, and I was startled at them. It was as though I had only just become conscious; I doubt that I had ever been fully conscious before ...

(Hudson, 1918; quoted in Conger, 1979, p. 9)

Over the last few years my personality has changed drastically, mostly due to pressures from my peers to conform, although I am happier with my new 'image' than I was before. However, I now feel the need to find my true personality, if that is possible, and to define myself. It is difficult not to do this by fitting into a stereotype, as I see many people doing, where the way they dress, their way of talking and even their values are defined by something as immaterial as their taste in music. I think quite deeply about my personality. From talking to my friends I think I am fairly unusual in this. Most people seem to take the way they are for granted whereas I see myself as having to work at myself to find a state in which I am happy ...

(Anna, aged 16, writing in 1994)

These two quotations are separated by nearly eighty years. The first is a reminiscence of the writer's mid-teens, and the other a contemporary account at a similar age. Yet they have features in common. Both indicate an intense awareness of and interest in themselves as people, coupled with a sense that they are undergoing a significant change from what they were. The writer W. H. Hudson recalls experiencing a sudden awakening prompted by a special occasion – his fifteenth birthday. For 16-year-old Anna the process has been more gradual, but with a recent intensification. (You have already read Anna's account in Chapter 5 (p. 189), where Dorothy Miell quotes her to illustrate changes in the way that children of different ages describe themselves.) One way of representing what both are talking about is in terms of *identity*. Both are seeking answers to the question 'Who am I?' According to some psychological accounts, adolescence is the stage in life when this issue is of central importance.

3.1 The influence of psychoanalysis

G. Stanley Hall's early portrayal of adolescence as a period of personal storm and stress (see Section 1) proved very influential in shaping perceptions and focusing subsequent psychological enquiry. Further weight has been added to it by the theories and writings of psychoanalysts. For example, Anna Freud, Sigmund's daughter, viewed adolescence as 'by its nature an interruption to peaceful growth' (Freud, 1958). For her, the onset of puberty saw the start of a process by which the adolescent needed to become *autonomous* and *detached* from the parents, a process characterized by rebellion, which in turn generates conflict within the family. The absence of such conflict was a clear indication that personal development was being stunted:

> We all know individual children who as late as the ages of 14, 15, or 16 show no such outer evidence of inner unrest. They remain as they have been during the latency [i.e. middle childhood] period, 'good' children, wrapped up in their family relationships, considerate sons of their mothers, submissive to their fathers, in accord with the atmosphere, ideas, and ideals of their childhood background.
>
> (Freud, 1968, p. 14; quoted in Conger, 1991, p. 20)

Another psychoanalytic interpretation has been provided by Peter Blos (1970). He portrayed adolescence as a *second individuation process* (the first one having occurred by the third year of life). The adolescent has to loosen the ties with and disengage from internalized loved ones within the family in order to allow engagement with new love objects in the world beyond the family. In order to achieve this disengagement, Blos claimed, the adolescent needs to reactivate earlier involvement and patterns of behaviour and this involves *regression*. Disengagement can lead to the experience of separation and loss and the creation of what he called 'object and affect hunger', a hunger which may be satisfied by intense emotional states, for example through delinquent activities, drugs and religion.

3.2 Erik Erikson's view of identity

Blos had an influence on the early career of Erik Erikson (1902–94) who went on to make a particular contribution to the study of identity formation in adolescence (Stevens, 1983).

Erikson trained and practised as a psychoanalyst in Austria before going to the US to escape the Nazi persecution. During World War Two

Erik Erikson

he worked at a rehabilitation clinic for war veterans and after that at the Austin Riggs Center in Massachusetts, with adolescent patients. These two experiences shaped his thinking about identity and its particular significance for adolescence, and he went on to incorporate this into a comprehensive account of developmental stages throughout the lifespan from birth to old age (Erikson, 1968).

Erikson regarded identity as 'a *subjective sense* of an *invigorating sameness* and *continuity*' (Erikson, 1968, p. 19, original italics), a recognition that we feel ourselves to be the same person through time and space. His contact with soldiers psychologically affected by the experience of war provided a telling contrast:

> What impressed me most was the loss in these men of a sense of identity. They knew who they were; they had a personal identity. But it was as if, subjectively, their lives no longer hung together – and never would again. There was a central disturbance of what I then started to call ego identity.
>
> (Erikson, 1965, p. 37)

This contrast between a sense of continuity characteristic of normal life and the loss of identity during wartime provided a framework for Erikson's subsequent work with adolescents. He coined the term *identity confusion* to describe the state found in 'severely conflicted young people whose sense of confusion is due, rather, to a war within themselves, and in confused rebels and destructive delinquents who war on their society' (Erikson, 1968, p. 17).

Erikson's account of the development of identity links to some of the ideas about the development of the self that you read about in Chapter 5. He saw its origins arising in infancy from the trustful relationship between parent and child; the infant incorporates or *interjects* the adults' images. Then, later in childhood, *identification* becomes the important mechanism, and the roles and values of others who are admired become incorporated. During adolescence the particular emphasis is on *identity formation*: the individual retains some of these earlier childhood identifications and rejects others in line with developing interests, abilities and values.

> The young person, in order to experience wholeness, must feel a progressive continuity between that which he has come to be during the long years of childhood and that which he promises to become in the anticipated future; between that which he conceives himself to be and that which he perceives others to see in him and to expect of him. Individually speaking, identity includes, but is more than, the sum of all the successive identifications of those earlier years when the child wanted to be, and often was forced to become, like the people he depended on. Identity is a unique product, which now meets a crisis to be solved only in new identifications with age mates and with leader figures outside of the family.
>
> (Erikson, 1968, p. 87)

FIGURE 4　Erikson's
developmental stages
are shown along the
horizontal axis. The vertical
axis indicates the
approximate age or
Freudian label for each
stage: I oral-sensory;
II muscular-anal;
III locomotor-genital;
IV latency; V puberty and
adolescence; VI young
adulthood; VII adulthood;
VIII maturity. (Adapted from
Erikson, 1968, p. 94.)

Erikson's developmental stages

One of Erikson's important contributions was his account of
development through the whole lifespan from birth to old age in terms
of eight stages. These are illustrated in Figure 4.

According to Erikson, each stage is characterized by its own particular
developmental 'task'. This can be represented in terms of a particular
conflict or crisis (shown in **bold type** in the figure) that needs to be
resolved if healthy development is to proceed. The term 'crisis' does not
carry the usual negative connotations, however; Erikson used it to
indicate an expected and necessary part of development, what he called
a *normative* crisis. So, in the first stage, infancy, the crisis is to do with
basic trust versus mistrust; in the fifth stage, adolescence, the task is to
establish a coherent identity at the expense of a sense of *identity
confusion* (sometimes known as *identity diffusion*).

	1	2	3	4	5	6	7	8
VIII								**Integrity** vs. **Despair**
VII							**Generativity** vs. **Stagnation**	
VI						**Intimacy** vs. **Isolation**		
V	Temporal perspective vs. Time confusion	Self-certainty vs. Self-consciousness	Role experimentation vs. Role fixation	Apprenticeship vs. Work paralysis	**Identity** vs. **Identity confusion**	Sexual polarization vs. Bisexual confusion	Leader- and followership vs. Authority confusion	Ideological commitment vs. Confusion of values
IV				**Industry** vs. **Inferiority**	Task identification vs. Sense of futility			
III			**Initiative** vs. **Guilt**		Anticipation of roles vs. Role inhibition			
II		**Autonomy** vs. **Shame, doubt**			Will to be oneself vs. Self-doubt			
I	**Trust** vs. **Mistrust**				Mutual recognition vs. Autistic isolation			

The crises characteristic of each stage are not independent of one another, however. What happens at each of the earlier stages has a bearing on the form that the crisis takes at subsequent stages. So, issues which have implications for the conflict between identity and identity confusion at the fifth stage are encountered at earlier stages in terms of the prevailing normative crisis of each stage. Some indication of these is provided in the lighter print in Figure 4 (note that only those cells which have a bearing on the fifth stage have been completed to make the figure more accessible). In the first year of life, for example, Erikson portrays the normative crisis as one of *trust* versus *mistrust*. It can be represented in terms of the trust generated through the mother's provision of life-sustaining care. The mutual recognition that this can generate forms a foundation of a sense of identity. Erikson argues that the absence or impairment of such trust and recognition 'can dangerously limit the capacity to feel *identical* when adolescent growth makes it incumbent on a person to abandon his childhood and to trust adulthood and, with it, the search for self-chosen loves and incentives' (Erikson, 1968, p. 105).

READING

Reading A at the end of this chapter is from Erikson's book *Identity: youth and crisis* (1968) where he offers his account of adolescence. The reading brings together some of the ideas that you have just been introduced to but in Erikson's own words.

As you read, note Erikson's view on the significance of the broader context within which young people experience the teenage years and the interrelationships of some of these. In these respects his ideas differ from other psychoanalytic accounts by introducing more of a cultural dimension.

The term *moratorium* is used often in Erikson's writings. It means a breathing space within which identity can be integrated without feeling under pressure.

Look out for examples of how the adolescent stage is set within the context of the crises of the preceding stages. Locate the stages referred to within Figure 4. Erikson reinforces the point that the experience of adolescence is influenced by how the crisis of each of the earlier stages was resolved. What relationships does he indicate?

Reflect on what you read here in terms of what has been said earlier in this chapter concerning how the adolescent experience is seemingly modified by the prevailing circumstances of an age cohort or cultural group. *Identity: youth and crisis* was published in 1968, a time of considerable social ferment in the US (and in many parts of Europe). Do you see any link with the way in which Erikson depicts adolescence? What are the possible implications of this?

Identity confusion (or diffusion) has an important place in the fifth stage. According to Erikson it can show itself in a number of ways:

- the problem of *intimacy* – a fear of losing identity by becoming involved in close personal relationships or commitments may lead adolescents to seek isolation or to establish over-formal relationships;
- diffusion of *time perspective* – anxieties about change and the prospect of becoming an adult are accompanied by a poor sense of time scales and a reluctance to plan for the future;
- diffusion of *industry* – an inability to concentrate on work or study or a preoccupation with a single activity;
- *negative identity* – rejection of the roles that are valued by parents or the community.

At this point you could look at your response to Activity 1 and see whether any of these tensions are reflected in your own experience.

Erikson's account has been influential as one of the most comprehensive, general theories of adolescence. But there is reason to be cautious about assuming that it can be universally applied. His views of adolescence were formed largely through experience with young people attending clinics on account of their significant problems and many of the examples of identity confusion that he cites come from this restricted population. Are the insights that come out of this work relevant to the experience of adolescents in general or do they have only a limited application?

Although some have criticized Erikson's methods and descriptions for being imprecise, impressionistic and unverifiable, others have explored ways of testing his ideas about identity formation more systematically and scientifically.

3.3 Research on identity formation

Such attempts are immediately faced with the problem of how to describe identity in terms that can be measured – how to *operationalize* it. Is it possible to find valid, reliable, observable manifestations of identity in behaviour? One psychologist who took up this challenge is the American James Marcia (1980), and he, in turn, has prompted others to extend his approach. I will use a selection of this research to illustrate both its potential and its limitations.

As you saw in Reading A, Erikson suggested that one task for the adolescent in the fifth stage is to find and become committed to some ideological world view and to a role in society. He highlighted a number of key developmental issues that could become the focus of an identity crisis: the choice of an occupation, decisions about religious or political commitments, sexual orientation and what behaviour is appropriate to a particular sex role. Marcia translated this into the following research question: what evidence is there that young people do consider alternatives and make commitments at this stage of development? He used semi-structured interviews to try to discover whether adolescents sought out knowledge and information that could lead to a personal choice – what he labelled *exploration*. He also looked for evidence of a genuine investment in a particular choice – what he called *commitment*. Taken together, these two dimensions offer the potential to categorize subjects in terms of four distinct *identity statuses* (Figure 5).

FIGURE 5 Identity statuses as related to dimensions of exploration and commitment.

	Commitment	
	Yes	No
Exploration — Yes	Identity achievement	Moratorium
Exploration — No	Foreclosure	Identity diffusion

How do these statuses relate to what adolescents said in the interviews? Marcia typified them in the following way:

1 *Identity diffusion* – some of those he interviewed had made no commitment nor did they appear to be attempting to arrive at one. In some cases there had been no active exploration of alternatives; in others there had been exploration in the past but it had not resulted in commitment.

2 *Foreclosure* – others had made a commitment and would defend it strongly, but it had been reached with few signs of an exploration or questioning of alternatives or of any crisis having been experienced. Instead, the beliefs and values of parents or of another influential adult had been adopted as providing the 'right way'.

3 *Moratorium* – Marcia adopted Erikson's term to classify those who are in an identity crisis, struggling, say, with issues to do with job choice or decisions about ideological issues and trying to make a commitment. Such adolescents are typically animated and anxious in their search for identity.

4 *Identity achievement* – here, a normative crisis has been experienced and resolved and a commitment entered into. After exploring alternatives, one has been selected which they believe fits their individuality best in the current circumstances. Marcia describes such adolescents as being thoughtful and reflective, open to new experiences and ideas and willing to judge them according to their own standards and values.

The following activity is designed to help you to check your understanding of these somewhat abstract identity statuses.

ACTIVITY 4

Allow about 10 minutes

ESTABLISHING IDENTITY STATUS

One question that Marcia asked in his interviews was 'Have you ever had any doubts about your religious beliefs?' Read the four responses below and attempt to classify them in terms of the four identity status categories described above.

(a) Yes, I have. I was thinking the other day about how, if there is a God, he can allow innocent people to die in floods and car crashes. I often find contradictions like that and it makes me rethink what I've been taught.

(b) I suppose some people think about things like that. But it doesn't bother me personally. When it comes to it, religions are all the same really.

(c) Yes. I've been reading about different religions around the world and I've gone to some services for different faiths. I've decided that Buddhism is the one for me; it seems to fit with the life I'd like to lead. I go to a Buddhist temple regularly, now.

(d) Not really. I've been going to church since I was quite small with my mum and dad and I find I believe what they've told me.

Check your answers with those given at the end of the chapter.

Now, consider possible progressions from one identity status to another. Is one more mature than the others?

Marcia and others have used this interview procedure and the fourfold classification to investigate a number of questions to do with the development of identity in adolescence:

(a) In what ways do identity statuses relate to the actual experiences of adolescents? For example, at any one time, does the same identity status apply across different aspects of an individual's life – vocation, religious beliefs, etc. – or can an individual be in different statuses for each aspect?

(b) Is there a developmental progression of identity statuses? For example, given the possible moves from one status to another, which of these indicates developmental progress, which moves are most likely to be experienced in practice, and under what conditions does change take place?

In a study done in North America, Sally Archer addressed the developmental issue. She interviewed children between the ages of 11 and 17 about occupational choice, religious beliefs, political philosophies and sex-role preferences (Archer, 1982). She found, not surprisingly perhaps, that 89 per cent of the 11 year olds' decisions were classifiable under the identity diffusion and foreclosure statuses. However, a less expected finding was that similar levels were recorded by the 13 and 15 year olds (87 per cent in both cases) and even amongst the 17 year olds, 81 per cent were classified in these two categories. So, although identity achievement increased significantly with age, it was far from being conspicuous in absolute terms, and the same was true for the active questioning and exploration of the moratorium status. In short, there was no clear-cut developmental progression for the school years.

Is greater movement found when the age-range is extended? Alan Waterman and colleagues (1974), in a longitudinal study, interviewed students at an American college in their first and, later, their fourth and final year.

TABLE 1 Identity status of American college students in occupational and ideological areas in their first and final years.

Identity status	Occupational (N=47)		Out of status	Into status
	Year 1	Year 4		
Achievement	7	19	2	14
Moratorium	8	0	8	0
Foreclosure	17	14	5	2
Diffusion	15	14	8	7
Identity status	Ideological (N=45)		Out of status	Into status
	Year 1	Year 4		
Achievement	5	20	0	15
Moratorium	4	1	4	1
Foreclosure	19	7	13	1
Diffusion	17	17	5	5

Source: adapted from Waterman *et al.* (1974), p. 390.

ACTIVITY 5

Allow about 10 minutes

CHARTING DEVELOPMENTAL TRENDS IN IDENTITY STATUS

Table 1 summarizes some of Waterman's data. The figures in the left-hand pair of columns show the number of students in each identity status for Marcia's occupational and ideological areas when interviewed in their first and final years at the college. The right-hand pair of columns shows the numbers of individuals who moved out of and into each status over the duration of the study – so, for example, 14 students moved into the identity achievement status for occupation and 2 who showed evidence of it in their first year were no longer categorized in that way in their final year.

What interpretation can be placed on these data?

What further questions are raised about issues of cohesion and change?

Comment

The first thing that stands out is that, in the two years considered separately, the spread of identity status was similar for both the occupational and ideological areas. In the first year, foreclosure was the most frequent for both areas (17 out of 47, and 19 out of 45), and foreclosure and diffusion together (32/47 and 36/45) were more frequently encountered than achievement and moratorium (similar to the pattern found by Archer with younger adolescents). Three years later the picture has changed. Achievement has become the largest single category for both occupation and ideology and the numbers in the moratorium status have all but disappeared. Many more participants became achievers than moved out of that category. (The increases in achievement status and decrease in moratorium status are all statistically significant at the 0.01 level of confidence.)

So, there is evidence here to suggest that some students had moved from a foreclosure position, where they appeared content to advance ideas derived from those in authority, to one of identity achievement where they had reached a position on their own account. The moratorium status is the most unstable, as might be expected.

It is notable, however, that even by the end of a four-year college course substantial numbers of these students in their early twenties were still classed in the least mature identity diffusion status (14/47 regarding occupation and 17/45 regarding ideological). In fact, 13 per cent of the sample were in the identity diffusion status in both areas and a further 33 per cent in one area only.

These data prompt further questions about the development of identity statuses:

Under what circumstances do people move from one status to another?

Do individuals explore a number of areas at a time or is exploration selective? Is it appropriate to think of changing identity in a global way, as reflecting a process of personal development, or would a truer picture need to take account of the influence of specific circumstances in the adolescent's social environment?

And to these questions may be added ones that arise from considering the nature of the sample being studied. How representative is a college sample like this of youth in general? And to what extent can findings from a North American sample be generalized to adolescents in other societies?

3.4 A question of time and place

The college where Waterman *et al.* carried out their research had a strong vocational orientation and aimed to develop work-related skills. This may help to account for the absence of students in the moratorium status for occupation in their final year. The researchers suggest that once the matter of occupation is settled, increasing emphasis can be placed on working out ideological beliefs; hence the increased numbers in the identity achievement status in year 4. A further possible influence on the degree of ideological exploration and commitment is that this study was conducted at the height of protests about American involvement in the Vietnam war; was the apparent shift away from foreclosure and towards achievement attributable, in part at least, to the circumstances of the moment? When Waterman (1982) subsequently carried out a similarly designed study in American liberal arts colleges at a time when the national political ferment had subsided somewhat, he found no systematic changes in commitments in the area of political ideology over an equivalent four-year period. The message seems to be that the wider social context plays a part in influencing the extent and nature of exploration and commitment. This, in turn, emphasizes the need for caution in seeking to generalize the results from research of this sort. What effects, for example, do high levels of unemployment and poor work prospects for young people have on occupational identity status?

The regular use of college students as participants in research of this type is usually because they are an accessible and compliant population, rather than because of any wider significance. But there are respects in which college students are likely to differ from others of their age: they are better educated, they may have moved away from the more direct influence of their parents (geographically, at least), and the nature of the courses they are following may well encourage a measure of exploration. Do these differences have implications?

Another longitudinal study by Archer and Waterman (Archer, 1989) sheds some light on the ways identity status can be strongly affected by social context. They followed 78 American 16 and 17 year olds through their last two years of high school and into the year after they left school. The interviews covered the by now familiar domains of vocational choice, religious beliefs, political ideologies and sex-role preferences. Table 2 overleaf shows the percentages in the four identity statuses for the four domains over the three years of the study.

The pattern of results in Table 2 is in keeping with the trends that have been described so far. There is considerable stability over the three years, with diffusion and foreclosure by far the most frequently found statuses. Overall, there is no sign of an increase in identity achievement with age – if anything, the opposite. However, of most interest here is what happened once this sample had left school. Some went on to college, others into work and some combined the two. When these three groups were compared in terms of identity status, diffusion was most frequently expressed by those in work and by males who were combining work and college. Identity achievement and moratorium by contrast, were primarily found among those at college, though even in that sub-group it represented a minority of their identity behaviour.

Other research has also highlighted the ways in which identity status is linked to context, though it is hard to find a consistent pattern. Munro and Adams (1977) compared the identity statuses of college students and people of the same age who were in work. In areas of religious belief and political ideology, those in work were more frequently in the achievement status and those at college more often in the diffusion status. In other words, this is further evidence that college-based samples differ in significant ways from the rest of the population, though not in a clear direction.

TABLE 2 The percentages of identity statuses for each domain at year intervals from 16 to 18.

Domain	Identity status			
	Diffusion	Foreclosure	Moratorium	Achievement
Junior year				
Vocational choice	37	32	19	12
Religious beliefs	40	43	1	16
Political ideology	80	19	1	0
Sex-role orientation	7	89	1	3
Senior year				
Vocational choice	26	48	10	16
Religious beliefs	44	48	0	8
Political ideology	82	16	0	2
Sex-role orientation	1	93	0	6
First year after high school				
Vocational choice	30	45	13	12
Religious beliefs	53	39	4	4
Political ideology	89	8	1	1
Sex-role orientation	6	88	1	4

Source: Archer (1989), p. 351.

Archer's (1989) findings (Table 2) also serve to highlight the issue of cohesion. At any one time, identity status varies across the four domains: at the age of 16, 80 per cent show diffusion with respect to political ideology, compared with 40 per cent regarding religious beliefs and only 7 per cent regarding sex-role orientation. In fact, few individuals in Archer's sample were actually diffuse or foreclosed in all four domains in any given year; they typically demonstrated several identity statuses at the same time. This cautions against making global statements about the development of identity. Rather, adolescent development appears to be differentiated, whereby young people can have achieved identity in one area, while still struggling in others.

A further limitation of this line of research is the regular use of the four domains of vocational plans, religious beliefs, political ideologies and sexual orientation, following Marcia's lead. Some of these domains may be of little or no personal significance to the participants. For example, Noller and Callan (1991) have suggested that the high levels of identity diffusion often to be found surrounding political ideology (as in Archer's data in Table 2) are attributable to a general low level of interest shown by young people in politics. One study conducted in the UK in the 1980s concluded that the overwhelming majority of young people appeared to be politically illiterate (McGurk, 1987).

3.5 A role for intervention in identity development?

One interpretation that might be placed on some of the evidence outlined in this section is that adolescents do not engage in activity to do with identity as much as Erikson's theory suggests. The teenage years are characterized by diffusion and foreclosure; the more developed statuses of moratorium and, in particular, identity achievement are less apparent. Does this mean that Erikson's theory was wrong and adolescent development takes a different course from the one he portrays, or alternatively is it that his theory is right but that many young people merely fail to engage with important tasks of adolescence that are prerequisites for becoming 'fulfilled' and 'successful' adults? There is certainly evidence of positive correlations between the more developed identity statuses of achievement and moratorium and a variety of measures of 'desirable' personality attributes and social behaviour. From this Archer concluded that 'identity achievement most consistently appears to be the decision-making mode individuals should strive to implement' (Archer, 1989, p. 349). However, this needs to be set against evidence that, for example, the foreclosure status is associated with good study habits, good behaviour, low levels of drug and alcohol use, etc. In short, we may be dealing not with a scientifically verifiable progression towards more mature personal identity, but with a model of change in personal identity founded on a set of values about age-and-stage-appropriate attributes. Archer herself translates the evidence that identity statuses reflect social values into a case for positive intervention:

> With the unpredictability of a fast paced world in which family roles and viable careers may be redefined within a decade, it would appear that flexibility, exploration, cognitive weighing of alternatives, making choices from among feasible options, and periodically reassessing one's decisions are becoming basic, mental health, survival skills for many individuals, at least in post-industrial societies.
>
> (Archer, 1989, p. 347)

This combination of circumstances – a need to examine alternatives and accommodate change on the one hand and significant numbers of adolescents apparently not demonstrating such skills in the area of identity formation on the other – prompts Archer to advocate 'identity intervention' to provide tools to enhance the ability to adjust to changing conditions. She suggests that this may be done in a number of ways through the school curriculum (e.g. the encouragement of inductive reasoning and the exploration of alternatives) and also through democratic parenting techniques from an early age. However, Archer is keen not to be prescriptive, recognizing that direct intervention is likely to be most effective when individuals perceive themselves to be in need of and ready for change.

SUMMARY OF SECTION 3

- Thinking about and establishing identity is widely seen as a key task of adolescence.

- Erik Erikson's account of identity portrays the stage of adolescence as featuring the normative crisis of identity versus identity confusion.

- James Marcia's empirical studies of Erikson's ideas employ four identity statuses to chart the development of identity.

- Research indicates that there is no clear pattern of cohesion and development in identity status, which appears to be influenced by specific social contexts of adolescent development.

- Acknowledgement that adolescent development is a social process, the goals of which are shaped by values and expectations, has prompted some to advocate positive intervention in adolescent personal development.

4 CRISIS? WHAT CRISIS?

The previous section provided an account of a line of enquiry prompted by one psychoanalytically inspired theory of adolescent development, that of Erikson. Although psychoanalytic accounts of the adolescent experience vary in detail and emphasis, they mostly share three underlying assumptions (Coleman and Hendry, 1990):

- adolescence is a period during which the personality is especially vulnerable;

- if the psychological defences cannot cope with inner conflicts and tensions then maladaptive behaviour is likely to result;

- disengagement is necessary if mature emotional and sexual relationships are to be established outside the family.

To what extent is this representation of adolescents and adolescence generally true? Is adolescence a time of turmoil for all young people? Or is the picture that derives from psychoanalytic theories distorted by the particularly selective sample of young people who are to be found in clinics and consulting rooms? Adelson (1964), for example, has argued that popular views of adolescence are shaped by two caricatures. One, the noble idealist, betrayed, exploited or neglected by the adult world – what he labels the 'visionary-victim' – derives from the sensitive, articulate, intense, intelligent, middle-class adolescent who forms the almost exclusive bedrock for the psychoanalytic theory of adolescence. The other is the sinister, amoral delinquent – the 'victimiser' – who is the stuff of newspaper articles and an identifiable character in novels, films and soap operas.

4.1 An empirical approach

If these are, indeed, descriptions based on highly selective groups, then what scope is there for developing a theory that reflects the actual experience of adolescence for teenagers in general? One answer is to approach the question empirically by taking a representative population and seeking information on particular experiences within a given social and cultural setting. What is the actual experience of family discord, emotional states and so on? Where these occur, are they more frequent and more intense during the adolescent years than at other stages of development? A valuable source of data relating to these questions is studies of large, representative samples, known as *epidemiological* studies, like the one carried out in the Isle of Wight by Michael Rutter and colleagues (Rutter *et al.*, 1970, 1976). You have already encountered this study in Chapter 2 (p. 47).

4.2 Evidence from the Isle of Wight study

During the 1960s a team of researchers gathered data on the physical health, educational performance, psychological state and family backgrounds of a large number of children on the island. They were subsequently followed up when 14–15 years old, and a sub-sample of 200 was selected at random for more intensive investigation, which included being interviewed by a psychiatrist. Their parents were also interviewed about relations with their adolescent children. They were asked about the frequency and nature of disagreements and arguments; difficulties in 'getting through' to their children and talking with them about their feelings and plans; and the extent to which the teenagers avoided being involved in family activities. Table 3 shows the extent to which these parents reported such examples of what might be summarized as alienation.

TABLE 3   Parental report of parent–child alienation in the Isle of Wight general population sample (*N*=192).

	Boys (*N*=98)	Girls (*N*=94)
Any altercation with parents	18%	19%
Any communication difficulties with child	24%	9%
Any physical withdrawal of child	12%	7%

Source: adapted from Rutter *et al.* (1976), p. 39.

ACTIVITY 6
Allow about 5 minutes

ANALYSING ALIENATION

Study the data in Table 3 and suggest interpretations that might be placed on them.

What further questions do they raise?

Comment

Overall there seems little evidence of serious or widespread alienation. Only one in six parents reported any altercations with their children and only one in ten of the children were said to withdraw from family activities. A noteworthy feature of the figures on communication difficulties is that nearly a quarter of the boys' parents report them, compared with fewer than one in ten of the girls' parents (a difference which is statistically significant at the 0.05 level).

In the same interviews the great majority of parents said that they approved of their children's friends, and although there were more frequent reports of disapproval of their teenager's clothes (24% of boys and 34% of girls) and hairstyles (46% of boys and 29% of girls), this did not always escalate into rows.

But parents provide only one side of the story. Might the adolescents themselves provide a different and perhaps more accurate view of the situation, since they would have less to lose by acknowledging weaknesses and failures in family relationships? Table 4 summarizes what they reported.

TABLE 4   Fourteen year olds' reports of parent–child alienation in the Isle of Wight general population sample (N=192).

	Boys (N=98)	Girls (N=94)
Any disagreements with parents	32%	27%
Any altercations with parents	42%	30%
Any criticism of mother	27%	37%
Any criticism of father	32%	31%
Any rejection of mother	3%	2%
Any rejection of father	5%	9%

Source: Rutter *et al.* (1976), p. 40.

At first sight these figures suggest a rather different story from that presented by the parents, but the variations are less dramatic than they might appear. The criticisms of parents reported by about one in three were instances of any critical remarks made during the interview, so two-thirds made no criticisms at all. Outright rejection was very uncommon indeed. And where there were arguments – a minority in any case – these were usually reported as being infrequent.

4.3 Evidence from the NCDS

A similar picture comes from another large population study in the UK, the National Child Development Study (Ghodsian and Lambert, 1978; and see also Chapter 2, p. 49). Interviews with over eleven thousand 16 year olds throughout England and Wales found that 89 per cent of boys and 87 per cent of girls said that they got on well with their mothers, and 74 per cent of the boys and 80 per cent of the girls that they got on well with their fathers. Table 5 shows the responses of their parents when presented with a list of common areas of disagreement and asked how often, if at all, they were actually the subject of argument. These figures, too, paint a largely harmonious picture.

TABLE 5 Disagreements between parents and their 16-year-old children.

	Often	Sometimes	Never or hardly ever
Choice of friends of the same sex	3%	16%	81%
Choice of friends of the opposite sex	2%	9%	89%
Dress or hairstyle	11%	35%	54%
Time of coming in at night or going to bed	8%	26%	66%
Places gone to in own time	2%	9%	89%
Doing homework	6%	18%	76%
Smoking	6%	9%	85%
Drinking	1%	5%	94%

Source: Fogelman (1976), p. 36.

The general pattern reported by both these UK epidemiological studies is similar to that found in large-scale surveys in the US. About three-quarters of US families are reported to enjoy warm and pleasant relations during the adolescent years and the great majority of teenagers say they admire their parents, feel loved and appreciated by them and are reassured that they can turn to them for advice (Steinberg, 1990). Where there are disagreements and arguments there is a comparable pattern – domestic disputes over household chores, times to be back home, completing homework and the like. It is worthy of note that a comparison of data from studies completed since the 1920s indicates that this pattern is remarkably consistent (Montemayor, 1983).

If these signs of alienation are not so great in absolute terms do they, nonetheless, increase in frequency during adolescence? Is there a developmental trend? It seems that there is an increase from childhood to adolescence and a decrease afterwards. Montemayor (1983) gives some sense of the magnitude of the difference when he estimates that, typically, parents and teenagers quarrel about twice a week whereas husbands and wives do so once a week. The longitudinal design of the Isle of Wight study also provides an opportunity to compare how relationships are portrayed in the mid-teens and how they had been when those same children were younger. This comparison indicated that half of the 14 year olds who withdrew from the family (see Table 3) were behaving in a similar fashion earlier in their childhood. And where communication difficulties with boys were concerned these, too, had been present for some time previously in the great majority of cases (Rutter, 1979). In other words, in many instances problems reported in adolescence had a history in earlier childhood.

This evidence indicates, then, that though there may be some increase in levels of conflict between parents and their adolescent children, it is not great in the large majority of families in the representative samples studied in this research. According to one review of the evidence, in only one in ten families is there a dramatic deterioration in parent–child relationships during adolescence (Steinberg, 1990). Does this state of relative harmony mean that detachment is not taking place, or is it that in the majority of families it is happening in a more ordered and controlled way which serves to avoid major confrontation and upset? Certainly conflict and hostility are not productive. For example, on the strength of a summary of research findings, Steinberg (1990) lists the following as being positively associated with relatively close relations between parents and their adolescents: greater self-reliance, higher self-esteem, better school performance, less deviant behaviour, fewer social problems and less depression.

4.4 Inner turmoil?

The data described so far in this section have been concerned with teenagers' relationships within the family. But what about their own feelings – did they experience the heightened inner turmoil supposedly characteristic of this stage? When the Isle of Wight sample was interviewed by a psychiatrist, 42 per cent of the boys and

48 per cent of the girls reported that they 'sometimes felt miserable and unhappy to the extent that they were tearful or wanted to get away from it all' (Rutter, 1976, p. 41). But when the same individuals recorded their responses to descriptions of feelings on an inventory, only about 20 per cent described themselves as 'often feeling miserable or depressed'. A helpful comparison here is with how their mothers responded to the same statement; 14 per cent checked the same description. So there would appear to be some heightening of emotion in adolescence, but not to a dramatic extent. Overall, Rutter *et al.* concluded that 'many 14 to 15 year olds experience quite marked feelings of affective disturbance which could well be described as "inner turmoil"' (Rutter *et al.*, 1976, p. 42).

A similar, though perhaps rather more muted, conclusion was reached in a study which sought to obtain data on day-to-day emotional states as they were being experienced (see Research Summary 1).

RESEARCH SUMMARY 1
DAILY EMOTIONAL STATES

Reed Larson and Claudia Lampman-Petraitis equipped 473 North American children aged 9 to 15 with an electronic pager. The pager was activated at random times on seven occasions every day, for a week. On hearing the signal the child had to record, on a report form, how they were feeling at that time. The form contained six scales (e.g. happy–unhappy, cheerful–irritable, friendly–angry) and they had to indicate a position on a seven-point scale between −3 and +3.

The scores were analysed in terms of two claims about typical emotional states during adolescence. The researchers found no variation over the 9–15 age-range in the amount of variability of emotional states during the course of a day. The 15 year olds did not report greater swings in moods than the younger children. However, there was some relationship between age and average mood. There were fewer occasions when the older participants reported extreme positive states and more occasions when they reported mildly negative ones. For these adolescents there were fewer occasions when they felt on top of the world and more when they felt mildly negative.

(Larson and Lampman-Petraitis, 1989)

4.5 Depression

In seeking to put the notion of inner turmoil into perspective as it relates to adolescents in general, it is important not to ignore the changing pattern of psychiatric disorder reported during adolescence (Rutter and Rutter, 1992). In particular, evidence from both epidemiological studies and clinical enquiries shows that there is a dramatic rise in the rate of overt depression and depression-related disorders at this time. Features of these include negative thoughts about the self, the world and the future; and a reduced capacity to work, or engage in leisure activities or social relationships. A number of explanations have been offered to account for the developmental trend, including: genetic factors which predispose depression to somehow 'switch on' during this period; hormonal changes associated with puberty increasing vulnerability to depression; and the changes in cognitive competence described in Section 1 which allow the adolescent greater access to the uncertainties of life and the range of alternative solutions open to them. Rutter and Rutter (1992) conclude that a satisfactory explanation has yet to be found. It is important, once again, to acknowledge that in making the case that adolescence is not, necessarily, a time of storm and stress for the majority, it can be a period of considerable personal turmoil for some.

4.6 Coleman's focal theory

How, then, can we explain the contradiction between the amount of overall change experienced during the adolescent years and the apparent relative resilience of the majority of those involved in such change? One attempt is the *focal theory* of John Coleman (Coleman, 1974; Coleman and Hendry, 1990). This theory grew out of a UK study in which girls and boys aged 11, 13, 15 and 17 completed various identical tests aimed at establishing their attitudes to a range of relationships, including those with parents, peers and the opposite sex. The responses were analysed in terms of whether they were constructive (where the relationship was seen as being in some way helpful, valuable, supportive or enjoyable), or negative (destructive, unhelpful, irritating, or to be avoided). Attitudes to the relationships changed with age, but Coleman was particularly struck by the evidence that concerns about different issues reached a peak at different points in adolescence.

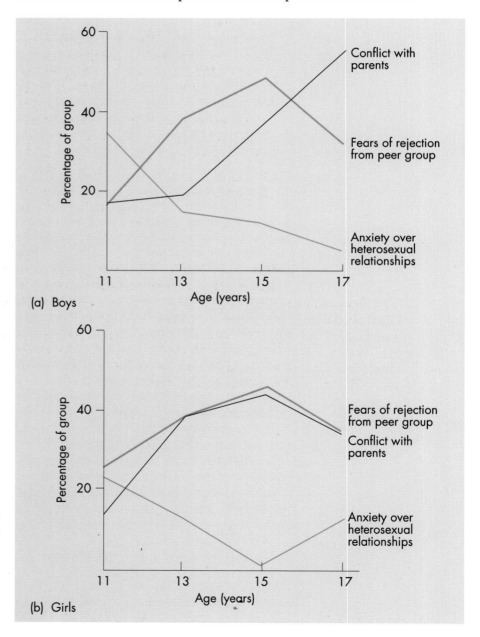

FIGURE 6 Negative expressions for different themes as a function of age: (a) boys; (b) girls. ((a) from Coleman and Hendry (1990), p. 206; (b) compiled from data in Coleman (1974).)

ACTIVITY 7

Allow about 5 minutes

ANALYSING PEAKS AND TROUGHS

Figure 6a summarizes some of the data provided by the boys in Coleman's study and Figure 6b the comparable data for the girls. The horizontal axis of the graph shows the four age points at which he collected data on attitudes. The vertical axis shows the percentage of each group giving negative responses. Lines are plotted for what Coleman claims are among the most important themes: conflict with parents, fears of rejection from peer group, and anxiety over heterosexual relationships.

What do the data appear to indicate?

Comment

Attitudes to these three sorts of relationship change with age. But, more importantly, concerns about different issues reach a peak at different times. The data for boys (Figure 6a) indicate that for conflict with parents there is an increase between 13 and 15 and yet more at 17, for fears of rejection from the peer group the peak is at 15, whereas anxiety over heterosexual relationships appears to be at its highest at the age of 11 and then to diminish.

For girls (Figure 6b) the picture is similar but not identical: the peak for fears of rejection from the peer group is also at 15, as is that for conflict with parents, and the anxiety over heterosexual relationships is highest at 11, as it is for the boys.

Coleman's interpretation of this and related evidence points to the way in which particular sorts of relationship patterns become prominent at certain ages, with no pattern being specific to one age only. These patterns overlap and different issues come into focus, as it were, at different times. Accordingly, he calls this the *focal* model and contrasts it with the 'storm and stress' model where the implication is that disruption occurs at the same time in all areas. The two models are contrasted in Figure 7.

FIGURE 7 (a) 'Storm and stress' model contrasted with (b) focal model. Each curve represents a different issue or relationship. (Coleman, 1974, pp. 150, 153.)

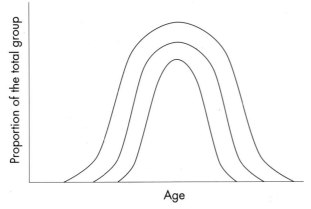

(a) 'Storm and stress' model

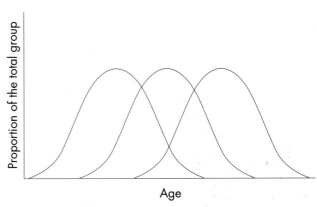

(b) Focal model

The focal model emerged from data from a cross-sectional study, but Coleman argues that it can also represent the progress of the individual through adolescence. Certain issues may be particularly pressing at certain times; other issues will not have disappeared but, rather, they may remain as residual sources of anxiety or conflict. So the adolescent spreads the process of adaptation over a span of years, resolving one issue at a time so that the stresses are not concentrated. For example, where puberty and the growth spurt occur within the normal range, individuals can adjust to these changes before other pressures occur, such as those from relationships with parents and teachers. For the late maturers the combination of puberty-related stresses with parental/teacher pressures may increase the probability of problems (Coleman, 1993). Figure 8 illustrates what happens when a number of different pressures become focused more closely together.

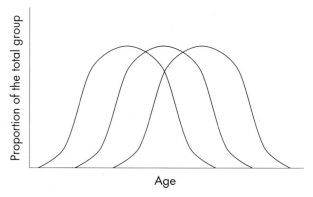

FIGURE 8   Focal model of an atypical group. (Coleman, 1974, p. 153.)

Coleman claims that adolescents are not merely passive responders to events but may actually determine their own rate of development:

> In any one day a teenager may choose to confront a parent over the breakfast table, to argue with a sibling, to accept the suggestion of a best friend, to stand up to an authoritarian teacher, to conform to peer group pressure, to resist the persuasion of a boyfriend or girlfriend, and so on. Every one of these situations offers the young person a choice, and all may well have a bearing on the inter-personal issues with which the focal model is concerned. We believe that most young people pace themselves through the adolescent transition. Most of them hold back on one issue, while they are grappling with another. Most sense what they can and cannot cope with, and will, in the real sense of the term, be an active agent in their own development.
>
> (Coleman and Hendry, 1990, pp. 213–14)

4.7 Criticisms of focal theory

Although focal theory has been described as 'the only influential theory [of adolescence] to emerge in recent years' (Jackson and Bosma, 1992, p. 331) it is not without its critics. There is a need for more evidence, particularly from longitudinal research, to test Coleman's claim that what appears cross-sectionally is also true of the development of individuals. But even if this does show that, typically, one issue is coped with at a time, is this necessarily an indication of stability? Some situations of family stress may be such that there is little option but to focus on them alone, even though this may be associated with a range of other problem behaviours (Jackson and Bosma, 1992).

In this section I have illustrated how the representation of adolescence as a period of 'storm and stress' has fallen out of favour as evidence has come forward from a number of studies to indicate that this is not the experience of the great majority of young people. This is not to say that important transitions do not take place, but rather that they are managed by the individuals themselves, and by those who retain a measure of control over their development – parents, teachers and other significant adults – so that the level of adaptation and change that is required is containable and compatible with positive development. In the final section we will look at the role that the family may play in this process.

> ### SUMMARY OF SECTION 4
>
> - Psychoanalytic theories promoted the view of normal adolescence as a period characterized by 'storm and stress'.
> - Evidence from representative samples of adolescents shows that while there may be some increase in levels of tension and conflict within the family, a serious deterioration in relationships is restricted to a small percentage.
> - Some degree of inner turmoil appears to be a feature of many adolescents' experience.
> - Coleman's focal theory offers one resolution of the apparent mismatch between popular conceptions of adolescence and actual experience.

5 ADOLESCENCE AND FAMILY RELATIONSHIPS

The data from large representative samples have shown how adolescence may proceed without necessarily being marked by storm and stress. At the same time they do indicate that this is a period when young people are subject to more conflict, confusion and stress. It is also a time when there are opportunities to be explored and commitments made. Much of this activity typically takes place in the context of the family and so it is appropriate to consider the role that family relationships play in the experience of this transition.

Arguably, one of the limitations of some accounts of adolescence is their focus on the young person's experience of transition, change and crisis independently of the family contexts in which those processes are embedded. An alternative to this individualistic approach would emphasize the issues of adolescence as emerging from patterns of family structures and relationships and more broadly from the place of the individual within the community and wider society. For example, instead of seeing the task of adolescence as creating distance from parental influences and preparing for a more autonomous and independent life, this task would be recast as a process of two-way negotiation between the adolescent and parents who are themselves undergoing a role and identity change which might be characterized as being from 'caregiver to young child' to 'guide and mentor to an emerging adult'.

One way of illustrating this approach is through studies of parenting styles and adolescent experience. For example, take the contrast between authoritarian styles on the one hand and democratic ones on the other (see Chapter 3). One summary of evidence (Noller and Callan, 1991) indicates that where parents are authoritarian, their adolescent children are less likely to explore alternative identities, more likely to adopt externally imposed moral standards rather than develop their own internalized moral code, and likely to have lower self-confidence and self-esteem. Where parents adopt a democratic style the adolescents are better able to make their own decisions and plans and, though they have the choice, they tend to identify with their parents and adopt their values.

Some studies have focused specifically on how identity status (using Marcia's categories) is linked to qualities of parent–adolescent relationships. So, foreclosures appear to have the closest relationships with parents, while those in the identity diffusion status see their parents as indifferent and rejecting. Family conflict is higher where adolescents are in the moratorium and identity achievement statuses. There is, however, a problem with how to interpret these associations. First, it is difficult to assign these status labels with confidence given that individuals change in and out of them. More importantly, the direction of the relationship is hard to determine – is the status a reaction to parental styles, or is parental style a response to the types of adolescent behaviour that are associated with the status?

This description of cyclical processes of cause and effect in parent–adolescent relationships should remind you of the discussion of this theme in Chapter 2. A *transactional model* applies as strongly to relationships at this age as it does for those with much younger children. Descriptions of parental style as 'authoritarian' or 'democratic' suggest a rather static, one-sided, unyielding view of what goes on in the family – that parents hold rigidly to a set of standards, rules and ways of treating their offspring against which adolescents react variously in terms of conformity, protest and rebellion. Is this actually what happens? Within a family life-cycle perspective we need to recognize that parents are not fixed while children develop; parents are also changing, relinquishing some responsibilities as they take on new ones. The 'crisis' of adolescence in the family can be experienced as strongly in parents as in the young people themselves, and understanding their way of responding to that crisis becomes just as important as the adolescent's own experience.

Within this perspective the emphasis is on *negotiation*, whereby at adolescence, for example, parent–child relationships are transformed so that close ties can be maintained which incorporate mutual recognition of the growing individuality of the adolescent. There is a process of redefining the relationship to which both child and parent contribute. In this view, adolescent crisis is 'co-constructed' through a failure of mutual adaptation.

James Youniss and Jacqueline Smollar have provided insights into this process through a series of studies of communication and relationships between American teenagers (aged 15–18) and their parents (Youniss and Smollar, 1985). They were interested in how open and understanding the two 'sides' were of each other's points of view; to what extent they were cautious about what they said to one another; how they dealt with disagreements and whether these were settled to the satisfaction of both parties; and the extent to which parents tried to impose their solutions on their adolescent children. What struck Youniss and Smollar was the way in which both parents and adolescents were active in redefining and renegotiating their relationship in a reciprocal way.

READING

You should now turn to Reading B by Youniss and Smollar at the end of this chapter. This summarizes how the researchers derived their ideas about transformations, and in particular the concept of *emancipation*, from adolescents' accounts of their relationship with their parents.

Note the way that the data from the interviews are interpreted in terms of the changing agenda of relationships, the role of parental authority and the possibility that transformation renders detachment inappropriate.

Finally, consider the status of this perspective on adolescence alongside the other formulations reviewed in this chapter. What are the distinctive features of Erikson's identity theory and Coleman's focal theory compared with a perspective based around transformations in family relationships?

In reviewing these different approaches to adolescence you may be reminded of the words of caution earlier in this chapter about the dangers of generalizing from samples drawn from a particular section of society, at a particular point in time, whose experience is then interpreted within given frameworks of contemporary psychology.

Awareness of these limitations of the approaches covered here does not undermine the enterprise entirely, but it does suggest that rather than attempting a single unified theory of adolescence, a more profitable endeavour would take the variability of adolescent experiences as a starting point in order to better illuminate the range of pathways along which individuals travel from the status of child to adult.

SUMMARY OF SECTION 5

- The role of the family – and notably parents – in the experience of the changes of adolescence may be a critical consideration in how the transition is experienced.
- The *transactional model,* with its emphasis on negotiation, offers one way of understanding the process by which the adolescent experience may avoid being a seriously confrontational or stormy one.

---

6 CONCLUSION

Adolescence is marked by changes of many sorts – of physiology, cognitive functioning, personal identity, social relationships with family and peers – and, often, these take place within a changing cultural context. Demands, expectations, opportunities and sanctions vary over time and place. Your reflections on your own experiences of adolescence as prompted by Activity 1 and the comparison of those with what you see going on around you today possibly highlighted some of those points. And throughout the chapter questions have been raised about the extent to which findings hold beyond the time and place in which they were gathered. All this renders neat generalizations and tidy conclusions as impossible as they are undesirable – but the challenge still remains of understanding the processes at work throughout the life-cycle.

Answers to Activity 4

(a) Moratorium – there is evidence of exploration of religious beliefs in the light of dilemmas prompted by everyday experience. As yet these dilemmas are unresolved and commitment to the beliefs seems insecure.

(b) Identity diffusion – there are few, if any, signs of either exploration or commitment.

(c) Identity achievement – after a period of active exploration a commitment appears to have been made to a particular set of beliefs. Note though, that this doesn't necessarily mean the end to exploration; commitments of this sort may well be temporary and be followed by a further period of moratorium resulting in a new commitment.

(d) Foreclosure – here there is commitment but based on little or no exploration, rather the adoption of beliefs direct from parents.

You may question aspects of the above answers; they do not claim to be infallible and signs of doubt about the appropriate label merely serve to illustrate some of the difficulties faced by researchers both in coding interview responses in a reliable way and developing measures that are valid.

FURTHER READING

COLEMAN, J. C. (ed.) (1992, 2nd edn) *The School Years: current issues in the socialisation of young people*, London, Routledge.

COLEMAN, J. C. and HENDRY, L. (1990, 2nd edn) *The Nature of Adolescence*, London, Routledge.

KROGER, J. (1989) *Identity in Adolescence,* London, Routledge.

REFERENCES

ADELSON, J. (1964) 'The mystique of adolescence', *Psychiatry*, **27**, pp. 1–5.

ARCHER, S. L. (1982) 'The lower age boundaries of identity development', *Child Development,* **53**, pp. 1551–6.

ARCHER, S. L. (1989) 'The status of identity: reflections on the need for intervention', *Journal of Adolescence*, **12**, pp. 345–59.

ARIES, P. (1962) *Centuries of Childhood*, London, Cape.

BLOS, P. (1970) *The Young Adolescent: clinical studies*, London, Collier Macmillan.

BROOKS-GUNN, J. and REITER, E. O. (1990) 'The role of pubertal processes' in FELDMAN, S. S. and ELLIOTT, G. R. (eds) *At the Threshold: the developing adolescent,* Cambridge (Mass.), Harvard University Press.

BROOKS-GUNN, J. and WARREN, M. (1985) 'The effects of delayed menarche in different contexts: dance and nondance students', *Journal of Youth and Adolescence,* **14**, pp. 285–300.

COLEMAN, J. C. (1974) *Relationships in Adolescence*, London, Routledge and Kegan Paul.

COLEMAN, J. C. (1993) 'Adolescence in a changing world' in JACKSON, S. and RODRIGUES-TOME, H. (eds) *Adolescence and its Social Worlds*, Hove, Lawrence Erlbaum Associates.

COLEMAN, J. C. and HENDRY, L. (1990, 2nd edn) *The Nature of Adolescence*, London, Routledge.

CONGER, J. J. (1979) *Adolescence: generation under pressure*, London, Harper and Row.

Conger, J. J. (1991, 4th edn) *Adolescence and Youth: psychological development in a changing world*, New York, HarperCollins Publishers.

Elder, G. H., Modell, J. and Parke, R. D. (1993) 'Studying children' in Modell, J. and Parke, R. D. (eds) *Children in Time and Space*, Cambridge, Cambridge University Press.

Erikson, E. H. (1965) *Childhood and Society*, Harmondsworth, Penguin Books.

Erikson, E. H. (1968) *Identity: youth and crisis,* London, Faber and Faber.

Fogelman, K. (ed.) (1976) *Britain's Sixteen-year-olds*, London, National Children's Bureau.

Freud, A. (1958) 'Adolescence', *Psychoanalytic Study of the Child,* **13**, pp. 255–78.

Ghodsian, M. and Lambert, L. (1978) 'Mum and dad are not so bad: the views of sixteen-year-olds on how they get on with their parents', *Journal of the Association of Educational Psychologists*, **4**, pp. 27–33.

Hall, G. S. (1904) *Adolescence: its psychology, and its relations to anthropology, sex, crime, religion and education* (2 vols), New York, Appleton.

Harley, G. W. (1941) 'Notes on the Poro in Liberia' in Sommer, B. B. (ed.) *Puberty and Adolescence*, New York, Oxford University Press.

Jackson, S. and Bosma, H. A. (1992) 'Developmental research on adolescence: European perspectives for the 1990s and beyond', *British Journal of Developmental Psychology*, **10**, pp. 319–37.

Jones, M. C. (1957) 'The later careers of boys who were early or late maturing', *Child Development*, **28**, pp. 113–28.

Keating, D. P. (1980) 'Thinking processes in adolescence' in Adelson, J. (ed.) *Handbook of Adolescent Psychology*, New York, John Wiley.

Keating, D. P. (1990) 'Adolescent thinking' in Feldman, S. S. and Elliott, G. R. (eds) *At the Threshold: the developing adolescent*, Cambridge (Mass.), Harvard University Press.

Kett, J. (1977) *Rites of Passage: adolescence in America, 1790 to the present*, New York, Basic Books.

Larson, R. and Lampman-Petraitis, C. (1989) 'Daily emotional states as reported by children and adolescents', *Child Development*, **60**, pp. 1250–60.

McGurk, H. (ed.) (1987) *What Next?*, London, Economic and Social Research Council.

Marcia, J. E. (1980) 'Identity in adolescence' in Adelson, J. (ed.) *Handbook of Adolescent Psychology*, New York, John Wiley.

Modell, J. and Goodman, M. (1990) 'Historical perspectives' in Feldman, S. S. and Elliott, G. R. (eds) *At the Threshold: the developing adolescent*, Cambridge (Mass.), Harvard University Press.

MONTEMAYOR, R. (1983) 'Parents and adolescents in conflict: all families some of the time and some families most of the time', *Journal of Early Adolescence*, **3**, pp. 83–103.

MUNRO, G. and ADAMS, G. R. (1977) 'Ego-identity formation in college students and working youth', *Developmental Psychology*, **13**, pp. 523–4.

MUSSEN, P. H. and JONES, M. C. (1957) 'Self conceptions, motivations and interpersonal attitudes of late and early maturing boys', *Child Development*, **28**, pp. 243–56.

NOLLER, P. and CALLAN, V. (1991) *The Adolescent in the Family*, London, Routledge.

RICHARDS, M. H., BOXER, A. M., PETERSEN, A. C. and ALBRECHT, R. (1990) 'Relation of weight to body image in pubertal girls and boys from two communities', *Developmental Psychology*, **26**, pp. 313–21.

RUTTER, M. (1979) *Changing Youth in a Changing Society*, London, Nuffield Provincial Hospitals Trust.

RUTTER, M. and RUTTER, M. (1992) *Developing Minds*, Harmondsworth, Penguin Books.

RUTTER, M., GRAHAM, P., CHADWICK, O. F. D. and YULE, W. (1976) 'Adolescent turmoil: fact or fiction?' *Journal of Child Psychology and Psychiatry*, **17**, pp. 35–56.

RUTTER, M., TIZARD, J. and WHITMORE, K. (eds) (1970) *Education, Health and Behaviour*, London, Longman.

SIMMONS, R. and ROSENBERG, F. (1975) 'Sex, sex-roles, and self-image', *Journal of Youth and Adolescence*, **4**, pp. 229–58.

STEINBERG, L. (1990) 'Autonomy, conflict, and harmony in the family relationship' in FELDMAN, S. S. and ELLIOTT, G. R. (eds) *At the Threshold: the developing adolescent*, Cambridge (Mass.), Harvard University Press.

STEVENS, R. (1983) *Erik Erikson*, Milton Keynes, Open University Press.

TANNER, J. M. (1962, 2nd edn) *Growth at Adolescence*, Oxford, Basil Blackwell.

TANNER, J. M. (1973) 'Growing up', *Scientific American*, **229**, pp. 35–43.

TANNER, J. M. (1989, 2nd edn) *Foetus into Man*, Castlemead Publications.

WATERMAN, A. S. (1982) 'Identity development from adolescence to adulthood: an extension of theory and a review of research', *Developmental Psychology*, **18**, pp. 341–58.

WATERMAN, A. S., GEARY, P. S. and WATERMAN, C. K. (1974) 'Longitudinal study of changes in ego identity status from the freshman to the senior year at college', *Developmental Psychology*, **10**, pp. 387–92.

YOUNISS, J. and SMOLLAR, J. (1985) *Adolescent Relations with Mothers, Fathers, and Friends*, Chicago, University of Chicago Press.

READINGS

Reading A   Adolescence

Erik Erikson

As technological advances put more and more time between early school life and the young person's final access to specialized work, the stage of adolescing becomes an even more marked and conscious period and, as it has always been in some cultures in some periods, almost a way of life between childhood and adulthood. Thus in the later school years young people, beset with the physiological revolution of their genital maturation and the uncertainty of the adult roles ahead, seem much concerned with faddish attempts at establishing an adolescent subculture with what looks like a final rather than a transitory or, in fact, initial identity formation. They are sometimes morbidly, often curiously, preoccupied with what they appear to be in the eyes of others as compared with what they feel they are, and with the question of how to connect the roles and skills cultivated earlier with the ideal prototypes of the day. In their search for a new sense of continuity and sameness, which must now include sexual maturity, some adolescents have to come to grips again with crises of earlier years before they can install lasting idols and ideals as guardians of a final identity. They need, above all, a moratorium for the integration of the identity elements ascribed in the foregoing to the childhood stages: only that now a larger unit, vague in its outline and yet immediate in its demands, replaces the childhood milieu – 'society'. A review of these elements is also a list of adolescent problems.

If the earliest stage bequeathed to the identity crisis an important need for trust in oneself and in others, then clearly the adolescent looks most fervently for men and ideas to have *faith* in, which also means men and ideas in whose service it would seem worth while to prove oneself trustworthy.

At the same time, however, the adolescent fears a foolish, all too trusting commitment, and will, paradoxically, express his need for faith in loud and cynical mistrust.

If the second stage established the necessity of being defined by what one can *will* freely, then the adolescent now looks for an opportunity to decide with free assent on one of the available or unavoidable avenues of duty and service, and at the same time is mortally afraid of being forced into activities in which he would feel exposed to ridicule or self-doubt. This, too, can lead to a paradox, namely, that he would rather act shamelessly in the eyes of his elders, out of free choice, than be forced into activities which would be shameful in his own eyes or in those of this peers.

If an unlimited *imagination* as to what one *might* become is the heritage of the play age, then the adolescent's willingness to put his trust in those peers and leading, or misleading, elders who will give imaginative, if not illusory, scope to his aspirations is only too obvious. By the same token, he objects violently to all 'pedantic' limitations on his self-images and will be ready to settle by loud accusation all his guiltiness over the excessiveness of his ambition.

Finally, if the desire to make something work, and to make it work well, is the gain of the school age, then the choice of an occupation assumes a significance beyond the question of remuneration and status. It is for this reason that some adolescents prefer not to work at all for a while rather than be forced into an otherwise promising career which would offer success without the satisfaction of functioning with unique excellence.

In any given period in history, then, that part of youth will have the most affirmatively exciting time of it which finds itself in the wave of a technological, economic, or ideological trend seemingly promising all that youthful vitality could ask for.

Adolescence, therefore, is least 'stormy' in that segment of youth which is gifted and well trained in the pursuit of expanding technological trends, and thus able to identify with new roles of competency and invention and to accept a more implicit ideological outlook. Where this is not given, the adolescent mind becomes a more explicitly ideological one, by which we mean one searching for some inspiring unification of tradition or anticipated techniques, ideas, and ideals. And, indeed, it is the ideological potential of a society which speaks most clearly to the adolescent who is so eager to be affirmed by peers, to be confirmed by teachers, and to be inspired by worthwhile 'ways of life'. On the other hand, should a young person feel that the environment tries to deprive him too radically of all the forms of expression which permit him to develop and integrate the next step, he may resist with the wild strength encountered in animals who are suddenly forced to defend their lives. For, indeed, in the social jungle of human existence there is no feeling of being alive without a sense of identity.

Source: Erikson, E. H. (1968) 'Adolescence', *in* Identity: youth and crisis, *London, Faber and Faber, pp. 128–30.*

Reading B Emancipation

James Youniss and Jacqueline Smollar

The evidence in our results is that adolescents do experience a kind of emancipation in which they perceive differences between their present and past relations with their parents.

Adolescents were able to articulate the contrast crisply: 'I used to listen to everything [my father said] and thought he was always right. Now I have my own opinions'. Some adolescents stated this insight further in that they were conscious of the complementary nature of the way in which their dependence was conjoined to parental protectiveness: 'She looked out for me'. 'He was concerned for my safety'. 'I know he's there to help'. 'I used to be daddy's little girl'. 'I was mommy's nice boy'.

Insights about emancipation were expressed a second way. Adolescents perceived that their parents do not know everything and that they are persons rather than impenetrable figures in the following statements: 'I realize he's not perfect, but still he's a good man'. 'I'm a little bit more understanding of what it's like to be an adult'. And, 'I'm aware of my father as a person rather than a role; I know his faults and strengths as a person'. The piercing of this mystique about parents is accompanied by adolescents seeing their parents treating them more as persons than just as sons and daughters: 'He deals with me as a person, not as a child'. 'Now I'm really not a little girl he's beginning to realize it'. 'He treats me more as an equal'. 'He sees me as someone he can talk to – not an equal'. And, 'He still has the upper hand, but treats me more seriously'.

The question then turns to what occurs after these insights have been made and adolescents have some understanding of how much of who and what they are is owed to the parental relationships. Here, the results are equally clear. Adolescents do not necessarily turn away from the relationship or reject it as no longer important. Instead, parental authority retains its hold as the relationship is transformed into a balance of dependence and freedom. For example, 'We can talk a little now. I am not afraid to do something against his will … I talk to him more'. 'Ask him more advice but not on personal matters. I still want to be nurtured and protected. I want his approval'. And, 'We're closer. I can be more open now. I'm still reserved but will air opinions. I'm still careful what I say. He feels closer to me. He will be more open and say what he's feeling if I initiate it. He may be a little afraid because I'm growing up and he can't be [the] full authority'.

In excerpts such as these, the transformation seems to have begun from both the parents' and the adolescents' sides. The parents retain authority by giving more freedom to adolescents by recognizing their personal needs and capabilities. In turn, adolescents act more individualistically while still relying on their parents for advice and guidance. It is clear that parental relationships have not been discarded nor have they lost their binding power. In fact, the adolescents said that the transformation helped to bring them and their parents closer.

But even in the cases where the transformation seems to be one-sided – the adolescents view parents as persons – these adolescents still desired to retain their relationships. For instance, these adolescents said: 'It was better 5 years ago. I get more defensive and fresh. He's being more pushy'. 'I'm not afraid to say things now. I still feel respect and look up to him'. Or, 'Now I'm angry. I still see him as my father. He gives me more freedom, but still demands a certain amount of respect from me'. And, 'We did not get along at all when I was 14. Now we get along better. I don't show when I'm mad; I try to understand him'. 'I know he won't change. He still treats me like I'm 13 and expects me to listen to him'.

A further clarification may be seen in the sort of escalation of authority that parents use as their sons and daughters proceed closer to adulthood. Although parents grant adolescents more freedom, the adolescents said their parents worry more about such things as their school performance and keeping out of trouble: 'He's being more pushy … about school. He does more prying into my business. Still I respect him'. 'I know he's there to help. Sees me as his little girl. He respects me more; knows I'm older … But he's more demanding [and] expects more of me'. And, 'He respects me more, knows I'm older and want to be on my own more. He's more demanding; expects more of me'.

We suggest that our findings as a whole, which are resketched through the foregoing excerpts, help to clarify the concept of emancipation in several ways. The awareness by adolescents of their childhood dependence on the parental relationship leads not to detachment but to a transformation that allows the relationship to be retained. Adolescents are given, or take, greater responsibility for themselves but still seek the endorsement of their parents. One reason parents retain, and are granted, authority is that the stakes for adolescents are higher as adolescents move closer to adulthood. Parents raise their expectations, and adolescents seem to sense that they need their parents' guidance even more as they come closer to adulthood. While the alternative of detachment may occur in some instances, it is hardly the rule for the adolescents in our samples. The typical case seems to be that of a persisting relationship in which the old complementary nature of the roles is modified, but in which parental authority coexists alongside greater agency for the self.

Source: Youniss, J. and Smollar, J. (1985) 'Emancipation', *in* Adolescent Relations with Mothers, Fathers, and Friends, *Chicago, University of Chicago Press, pp. 162–3.*

READING STUDYING RELATIONSHIPS AND SOCIAL UNDERSTANDING

Judy Dunn

CONTENTS

1	THE BEGINNINGS OF THE SIBLING RELATIONSHIP	337
2	THE BEGINNINGS OF SOCIAL UNDERSTANDING	340
3	THE PENNSYLVANIA STUDY OF SOCIAL UNDERSTANDING	342
4	RELATIONSHIPS OVER TIME	344
5	THE COLORADO SIBLING STUDY	345
6	IN CONCLUSION	346
	REFERENCES	347

Judy Dunn is Professor of Human Development at the Pennsylvania State University. From the early 1970s she has studied children's development, particularly their social and emotional development.

In the following chapter, written in 1993, she provides a brief personal history of her main research studies, indicating how each led on to the subsequent research and describing some of the key decisions about their aims, their design and their findings.

Any parent with more than one young child, or anyone who spends much time with young children, cannot fail to notice the great individual differences between them: differences in personality, in emotional expressiveness, in interest in other people, in style of relating to others, or in playing. My own interest in doing research on children originally began when I had three of my own very close in age – all within 18 months. I was fascinated by the differences between the three and by the differences in how other people related to each of them.

I then became involved with Martin Richards in a longitudinal study of 80 children in Cambridge, in which we focused specifically on individual differences in the newborn period and attempted to trace the children's social development over the next five years (Dunn, 1977). My research training and background had been in ethology (the study of animal behaviour). While I had very strong reservations about simplistic extrapolations from animal work to humans (common in the 1970s), it seemed to me crucial to study children within their own families, rather than in an experimental setting. There were two grounds for this.

First, if we wish to understand the significance of children's social experiences in daily life, it is these experiences that we must try to describe and measure. We should attempt to capture what *actually* happens to children, rather than to standardize the circumstances in which we study them. There will obviously be problems in drawing *causal* conclusions from such descriptions, but they are an essential part of any research attempt to understand the impact of family experiences.

Secondly, if we want to understand children's emotional and social development and their experiences – not just the causes of unhappiness and insecurity, but what excites, amuses and interests children – then it is crucial to study them in situations of emotional significance to them, that is, with their family and friends. My belief in the importance of these two issues, and the value of naturalistic studies – at least in research on early childhood – has grown over the last fifteen years, for reasons to which I will return.

In the project with Martin Richards we studied the children with their mothers, following the conventional approach to children's family experiences, which in the 1970s (and even now) was based on the assumption that the central and key relationship in children's early development was that between mother and child. But in the course of the home observations on which the study was based, I became increasingly struck by what I noticed happening between the baby and his or her *older sibling*. Two-thirds of the sample were secondborn children, and my impression was not just that the babies were very interested in their older siblings, but that the interactions between the two young children were very different from those between either child and parent and they suggested a quite different social repertoire and communication style. I decided to plan a prospective study of young siblings, to understand these interactions more fully.

1   THE BEGINNINGS OF THE SIBLING RELATIONSHIP

The idea that the birth of a sibling is linked to rivalry and disturbance is one that is commonly expressed in clinical writing from Freud on, so I assumed that there was extensive documentation of the beginnings of that relationship in the research literature. To my surprise I could find no systematic prospective studies which followed children over the period when a sibling was born, with the exception of one very brief study of 8-month child pairs. So I planned a study that began *before* the birth of a sibling, and followed young siblings for the first 14 months of their life together.

There were two sets of questions that I wanted to answer in this study. First, there were questions about the *relationships* in the family:

(a) What was the nature of the relationship that very young siblings formed with one another?

(b) How did the relationships between parent and firstborn children change with the arrival of a second?

(c) How was the quality of the relationship that developed between the siblings linked to each child's relationships with the parents?

Secondly, there were *clinical* issues:

(a) Which children became disturbed or upset by the change in their family lives?

(b) Could we predict who was most vulnerable?

(c) Which aspects of the changes in their lives were associated with disturbance?

(d) What significance did signs of upset in the early months have for the children's later well-being and their relationships?

Judy Dunn with her three children, who sparked off her interest in individual differences in siblings.

To begin to answer these questions, *longitudinal* research was clearly needed. As both sets of questions are concerned with individual differences in children, whatever form the study took we would need to work with a sample sufficiently large to begin to examine these. But what methods and strategies would best describe young children's daily experiences and characteristic behaviour and their relations with their families? Any one method of observing children or interviewing parents can give us only part of the picture, and both interviews and observations are potentially biased sources of information. The presence of an observer is intrusive and there are some aspects of siblings' behaviour an observer is unlikely to see in the limited time she is present; for instance, the way in which a firstborn reacts to a sibling in danger. And a parent's account of a child's behaviour will give their particular view of the child. This is in itself very interesting and significant, yet it might well differ from the description given by another person.

So, when I began to work with Carol Kendrick (later published as Dunn and Kendrick, 1982), we decided to use both observations and interviews, and to employ a variety of ways of describing the behaviour. We also decided to look systematically at the relation between the information from these different sources of information, to assess the extent of agreement between them and to help clarify which kinds of questions are most usefully answered by observations and which by interviews.

The children were observed at home over the period before and after a second child was born (see Figure 1), and their mothers were interviewed extensively. Four big issues have to be faced in planning any observational study:

(a) How to minimize the intrusion into people's lives.

(b) How to capture a representative slice of behaviour and interaction.

(c) How to achieve good agreement about descriptive units.

(d) And, by far the most important, how to develop an observational scheme that would adequately capture the behaviour you want to describe.

For this study, we decided to use a variety of descriptive units, including measures that described both single acts and also broader categories such as joint play. In addition, we kept a narrative record of particular aspects that interested us, such as the details of pretend play, and included ratings of the emotion the children expressed.

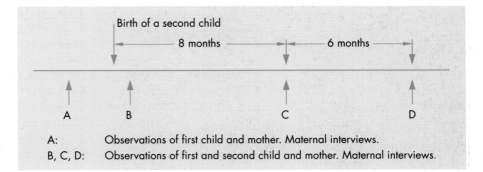

FIGURE 1 Design of the Cambridge Sibling Study.

A decision that turned out to be particularly useful was the choice to record the family conversations with sound recorders; conversations can be reliably and accurately recorded and transcribed and are then open to being coded in a wide variety of ways,

The findings of the study gave rise to two different but related lines of research which I have continued to pursue in subsequent studies. First, the *relationships* issue: the question of how and why sibling–child, parent–child (and in later studies also friend–child) relationships differ, how they influence one another, and how they develop over time. The observations in this first sibling study indicated that the patterns of influence between relationships involve complex and diverse processes (a lesson learnt from the diversity of the methods we had chosen to use). The later studies (see below) have further highlighted the importance of describing social processes at different levels including, for instance, affective expression and conversational exchanges.

The second line of research that grew out of the first sibling study was more unexpected. I described the early stages of this interest in the preface to my 1988 book, *The Beginnings of Social Understanding*:

> Sitting in the kitchens and living rooms of the families, watching the games, jokes, and disputes between the siblings and their complex relationships with the parents, I became fascinated with the glimpses of understanding that much of the children's social behaviour appeared to reflect. Not only the firstborn children, but most surprisingly some of their younger siblings early in the second year showed a clear practical grasp of how to annoy or comfort the other child. This suggested powers of understanding in these young children well beyond those we might expect from studies of children outside the familiar emotional world of the family – but the incidents involving the younger siblings were too few to provide more than provocative anecdotes. I decided to pursue the issue with systematic studies of children's understanding of the feelings and behaviour of others in their family world, observing the children within the drama and excitement of family life …

(Dunn, 1988)

2 THE BEGINNINGS OF SOCIAL UNDERSTANDING

In the study that resulted in that 1988 book, Penny Munn and I used two different strategies to examine the developments in children's understanding of others over the second and third years. One approach was to study a small number of children intensively: we followed six children from 14 to 24 months, and a further six children from 24 to 36 months (Studies 1 and 3 in Figure 2).

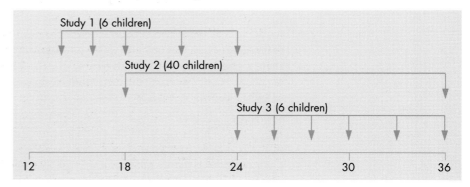

FIGURE 2 Design of studies contributing to *The Beginnings of Social Understanding.*

With this design we were able to look in detail at the developmental changes in the second and third year. However, to examine how general these patterns were we needed a larger number of families, and in Study 2 we focused on 40 families seen at 18, 24, and 36 months. The siblings in this study – the Cambridge Sibling Study – were later followed up through middle childhood (see Section 4 below).

The methods of observation we chose were very similar to those used in the work I did with Carol Kendrick, studying the arrival of a sibling. We paid particular attention to details of certain social situations that would illuminate the changing nature of children's understanding of their social world, arguments and conflict, teasing, jokes, fantasy play, and co-operative exchanges. The coding of conversations assumed major importance.

The evidence from the observations of children's behaviour in these situations and in conversations with their mothers and siblings demonstrated both the subtlety of children's understanding of others, and the significance of children's family relationships as the context in which such understanding is revealed and fostered. The project led to a model of the growth of social understanding in which development starts from the child's interest in and responsiveness to the feelings and behaviour of others, and, subsequently, key contributions are made first by the children's intense self-concern in the context of family relationships and second by children's participation in the moral discourse of the family. In discussing the findings my concern was not to demonstrate that children show certain capabilities several months or years earlier than previously suspected, but rather to explore the questions of *why* and *how* such abilities develop and are demonstrated.

The observations and arguments showed that there are notable features of this development that are neglected by current theories of moral and sociocognitive development: that the growth of understanding involves more than an unfolding of cognitive abilities, and self-concern and affective experience play central roles in the interactions in which moral and social rules are articulated and fostered. The development of these ideas depended crucially on the illumination we had gained from the naturalistic observations.

At the time that I was emphasizing the subtlety of children's social understanding as revealed in their family interactions and the role of relationships in its development, cognitive developmental psychologists working within a strictly experimental paradigm were becoming interested in the growth of children's understanding of others' mental states and beliefs – their 'theory of mind'. There was (and still is) plenty of controversy about the limitations of young children's understanding of 'other minds', and about the course of its development. But generally it was held that most 4 year olds had some grasp of 'other minds', but 3 year olds did not. The observations I had made of children in the second and third year made me eager to examine the possibility that studying children within their own families might actually give a different and useful perspective on the growth of understanding others' inner states. I also wanted to examine the patterns of individual differences in this understanding, until then completely neglected in the 'stage' approach to children's developing understanding.

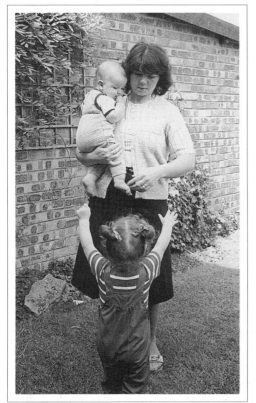

Over the next few years, then, I pursued two sets of questions, both of which had grown out of my initial work with siblings and mothers. The first set concerned the development of children's understanding. How does children's understanding of others change as they grow from 2 year olds to become sophisticated school-aged children? Do their interaction and conversation within their real-life relationships show consistent links with their performance on tests of understanding 'other minds', such as the false belief tests? Do they, in fact, show similar understanding within their different relationships (with mother, sibling, and friend, for instance), or does the affective quality of the relationship influence the kinds of understanding the children show? The second set of questions concerned the *relationships* between siblings and parents. Do children's early relationship experiences with their siblings show any systematic links with their later development or relationships? Does growing up with a hostile, critical sibling, for example, affect a child's perception of herself, or her adjustment? And more broadly, why do siblings within the same family differ so much from one another? We know from large-scale studies that siblings differ strikingly in personality, in adjustment, in intellectual style. Yet they share 50 per cent of their genes and are brought up by the same parents. The question presents a major challenge to those studying family influence, because many of the variables we have thought to be central in influencing children's development, such as the mental health of their parents, the quality of the marital relationship, parents' educational background, the neighbourhood, and social class of the family are apparently shared by the siblings, who nevertheless grow up to be so different from one another. What, then, are the experiences within the family that are not shared by the siblings, yet influence their development?

To answer these questions, we had to face a range of different methodological issues. What kind of observations would be sensitive to differences in understanding? How revealing or appropriate would observational techniques be with school-aged children? Could we use open-ended interviews with success? I addressed these questions, and the methodological problems that attended them, in three rather different longitudinal studies, on which I will briefly comment next.

3 THE PENNSYLVANIA STUDY OF SOCIAL UNDERSTANDING

This study focused on the development of children's understanding of others' feelings, mental states and social rules over the third and fourth years, and the links between this understanding and the children's close dyadic relationships with family members and with friends; we then followed the children up through their first two years at school. We used both the conventional measures of emotion understanding (e.g., Denham, 1986) and of 'other minds' (like the false belief tests, e.g., Bartsch and Wellman, 1989), and also examined the understanding that was reflected in their interactions in close relationships. The outline of the study is given in Figure 3.

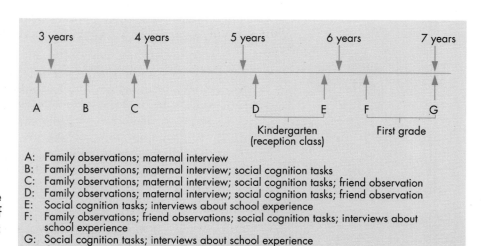

FIGURE 3 The Pennsylvania study of social understanding: timing of visits.

A: Family observations; maternal interview
B: Family observations; maternal interview; social cognition tasks
C: Family observations; maternal interview; social cognition tasks; friend observation
D: Family observations; maternal interview; social cognition tasks; friend observation
E: Social cognition tasks; interviews about school experience
F: Family observations; friend observations; social cognition tasks; interviews about school experience
G: Social cognition tasks; interviews about school experience

First, there was the thorny question of which observational techniques would be sensitive to developments in social and emotional understanding. We chose to focus in detail on conversational interaction; the grounds for this were several and varied. For example, a number of lines of evidence from our previous studies had suggested that individual differences in the frequency with which children had participated in conversations about why people behave the way they do, and about feelings, were linked over time to differences in emotional understanding and relationships (Dunn and Kendrick, 1982; Dunn *et al.*, 1991). Moreover, much of the explicit transmission and discussion of social rules is through talk.

Secondly, I chose again to focus on the particular kinds of social interaction which had proved especially revealing of children's sociocognitive abilities – namely conflicts, pretend play, conversations about inner states and social rules, and humorous exchanges (in which violations of expectations about behaviour frequently form the core of the joke). Thirdly, we studied each child with three different social partners – mother, sibling, close friend – because this would enable us to examine how the qualities of particular relationships were or were not linked to the social understanding children revealed, and to see whether there were differences across three relationships in the nature and significance of understanding demonstrated. I also included a new focus on *moral* understanding, employing both brief interviews with the children and a focus on their use of excuses and justifications in disputes.

Among a host of findings in the study a number of themes stand out, five of which can serve as illustrations. First, individual differences in children's interactions with their family and friends *did* relate to their ability to understand emotions and 'other minds' as assessed more formally. For example, it was the children who had engaged in much pretend play with their siblings as 2 year olds who were particularly successful at understanding other minds in the formal assessments seven months later, who were likely to take account of an antagonist's point of view when in disputes, and who, one year later, in interaction with a friend, were likely to communicate in an especially 'connected' way.

Secondly, it appeared that a variety of different processes were implicated in the development of social understanding, including not only frequent engagement in pretend play with a sibling, but discourse processes such as participation in talk about why people behave the way they do, and also the quality of the relationship between *other* members of the family. For example, in families in which mother and older sibling were intensely involved with one another, the younger children performed well on the 'other minds' tasks.

Thirdly, there were interesting differences in children's behaviour and interview responses in the context of their different relationships. For example, the same child used very different types of argument with his or her friend and with family members. This suggests we should think about social understanding as an 'emergent property' of relationships, rather than as a 'within-child' characteristic, as other models of social competence have envisaged.

Fourthly, there were longer-term patterns of connection from the earliest observations and tests to the understanding that children showed in the school years. For example, differences in our assessments of emotional understanding performed when the children were only 40 months old showed clear links with the differences in their emotional understanding assessed in tests when they were 7 year olds.

Finally, in many of the aspects of the children's development that we studied, we found that *child–child* interaction – both sibling and friend relationships – became more strongly implicated in the development of individual differences as the children grew up. This was so, for instance, in the differences in children's talk about mental states, in their understanding of emotions, and in their perceptions of their own self competence.

4   RELATIONSHIPS OVER TIME

The importance of children's experiences with siblings and friends introduces the issue of the longer-term significance of children's early experiences with their siblings. In the follow-up phase of the Cambridge Sibling Study I was not able to include detailed naturalistic observations but had to rely on interviews and self-reports. What Lynn Beardsall and I found when we visited the children in middle childhood and adolescence (see Figure 4) was that there were indeed links between the quality of the relationship between the siblings in the pre-school period and the children's outcome in a number of domains. For example, early adolescents who had grown up with a sibling who had been unfriendly or hostile and aggressive in the pre-school years were more likely to show worrying, anxious or depressed behaviour or aggressive behaviour than those whose siblings had been friendly and affectionate.

There was considerable continuity in the quality of the sibling relationship itself from this early period, in spite of the major developmental changes and transitional experiences the children went

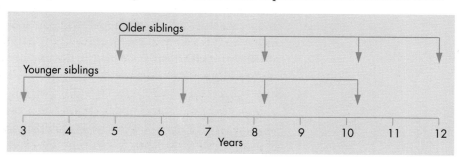

FIGURE 4   Cambridge Sibling Study follow-up: timing of visits.

through between the pre-school and early adolescent phases. But there were also marked changes in some children's sibling relationships, and analyzing these revealed some important general themes. First, in the face of negative life events (such as major maternal illness, or trouble at school), most siblings grew closer together and provided real support for one another. Secondly, the social and economic circumstances of the family appeared to have an increasing impact on the family relationships as the children grew to adolescence. In working-class families with boys, especially, sibling relationships became less intimate and supportive over time. Gender, too, appeared to be more strongly linked to differences in the quality of the sibling and friend relationships as the children reached adolescence. A sample of 80 children is too small to generalize from with confidence about social class and gender effects. However, the questions and issues raised about the changing impact of the world outside the family upon these intimate relationships as children grow up certainly deserve more attention. So, too, do some other surprising sources of change: we found, for instance, that the children's new friendships in middle childhood had a consistently negative impact on their sibling relationships, according to both siblings and mothers.

5 THE COLORADO SIBLING STUDY

Finally, that other quite different set of questions about family relationships: the matter of why siblings are so different from one another. This question was posed by the behavioural geneticists who had first drawn attention to the challenge it presented for family researchers (Plomin and Daniels, 1987).

I was fortunate enough to have a chance to participate in a large-scale study of families that gave us the opportunity to work on this question – the Colorado Adoption Project (DeFries *et al.*, 1994). Robert Plomin and I set out to try to describe and measure the differential experiences of children growing up within the same family, and to relate these differences to the siblings' outcome. With this sample, which included both biological and adopted siblings, we could also begin to examine the extent to which the genetic similarity of biological (as opposed to adopted) siblings contributed to their behavioural similarities. The methodological issues that the study presented were rather different from those described so far. We had to work with a much larger sample than the 50 or so families in the earlier studies, in order to have the statistical power to conduct the genetic analyses. And this ruled out the possibility of extensive naturalistic observations.

We documented a number of different sources of experience that differed sharply for some sibling pairs: they were treated differently by both mothers and fathers, they had quite different experiences *within* the sibling relationship itself, and they also had different experiences in their peer relationships outside the family. Most importantly, some of these were linked to differences in the children's outcome in middle childhood and early adolescence. For example, differences in mothers' affection and interest in their two children, which in some families were quite marked, showed considerable stability over time as the children grew up, and were associated over time with the development of externalizing behaviour. Children whose sibling was receiving more affection and attention from their mother were more likely to show aggressive, difficult or conduct-disordered behaviour than children who had not received less maternal affection or attention than their siblings. It appears that *relative* differences in how much loved you feel compared with your sibling may be of particular significance in adjustment.

6 IN CONCLUSION

What has been learned through the focus in these studies on children in their own world – a world of emotional relationships? Perhaps the most important lessons for developmentalists are these:

- that children can be remarkably interested in and sophisticated about their social worlds, from early in the pre-school years;
- that emotional experiences, family talk, and the quality of close relationships may play a significant role in the development of this sophisticated understanding;
- that the early relationship between siblings shows not only concurrent associations with children's sociocognitive development, but long-term associations with children's later relationships, patterns that link pre-school and adolescent periods in development;
- that as children grow into early adolescence, the world outside the family (whether it is a matter of current views on gender, or of difficult socio-economic circumstances) has growing impact even on intimate family relationships;
- that child–child relationships grow in significance as children grow from toddlers to school children, in terms of their emotional relationships *and* in terms of their understanding.

More generally, the significance of children's relationships for all aspects of their development underlies a key issue that stands out from these studies: if we are to make progress in understanding children's development we should surely include a focus on the relationships within which that development takes place. Naturalistic studies have a special value for such research in childhood.

REFERENCES

BARTSCH, K. and WELLMAN, H. (1989) 'Young children's attribution of action to beliefs and desires', *Child Development,* **60**, pp. 946–64.

DeFRIES, J. C., PLOMIN, R. and FULKER, D. W. (1994) *Nature and Nurture in Middle Childhood,* Oxford, Blackwell.

DENHAM, S. A. (1986) 'Social cognition, prosocial behaviour, and emotion in pre-schoolers: contextual validation', *Child Development,* **57**, pp. 194–201.

DUNN, J. (1988) *The Beginnings of Social Understanding,* Oxford, Blackwell.

DUNN, J. B. (1977) 'Patterns of early interaction: continuities and consequences' in H. R. SCHAFFER (ed.) *Studies of Mother–infant Interaction*, New York, Academic Press (pp. 457–74).

DUNN, J. and KENDRICK, C. (1982) *Siblings: love, envy and understanding,* Cambridge (Mass.), Harvard University Press.

DUNN, J., BROWN, J. R. and BEARDSALL, L. (1991) 'Family talk about emotions, and children's later understanding of others' emotions', *Developmental Psychology,* **27**, pp. 448–55.

PLOMIN, R., and DANIELS, D. (1987) 'Why are children of the same family so different from each other?', *The Behavioural and Brain Sciences*, **10**, pp. 1–16.

ACKNOWLEDGEMENTS

Grateful acknowledgement is made to the following for permission to reproduce material in this book:

Chapter 1

Figure, table and photograph

Figure 1: Belsky, J. (1984) *Child Development*, **55**, University of Chicago Press, © The Society for Research in Child Development Inc.

Table 2: Belsky, J. (1988) 'Effects of infant day care reconsidered' in *Early Childhood Research Quarterly*, **3**, Ablex Publishing Corporation.

p. 6 photograph: Hermann Kacher.

Chapter 2

Text

Richman, N., Stevenson, J. and Graham, P. J. (1982) *Pre-School to School: a behavioural study*, Academic Press Ltd; Rutter, M. (1968) 'A children's behaviour questionnaire for completion by teachers', copyright © 1968 Professor Rutter.

Figure, tables and photograph

Figure 5: Sameroff, A. J. (1987) 'The social context of development' in Eisenberg, N. (ed.) *Contemporary Topics in Developmental Psychology*, John Wiley and Sons, Inc., reprinted by permission of John Wiley and Sons, Inc.

Tables 1, 2, 3 and 4: Richman, N., Stevenson, J. and Graham, P. J. (1982) *Pre-School to School: a behavioural study*, Academic Press Ltd; *Table 6*: Crockenburg, S. B. (1981) 'Infant irritability, mother responsiveness, and social support influences on the security of infant–mother attachment', *Child Development*, **52**, University of Chicago Press, copyright © Society for Research in Child Development, Inc.

p. 63 photograph: reproduced by courtesy of Lynne Murray, Winnicott Research Unit, University of Cambridge.

Chapter 3

Figures and photograph

Figure 1: from *Familes in the Future: study commission on the family*, Family Policy Studies Centre; *Figure 2*: White, D. and Woollett, A. (1992) *Families: a context for development*, Falmer Press, copyright © 1992 David White and Anne Woollett; *Figure 3*: reprinted by permission of the publishers from *Siblings: love, envy and understanding*, Cambridge (Mass.), Harvard University Press, copyright © 1982 by Judy Dunn and Carole Kendrick.

p. 105 photograph: Hulton Deutsch Collection.

'Emancipation' in *Adolescent Relations with Mothers, Fathers and Friends*, University of Chicago Press, © 1985 by The University of Chicago.

Figures and photograph

Figure 1: Coleman, J. and Hendry, L. (1990) *The Nature of Adolescence*, Routledge, © 1990 John Coleman and Leo Hendry; *Figure 2:* Richards, M. H., Boxer, A. M., Petersen, A.C. and Albrecht, R. (1990) 'Weight and body image' in *Developmental Psychology*, **26**, p. 317, American Psychological Association, copyright © 1990 by the American Psychological Association, reprinted by permission; *Figure 3*: Tanner, J. M. (1989, 2nd edn) *Foetus Into Man*, Castlemead Publications; *Figure 4*: Erikson, E. (1968) *Identity: youth and crisis*, W. W. Norton & Co. Inc., copyright © 1968 W. W. Norton, New York and The Hogarth Press, London; *Figures 7 and 8*: Coleman, J. C. (1974) *Relationships in Adolescence*, Routledge, © John C. Coleman 1974.

p. 303 photograph: Courtesy of The Harvard University Office of News and Public Affairs.

Tables

Table 1: Waterman, A. S., Geary, P. S. and Waterman, C. K. (1974) 'Longitudinal study of changes in ego identity status from the freshman to the senior year at college' in *Developmental Psychology*, **10**, p. 390, American Psychological Association, copyright © 1974 by the American Psychological Association, adapted by permission; *Table 2*: Archer, S. L. (1989) 'The status of identity: reflections on the need for intervention', *Journal of Adolescence*, **12**, p. 351, Academic Press Ltd; *Tables 3 and 4*: Rutter, M., Graham, P., Chadwick, O. F. D. and Yule, W. (1976) 'Adolescent turmoil: fact or fiction?', *Journal of Child Psychology*, **17**, Elsevier Science Ltd, reprinted with the kind permission of Elsevier Science Ltd, The Boulevard, Langford Lane, Kidlington OX5 1GB, UK; *Table 5*: Fogelman, K. (1976) *Britain's Sixteen-Year-Olds*, National Children's Bureau, © NCB 1976.

NAME INDEX

Adelson, J. 314
Ainsworth, M. 3, 3–16, 18, 28–30
Archer, S. 308–9, 310, 311, 312, 313

Baldwin, J. M. 195
Bannister, D. 221, 222
Barkley, R. 69–71, 73
Baumrind, D. 90–1, 93, 94, 95, 100, 101
Bell, R. Q. 68–9
Belsky, J. 19–20, 21, 27, 28
Bem, S. 214, 215, 218–20, 228–9
Blatchford, P. 269–70, 271
Bowlby, J. vii, 3, 5–9, 12, 13, 16, 19, 28, 35
Brody, L.R. 176, 177, 185–6
Bruner, J. 260
Burgoyne, J. 174, 183–5

Camras, L. A. 149
Chess, S. 73
Cole, M. and S. R. 105–6, 108, 110
Cole, P. 170, 171, 172
Coleman, J. C. 288, 314, 320–2, 325
Connolly, J. 249–50, 252
Cooley, C. 193, 195, 198, 205
Coopersmith, S. 200–1
Corsaro, W. 259, 261–3, 264
Cox, T. 63, 64
Crockenburg, S. B. 75–6
Curry, N. 257, 258–9

Darwin, Charles 140, 141, 142, 143, 164
Dunn, J. viii, ix, 24, 30, 119, 120–3, 151–6, 157, 159, 164, 165, 166, 193, 207–8, 211, 250–2, 336

Erikson, E. viii, 288, 302–6, 314, 325, 330–1
Erwin, P. 275

Fein, G. 246–8
Ferguson, D. N. 116
Freud, A. 302
Freud, S. 5, 133, 213–14, 220, 337

Geertz, C. 190–1
Goldfarb, W. 8, 10, 11, 68

Hall, G. S. 295, 302
Harkness, S. 109–10

Harlow, H. 9
Harris, P. viii, 151, 162, 163, 164–5, 171, 172, 174–5
Harter, S. 194, 200, 201–4, 204–5, 223, 224
Haviland, J. 143, 147, 176
Herbert, M. 47
Hetherington, E. M. 115
Hobbs, T. 133
Hoffman, L. 107
Hughes, M. 97, 98

Isaacs, S. 232–3
Izard, C. E. 157

James, W. 192, 194, 195, 204, 224

Keating, D. P. 290
Kelly, E. 274–5
Kendrick, C. 24, 25, 119, 121, 123, 193, 207–8, 211, 338, 340, 343
Kessen, W. 60
Klein, M. 261
Kohlberg, L. 209–10, 274
Kuhn, D. 210

Larson, R. 319
Lelwica, M. 143
Lerner, J. V. 108–9
LeVine, R. 102–3, 104
Locke, J. 132
Lorenz, K. 6
Lowenfeld, M. 261
Lucey, H. 98–9

Maccoby, E. 190, 192, 198, 204
McMillan, M. 232
Main, M. 32–3
Malatesta, C. 147, 148, 157, 176
Marcia, J. 306–8, 309, 314, 324
Mead, G. H. viii, 195, 196–7, 221, 224, 232, 242–3, 245, 246, 247, 253, 265, 285
Meltzer, B. 243
Morgan, D. 86, 130–1
Murray, L. 61–3, 64

Neill, A. S. 232

Oates, J. 183
Opie, I. 237, 267, 268, 271

Parten, M. 233–4, 235
Piaget, J. viii, 195–6, 209, 232, 236–7, 239–41, 245, 253, 265, 272–6, 283
Pollard, A. 244, 245, 246, 274
Pope Edwards, C. 99, 103–4

Richards, M. 298, 336, 337
Richman, N. 42, 52, 53, 54, 56, 57, 58–9, 62, 64, 67, 74
Robertson, J. and J. 8
Rosenberg, M. 222–3
Rutter, M. 11–12, 47, 48, 49, 52, 57, 74, 75, 77, 115, 293, 315, 317, 318, 319

Saarni, C. 170, 171, 172
Sachs, J. 259, 260
Sameroff, A. J. 72–3
Schaffer, R. 86–7, 88, 94, 97, 100, 101, 145
Sluckin, A. 267–9, 270, 271, 274
Smith, P. 232, 233, 236
Statham, J. 218, 219
Steinberg, L. 318
Stratton, P. 65–6
Super, C. M. 109–10
Swaffer, R. 65–6

Tanner, J. 295, 296, 297
Thomas, A. 73
Tizard, B. 10, 11, 19, 49, 68, 97, 98
Trevarthen, C. 150

Vygotsky, L. viii, 232, 241–2, 245, 249

Walkerdine, V. 98–9
Waterman, A. 309, 310, 311
Waters, E. 75–6
Watson, J. B. 132
Whiting, B. 99, 103–4, 105, 106, 213, 215–16
Winnicott, D. 261

Yarrow, M. R. 144
Youniss, J. 325, 331–3

Zahn-Waxler, C. 144

SUBJECT INDEX

abused children
　and emotional expression 149
　mothers of 65–6
adolescence viii–ix, 288–333
　absence of in pre-industrial
　society 291–2
　as an identity crisis 301–14
　behaviour disorders in 9
　and cognitive development
　289–90, 295, 319
　discovery of 291–2
　epidemiological studies of
　315–18
　Erikson's view of identity in
　302–6, 314
　and family relationships 290,
　323–6
　focal theory of 319–22, 325
　　criticisms of 322–3
　and inner turmoil 318–19, 323
　Isle of Wight study 315
　and moral development 273,
　274
　personal perspective on 293–4
　physical changes occurring
　during 288–9
　psychoanalytic theory of 302,
　314
　relations with parents 315–18,
　320, 321, 323–6
　　and emancipation 325,
　　331–3
　and self-esteem 205, 300, 301,
　318, 324
　and sense of self 198
　sibling relationships in 344,
　345, 346
　as a social creation 293
　storm and stress model of 302,
　321, 323
　subculture 330
　variability issues 290–1
　and the 'victimiser' 314
　and the 'visionary-victim' 314
　weight and dieting during
　298–300
　see also puberty
Adult Attachment Interview (AAI)
32–4
adults
　and emotion 137–8, 168–9
　and play activity 284

Africa
　children's games 242, 254–5
　parental expectations of
　children 106–8, 126
　rite of passage in Liberia 289
　socialization and parental roles
　in 102–3, 105–6
age
　and adolescence 289
　as criterion for defining
　disturbing behaviour 47, 49, 50,
　52
　and emotional understanding
　172
　of maturity, implications of
　297–300, 322
　and moral development 272–3
　of onset of the menarche 296–7
　and parental control 100, 101
　play and social competence 253
agenda setters 274
aggressive behaviour, and
parental style 68, 68–9
anger
　of children after marital
　separation 184
　displays of in young children,
　and sense of self 197–8
　expression of
　　and culture 169
　　and gender 185, 186
antisocial behavioural difficulties
48, 56
　and parental control 64
anxious/ambivalent children
(Type C) 14, 16, 17, 18
　internal working model 29, 31
　parents of 32
anxious/avoidant children (Type
A) 14, 16, 17, 18
　internal working model 29
　parents of 32
attachment vii, 2–35
　in adult life 32–4
　beyond infancy 28–34
　and difficult behaviour 75–6
　internal working model vii, 2,
　3, 28–32, 34, 35
　　and disturbed behaviour 65,
　　67
　lifespan dimension of 3
　and maternal depression 64

and maternal deprivation 3,
6–9, 13
　critique of 9–13
　multiple relationships within
　families 113
　patterns 13–18
　　cross-cultural comparisons
　　16–17, 18
　proximity-promoting behaviours
　5, 12
　recalling early attachments 4
　young children 4–28
　　and other family members
　　23–6
　see also insecure attachments;
　secure attachments
authoritarian (autocratic) parental
style 91, 92, 93, 94, 96
　and adolescent experience 324
authoritative parental style 91, 92,
93, 94, 95, 96
autistic children 161
autonomous-secure adults 32, 33

babies see infants
Balinese society, definition of the
self 190–1
behaviourism, and socialization 87
belief, and emotional development
161–3, 164, 165, 166, 167, 177
black families, role of
grandmothers 26
blame, attribution of 157, 158
boarding school, coping strategies
for homesickness 174–5
boys
　adolescent
　　and age of maturity 298, 300
　　and focal theory 320, 321
　　relations with parents
　　316–17
　　and sibling relationships 345
　　weight 299
　and authoritative parental style
　93, 94
　disruption and distortion of
　affectional bonds 12, 115–16
　disturbing behaviour in 49, 57,
　59
　　and maternal attitudes 66–7
　　and parental discord 117, 124
　　and temperament 74

effects of divorce and parental discord on 115–16, 185
and emotional expression 147–8, 176, 185, 186
    regulation of 170, 171, 173
    talking about emotions 159, 176
and gender identity 213, 214
and non-sexist childraising 219
and physical change 295, 296
and play 257, 258, 259
and sibling relationships 122
and socio-dramatic play 256

Cambridge Sibling Study 24, 250–2, 336, 338–9, 340–1
caregivers
    and emotion in infancy 136
    and empathy in infants 143–5
    infant recognition of emotion in 142–3
    and the internal working model 28–30, 34
    sensitivity 2
    shared care of young children 10–12, 13
    see also mothers
categorical self (self-as-object) viii, 188, 194–5, 196–7, 199, 220, 221
    and gender identity 206
child labour, in Africa 102–3
'Child Study' movement 292
childminders 22
clay-moulding model of socialization 132
cognitive development
    and adolescence 289–90, 295, 319
    effects of institutional care on 11
    and emotion 139, 151, 167, 177
    and gender identity 209–11, 215
    and play 233, 284
Colorado Sibling Study 345–6
concrete operations, stage of 290
conflict
    in adolescence 302
    model of socialization 87, 133
    and parental control 98, 100, 101
    parental discord and disturbing behaviour 115–18
conjugal nuclear families 85, 87
constructive play 238, 283, 284

contingency, in mother–child relationships 70
critical period, of imprinting 5, 9
cross-cultural studies
    of attachment patterns 16–17, 18
    of disturbing behaviour 51
    of facial expression of emotions 141–2
    of role of grandparents 26
    of socialization 102–10, 111
    of socio-dramatic play 258–9
cultural identity, and play 257–9, 264, 276
cultural relativism 219
culture
    and adolescence 291
        self-image in 300
    and gender identity 215–16
    in the playground 267–72, 276
    and the regulation of emotion 136, 137–8, 169, 170
    and sense of self 190–1, 192
    and socialization 102–10
    see also cross-cultural studies

day care, effects on young children 2, 19–22
depression
    in adolescence 319
    in children after marital separation 184
    maternal and problem behaviour 57, 62–4, 67
    post-natal
        and emotional development 136, 149–50
        and infant development 62
desires, and emotional development 161–3, 164, 165, 166, 167, 177
direction of effect 68–71
dismissing-detached adults 32, 33, 34
disorganized children (Type D), internal working model 31–2
disputes, and parental control 98, 100
disruption
    of affectional bonds 12, 115–16
    of relationships 12
distortion, of relationships 12, 115–19
disturbing behaviour vii, 42–78
    and attachment 75–6

context-embedded 50–2, 59
deciding what constitutes 46–8, 50–2
degree of stability in 53–7, 59
and directions of effect 68–71
effects of medication on mother–child interactions 70–1
incidence of 52–3
Isle of Wight study 47–8, 48–9, 52
medical model of 44–5, 58
multiple pathways to 77
National Child Development Study of 49
normatively defined 49, 50, 59
and parental discord 115–18
and protective factors 74–5, 78
risk factors in 57–9, 68, 74, 75, 78, 114
role of the child in 68–78
role of the family in 60–7
social environment model of 45, 58, 68
and temperament 73–6
thinking about 42–5
Thomas Coram Research Unit Study of 49
transactional model of 72–3, 78
Waltham Forest study 52
division of labour, by gender 216
divorce vii, 86
    and adolescence 290
    and grandparents 26
    impact on children 114–15, 119, 124, 184, 185
    and sibling relationships 122
    see also marital separation
drug therapy, and mother–child interactions 70–1, 78
dyadic relationships 111, 113, 120, 342

economic factors
    and attachment 28
    and the concept of adolescence 291–2
education, and adolescence 291
egocentric empathy 144, 164
egocentricity, and play 240, 245
18 month olds
    play and social competence 250, 251
    sense of self 197
emancipation, and adolescents'

relationships with parents 325, 331–3
emotion viii, 136–86
   in adolescence 318–19
   and adults 137–8
   appearance-reality distinction 172
   and belief 161–3, 164, 165, 166, 167, 177
   and change from childhood to maturity 138
   co-regulation in emotional development 149–50
   controlling 168–75
   coping strategies 168, 169
      and children's reactions to trauma 136, 173–5, 178
      and play 263
   cultural regulation of 136, 137–8
   and desires 161–3, 164, 165, 166, 167, 177
   display rules 136, 148, 169, 170–1, 173, 176, 178
   and empathy 136, 143–5, 150, 152, 154, 160, 163, 164, 177
   expression of 141–2, 145, 176, 185
      controlling 168–75
      facial 136, 140, 141–3, 147, 166, 169, 185, 186
   and family relationships 136, 151–9
   and gender 136, 147–8, 168, 170–1, 176–7, 178, 185–6
   imaginative understanding of 163, 164–6
   in infancy 136, 140–50, 177
   'negative' and 'positive' emotion 138
   psychoanalysis and emotional development 183
   psychological study of 139
   recognition of 136, 142–3, 145–9, 150
   recognition of in others 138–9
   showing and hiding feelings 170–3
   and social referencing 136, 146–8, 150, 170, 173, 177
   and social understanding 151–60, 175, 341, 343
   and socialization 136, 145–9, 169
      and gender 185–6
   talking about, and social understanding 156–9

understanding complex 166–7
   see also theory of mind
emotional contagion 144, 164
emotional tension, and thematic fantasy play 261–3, 264
empathy, and emotion 136, 143–5, 150, 152, 154, 160, 163, 164, 177
employment prospects, and adolescence 291
environmental contexts, in socialization 108–9
Erikson's developmental stages 304–5
ethnic background, and adolescence 291
ethnocentric fallacy 102, 108
existential self (self-as-subject) viii, 188, 192–4, 196, 199
extended families 85, 131

facial expression, and emotion 136, 140, 141–3, 147, 166, 169, 185, 186
false-belief paradigm 161
families
   different structures 84–5, 130–1
   and households 131
   importance of early experiences within and play 232
   life-cycles 86
   and problem behaviour in children 60–7
   relationships
      in adolescence 290, 323–6
      multiple influences in 111–23
   role of different family members in development of young children 2, 34–5
   and socialization 84–111
   unity and diversity in 131
fathers
   attitudes and problem behaviour 59
   and parental control 100–1
   relations with adolescent children 316, 317
   and sensitivity 18
   young children's relationships with 23
   see also parental style
feral (wild) children 195–7
first-born children
   and the birth of a sibling 159, 338–9
   and sibling relationships 119, 121–3

focal theory, and adolescence 319–23, 325
foreclosure identity status
   in adolescence 307, 308, 309–10, 311, 312, 313, 327
      and relationships with parents 324
formal operations, stage of 290
4 year olds
   and gender identity 209
   and social understanding 341

games
   game stage of play 239, 240, 243
   with rules 272, 276, 283
gender
   and adolescence 291
   and children with disturbing behaviour 49, 74
   developing ideas about 208–13
   division of labour by 216
   and emotion 136, 147–8, 170–1, 176–7, 178, 185–6
   in everyday interaction 207–8
   identity viii, 188, 206–20
      and clothing 215–16
      identifying with same-sex parent 213–14
      learning gender appropriate behaviour 213–20
      and media images 216–20
      and non-sexist childraising 219–20
      and play 257, 258, 264, 276
      and the self 221
      social context of 211–13
      stability and constancy 208–13, 220
   and sibling relationships 122
      in adolescence 345
   see also boys; girls
gender schema theory 214–15, 218–20, 228–9
'generalized other', concept of the 244, 245, 265, 278, 285
girls
   adolescent
      and age of maturity 298
      and focal theory 320, 321
      physical changes at puberty 295, 296–7
      relations with parents 316–17
      weight and dieting 298, 299
   effects of marital separation on 185

and emotional expression 147–8,
176, 186
    regulation of 170, 171, 173,
    176
    talking about emotions 159
and gender identity 212, 214,
220
and non-sexist childraising 219
and parental discord 117
and play 257, 258
    school playtimes 271
    socio-dramatic play 256
goodness of fit
    and disturbing behaviour 7, 51,
    73, 78
    and socialization 108, 110, 111,
    125
grandparents, young children's
relationships with 25–6

Harter's Self-Perception Profile
for Children 201–5, 206
heterosexual relationships in
adolescence, anxiety over 320, 321
homesickness, coping strategies
174–5
households, and families 131
housing, and problem behaviour 57
humour 155–6, 160
hyperactive children, interaction
with mothers 69–71, 73, 78

identification, in childhood 303
identity, in adolescence 301–14,
325, 330
identity achievement status
    in adolescence 307, 309, 310,
    311, 312, 313, 326
        and relations with parents
        324
identity confusion (diffusion)
    in adolescence 303, 304, 305,
    306, 307, 309, 310, 311, 312, 313,
    326
        and relations with parents
        324
identity formation, in adolescence
303
identity intervention, in
adolescence 313
identity statuses, in adolescence
307, 308–13, 314, 324
ideological identity status, in
adolescence 309

imaginary companions 285–6
imitation
    as a product of accommodation
    239
    and sense of self 193–4, 195,
    284
imprinting 6
independence, and parental style
91, 93
India, parental roles in 104
individual differences
    between siblings 341–2
    between young children 336
    in the development of the self
    253
industry, diffusion of, in
adolescence 306
infants
    attachment in 4–21
        proximity-promoting
        behaviours 5, 12
    cross-cultural comparisons of
    socialization 109–10
    development of identity in 303
    effects of disruption on 61–3
    emotion in 136, 140–50, 177
    and the self as subject 192–4
insecure attachments 2
    anxious/ambivalent (Type C) 14,
    16, 17, 18, 29, 31
    anxious/avoidant (Type A) 14,
    16, 17, 18, 29
    disorganized (Type D) 14, 18
    internal working model 34
    and maternal depression 62, 67,
    75
    and non-maternal care 19–20
    and problem behaviour 75–6
institutional care, and attachment
8, 10–12, 68
inter-modal mapping 142
internal working model vii, 2, 3,
28–32, 34, 35
    and disturbed behaviour 65, 67
intimacy, and adolescence 306
Isle of Wight study
    of adolescence 315
    of disturbing behaviour 47–8,
    48–9
isolates 274

jokes 155–6, 160, 177

Kenya
    Embu parents' perceptions of
    problem behaviour 51
    Kokwet society socialization in
    109–10
    parental roles in Gusii society
    105, 106

labour
    child labour in Africa 102–3
    division of, by gender 216
laissez-faire model of socialization
132
language
    and emotional development 136,
    157, 158, 160, 177, 186
        and gender 186
    and play 242, 255
    and sense of self 195
language disorders, children with
77
Liberia, rite of passage in 289
linguistic development, effects of
institutional care on 11
links, in the mother–child
relationship 63
lone parent families 85
    and grandparents 25
looking-glass self 195–8, 205

Malawi
    children's play in 242
    play of Ngoni boys 242, 258
marital relationships
    and the birth of a child 120
    and problem behaviour 57, 58,
    59, 114–19
    remarriage vii, 86, 115
marital separations vii, 114, 117
    children's reactions to 183–5
    see also divorce
mastery stage, of play 239, 240
maternal depression
    and emotional development
    149–50
    post-natal
        and emotional development
        136, 149–50
        and infant development 62
    and problem behaviour 57, 62–4,
    67
maternal deprivation hypothesis 3,
6–9, 13, 60
    critique of 9–13

and disturbing behaviour in children 45
media images, and gender identity 216–20, 257
medical model, of disturbing behaviour 44–5, 58
menarche, onset of 295, 296–7
mental health workers' perceptions of problem behaviour 50
monotropism 7, 10
moral development
    ages and stages in 272–3
    constraint-based 273, 274, 276
    and mutual respect 273, 274
    and play 239, 265, 272–6, 277
    and social understanding 341
moral understanding 343
moratorium status
    in adolescence 305, 307, 309, 310, 312, 313, 326, 330
        and relations with parents 324
mothers
    of abused children 65–6
    attitudes and problem behaviour 59, 65–7
    and the birth of a sibling 159
    of children with special needs 65–7
    and children's gender identity 212, 213
    and disturbed behaviour in children, transactional model 72–3
    and emotional development
        and gender 176
        post-natal depression 149–50
        social referencing of emotion 146–8
        talking about emotions 156–7, 158–9
    of hyperactive children 69–71, 73, 78
    maternal behaviour cultural differences in 104
    maternal responsibility and problem behaviour 60–1, 67
    maternal responsiveness and problem behaviour 61–4, 67, 75–6
    mental state and problem behaviour 57, 61–4
    and parental control 97–101
    relations with adolescent

children 316, 317
    sensitive mothering 2, 13–14, 17–18, 20, 99
    and sibling relationships 121–3, 337, 338–9, 343, 346
    speech of 100
    working mothers of young children and attachment 19–21
    see also maternal depression; maternal deprivation hypothesis; parental styles

narrative thought, and thematic fantasy play 260
National Child Development Study
    of adolescence 316–17
    of disturbing behaviour 49
negative identity, in adolescence 306
neurotic behavioural difficulties 48, 56–7
non-conjugal nuclear families 85
normative crisis 304, 305
Nso people (Cameroon), parental expectations of children 106–8, 126
nuclear families 85, 131
    sibling relationships 23
nurseries, day care in 22

object-relations theory, and gender identity 214
occupation of parents, and problem behaviour 57
occupational identity status, in adolescence 308, 309, 311, 331
Oedipus complex 214

paradigmatic thought, and thematic fantasy play 260
parental control 84
    and socialization 97–101
parental discord
    and disturbing behaviour 115–18
    impact on children 118–19, 124
parental expectations of children 106–8
parental goals and behaviour, cultural differences in 103–6
parental style
    and adolescent experience 324–5
    and attributes of parents 95–6
    authoritarian (autocratic) 91,

92, 93, 94, 96, 324
    authoritative 91, 92, 93, 94, 95, 96
    and children's behaviour 93–6, 125, 275
    consistent use of particular 96
    fluctuation over time 96
    and individual characteristics of the child 96
    permissive 91, 92, 93, 96, 132
    permissiveness-restrictiveness in 88–9, 90
    and problem behaviour 68–9
    and social context 95
    and socialization viii, 88–96, 275
    warmth–coldness in 88, 90
parents
    attitudes to problem behaviour 58, 59
    and displays of emotion 138
    and gender identity 211, 215
    identifying with same-sex 213–14
    and moral development 275
    and non-sexist childraising 219
    patterns of adult attachment 32–4
    perceptions of problem behaviour 50, 51
    relations with adolescent children 315–18, 320, 321, 323–6
        and emancipation 325, 331–3
    and self-esteem 205, 206
    and sibling relationships 341–2
    see also divorce; marital separation
peer groups
    in adolescence, fears of rejection by 320, 321
    and gender identity 216
    influence of 125
    and play 232, 233
    relationships with
        and moral development 273, 275–6, 277
        and siblings 344, 345, 346
        and self-esteem 205, 206
Pennsylvania Study of Social Understanding 159, 342–4
permissive parental style 91, 92, 93, 96, 132
personality and self-esteem 200

play viii, 232–86
    associative 233, 234
    of boys and emotional expression
    186
    co-operative 233, 234, 238
    constructive 238, 283, 284
    content of 254–64
    effects of divorce on patterns of
    115
    fantasy 236, 237, 238
    friendship groups (Goodies,
    Jokers and Gangs) 244, 278
    games with rules 272, 276, 283
    and the 'generalized other' 244,
    245, 265, 278, 285
    imaginative 236
    importance of and early
    experiences in families 232
    kapenta game 254–5
    Mead's theory of 242–3, 244,
    245, 247
    in middle childhood 265–77
    and moral development 239,
    265, 272–6, 277
    parallel activity 233, 234
    Piaget's theory of 239–41, 245,
    272–6, 283
    playground behaviour 266,
    267–72
        and moral development 272–6
    'playtime' at school 235
    practice play 283
    pretend 235, 236
        and gender identity 208
        and imaginative
        understanding 136, 164–6,
        167, 177
        self-building potential of 246
        in siblings 250–2, 343
        and societal knowledge 263–4
    as a product of assimilation 239
    role-play 236, 238, 243, 245,
    247–8, 250, 283, 284–5
    with rules 236, 238
    script knowledge in 259–60, 261,
    264
    and sense of self viii, 195, 242–3,
    245, 247, 253, 257–8, 284–5
    and social competence 249–52,
    254, 264, 278
    and social development 238, 239,
    254, 267–72, 276, 283
    social participation in 233–5,
    238

    and social perspective-taking
    skills 239–40, 245–9, 254
    and socialization 232, 233, 258
    solitary independent 233, 234
    symbolic 236, 238, 283
    thematic fantasy viii, 232,
    255–6, 260–3, 264, 276
    and theory of mind 240–1
    Vygotsky's theory of 241–2, 245
    see also socio-dramatic play
play stage 239, 240, 243
political ideology, and identity
status in adolescence 306, 308, 312
post-natal depression
    and emotional development 136,
    149–50
    and infant development 62
poverty
    and child care by relations 25
    and secure attachments 27
practice play 283
pre-school children
    dimensions of behaviour 90
    and emotional expression 178
    and socio-dramatic play 246–9,
    254, 283
    and symbolic play 283
preformationism 132
preoccupied-entangled adults 32,
33, 34
pride, feelings of 166–7, 185
privation, of affectional bonds
11–12, 115
problem behaviour *see* disturbing
behaviour
protective factors, and disturbing
behaviour 74–5, 78
proximity-promoting behaviours 5,
12
psychoanalysis, and emotional
development 183
psychodynamic explanations, of
gender appropriate behaviour
213–14
puberty 295–301
    physical changes during 295–7,
    301
        and focal theory 322
        psychological implications of
        297–300
    as rite of passage 289
punishment
    and the Nso people (Cameroon)
    107–8
    and problem behaviour 59

racism, in the playground 274–5
rage *see* anger
reconstituted families 85
regression, in adolescence 302
relatives 131
    care of young children by 22, 25
religious beliefs, and identity
status in adolescence 306, 308, 312
remarriage vii, 86, 115
responders 274
risk factors 42
    in disturbing behaviour 57–9,
    74, 75, 114
role-play 236, 238, 243, 245, 247–8,
250, 283, 284–5

script knowledge, in play 259–60,
261, 264
secure attachments 2, 5
    and non-maternal care 19–20
    and poverty 27
securely attached children (Type B)
14, 16–17, 18
    internal working model 29
    parents of 32
self
    in Balinese society 190–1
    becoming aware of the 221
    categorical (self-as-object) viii,
    188, 194–5, 196–7, 199, 220, 221
    developing a sense of viii,
    188–229
        game stage 285
        and play viii, 195, 242–3,
        245, 247, 253, 257–8, 284–5
        play stage 284–5
        preparatory stage 284
    evaluations of 199–200
    existential (self-as-subject) viii,
    188, 192–4, 196, 199
    looking-glass self 195–8, 205
    Western view of the 191, 192
self-awareness 290
self-descriptions 188–9
    developmental sequences in 223
    psychological 222–4
    and self-esteem 221–4
self-esteem 188, 199–206
    in adolescence 205, 300, 301,
    318, 324
    developing a sense of 204–6
    measuring 200–4
    and self-description 221–4
self-identity, development of viii

self-image, in adolescence 300
self-recognition, development of 197
self-reflection 290
sensitive mothering 2, 13–14,
17–18, 20, 99
sensitive period, and attachment 9
separation *see* marital separations;
maternal deprivation hypothesis
sex differences *see* gender
sex-role orientation, and identity
status in adolescence 306, 308, 312
sexism, in the playground 274–5
sexual activity, and adolescence 291
sexual characteristics, development
of in puberty 295–7
sexual relationships
    in adolescence
        anxiety over 320, 321
        and early maturity 298
shame, feelings of 166–7
siblings
    biological and adopted 345
    birth of new baby 158–9, 337,
    338–9
        and attachment 24–5
        and gender identity 207
    Cambridge Sibling Study 24,
    250–2, 336, 338–9, 340–1
    Colorado Sibling Study 345–6
    individual differences between
    341–2
    play and social competence
    250–2
    pretend play and talks about
    feelings 165
    relationships
        in adolescence 344, 345, 346
        emotional 152–5, 158
        in the family 337
        and mothers 121–3, 337,
        338–9, 343, 346
        over time 344–5
        with parents 341
        and social understanding
        336–46
        young children 23–5, 119–23,
        124, 125
    young children's responses to
    sibling distress 152–4
social background, and problem
behaviour 57, 59
social class
    and adolescence 291

and children with disturbing
behaviour 49
and parental control 99
social competence
    individual differences in 252–3
    and parenting styles 275
    and play viii, 232, 249–52, 254,
    264, 278
social conditions, and attachment
28
social context
    and identity status 311
    and parental style 95
social development
    and play 232, 233, 238, 239, 276,
    283
        in the playground 269–72
social environment model, of
disturbing behaviour 45, 58, 68
social interactions, effects of divorce
on patterns of 115
social learning theory, and gender
identity 214, 215, 220
social perspective-taking skills, and
play 239–40, 245–9, 254
social roles, and the self 191, 195,
197, 199
social skills
    and playground culture 271
    and social competence 254
social understanding
    as an 'emergent property' of
    relationships 344
    and emotion 151–9, 151–60, 175,
    341, 343
    Pennsylvania study of 342–4
social world, and the self 195–7, 199
socialization viii, 84–111
    clay-moulding model 132
    conflict model of 87, 133
    cross-cultural studies of 102–10,
    111
    and emotional development 136,
    145–9, 169
        and gender 185–6
    and gender identity 213, 215–16
    laissez-faire model of 132
    models of 86–7, 132–3
    and parental control 97–101
    and parental style viii, 88–96,
    275
    and play 232, 233, 258
    transactional model 87, 94
society, playing at 255, 263–4

socio-dramatic play viii, 232, 236,
237–8, 242, 245, 246–9, 254, 276
    cross-cultural studies of 258–9
    intellectual benefits of 284
    scripted events in 259–60, 261,
    264
    and thematic fantasy play 255–6,
    260–3, 264
    and toys 256
special needs, mothers of children
with 65
step-families 85, 86, 114, 290
Strange Situation technique 14–17,
18, 20
    and children in day care 22
    insecure attachment in 62, 76
    and sibling relationships 25
    and social referencing of emotion
    146
    variants of, with older children
    31
symbolic interactionism 195
    and play 242, 246, 253, 254
symbolic play 283

teachers, perceptions of problem
behaviour 50
teasing 154–5, 156, 177
teenagers, effects of marital
separation 184–5
television, childrens' and gender
stereotyping 218
temperament
    and attachment 28
    of children 42
    and disturbing behaviour 73–6
    and environmental context 108,
    109
    and parent-child relations in
    infancy 94
    and sibling relationships 122
thematic fantasy play viii, 232,
255–6, 260–3, 264, 276
theory of mind
    and emotion viii, 136, 151,
    160–1, 162, 167, 172
    and play 240–1
    and social understanding 341
Thomas Coram Research Unit
Study
    on child care 22, 25
    of disturbing behaviour 49

3 year olds
emotional development 151, 152,
153, 154
and gender identity 209, 210
monitoring emotional
expressions 171
play and social competence 250,
251
and social understanding 341
socio-dramatic play 260
time perspective, and adolescence
306
toys, and socio-dramatic play 256
training, and adolescence 291
transactional model 42
of disturbing behaviour 72–3, 78
and family relationships in
adolescence 324–5, 326
of socialization 87, 94, 111
in cross-cultural perspective
108–11
and gender 186
trust versus mistrust 305

2 year olds
and the birth of a sibling 158–9
emotional development 153, 154,
156
and gender identity 206, 208,
210, 220
play and social competence 250,
251, 253
sense of self 197
and social understanding 341,
343
socio-dramatic play 260

United States
environmental context of
socialization 109–10
parental roles in Orchard Town
104, 105, 106
parents' perceptions of problem
behaviour 51
unresolved-disorganized adults 32,
33, 34

'victimisers' 314
'visionary-victims' 314
wild (feral) children 195–7
Zambia, children's game (kapenta)
254–5
ZPD (zone of proximal
development) 241–2